ANTENATAL AND POSTNATAL MENTAL HEALTH

D1387498

Clinical management and service guidance

National Clinical Practice Guideline Number 45

National Collaborating Centre for Mental Health
commissioned by the

National Institute for Health & Clinical Excellence

published by
The British Psychological Society and Gaskell

British Library Cataloguing-in-Publication Data

A catalogue record for this book is available from
the British Library.

ISBN-: 978-1-85433-454-1

Printed in Great Britain by Alden Press.

developed by   National Collaborating Centre for Mental Health
Royal College of Psychiatrists' Research and Training Unit
4th Floor, Standon House
21 Mansell Street
London
E1 8AA

commissioned by   National Institute for Health and Clinical Excellence
MidCity Place, 71 High Holborn
London
WCIV 6NA
www.nice.org.uk

published by   The British Psychological Society
St Andrews House
48 Princess Road East
Leicester
LE1 7DR
www.bps.org.uk

and

The Royal College of Psychiatrists
17 Belgrave Square
London
SW1X 8PG
www.rcpsych.ac.uk

The
British
Psychological
Society

RC
PSYCH
ROYAL COLLEGE OF
PSYCHIATRISTS

CONTENTS

Contents

GUIDELINE DEVELOPMENT GROUP MEMBERSHIP

Dr Dave Tomson
Guideline Development Group Chair
GP and Consultant in patient-centred primary care, North Shields

Mr Stephen Pilling
Facilitator, Guideline Development Group
Joint Director, National Collaborating Centre for Mental Health
Director, Centre for Outcomes, Research and Effectiveness, University
College London
Consultant Clinical Psychologist, Camden and Islington Mental Health
and Social Care Trust

Dr Fiona Blake
Consultant Psychiatrist, Cambridge University Hospitals, NHS Foundation Trust

Ms Rachel Burbeck
Systematic Reviewer (from July 2005), National Collaborating Centre for
Mental Heath

Dr Sandra Elliott
Consultant Clinical Psychologist, South London and Maudsley NHS Trust

Dr Pauline Evans
Service user representative, Guideline Development Group
Senior Lecturer in Health and Social Care, University of Gloucestershire

Ms Josephine Foggo
Project Manager (until August 2005), National Collaborating Centre for
Mental Health

Dr Alain Gregoire
Consultant Perinatal Psychiatrist, Hampshire Partnership, NHS Trust and University
of Southampton

Dr Jane Hamilton
Consultant Psychiatrist in Maternal Health, Sheffield Care Trust

Mrs Claire Hesketh
Primary Care Mental Health Services Manager, Northumberland, Tyne and Wear
NHS Trust

Ms Rebecca King
Project Manager (August 2005 to August 2006), National Collaborating Centre
for Mental Health

Dr Elizabeth McDonald
Consultant Perinatal Psychiatrist, East London and the City Mental Health
NHS Trust

Ms Rosa Matthews
Systematic Reviewer (until July 2005), National Collaborating Centre for
Mental Health

Dr Ifigeneia Mavranezouli
Health Economist, National Collaborating Centre for Mental Health

Mr Patrick O'Brien
Obstetrician, University College London Hospitals NHS Foundation Trust

Dr Donald Peebles
Obstetrician, University College London Hospitals NHS Foundation Trust

Dr Catherine Pettinari
Project Manager (August 2006–present), National Collaborating Centre
for Mental Health

Mrs Sue Power
Team Manager for Community Mental Health Team, Vale of Glamorgan
County Council

Mrs Yana Richens
Consultant Midwife, University College London Hospitals NHS Foundation Trust

Mrs Ruth Rothman
Specialist Health Visitor for Postnatal Depression and Clinical Lead for Mental
Health, Southend Primary Care Trust

Ms Fiona Shaw
Service user representative, Guideline Development Group and author

Ms Sarah Stockton
Information Scientist, National Collaborating Centre for Mental Health

Dr Clare Taylor
Editor, National Collaborating Centre for Mental Health

Ms Lois Thomas
Research Assistant (until September 2005), National Collaborating Centre for
Mental Health

Dr Clare Thormod
GP, London

Ms Jenny Turner
Research Assistant (from November 2005), National Collaborating Centre for
Mental Health

ACKNOWLEDGEMENTS

The antenatal and postnatal mental health Guideline Development Group and review team at the National Collaborating Centre for Mental Health would like to thank the following people:

Those women who have experienced mental health problems in the antenatal or postnatal period who contributed testimonies that have been included in this guideline
Those who acted as advisers on specialist topics or have contributed to the process by reviewing drafts of the guideline:
Mr Stephen Bazire
Dr Roch Cantwell
Dr Margaret Oates

Speakers at an infant mental health day:
Dr Eia Asen
Mr Robin Balbernie
Professor Vivette Glover
Dr Sebastian Kraemer
Dr Tessa Leverton
Dr Veronica O'Keane
Dr Susan Pawlby

Speakers in a consensus conference on the pharmacological management of mental disorders in pregnancy and lactating women:
Professor David Chadwick
Professor Nicol Ferrier
Dr Peter Haddad
Dr Elizabeth McDonald
Dr Patricia McElhatton
Mr Patrick O'Brien

Development of the specialist perinatal services survey:
Dr Sonia Johnson
Dr Alain Gregoire

Development of the primary care trust survey:
Ms Susannah Pick

Responders to the primary care trust and specialist perinatal services surveys

Editorial assistance
Ms Emma Brown

1. EXECUTIVE SUMMARY

KEY PRIORITIES FOR IMPLEMENTATION

The following recommendations have been identified as recommendations for implementation.

Prediction and detection

● At a woman's first contact with services in both the antenatal and postnatal periods, healthcare professionals (including midwives, obstetricians, health visitors and GPs) should ask questions about:
  – past or present severe mental illness including schizophrenia, bipolar disorder, psychosis in the postnatal period and severe depression
  – previous treatment by a psychiatrist/specialist mental health team including inpatient care
  – a family history of perinatal mental illness.

Other specific predictors, such as poor relationships with her partner, should not be used for the routine prediction of the development of a mental disorder.

● At a woman's first contact with primary care, at her booking visit and postnatally (usually at 4 to 6 weeks and 3 to 4 months), healthcare professionals (including midwives, obstetricians, health visitors and GPs) should ask two questions to identify possible depression.
  – During the past month, have you often been bothered by feeling down, depressed or hopeless?
  – During the past month, have you often been bothered by having little interest or pleasure in doing things?

A third question should be considered if the woman answers 'yes' to either of the initial questions.
  – Is this something you feel you need or want help with?

Psychological treatments

● Women requiring psychological treatment should be seen for treatment normally within 1 month of initial assessment, and no longer than 3 months afterwards. This is because of the lower threshold for access to psychological therapies during pregnancy and the postnatal period arising from the changing risk–benefit ratio for psychotropic medication at this time.

Explaining risks

● Before treatment decisions are made, healthcare professionals should discuss with the woman the absolute and relative risks associated with treating and not treating the mental disorder during pregnancy and the postnatal period. They should:
  – acknowledge the uncertainty surrounding the risks
  – explain the background risk of fetal malformations for pregnant women without a mental disorder
  – describe risks using natural frequencies rather than percentages (for example, 1 in 10 rather than 10%) and common denominators (for example, 1 in 100 and 25 in 100, rather than 1 in 100 and 1 in 4)
  – if possible use decision aids in a variety of verbal and visual formats that focus on an individualised view of the risks
  – provide written material to explain the risks (preferably individualised) and, if possible, audio-taped records of the consultation.

Management of depression

● When choosing an antidepressant for pregnant or breastfeeding women, prescribers should, while bearing in mind that the safety of these drugs is not well understood, take into account that:
  – tricyclic antidepressants, such as amitriptyline, imipramine and nortriptyline, have lower known risks during pregnancy than other antidepressants
  – most tricyclic antidepressants have a higher fatal toxicity index than selective serotonin reuptake inhibitors (SSRIs)
  – fluoxetine is the SSRI with the lowest known risk during pregnancy
  – imipramine, nortriptyline and sertraline are present in breast milk at relatively low levels
  – citalopram and fluoxetine are present in breast milk at relatively high levels
  – SSRIs taken after 20 weeks' gestation may be associated with an increased risk of persistent pulmonary hypertension in the neonate
  – paroxetine taken in the first trimester may be associated with fetal heart defects
  – venlafaxine may be associated with increased risk of high blood pressure at high doses, higher toxicity in overdose than SSRIs and some tricyclic anti-depressants, and increased difficulty in withdrawal
  – all antidepressants carry the risk of withdrawal or toxicity in neonates; in most cases the effects are mild and self-limiting.
● For a woman who develops mild or moderate depression during pregnancy or the postnatal period, the following should be considered:
  – self-help strategies (guided self-help, computerised cognitive behavioural therapy or exercise)
  – non-directive counselling delivered at home (listening visits)
  – brief cognitive behavioural therapy and interpersonal psychotherapy.

Organisation of care

- Clinical networks should be established for perinatal mental health services, managed by a coordinating board of healthcare professionals, commissioners, managers, and service users and carers. These networks should provide:
  - a specialist multidisciplinary perinatal service in each locality, which provides direct services, consultation and advice to maternity services, other mental health services and community services; in areas of high morbidity these services may be provided by separate specialist perinatal teams
  - access to specialist expert advice on the risks and benefits of psychotropic medication during pregnancy and breastfeeding
  - clear referral and management protocols for services across all levels of the existing stepped-care frameworks for mental disorders, to ensure effective transfer of information and continuity of care
  - pathways of care for service users, with defined roles and competencies for all professional groups involved.

1.1 PRINCIPLES OF CARE FOR ALL WOMEN WITH MENTAL DISORDERS DURING PREGNANCY AND THE POSTNATAL PERIOD

1.1.1 Providing and using information effectively

1.1.1.1 Women with an existing mental disorder who are pregnant or planning a pregnancy, and women who develop a mental disorder during pregnancy or the postnatal period, should be given culturally sensitive information at each stage of assessment, diagnosis, course and treatment about the impact of the disorder and its treatment on their health and the health of their fetus or child. This information should cover the proper use and likely side effects of medication.

1.1.1.2 Healthcare professionals should work to develop a trusting relationship with the woman, and where appropriate and acceptable to the woman, her partner and family members and carers. In particular, they should:
- explore the woman's ideas, concerns and expectations and regularly check her understanding of the issues
- discuss the level of involvement of the woman's partner, family members and carers, and their role in supporting the woman
- be sensitive to the issues of stigma and shame in relation to mental illness.

1.1.1.3 Healthcare professionals should ensure that adequate systems are in place to ensure continuity of care and effective transfer of information, to reduce the need for multiple assessments.

1.1.1.4 Healthcare professionals should discuss contraception and the risks of pregnancy (including relapse, risk to the fetus and risks associated with stopping or changing medication) with all women of child-bearing potential who have an existing mental disorder and/or who are taking psychotropic medication. Such women should be encouraged to discuss pregnancy plans with their doctor.

1.1.2 Supporting partners, families and carers

1.1.2.1 Healthcare professionals should assess and, where appropriate address, the needs of the partner, family members and carers of a woman with a mental disorder during pregnancy and the postnatal period, including:
● the welfare of her infant, and other dependent children and adults
● the impact of any mental disorder on relationships with her partner, family members and carers.

1.1.3 Considerations for adolescents

1.1.3.1 Healthcare professionals working with adolescents experiencing a mental disorder during pregnancy or the postnatal period should:
● be familiar with local and national guidelines on confidentiality and the rights of the child
● obtain appropriate consent, bearing in mind the adolescent's understanding (including Gillick competence[1]), parental consent and responsibilities, child protection issues, and the use of the Mental Health Act and of the Children Act (1989).

1.2 PREDICTION, DETECTION AND INITIAL MANAGEMENT OF MENTAL DISORDERS

1.2.1 Prediction and detection

1.2.1.1 In all communications (including initial referral) with maternity services, healthcare professionals should include information on any relevant history of mental disorder.

1.2.1.2 At a woman's first contact with services in both the antenatal and postnatal periods, healthcare professionals (including midwives, obstetricians, health visitors and GPs) should ask about:
● past or present severe mental illness including schizophrenia, bipolar disorder, psychosis in the postnatal period and severe depression
● previous treatment by a psychiatrist/specialist mental health team including inpatient care
● a family history of perinatal mental illness.

---

[1]Also known as the Fraser competence rule after the judge presiding over the original case.

Other specific predictors, such as poor relationships with her partner, should not be used for the routine prediction of the development of a mental disorder.

1.2.1.3　At a woman's first contact with primary care, at her booking visit and post-natally (usually at 4 to 6 weeks and 3 to 4 months), healthcare profession-als (including midwives, obstetricians, health visitors and GPs) should ask two questions to identify possible depression.

- During the past month, have you often been bothered by feeling down, depressed or hopeless?
- During the past month, have you often been bothered by having little interest or pleasure in doing things?

A third question should be considered if the woman answers 'yes' to either of the initial questions.

- Is this something you feel you need or want help with?

1.2.1.4　Healthcare professionals may consider the use of self-report measures such as the Edinburgh Postnatal Depression Scale (EPDS), Hospital Anxiety and Depression Scale (HADS) or Patient Health Questionnaire-9 (PHQ-9) as part of a subsequent assessment or for the routine monitoring of outcomes.

1.2.2　Referral and initial care

1.2.2.1　After identifying a possible mental disorder in a woman during pregnancy or the postnatal period, further assessment should be considered, in consul-tation with colleagues if necessary.

- If the healthcare professional or the woman has significant concerns, the woman should normally be referred for further assessment to her GP.
- If the woman has, or is suspected to have, a severe mental illness (for example, bipolar disorder or schizophrenia), she should be referred to a specialist mental health service, including, if appropriate, a specialist perinatal mental health service. This should be discussed with the woman and preferably with her GP.
- The woman's GP should be informed in all cases in which a possible current mental disorder or a history of significant mental disorder is detected, even if no further assessment or referral is made.

1.2.2.2　If a woman has a current mental disorder or a history of severe mental illness, she should be asked about her mental health at all subsequent contacts.

1.2.2.3　A written care plan covering pregnancy, delivery and the postnatal period should be developed for pregnant women with a current or past history of severe mental illness, usually in the first trimester. It should:

- be developed in collaboration with the woman and her partner, family and carers, and relevant healthcare professionals

- include increased contact with specialist mental health services (including, if appropriate, specialist perinatal mental health services)
- be recorded in all versions of the woman's notes (her own records and maternity, primary care and mental health notes) and communicated to the woman and all relevant healthcare professionals.

1.2.2.4 Women who need inpatient care for a mental disorder within 12 months of childbirth should normally be admitted to a specialist mother and baby unit, unless there are specific reasons for not doing so.

1.2.2.5 Managers and senior healthcare professionals responsible for perinatal mental health services (including those working in maternity and primary care services) should ensure that:

- there are clearly specified care pathways so that all primary and secondary healthcare professionals involved in the care of women during pregnancy and the postnatal period know how to access assessment and treatment
- staff have supervision and training, covering mental disorders, assessment methods and referral routes, to allow them to follow the care pathways.

1.3 PREVENTION OF MENTAL DISORDERS

1.3.1.1 For pregnant women who have symptoms of depression and/or anxiety that do not meet diagnostic criteria but significantly interfere with personal and social functioning, healthcare professionals should consider:

- for women who have had a previous episode of depression or anxiety, offering individual brief psychological treatment (four to six sessions), such as interpersonal psychotherapy (IPT) or cognitive behavioural therapy (CBT)
- for women who have not had a previous episode of depression or anxiety, offering social support during pregnancy and the postnatal period; such support may consist of regular informal individual or group-based support.

1.3.1.2 Psychosocial interventions (for example, group psychoeducation) designed specifically to reduce the likelihood of developing a mental disorder during pregnancy or the postnatal period should not be part of routine antenatal and postnatal care.

1.3.1.3 Single-session formal debriefing focused on the birth should not be routinely offered to women who have experienced a traumatic birth. However, maternity staff and other healthcare professionals should support women who wish to talk about their experience, encourage them to make use of natural support systems available from family and friends, and take into account the effect of the birth on the partner.

1.3.1.4 Mothers whose infants are stillborn or die soon after birth should not be routinely encouraged to see and hold the dead infant. These women should be offered an appropriate follow-up appointment in primary or secondary care.

1.4 CARE OF WOMEN WITH A MENTAL DISORDER DURING PREGNANCY AND THE POSTNATAL PERIOD

1.4.1 Treating pregnant and breastfeeding women: balancing risks and benefits

1.4.1.1 Women requiring psychological treatment should be seen for treatment normally within 1 month of initial assessment, and no longer than 3 months afterwards. This is because of the lower threshold for access to psychological therapies during pregnancy and the postnatal period arising from the changing risk–benefit ratio for psychotropic medication at this time.

1.4.1.2 Discussions about treatment options with a woman with a mental disorder who is planning a pregnancy, pregnant or breastfeeding should cover:
- the risk of relapse or deterioration in symptoms and the woman's ability to cope with untreated or subthreshold symptoms
- severity of previous episodes, response to treatment and the woman's preference
- the possibility that stopping a drug with known teratogenic risk after pregnancy is confirmed may not remove the risk of malformations
- the risks from stopping medication abruptly
- the need for prompt treatment because of the potential impact of an untreated mental disorder on the fetus or infant
- the increased risk of harm associated with drug treatments during pregnancy and the postnatal period, including the risk in overdose
- treatment options that would enable the woman to breastfeed if she wishes, rather than recommending she does not breastfeed.

1.4.1.3 When prescribing a drug for a woman with a mental disorder who is planning a pregnancy, pregnant or breastfeeding, prescribers should:
- choose drugs with lower risk profiles for the mother and the fetus or infant
- start at the lowest effective dose, and slowly increase it; this is particularly important where the risks may be dose related
- use monotherapy in preference to combination treatment
- consider additional precautions for preterm, low birthweight or sick infants.

1.4.1.4 When stopping a drug in a woman with a mental disorder who is planning a pregnancy, pregnant or breastfeeding, take into account:
- NICE guidance on the specific disorder (see NICE, 2002, 2004a, 2004b, 2004c, 2005a, 2005c, 2006)

15

- the risk to the fetus or infant during the withdrawal period
- the risk from not treating the disorder.

1.4.2 Discussing and explaining the risk of treatments

1.4.2.1 Before treatment decisions are made, healthcare professionals should discuss with the woman the absolute and relative risks associated with treating and not treating the mental disorder during pregnancy and the postnatal period. They should:
- acknowledge the uncertainty surrounding the risks
- explain the background risk of fetal malformations for pregnant women without a mental disorder
- describe risks using natural frequencies rather than percentages (for example, 1 in 10 rather than 10%) and common denominators (for example, 1 in 100 and 25 in 100, rather than 1 in 100 and 1 in 4)
- if possible use decision aids in a variety of verbal and visual formats that focus on an individualised view of the risks
- provide written material to explain the risks (preferably individualised) and, if possible, audio-taped records of the consultation.

1.4.3 Specific considerations for the use of psychotropic drugs during pregnancy and the postnatal period

Antidepressants

1.4.3.1 If a woman taking paroxetine is planning a pregnancy or has an unplanned pregnancy, she should be advised to stop taking the drug.

1.4.3.2 When choosing an antidepressant for pregnant or breastfeeding women, prescribers should, while bearing in mind that the safety of these drugs is not well understood, take into account that:
- tricyclic antidepressants, such as amitriptyline, imipramine and nortriptyline, have lower known risks during pregnancy than other anti-depressants
- most tricyclic antidepressants, have a higher fatal toxicity index than selective serotonin reuptake inhibitors (SSRIs)
- fluoxetine is the SSRI with the lowest known risk during pregnancy
- imipramine, nortriptyline and sertraline are present in breast milk at relatively low levels
- citalopram and fluoxetine are present in breast milk at relatively high levels
- SSRIs taken after 20 weeks' gestation may be associated with an increased risk of persistent pulmonary hypertension in the neonate
- paroxetine taken in the first trimester may be associated with fetal heart defects

- venlafaxine may be associated with increased risk of high blood pressure at high doses, higher toxicity in overdose than SSRIs and some tricyclic antidepressants, and increased difficulty in withdrawal
- all antidepressants carry the risk of withdrawal or toxicity in neonates; in most cases the effects are mild and self-limiting.

Benzodiazepines

1.4.3.3 Benzodiazepines should not be routinely prescribed for pregnant women, except for the short-term treatment of extreme anxiety and agitation. This is because of the risks to the fetus (for example, cleft palate) and the neonate (for example, floppy baby syndrome). Consider gradually stopping benzodiazepines in women who are pregnant.

Antipsychotics

1.4.3.4 Women taking antipsychotics who are planning a pregnancy should be told that the raised prolactin levels associated with some antipsychotics (notably amisulpride, risperidone and sulpiride) reduce the chances of conception. If prolactin levels are raised, an alternative drug should be considered.

1.4.3.5 If a pregnant woman is taking clozapine, switching to another drug and careful monitoring should be considered. Clozapine should not be routinely prescribed for women who are pregnant (because there is a theoretical risk of agranulocytosis in the fetus) or for women who are breast-feeding (because it reaches high levels in breast milk and there is a risk of agranulocytosis in the infant).

1.4.3.6 When deciding whether to prescribe olanzapine to a woman who is pregnant, risk factors for gestational diabetes and weight gain, including family history, existing weight and ethnicity, should be taken into account.

1.4.3.7 Depot antipsychotics should not be routinely prescribed to pregnant women because there is relatively little information on their safety, and their infants may show extrapyramidal symptoms several months after administration of the depot. These are usually self-limiting.

1.4.3.8 Anticholinergic drugs should not be prescribed for the extrapyramidal side effects of antipsychotic drugs except for acute short-term use. Instead, the dose and timing of the antipsychotic drug should be adjusted, or the drug changed.

Valproate

1.4.3.9 Valproate should not be routinely prescribed to women of child-bearing potential. If there is no effective alternative, the risks of taking valproate

17

during pregnancy, and the importance of using adequate contraception, should be explained.

1.4.3.10 Valproate should not be prescribed to women younger than 18 years because of the risk of polycystic ovary syndrome and increased risk of unplanned pregnancy in this age group.

1.4.3.11 If a woman who is taking valproate is planning a pregnancy, or is pregnant, she should be advised to stop taking the drug. Where appropriate in the treatment of bipolar disorder, an alternative drug (usually an antipsychotic) should be considered.

1.4.3.12 If there is no alternative to valproate, doses should be limited to a maximum of 1 gram per day, administered in divided doses and in the slow release form, with 5 mg/day folic acid. However, it is not clear how the serum level of valproate affects the risk of abnormalities.

Lithium

1.4.3.13 Lithium should not be routinely prescribed for women, particularly in the first trimester of pregnancy (because of the risk of cardiac malformations in the fetus) or during breastfeeding (because of the high levels in breast milk).

1.4.3.14 If a woman taking lithium is planning a pregnancy, and is well and not at high risk of relapse, she should be advised to stop taking the drug because of the risk of cardiac malformations in the fetus.

1.4.3.15 If a woman who is taking lithium becomes pregnant:
- if the pregnancy is confirmed in the first trimester, and the woman is well and not at high risk of relapse, lithium should be stopped gradually over 4 weeks; it should be explained that this may not remove the risk of cardiac defects in the fetus
- if the woman is not well or is at high risk of relapse, the following should be considered:
  - switching gradually to an antipsychotic, or
  - stopping lithium and restarting it in the second trimester if the woman is not planning to breastfeed and her symptoms have responded better to lithium than to other drugs in the past, or
  - continuing with lithium if she is at high risk of relapse.

1.4.3.16 If a woman continues taking lithium during pregnancy, serum lithium levels should be checked every 4 weeks, then weekly from the 36th week, and less than 24 hours after childbirth; the dose should be adjusted to keep serum levels towards the lower end of the therapeutic range, and the woman should maintain adequate fluid intake.

1.4.3.17 Women taking lithium should deliver in hospital, and be monitored during labour by the obstetric team. Monitoring should include fluid balance, because of the risk of dehydration and lithium toxicity (in prolonged labour, it may be appropriate to check serum lithium levels).

Carbamazepine and lamotrigine

1.4.3.18   If a woman who is taking carbamazepine or lamotrigine is planning a pregnancy or has an unplanned pregnancy, healthcare professionals should advise her to stop taking these drugs because of the risk of neural tube defects and other malformations in the fetus. If appropriate an alternative drug (such as an antipsychotic) should be considered.

1.4.3.19   Carbamazepine or lamotrigine should not be routinely prescribed for women who are pregnant because of the lack of evidence of efficacy and the risk of neural tube defects in the fetus.

1.4.3.20   Lamotrigine should not be routinely prescribed for women who are breast-feeding because of the risk of dermatological problems in the infant, such as Stevens–Johnson syndrome.

1.4.4   Special considerations arising from the use of psychotropic drugs during early pregnancy or while breastfeeding

1.4.4.1   If a pregnant woman was taking drugs with known teratogenic risk (lithium, valproate, carbamazepine, lamotrigine and paroxetine) at the time of conception and/or in the first trimester, healthcare professionals should:

●   confirm the pregnancy as quickly as possible

●   offer appropriate screening and counselling about the continuation of the pregnancy, the need for additional monitoring and the risks to the fetus if the woman continues to take medication

●   undertake a full paediatric assessment of the newborn infant

●   monitor the infant in the first few weeks after delivery for adverse drug effects, drug toxicity or withdrawal (for example, floppy baby syndrome, irritability, constant crying, shivering, tremor, restlessness, increased tone, feeding and sleeping difficulties and, rarely, seizures); if the mother was prescribed antidepressants in the last trimester, these may result from serotonergic toxicity syndrome rather than withdrawal.

1.4.4.2   Infants of mothers who are breastfeeding while taking psychotropic medication should be monitored for adverse reactions.

1.4.5   Sleep problems

1.4.5.1   Pregnant women with a mental disorder who have sleep problems should initially be given general advice about sleep hygiene (including bedtime routines, the avoidance of caffeine, and the reduction of activity before sleep). For women with serious and chronic problems, low-dose chlorpromazine or low-dose amitriptyline may be considered.

1.4.6   Electroconvulsive therapy (ECT)

1.4.6.1   A course of ECT should be considered for pregnant women with severe depression, severe mixed affective states or mania in the context of bipolar disorder, or catatonia, whose physical health or that of the fetus is at serious risk.

1.4.7   Rapid tranquillisation

1.4.7.1   A pregnant woman requiring rapid tranquillisation should be treated according to the NICE clinical guidelines on the short-term management of disturbed/violent behaviour, schizophrenia and bipolar disorder (see NICE [2005d, 2002, 2006] for details), except that:

● she should not be secluded after rapid tranquillisation
● restraint procedures should be adapted to avoid possible harm to the fetus
● when choosing an agent for rapid tranquillisation in a pregnant woman, an antipsychotic or a benzodiazepine with a short half-life should be considered; if an antipsychotic is used, it should be at the minimum effective dose because of neonatal extrapyramidal symptoms; if a benzodiazepine is used, the risks of floppy baby syndrome should be taken into account
● during the perinatal period, the woman's care should be managed in close collaboration with a paediatrician and an anaesthetist.

1.4.8   Guidance for specific disorders

This section recommends how NICE guidance on specific mental disorders may be adapted for women who are planning a pregnancy, pregnant or breastfeeding. It should be read in conjunction with the rest of the advice in section 1.4.

Depression
This section should be read in conjunction with the NICE clinical guideline on the management of depression in primary and secondary care (see NICE, 2004a).

Women being treated for depression who are planning a pregnancy or have an unplanned pregnancy
1.4.8.1   If a woman being treated for mild depression is taking an antidepressant, the medication should be withdrawn gradually and monitoring ('watchful waiting') considered. If intervention is then needed the following should be considered:

● self-help approaches (guided self-help, computerised CBT [C-CBT], exercise) or
● brief psychological treatments (including counselling, CBT and IPT).

1.4.8.2   If a woman is taking an antidepressant and her latest presentation was a moderate depressive episode, the following options should be discussed with the woman, taking into account previous response to treatment, her preference, and risk:
● switching to psychological therapy (CBT or IPT)
● switching to an antidepressant with lower risk.

1.4.8.3   If a woman is taking an antidepressant and her latest presentation was a severe depressive episode, the following options should be discussed with the woman, taking into account previous response to treatment, her preference, and risk:
● combining drug treatment with psychological treatment, but switching to an antidepressant with lower risk
● switching to psychological treatment (CBT or IPT).

Pregnant or breastfeeding women who have a new episode of depression
1.4.8.4   For a woman who develops mild or moderate depression during pregnancy or the postnatal period, the following should be considered:
● self-help strategies (guided self-help, C-CBT or exercise)
● non-directive counselling delivered at home (listening visits)
● brief CBT or IPT.

1.4.8.5   Antidepressant drugs should be considered for women with mild depression during pregnancy or the postnatal period if they have a history of severe depression and they decline, or their symptoms do not respond to, psychological treatments.

1.4.8.6   For a woman with a moderate depressive episode and a history of depression, or with a severe depressive episode during pregnancy or the postnatal period, the following should be considered:
● structured psychological treatment specifically for depression (CBT or IPT)
● antidepressant treatment if the woman has expressed a preference for it
● combination treatment if there is no response, or a limited response to psychological or drug treatment alone, provided the woman understands the risks associated with antidepressant medication.

Treatment-resistant depression
1.4.8.7   For pregnant women with treatment-resistant depression, a trial of a different single drug or ECT should be considered before combination drug treatment. Lithium augmentation should be avoided.

Generalised anxiety disorder (GAD)

This section should be read in conjunction with the NICE clinical guideline on the management of anxiety in primary, secondary and community care (see NICE [2004c] for details).

Women with GAD who are planning a pregnancy or pregnant

1.4.8.8   If a woman is planning a pregnancy or becomes pregnant while being treated with medication for GAD, the following should be considered:

● stopping medication and starting CBT if it has not already been tried

● if necessary, switching to a safer drug, if the decision is to maintain medication.

Women who have a new episode of GAD

1.4.8.9   A woman who has a new episode of GAD during pregnancy should be treated according to the NICE guideline on anxiety, and CBT should be offered.

Panic disorder

This section should be read in conjunction with the NICE clinical guideline on the management of anxiety in primary, secondary and community care (see NICE [2004c] for details).

Women with panic disorder who are planning a pregnancy or pregnant

1.4.8.10   If a woman is planning a pregnancy or becomes pregnant while being treated for panic disorder, the following should be considered:

● stopping medication and starting CBT if it has not already been tried

● if necessary, switching to a safer drug, if the decision is to maintain medication.

Women who have a new episode of panic disorder

1.4.8.11   For women who have a new episode of panic disorder during pregnancy, psychological therapy (CBT), self-help or C-CBT should be considered before starting drug treatment.

1.4.8.12   For women who have a new episode of panic disorder during pregnancy, paroxetine should not be started and a safer drug should be considered.

Obsessive–compulsive disorder

This section should be read in conjunction with the NICE clinical guideline on the treatment and management of obsessive–compulsive disorder (OCD) (see NICE [2005c] for details).

Women with OCD who are planning a pregnancy or pregnant

1.4.8.13   A woman with OCD who is planning a pregnancy or pregnant should be treated according to the NICE clinical guideline on OCD except that:

● if she is taking medication alone, stopping the drug and starting psychological therapy should be considered

- if she is not taking medication, starting psychological therapy should be considered before drug treatment
- if she is taking paroxetine, it should be stopped and switching to a safer antidepressant considered.

1.4.8.14   A pregnant woman with OCD who is planning to breastfeed should be treated according to the NICE clinical guideline on OCD, except that the use of a combination of clomipramine and citalopram should be avoided if possible.

Women who have a new episode of OCD while breastfeeding

1.4.8.15   A woman who has a new episode of OCD while breastfeeding should be treated according to the NICE clinical guideline on OCD, except that the combination of clomipramine and citalopram should be avoided because of the high levels in breast milk.

Post-traumatic stress disorder

This section should be read in conjunction with the NICE clinical guideline on the management of post-traumatic stress disorder (PTSD) (see NICE [2005a] for details).

Women with PTSD who are planning a pregnancy or pregnant

1.4.8.16   A woman with PTSD who is planning a pregnancy or pregnant should be treated according to the NICE clinical guideline on PTSD, except that if she is taking an antidepressant the drug should be stopped and trauma-focused psychological therapy (for example, CBT or eye movement desensitisation and reprocessing therapy) offered.

1.4.8.17   For a woman with PTSD who is planning a pregnancy or pregnant, adjunctive olanzapine should not be prescribed.

Eating disorders

This section should be read in conjunction with the NICE clinical guideline on the treatment and management of eating disorders (see NICE [2004b] for details).

Women with anorexia nervosa

1.4.8.18   A woman with anorexia nervosa who is planning a pregnancy, has an unplanned pregnancy or is breastfeeding should be treated according to the NICE clinical guideline on eating disorders.

Women with binge eating disorder

1.4.8.19   A woman with binge eating disorder who is taking an antidepressant and is planning a pregnancy, has an unplanned pregnancy or is breastfeeding should be treated according to the section on depression in this guideline (recommendations 1.4.8.1–7).

Women with bulimia nervosa

1.4.8.20 If a woman who is taking medication for bulimia nervosa is planning a pregnancy or pregnant, healthcare professionals should consider gradually stopping the medication after discussion with her. If the problem persists, referral for specialist treatment should be considered.

Women who have an episode of bulimia nervosa while breastfeeding

1.4.8.21 If a woman has an episode of bulimia nervosa while breastfeeding, psychological treatment should be offered, rather than fluoxetine at 60 mg. If a woman is already taking fluoxetine at 60 mg, she should be advised not to breastfeed.

Bipolar disorder

These recommendations are from the NICE clinical guideline on the management of bipolar disorder (see NICE [2006] for details).

Pregnant women with bipolar disorder who are stable on an antipsychotic

1.4.8.22 If a pregnant woman with bipolar disorder is stable on an antipsychotic and likely to relapse without medication, she should be maintained on the antipsychotic, and monitored for weight gain and diabetes.

Women with bipolar disorder planning a pregnancy

1.4.8.23 If a woman who needs antimanic medication plans to become pregnant, a low-dose typical or atypical antipsychotic should be the treatment of choice.

1.4.8.24 If a woman with bipolar disorder planning a pregnancy becomes depressed after stopping prophylactic medication, psychological therapy (CBT) should be offered in preference to an antidepressant because of the risk of switching to mania associated with antidepressants. If an antidepressant is used, it should usually be an SSRI (but not paroxetine) and the woman should be monitored closely.

Women with bipolar disorder who have an unplanned pregnancy

1.4.8.25 If a woman with bipolar disorder has an unplanned pregnancy and is stopping lithium as prophylactic medication, an antipsychotic should be offered.

Pregnant women with acute mania or depressive symptoms
  Acute mania

1.4.8.26 If a pregnant woman who is not taking medication develops acute mania, a typical or an atypical antipsychotic should be considered. The dose should be kept as low as possible and the woman monitored carefully.

1.4.8.27   If a pregnant woman develops acute mania while taking prophylactic medication, prescribers should:
- check the dose of the prophylactic agent and adherence
- increase the dose if the woman is taking an antipsychotic, or consider changing to an antipsychotic if she is not
- if there is no response to changes in dose or drug and the patient has severe mania, consider the use of ECT, lithium and, rarely, valproate.

1.4.8.28   If there is no alternative to valproate, augmenting it with antimanic medication (but not carbamazepine) should be considered.

Depressive symptoms

1.4.8.29   For mild depressive symptoms in pregnant women with bipolar disorder the following should be considered, in this order:
- self-help approaches such as guided self-help and C-CBT
- brief psychological treatments (including counselling, CBT and IPT).

1.4.8.30   For moderate to severe depressive symptoms in pregnant women with bipolar disorder the following should be considered:
- psychological treatment (CBT) for moderate depression
- combined medication and structured psychological treatments for severe depression.

1.4.8.31   If prescribing medication for moderate to severe depressive symptoms in a pregnant woman with bipolar disorder, quetiapine alone, or SSRIs (but not paroxetine) in combination with prophylactic medication should be preferred because SSRIs are less likely to be associated with switching to mania than the tricyclic antidepressants. Monitor closely for signs of switching and stop the SSRI if the woman starts to develop manic or hypomanic symptoms.

Care in the perinatal period

1.4.8.32   After delivery, if a woman with bipolar disorder who is not on medication is at high risk of developing an acute episode, prescribers should consider establishing or reinstating medication as soon as the woman is medically stable (once the fluid balance is established).

1.4.8.33   If a woman maintained on lithium is at high risk of a manic relapse in the immediate postnatal period, augmenting treatment with an antipsychotic should be considered.

Women with bipolar disorder who wish to breastfeed

1.4.8.34   Women with bipolar disorder who are taking psychotropic medication and wish to breastfeed should be offered a prophylactic agent that can be used when breastfeeding. The first choice should be an antipsychotic.

Schizophrenia

This section should be read in conjunction with the NICE clinical guideline on the treatment and management of schizophrenia (see NICE [2002] for details).

Women with schizophrenia who are planning a pregnancy or pregnant

1.4.8.35   Women with schizophrenia who are planning a pregnancy or pregnant should be treated according to the NICE clinical guideline on schizophrenia, except that if the woman is taking an atypical antipsychotic consideration should be given to switching to a low-dose typical antipsychotic, such as haloperidol, chlorpromazine or trifluoperazine.

Women with schizophrenia who are breastfeeding

1.4.8.36   A woman with schizophrenia who is breastfeeding should be treated according to the NICE clinical guideline on schizophrenia, except that women receiving depot medication should be advised that their infants may show extrapyramidal symptoms several months after administration of the depot. These are usually self-limiting.

1.5   THE ORGANISATION OF SERVICES

1.5.1.1   Clinical networks should be established for perinatal mental health services, managed by a coordinating board of healthcare professionals, commissioners, managers, and service users and carers. These networks should provide:
- a specialist multidisciplinary perinatal service in each locality, which provides direct services, consultation and advice to maternity services, other mental health services and community services; in areas of high morbidity these services may be provided by separate specialist perinatal teams
- access to specialist expert advice on the risks and benefits of psychotropic medication during pregnancy and breastfeeding
- clear referral and management protocols for services across all levels of the existing stepped-care frameworks for mental disorders, to ensure effective transfer of information and continuity of care
- pathways of care for service users, with defined roles and competencies for all professional groups involved.

1.5.1.2   Each managed perinatal mental health network should have designated specialist inpatient services and cover a population where there are between 25,000 and 50,000 live births a year, depending on the local psychiatric morbidity rates.

1.5.1.3   Specialist perinatal inpatient services should:
- provide facilities designed specifically for mothers and infants (typically with 6–12 beds)
- be staffed by specialist perinatal mental health staff
- be staffed to provide appropriate care for infants
- have effective liaison with general medical and mental health services

- have available the full range of therapeutic services
- be closely integrated with community-based mental health services to ensure continuity of care and minimum length of stay.

1.6   RESEARCH RECOMMENDATIONS

The Guideline Development Group has made the following recommendations for research, based on its review of evidence, to improve NICE guidance and patient care in the future.

1.6.1   Decision aids for helping pregnant and breastfeeding women to make decisions about their care

A randomised controlled trial should be conducted to compare usual care with usual care plus the use of decision aids designed to help pregnant and breastfeeding women with mental disorders to make informed decisions about their care. Outcomes should include the development of agreed care plans, the successful implementation of the agreed care plans, and satisfaction with the care plan and the communication about the planning.

Why this is important
Psychotropic drugs carry teratogenic risks during pregnancy and are often present in breast milk. It is therefore important that women are enabled to make informed decisions about treatment choices.

1.6.2   Interventions for women with subthreshold symptoms of depression and/or anxiety

A randomised controlled trial should be conducted to compare the efficacy and cost effectiveness of an intervention for women with chronic subthreshold symptoms of depression and anxiety with usual maternity and primary care. The intervention should be a brief psychoeducational intervention. Primary outcome measures may include symptoms of depression and anxiety, and there should be a 1-year follow-up period.

Why this is important
Depression and anxiety in the postnatal period can have a serious impact on a woman's ability to cope with day-to-day life, including looking after her infant and other children in the family. Even subthreshold symptoms can affect a woman's general functioning and the development of her infant. Treating subthreshold

symptoms may prevent escalation of symptoms into a diagnosis of depression or anxiety, and also improve a woman's ability to cope.

1.6.3   Assessing managed perinatal networks

An evaluation of managed perinatal networks should be undertaken to compare the effectiveness of different network models in delivering care. It should cover the degree of integration of services, the establishment of common protocols, the impact on patients' access to specified services and the quality of care, and staff views on the delivery of care.

Why this is important
Although only a relatively small number of women have a serious mental disorder during pregnancy and the postnatal period, those who do may need specialist care, including access to knowledge about the risks of psychotropic medication, specialist inpatient beds and additional intrapartum care. Managed clinical perinatal networks may be a way of providing this level of care in a cost effective and clinically effective way by allowing access to specialist care for all women who need it, whether or not they live near a specialist perinatal team.

1.6.4   Prescription patterns

A study of the General Practice Research Database should be undertaken to assess the impact of pregnancy on changing psychotropic medication (including both switching and stopping medication). Outcomes should include relapse of mental disorders, exacerbation of symptoms, type and duration of treatment, and birth outcomes.

Why this is important
Most women with a mental disorder during pregnancy will be cared for in primary care. Knowing how pregnancy affects the pattern of psychotropic prescription would help to target educational campaigns for healthcare professionals caring for pregnant women.

1.6.5   Case finding for depression

A validation study should be undertaken of the 'Whooley questions' (During the past month, have you often been bothered by feeling down, depressed or hopeless? During the past month, have you often been bothered by having little interest or pleasure in doing things?) in women in the first postnatal year, examining the questions' effectiveness when used by midwives and health visitors compared with a psychiatric interview.

Why this is important

Depression in the first postnatal year is relatively common and may have a lasting impact on the woman, her baby and other family members. Case finding is most conveniently undertaken by healthcare professionals in regular contact with women, but they do not traditionally have training in mental health. The Whooley questions appear to offer a relatively quick and convenient way of case finding for healthcare professionals who are not specialists in mental health.

2. INTRODUCTION

This guideline has been developed to advise on the clinical management of and service provision for antenatal and postnatal mental health. The guideline recommendations have been developed after careful consideration of the best available evidence by a multidisciplinary team of healthcare professionals, women who have experienced mental health problems in the antenatal or postnatal period and guideline methodologists. It is intended that the guideline will be useful to clinicians and service commissioners in providing and planning high-quality care for women with antenatal and postnatal mental health problems while also emphasising the importance of the experience of care for women and their families and carers.

2.1 NATIONAL GUIDELINES

2.1.1 What are clinical practice guidelines?

Clinical practice guidelines are 'systematically developed statements that assist clinicians and patients in making decisions about appropriate treatment for specific conditions' (Mann, 1996). They are derived from the best available research evidence, using predetermined and systematic methods to identify and evaluate all the evidence relating to the specific condition in question. Where evidence is lacking, the guidelines will incorporate statements and recommendations based upon the consensus statements developed by the Guideline Development Group (GDG).

Clinical guidelines are intended to improve the process and outcomes of healthcare in a number of different ways. They can:

- provide up-to-date evidence-based recommendations for the management of conditions and disorders by healthcare professionals
- be used as the basis to set standards to assess the practice of healthcare professionals
- form the basis for education and training of healthcare professionals
- assist patients and carers in making informed decisions about their treatment and care
- improve communication between healthcare professionals, patients and carers
- help identify priority areas for further research.

2.1.2 Uses and limitations of clinical guidelines

Guidelines are not a substitute for professional knowledge and clinical judgement. They can be limited in their usefulness and applicability by a number of different factors: the availability of high-quality research evidence, the quality of the methodology used in the development of the guideline, the generalisability of research findings and the uniqueness of individual patients.

Although the quality of research in antenatal and postnatal mental health is variable, the methodology used here reflects current international understanding on the appropriate practice for guideline development (AGREE: Appraisal of Guidelines Research and Evaluation Instrument; www.agreecollaboration.org), ensuring the collection and selection of the best research evidence available and the systematic generation of treatment recommendations applicable to the majority of patients and situations. However, there will always be some patients for whom clinical guideline recommendations are not appropriate and situations in which the recommendations are not readily applicable. This guideline does not, therefore, override the individual responsibility of healthcare professionals to make appropriate decisions in the circumstances of the individual patient, in consultation with the patient and/or carer.

In addition to the clinical evidence, cost-effectiveness information, where available, is taken into account in the generation of statements and recommendations of the clinical guidelines. While national guidelines are concerned with clinical and cost effectiveness, issues of affordability and implementation costs are to be determined by the National Health Service (NHS).

In using guidelines, it is important to remember that the absence of empirical evidence for the effectiveness of a particular intervention is not the same as evidence for ineffectiveness. In addition, of particular relevance in mental health, evidence-based treatments are often delivered within the context of an overall treatment programme including a range of activities, the purpose of which may be to help engage the patient and provide an appropriate context for the delivery of specific interventions. It is important to maintain and enhance the service context in which these interventions are delivered, otherwise the specific benefits of effective interventions will be lost. Indeed, the importance of organising care, so as to support and encourage a good therapeutic relationship, is at times more important than the specific treatments offered.

2.1.3   Why develop national guidelines?

The National Institute for Health and Clinical Excellence (NICE) was established as a Special Health Authority for England and Wales in 1999, with a remit to provide a single source of authoritative and reliable guidance for patients, professionals and the public. NICE guidance aims to improve standards of care, to diminish unacceptable variations in the provision and quality of care across the NHS and to ensure that the health service is patient centred. All guidance is developed in a transparent and collaborative manner using the best available evidence and involving all relevant stakeholders.

NICE generates guidance in a number of different ways, two of which are relevant here. First, national guidance is produced by the Technology Appraisal Committee to give robust advice about a particular treatment, intervention, procedure or other health technology. Second, NICE commissions the production of national clinical practice guidelines focused upon the overall treatment and management of a specific condition. To enable this latter development, NICE established seven National Collaborating Centres in conjunction with a range of professional organisations involved in healthcare.

2.1.4   The National Collaborating Centre for Mental Health

This guideline has been commissioned by NICE and developed within the National Collaborating Centre for Mental Health (NCCMH). The NCCMH is led by a partnership between the Royal College of Psychiatrists' Research and Training Unit and the British Psychological Society's equivalent unit (Centre for Outcomes Research and Effectiveness).

2.1.5   From national guidelines to local protocols

Once a national guideline has been published and disseminated, local healthcare groups will be expected to produce a plan and identify resources for implementation, along with appropriate timetables. Subsequently, a multidisciplinary group involving commissioners of healthcare, primary care and specialist mental health professionals, patients and carers should undertake the translation of the implementation plan into local protocols. The nature and pace of the local plan will reflect local healthcare needs and the nature of existing services; full implementation may take a considerable time, especially where substantial training needs are identified.

2.1.6   Auditing the implementation of guidelines

This guideline identifies key areas of clinical practice and service delivery for local and national audit. Although the generation of audit standards is an important and necessary step in the implementation of this guidance, a more broadly based implementation strategy should be developed. Nevertheless, it should be noted that the Healthcare Commission will monitor the extent to which Primary Care Trusts (PCTs), trusts responsible for mental health and social care, and Health Authorities have implemented these guidelines.

2.2   THE NATIONAL ANTENATAL AND POSTNATAL MENTAL HEALTH GUIDELINE

2.2.1   Who has developed this guideline?

The GDG was convened by the NCCMH and supported by funding from NICE. The GDG consisted of two former service users, professionals from psychiatry, clinical psychology, general practice, midwifery, obstetrics, health visiting, social work services and management.

Staff from the NCCMH provided leadership and support throughout the process of guideline development, undertaking systematic searches, information retrieval, appraisal and systematic review of the evidence. Members of the GDG received training in the process of guideline development. The National Guidelines Support and Research Unit, also established by NICE, provided advice and assistance regarding aspects of the guideline development process.

All members of the group made formal declarations of interest at the outset, updated at every GDG meeting. GDG members met a total of 15 times throughout the process of guideline development. For ease of evidence identification and analysis, some members of the GDG became topic leads, covering identifiable treatment approaches. The NCCMH technical team supported group members, with additional expert advice from special advisers where necessary. All statements and recommendations in this guideline have been generated and agreed by the whole GDG.

2.2.2   For whom is this guideline intended?

This guideline will be of relevance to all women who suffer from antenatal and post-natal mental health problems.

The guideline covers the care provided by primary, secondary, tertiary and other healthcare professionals who have direct contact with, and make decisions concerning, the care of women with mental disorder in the antenatal and postnatal period.

Although this guideline will briefly address the issue of diagnosis, it will not make evidence-based recommendations or refer to evidence regarding diagnosis, primary prevention or assessment. In sum, the guideline is intended for use by:

● Professional groups who share in the treatment and care for women with a diagnosis of antenatal and postnatal mental health problems, including psychiatrists, clinical psychologists, mental health nurses, community psychiatric nurses (CPNs), other community nurses, general practitioners (GPs), midwives, obstetricians, health visitors, social workers, counsellors, practice nurses, occupational therapists, pharmacists and others.

● Professionals in other health and non-health sectors who may have direct contact with or are involved in the provision of health and other public services for those diagnosed with antenatal and postnatal mental health problems; these may include accident and emergency staff, paramedical staff, prison doctors, the police and professionals who work in the criminal justice and education sectors.

● Those with responsibility for planning services for people with a diagnosis of antenatal and postnatal mental health problems, and their carers, including directors of public health, NHS trust managers and managers in PCTs.

2.2.3   Specific aims of this guideline

The guideline makes recommendations for pharmacological treatments and the use of psychological and service-level interventions. Specifically it aims to:

● evaluate the role of specific pharmacological agents in the treatment and management of antenatal and postnatal mental health problems

● evaluate the role of specific psychological interventions in the treatment and management of antenatal and postnatal mental health problems

● evaluate the role of specific service-delivery systems and service-level interventions in the management of antenatal and postnatal mental health problems

- integrate the above to provide best-practice advice on the care of individuals with a diagnosis of antenatal or postnatal mental health problems through the different phases of illness, including the initiation of treatment, the treatment of acute episodes and the promotion of recovery
- consider economic aspects of various standard treatments for antenatal and postnatal mental health problems.

The guideline will not cover treatments that are not normally available on the NHS.

2.2.4   Other versions of this guideline

There are other versions of *Antenatal and Postnatal Mental Health: Clinical Management and Service Guidance*, including:
- the NICE guideline, which is a shorter version of this guideline, containing the key recommendations and all other recommendations
- the Quick Reference Guide, which is a summary of the main recommendations in the NICE guideline
- Understanding NICE Guidance, which describes the guidance using non-technical language. It is written chiefly for patients but may also be useful for family members, advocates or those who care for women with antenatal and postnatal mental health problems.

2.3   THE STRUCTURE OF THIS GUIDELINE

The guideline is divided into chapters, each covering a set of related topics. The first three chapters provide a summary of the clinical practice and research recommendations and a general introduction to guidelines and to the methods used to develop them. The fourth chapter provides an introduction to the topic of antenatal and postnatal mental health. Chapters 5 to 8 describe the evidence that underpins the recommendations.

Where appropriate, details about current practice, the evidence base and any research limitations are provided. Information is also given about both the interventions included and the included studies where appropriate. Summary evidence profiles are also provided. Clinical summaries bring the evidence together highlighting key issues. Recommendations related to each topic are presented at the end of the relevant section of the chapter. The CD-ROM which accompanies this publication includes fuller details of the included studies plus the excluded studies and reasons for exclusion, the full evidence profiles, and the forest plots (see below for details).

Appendices on CD-ROM

Content	Appendix
Characteristics of reviewed studies	Appendix 18
Evidence profiles	Appendix 19
Clinical evidence forest plots	Appendix 20

3. METHODS USED TO DEVELOP THIS GUIDELINE

3.1   OVERVIEW

The development of this guideline drew upon methods outlined by NICE (*Guideline Development Methods: Information for National Collaborating Centres and Guideline Developers*[2] [NICE, 2005b]). A team of health professionals, lay representatives and technical experts known as the GDG, with support from the NCCMH staff, undertook the development of a patient-centred, evidence-based guideline. There are six basic steps in the process of developing a guideline:

- define the scope, which sets the parameters of the guideline and provides a focus and steer for the development work
- define clinical questions considered important for practitioners and service users
- develop criteria for evidence searching and search for evidence
- design validated protocols for systematic review and apply to evidence recovered by search
- synthesise and (meta-) analyse data retrieved, guided by the clinical questions, and produce evidence profiles
- answer clinical questions with evidence-based recommendations for clinical practice.

The clinical practice recommendations made by the GDG are therefore derived from the most up-to-date and robust evidence for the clinical and cost effectiveness of treatments and services used in the management of mental health disorders in women during pregnancy and up to 1 year after delivery. In addition, to ensure a service user and carer focus, the concerns of service users and carers regarding clinical practice have been highlighted and addressed by recommendations agreed by the whole GDG.

3.2   THE SCOPE

Guideline topics are selected by the Department of Health (DH) and the Welsh Assembly Government, which identify the main areas to be covered by the guideline in a specific remit (see *The Guideline Development Process – An Overview for Stakeholders, the Public and the NHS*[3] [NICE, 2004e]). The remit for this guideline was translated into a scope document by staff at the NCCMH.

---

[2]Available from: www.nice.org.uk
[3]Available from: www.nice.org.uk

The purpose of the scope was to:
- provide an overview of what the guideline would include and exclude
- identify the key aspects of care that must be included
- set the boundaries of the development work and provide a clear framework to enable work to stay within the priorities agreed by NICE and the NCCMH and the remit from the DH/Welsh Assembly Government
- inform the development of the clinical questions and search strategy
- inform professionals and the public about the expected content of the guideline
- keep the guideline to a reasonable size to ensure that its development could be carried out within an 18-month period.

The draft scope was subject to consultation with stakeholders over a 4-week period. During the consultation period, the scope was posted on the NICE website (www.nice.org.uk). Comments were invited from stakeholder organisations and the Guideline Review Panel (GRP). Further information about the GRP can also be found on the NICE website. The NCCMH and NICE reviewed the scope in light of comments received, and the revised scope was signed off by the GRP.

3.3   THE GUIDELINE DEVELOPMENT GROUP

The GDG was made up of professionals in psychiatry, clinical psychology, midwifery, health visiting, social work and general practice, together with two former service users. The guideline development process was supported by staff from the NCCMH, who undertook the clinical and health economics literature searches, reviewed and presented the evidence to the GDG, managed the process and contributed to drafting the guideline.

3.3.1   Guideline Development Group meetings

Fifteen GDG meetings were held between 18 November 2004 and 29 September 2006. During each day-long GDG meeting, in a plenary session, clinical questions and clinical and economic evidence were reviewed and assessed, and recommendations formulated. At each meeting, all GDG members declared any potential conflict of interest, and service-user concerns were routinely discussed as part of a standing agenda.

3.3.2   Topic groups

The GDG divided its workload along clinically relevant lines to simplify the guideline development process, and GDG members formed smaller topic groups to undertake guideline work in that area of clinical practice. Topic Group 1 covered questions relating to pharmacological aspects of management of antenatal and postnatal mental health problems; Topic Group 2 covered the prediction and detection of mental disorder; Topic

Group 3 covered psychology and psychosocial interventions; and Topic Group 4 covered service delivery. These groups were designed to efficiently manage the large volume of evidence appraisal prior to presenting it to the GDG as a whole. Each topic group was chaired by a GDG member with expert knowledge of the topic area (one of the healthcare professionals). Topic groups refined the clinical questions, refined the clinical definitions of treatments, reviewed and prepared the evidence with the systematic reviewer before presenting it to the GDG as a whole and helped the GDG to identify further expertise in the topic. Topic-group leaders reported the status of the group's work as part of the standing agenda. They also introduced and led the GDG discussion of the evidence review for that topic and assisted the GDG Chair in drafting that section of the guideline relevant to the work of each topic group.

3.3.3 Service users and carers

Individuals with direct experience of services gave an integral service-user focus to the GDG and the guideline. The GDG included two service users. They contributed as full GDG members to writing the clinical questions, helping to ensure that the evidence addressed their views and preferences, highlighting sensitive issues and terminology relevant to the guideline and bringing service-user research to the attention of the GDG. In drafting the guideline, they contributed to identifying recommendations from the service-user perspective. In addition, testimonies were collected from other service users and healthcare professionals (see Section 3.8).

3.3.4 Special advisers

Special advisers, who had specific expertise in one or more aspects of treatment and management relevant to the guideline, assisted the GDG, commenting on specific aspects of developing the guideline and making presentations to the GDG. Appendix 2 lists those who agreed to act as special advisors.

3.3.5 Consensus conference and focus group

A consensus conference was held during the guideline development period in collaboration with the GDG developing the NICE guideline for the treatment and management of bipolar disorder. This was to discuss the use of psychotropic medication before, during and after pregnancy with invited experts from outside of the GDG, who gave presentations and commented on a draft position statement which formed the basis of Chapter 7. Invited experts are listed in Appendix 2.

Towards the end of the guideline development process, a focus group was held with healthcare professionals from primary care (GPs, health visitors and midwives) to aid understanding of how the guideline will impact on primary care in order to facilitate writing the quick reference guide (see Section 2.2.4).

3.4   CLINICAL QUESTIONS

Clinical questions were used to guide the identification and interrogation of the evidence base relevant to the topic of the guideline. Before the first GDG meeting, draft questions were prepared by NCCMH staff based on the scope and an overview of existing guidelines and modified during a meeting with the guideline Chair. They were then discussed by the GDG and amended as necessary. Where appropriate, the questions were refined once the evidence had been searched and, where necessary, sub-questions were generated. Questions submitted by stakeholders were also discussed by the GDG and the rationale for not including questions was recorded in the minutes. The final list of clinical questions is in Appendix 5.

For questions about interventions, the patient, intervention, comparison and outcome (PICO) framework was used. This structured approach divides each question into four components: the patients (the population under study), the interventions (what is being done), the comparisons (other main treatment options) and the outcomes (the measures of how effective the interventions have been) (see Text Box 1).

For questions relating to diagnosis, the PICO framework was not used, as such questions do not involve an intervention designed to treat a particular condition. Rather, the questions were designed to pick up key issues specifically relevant to diagnostic tests, for example their accuracy, reliability, safety and acceptability to the patient.

Text Box 1: Features of a well-formulated question on intervention effectiveness – the PICO guide

Patients/population	Which patients or population of patients are we interested in? How can they be best described? Are there subgroups that need to be considered?
Intervention	Which intervention, treatment or approach should be used?
Comparison	What is/are the main alternative/s to compare with the intervention?
Outcome	What is really important for the patient? Which outcomes should be considered: intermediate or short-term measures, mortality, morbidity and treatment complications, rates of relapse, late morbidity and readmission, return to work, physical and social functioning and other measures such as quality of life, general health status and costs?

In some situations, the prognosis of a particular condition is of fundamental importance over and above its general significance in relation to specific interventions. Areas where this is particularly likely to occur relate to assessment of risk, for example in terms of behaviour modification or screening and early intervention. In addition, questions related to issues of service delivery are occasionally specified in the remit from the DH/Welsh Assembly Government. In these cases, appropriate clinical questions were developed to be clear and concise.

To help facilitate the literature review, a note was made of the best study-design type to answer each question. There are four main types of clinical questions of relevance to NICE guidelines. These are listed in Text Box 2. For each type of question, the best primary study design varies, where 'best' is interpreted as 'least likely to give misleading answers to the question'.

However, in all cases, a well-conducted systematic review of the appropriate type of study is likely to always yield a better answer than a single study.

Deciding on the best design type to answer a specific clinical or public health question does not mean that studies of different design types addressing the same question were discarded.

Text Box 2: Best study design to answer each type of question

Type of question	Best primary study design
Effectiveness or other impact of an intervention	Randomised controlled trial (RCT); other studies that may be considered in the absence of an RCT are the following: internally/externally controlled before-and-after trial, interrupted time series
Accuracy of information (for example, risk factor, test, prediction rule)	Comparing the information against a valid gold standard in a randomised trial or inception cohort study
Rates (of disease, patient experience, rare side effects)	Cohort, registry, cross-sectional study
Costs	Naturalistic prospective cost study

3.5   SYSTEMATIC CLINICAL LITERATURE REVIEW

The aim of the clinical literature review was to systematically identify and synthesise relevant evidence from the literature in order to answer the specific clinical questions developed by the GDG. Thus, clinical practice recommendations are evidence based, where possible, and if evidence was not available, informal consensus methods were used (see Section 3.5.6) and the need for future research was specified.

3.5.1   Methodology

A stepwise, hierarchical approach was taken to locating and presenting evidence to the GDG. The NCCMH developed this process based on methods set out in *Guideline Development Methods: Information for National Collaborating Centres and Guideline Developers*[4] (NICE, 2005b) and after considering recommendations from a range of other sources. These included:

- Centre for Clinical Policy and Practice of the New South Wales Health Department (Australia)
- Clinical Evidence
- The Cochrane Collaboration
- New Zealand Guidelines Group
- NHS Centre for Reviews and Dissemination
- Oxford Centre for Evidence-Based Medicine
- Scottish Intercollegiate Guidelines Network (SIGN)
- United States Agency for Healthcare Research and Quality
- Oxford Systematic Review Development Programme
- GRADE Working Group.

3.5.2   The review process

After the scope was finalised, a more extensive search for systematic reviews and published guidelines was undertaken.

The GDG decided which questions were likely to have a good evidence base and which questions were likely to have little or no directly relevant evidence. In the absence of good evidence, recommendations were developed by informal consensus. For questions that were unlikely to have a good evidence base, a brief descriptive review was initially undertaken by a member of the GDG (see Section 3.5.6). For questions with a good evidence base, the review process depended on the type of clinical question.

Searches for evidence were updated between 6 and 8 weeks before the first consultation. After this point, studies were included only if they were judged by the GDG to be exceptional (for example, the evidence was likely to change a recommendation).

The search process for questions concerning interventions
For questions related to interventions, the initial evidence base was formed from well-conducted RCTs that addressed at least one of the clinical questions. Although there are a number of difficulties with the use of RCTs in the evaluation of interventions in mental health, the RCT remains the most important method for establishing treatment efficacy (this is discussed in more detail in appropriate clinical evidence chapters). For other clinical questions, searches were for the appropriate study design (see above).

---

[4]Available from: www.nice.org.uk

All searches were based on the standard mental-health-related bibliographic databases (EMBASE, MEDLINE, CINAHL, PsycINFO) for all trials potentially relevant to the guideline. Since the number of citations generated from a search for all RCTs was large (around 14,000), this search was run three times: once for citations up to 1994, once for citations from 1995 to 1999 and a third for citations from 2000 to 2004 (when the development process started). Update searches were undertaken a further two times during the development process. Additional searches were run for clinical questions not best answered by RCTs. These are noted in the review write-ups in the following chapters.

After the initial search results were scanned liberally to exclude irrelevant papers, the review team used a purpose-built 'study information' database to manage both the included and the excluded studies (eligibility criteria were developed after consultation with the GDG). Future guidelines will be able to update and extend the usable evidence base starting from the evidence collected, synthesised and analysed for this guideline.

In addition, searches were made of the reference lists of existing systematic reviews and included studies, as well as the list of evidence submitted by stakeholders. Known experts in the field, based both on the references identified in early steps and on advice from GDG members, were sent letters requesting relevant studies that were in the process of being published[5]. In addition, the tables of contents of appropriate journals were periodically checked during the development process for relevant studies.

Search filters
Search filters developed by the review team consisted of a combination of subject heading and free-text phrases. Specific filters were developed for the guideline topic and, where necessary, for each clinical question. In addition, the review team used filters developed for systematic reviews, RCTs and other appropriate research designs (see Appendix 6).

Study selection
All primary-level studies included after the first scan of citations were acquired in full and re-evaluated for eligibility at the time they were being entered into the study information database. Appendix 7 lists the standard inclusion criteria. More specific eligibility criteria were developed for each clinical question and are described in the relevant clinical evidence chapters. Eligible primary-level studies were critically appraised for methodological quality (see Appendix 8). The eligibility of each study was confirmed by at least one member of the appropriate topic group.

For some clinical questions, it was necessary to prioritise the evidence with respect to the UK context (that is, external validity). To make this process explicit, the

---

[5]Unpublished full trial reports were also accepted where sufficient information was available to judge eligibility and quality (see section on unpublished evidence).

topic groups took into account the following factors when assessing the evidence:

● participant factors (for example, gender, age and ethnicity)
● provider factors (for example, model fidelity, the conditions under which the intervention was performed and the availability of experienced staff to undertake the procedure)
● cultural factors (for example, differences in standard care and differences in the welfare system).

It was the responsibility of each topic group to decide which prioritisation factors were relevant to each clinical question in light of the UK context, and then decide how they should modify their recommendations.

Unpublished evidence
The GDG used a number of criteria when deciding whether or not to accept unpublished data. First, the evidence must have been accompanied by a trial report containing sufficient detail to properly assess the quality of the data. Second, the evidence must have been submitted with the understanding that data from the study and a summary of the study's characteristics would be published in the full guideline. Therefore, the GDG did not accept evidence submitted as commercial in confidence. However, the GDG recognised that unpublished evidence submitted by investigators might later be retracted by those investigators if the inclusion of such data would jeopardise publication of their research.

3.5.3   Synthesising the evidence

Outcome data were extracted from all eligible studies that met the quality criteria, using standardised forms (see Appendix 9 and Appendix 10). Where possible, meta-analysis was used to synthesise the evidence using Review Manager 4.2.8 (Cochrane Collaboration, 2005). If necessary, reanalyses of the data or sub-analyses were used to answer clinical questions not addressed in the original studies or reviews.

For a given outcome (continuous and dichotomous), where more than 50% of the number randomised to any group were not accounted for[6] by trial authors, the data were excluded from the review because of the risk of bias. However, where possible, dichotomous efficacy outcomes were calculated on an intention-to-treat basis (that is, a 'once-randomised-always-analyse' basis). This assumes that those participants who ceased to engage in the study – from whatever group – had an unfavourable outcome and means that the 50% rule was not applied to dichotomous outcomes where there was good evidence that those participants who ceased to engage in the study were likely to have an unfavourable outcome (in this case, early withdrawals were included in both the numerator and denominator). Adverse effects were entered into Review Manager as reported by the study authors because it was usually not possible to

---

[6]'Accounted for' in this context means that an appropriate method for dealing with missing data (for example, last observation carried forward [LOCF] or a regression technique) had been used.

determine whether early withdrawals had an unfavourable outcome. For the outcome 'leaving the study early for any reason', the denominator was the number randomised.

The number needed to treat to benefit (NNTB) or the number needed to treat to harm (NNTH) was reported for each outcome where the baseline risk (that is, control group event rate) was similar across studies. In addition, NNTs calculated at follow-up were only reported where the length of follow-up was similar across studies. When the length of follow-up or baseline risk varies (especially with low risk), the NNT is a poor summary of the treatment effect (Deeks, 2002).

Included/excluded studies tables, generated automatically from the study information database, were used to summarise general information about each study (see Appendix 18). Where meta-analysis was not appropriate and/or possible, the reported results from each primary-level study were also presented in the included studies table (and included, where appropriate, in a narrative review).

Consultation was used to overcome difficulties with coding. Data from studies included in existing systematic reviews were extracted independently by one reviewer and cross-checked with the existing data set. Where possible, two independent reviewers extracted data from new studies. Where double data extraction was not possible, data extracted by one reviewer was checked by the second reviewer. Disagreements were resolved with discussion. Where consensus could not be reached, a third reviewer resolved the disagreement. Masked assessment (that is, blind to the journal from which the article comes, the authors, the institution and the magnitude of the effect) was not used since it is unclear that doing so reduces bias (Jadad *et al.*, 1996; Berlin, 1997).

3.5.4 Presenting the data to the GDG

Summary characteristics tables and, where appropriate, forest plots generated with Review Manager, were presented to the GDG, in order to prepare an evidence profile for each review and to develop recommendations.

Evidence profile tables

An evidence profile table was used to summarise both the quality of the evidence and the results of the evidence synthesis (see Table 1 for an example evidence profile table). Each table included details about the quality assessment of each outcome: number of studies, the study design, limitations (based on the quality of individual studies; see Appendix 8 for the quality checklist and Appendix 18 for details about each study), information about the consistency of the evidence (see below for how consistency was measured), directness of the evidence (that is, how closely the outcome measures, interventions and participants match those of interest) and any other considerations (for example, effect sizes with wide confidence intervals (CIs) would be described as imprecise data). Each evidence profile also included a summary of the findings: number of patients included in each group, an estimate of the magnitude of the effect, quality of the evidence and the importance of the evidence. The quality of the evidence was based on the quality assessment

Table 1: Example evidence profile table

	Quality assessment					No. of patients		Summary of findings			
								Effect			
No. of studies	Quality of included studies	Consistency	Directness	Other modifying factors		CBT	Waitlist	Effect size	Likelihood of clinically important effect	Overall quality	Importance
Carbamazepine versus placebo											
Efficacy											
Mania: change score at endpoint (manic only)											
Weisler 2004 Weisler 2005	Sign: 1+ (−1)	None	Acute mania	Strong effect (+1)		134	146	WMD = −6.87 (−9.24, −4.49)	Very likely (favouring carbamaze-pine)	Moderate	Critical
Acceptability/tolerability											
Leaving treatment early for any reason											
Weisler 2004 Weisler 2005	Sign: 1+ (−1)	Significant heterogeneity (−1): random effects model used	Acute mania	None		134	146	RR (random effects) = 0.79 (0.59, 1.06)	Likely (favouring carbamaze-pine)	Low	Critical

components (study design, limitations to study quality, consistency, directness and any other considerations) and graded using the following definitions:

- **High** = Further research is very unlikely to change our confidence in the estimate of the effect.
- **Moderate** = Further research is likely to have an important impact on our confidence in the estimate of the effect and may change the estimate.
- **Low** = Further research is very likely to have an important impact on our confidence in the estimate of the effect and is likely to change the estimate.
- **Very low** = Any estimate of effect is very uncertain.

For further information about the process and the rationale of producing an evidence profile table, see GRADE Working Group (2004).

Forest plots

Each forest plot displayed the effect size and CI for each study as well as the overall summary statistic. The graphs were organised so that the display of data in the area to the left of the 'line of no effect' indicated a 'favourable' outcome for the treatment in question. Dichotomous outcomes were presented as relative risks with the associated 95% CI (for an example, see Figure 1). A relative risk (or risk ratio) is the ratio of the treatment event rate to the control event rate. A relative risk of 1 indicates no difference between treatment and control. In Figure 1, the overall relative risk of 0.73 indicates that the event rate (that is, non-remission rate) associated with intervention A is about three quarters of that with the control intervention, or in other words, the relative risk reduction is 27% (that is, 270 in 1,000).

The CI shows with 95% certainty the range within which the true treatment effect should lie, and can be used to determine statistical significance. If the CI does not cross the 'line of no effect', the effect is statistically significant.

Continuous outcomes were analysed as weighted mean differences (WMD), or as standardised mean differences (SMD) when different measures were used in different studies to estimate the same underlying effect (for an example, see Figure 2). If provided, intention-to-treat data, using a method such as 'last observation carried forward' (LOCF), were preferred over data from completers.

Figure 1: Example of a forest plot displaying dichotomous data

Review: NCCMH clinical guideline review (Example)
Comparison: 01 Intervention A compared to a control group
Outcome: 01 Number of people who did not show remission

Study or sub-category	Intervention A n/N	Control n/N	RR (fixed) 95% CI	Weight %	RR (fixed) 95% CI
01 Intervention A vs. control					
Griffiths1994	13/23	27/28		38.79	0.59 [0.41, 0.84]
Lee1986	11/15	14/15		22.30	0.79 [0.56, 1.10]
Treasure1994	21/28	24/27		38.92	0.84 [0.66, 1.09]
Subtotal (95% CI)	45/66	65/70		100.00	0.73 [0.61, 0.88]
Test for heterogeneity: Chi² = 2.83, df = 2 (P = 0.24), I² = 29.3%					
Test for overall effect: Z = 3.37 (P = 0.0007)					

0.2   0.5   1   2   5
Favours intervention Favours control

Figure 2: Example of a forest plot displaying continuous data

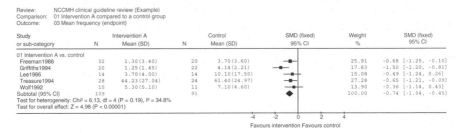

To check for consistency between studies, both the I^2 test of heterogeneity and a visual inspection of the forest plots were used. The I^2 statistic describes the proportion of total variation in study estimates that is due to heterogeneity (Higgins & Thompson, 2002). The I^2 statistic was interpreted in the following way:

● Greater than 50%: notable heterogeneity. (An attempt was made to explain the variation; for example, outliers were removed from the analysis or sub-analyses were conducted to examine the possibility of moderators. If studies with heterogeneous results were found to be comparable, a random-effects model was used to summarise the results [DerSimonian & Laird, 1986]. In the random effects analysis, heterogeneity is accounted for both in the width of CIs and in the estimate of the treatment effect. With decreasing heterogeneity, the random effects approach moves asymptotically towards a fixed-effects model.)

● 30 to 50%: moderate heterogeneity (both the chi-squared test of heterogeneity and a visual inspection of the forest plot were used to decide between a fixed- and random-effects model).

● Less than 30%: mild heterogeneity (a fixed-effects model was used to synthesise the results).

To explore the possibility that the results entered into each meta-analysis suffered from publication bias, data from included studies were entered, where there was sufficient data, into a funnel plot. Asymmetry of the plot was taken to indicate possible publication bias and investigated further.

Forest plots included lines for studies that were believed to contain eligible data even if the data were missing from the analysis in the published study. An estimate of the proportion of eligible data that were missing (because some studies did not include all relevant outcomes) was calculated for each analysis.

3.5.5   Forming the clinical summaries and recommendations

Once the evidence profile tables relating to a particular clinical question were completed, summary tables incorporating important information from the evidence profile and an assessment of the clinical significance of the evidence were produced (these tables are presented in the evidence chapters). Finally, the systematic reviewer, in conjunction with the topic group lead, produced a clinical summary.

In order to facilitate consistency in generating and drafting the clinical summaries, a decision tree was used to help determine, for each comparison, the likelihood of the effect being clinically significant (see Figure 3). The decision tree was designed to be used as one step in the interpretation of the evidence (primarily to separate clinically

Figure 3: Decision tree for helping to judge the likelihood of clinical significance

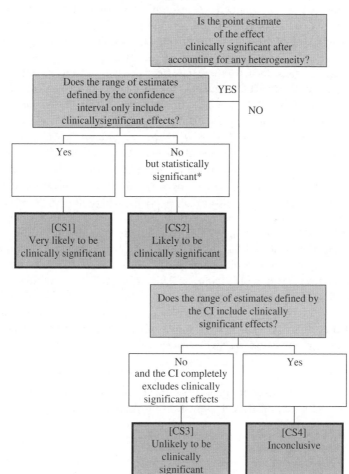

*Efficacy outcomes with large effect sizes and very wide CIs should be interpreted with caution and should be described as inconclusive (CS4), especially if there is only one small study.

important from clinically negligible effects) and was not designed to replace clinical judgement. For each comparison, the GDG defined *a priori* a clinically significant threshold, taking into account both the comparison group and the outcome.

As shown in Figure 3, the review team first classified the point estimate of the effect as clinically significant or not. For example, if a relative risk of 0.75 was considered to be the threshold, then a point estimate of 0.73 (as can be seen in Figure 1), would meet the criteria for clinical significance. Where heterogeneity between studies was judged problematic, in the first instance an attempt was made to explain the cause of the heterogeneity (for example, outliers were removed from the analysis or sub-analyses were conducted to examine the possibility of moderators). Where homogeneity could not be achieved, a random-effects model was used.

Where the point estimate of the effect exceeded the threshold, a further consideration was made about the precision of the evidence by examining the range of estimates defined by the CI. Where the effect size was judged clinically significant for the full range of plausible estimates, the result was described as *very likely to be clinically significant* (that is CS1). In situations where the CI included clinically unimportant values, but the point estimate was both clinically and statistically significant, the result was described as *likely to be clinically significant* (that is CS2). However, if the CI crossed the line of no effect (that is, the result was not statistically significant), the result was described as *inconclusive* (that is CS4).

Where the point estimate did not meet the criteria for clinical significance and the CI completely excluded clinically significant values, the result was described as *unlikely to be clinically significant* (that is, CS3). Alternatively, if the CI included both clinically significant and clinically unimportant values, the result was described as *inconclusive* (that is, CS4). In all cases described as inconclusive, the GDG used clinical judgement to interpret the results.

Once the evidence profile tables and clinical summaries were finalised and agreed by the GDG, the associated recommendations were produced, taking into account the trade-off between the benefits and risks as well as other important factors. These included economic considerations, values of the development group and society, and the group's awareness of practical issues (Eccles *et al.*, 1998).

3.5.6 Method used to answer a clinical question in the absence of appropriately designed, high-quality research

In the absence of RCTs (or high-quality research of a design appropriate to the clinical question), or where the GDG were of the opinion (on the basis of previous searches or their knowledge of the literature) that there were unlikely to be such evidence, an informal consensus process was adopted. This process focused on those questions that the GDG considered a priority.

Informal consensus
The starting point for the process of informal consensus was that a member of the topic group identified, with help from the systematic reviewer, a narrative review that

most directly addressed the clinical question. Where this was not possible, a brief review of the recent literature was initiated.

This existing narrative review or new review was used as a basis for beginning an iterative process to identify lower levels of evidence relevant to the clinical question and to lead to written statements for the guideline. The process involved a number of steps:

- A description of what is known about the issues concerning the clinical question was written by one of the topic group members.
- Evidence from the existing review or new review was then presented in narrative form to the GDG and further comments were sought about the evidence and its perceived relevance to the clinical question.
- Based on the feedback from the GDG, additional information was sought and added to the information collected. This may have included studies that did not directly address the clinical question but were thought to contain relevant data.
- If, during the course of preparing the report, a significant body of primary-level studies (of appropriate design to answer the question) were identified, a full systematic review was done.
- At this time, subject possibly to further reviews of the evidence, a series of statements that directly addressed the clinical question was developed.
- Following this, on occasions and as deemed appropriate by the development group, the report was then sent to appointed experts outside of the GDG for peer review and comment. The information from this process was then fed back to the GDG for further discussion of the statements.
- Recommendations were then developed.
- After this final stage of comment, the statements and recommendations were again reviewed and agreed upon by the GDG.

3.6   HEALTH ECONOMICS REVIEW STRATEGIES

The aim of the health economics literature review was to contribute to the guideline development process by providing evidence on the economic burden of mental disorders in the antenatal and postnatal period as well as on the relative cost effectiveness of different preventive and treatment options covered in the guideline. Where available, relevant evidence was collected and assessed in order to help the decision-making process.

This process was based on a preliminary analysis of the clinical evidence and had two stages:

- identification of areas with likely major resource implications within the scope of the guideline
- systematic review of existing data on the economic burden of mental disorders in the antenatal and postnatal period and evidence on cost effectiveness of interventions aimed at prevention and management of such disorders.

In addition, in areas with likely major cost implications where relevant data did not already exist, primary economic analyses based on decision-analytic economic modelling were undertaken alongside the guideline development process, in order to provide cost-effectiveness evidence and assist decision making.

3.6.1 Key economic issues

The following economic issues relating to the epidemiology and the management of mental disorders in the antenatal and postnatal period were identified by the GDG in collaboration with the health economist as primary key issues that should be considered in the guideline:

- the global economic burden of mental disorders experienced by women during pregnancy and in their first postnatal year, with specific reference to the UK
- cost effectiveness of psychological interventions for the prevention and treatment of depression in the postnatal period
- cost effectiveness of specialist perinatal mental health services for the management of women with mental disorders in the antenatal and postnatal period.

3.6.2   Systematic literature review

A systematic review of the health economics evidence was conducted. The aim of the review was threefold:

- to identify publications providing information on the economic burden of mental disorders during pregnancy and in the first postnatal year relevant to the UK context
- to identify existing economic evaluations of psychological interventions for the prevention and treatment of depression in the postnatal period, as well as of specialist perinatal mental health services for the management of women with mental disorders in the antenatal and postnatal period, that were transferable to the UK patient population and healthcare setting
- to identify studies reporting relevant health state utility data transferable to the UK population to facilitate a possible cost–utility modelling process.

Although no attempt was made to review systematically studies with only resource use or cost data, relevant UK-based information was extracted for future modelling exercises if it was considered appropriate.

3.6.3   Search strategy

For the systematic review of economic evidence, the standard mental-health-related bibliographic databases (EMBASE, MEDLINE, CINAHL, PsychINFO and HTA) were searched. For these databases, a health economics search filter adapted from the Centre for Reviews and Dissemination (CRD) at the University of York was used in combination with a general filter for antenatal- and postnatal-related mental disorders. The subject filter employed a combination of free-text terms and medical subject headings, with subject headings having been exploded. Additional searches were performed in specific health economics databases (NHS EED, OHE HEED). HTA and NHS EED databases were accessed via the Cochrane Library, using the general filter for antenatal- and postnatal-related mental disorders. OHE HEED was searched using a shorter, database-specific strategy. Initial searches were performed between

February and March 2005. The searches were updated regularly, with the final search between 6 and 8 weeks before the first consultation. Search strategies used for the health economics systematic review are presented in Appendix 6.

In parallel to searches of electronic databases, reference lists of eligible studies and relevant reviews were searched by hand, and experts in the field of antenatal and postnatal mental health and mental health economics were contacted in order to identify additional relevant published and unpublished studies. Studies included in the clinical evidence review were also screened for economic evidence.

3.6.4   Review process

The database searches for general health economics evidence for bipolar disorder resulted in 84 potentially eligible references. A further two possibly eligible references were found by hand searching. Full texts of all potentially eligible studies (including those for which relevance/eligibility was not clear from the abstract) were obtained. These publications were then assessed against a set of standard inclusion criteria by the health economist, and papers eligible for inclusion as economic evaluations were subsequently assessed for internal validity. The quality assessment was based on the 35-point checklist used by the *British Medical Journal* to assist referees in appraising full economic analyses (Drummond & Jefferson, 1996) (see Appendix 12).

3.6.5   Selection criteria

The following inclusion criteria were applied to select studies identified by the economic searches for further analysis:
● No restriction was placed on language or publication status of the papers.
● Studies published between 1985 and 2006 were included. This date restriction was imposed in order to obtain data relevant to current healthcare settings and costs.
● Only studies from Organisation for Economic Cooperation and Development (OECD) countries were included, as the aim of the review was to identify economic information transferable to the UK context.
● Selection criteria based on types of clinical conditions and patients were identical to the clinical literature review (see Appendix 12).
● Studies were included provided that sufficient details regarding methods and results were available to enable the methodological quality of the study to be assessed and provided that the study's data and results were extractable.
Additional selection criteria were applied in the case of economic evaluations:
● Only full economic evaluations that compared two or more options and considered both costs and consequences (that is cost–minimisation analysis, cost–consequences analysis, cost–effectiveness analysis, cost–utility analysis or cost–benefit analysis) were included in the review.

- Economic studies were considered only if they utilised clinical evidence derived from a meta-analysis, a well-conducted literature review, an RCT, a quasi-experimental trial or a cohort study.

3.6.6 Data extraction

Data were extracted by the health economist using an economic data extraction form (Appendix 13). Masked assessment, whereby data extractors are blind to the details of journal, authors, and so on, was not undertaken.

3.6.7 Presentation of the results

The economic evidence identified in the health economics systematic review is summarised in the respective chapters of the guideline, following presentation of the clinical evidence. Results of additional economic modelling undertaken alongside the guideline development process are also presented in the relevant chapters.

3.7 STAKEHOLDER CONTRIBUTIONS

Professionals, service users and companies have contributed to and commented on the guideline at key stages in its development. Stakeholders for this guideline include:
- service user/carer stakeholders: the national service user and carer organisations that represent people whose care is described in this guideline
- professional stakeholders: the national organisations that represent healthcare professionals who are providing services to service users
- commercial stakeholders: the companies that manufacture medicines used in the treatment of mental disorders
- PCTs
- DH and Welsh Assembly Government.
  Stakeholders have been involved in the guideline's development at the following points:
- commenting on the initial scope of the guideline and attending a briefing meeting held by NICE
- contributing possible clinical questions and lists of evidence to the GDG
- commenting on the first and second drafts of the guideline.

3.8 TESTIMONIES FROM WOMEN WITH MENTAL DISORDERS IN THE ANTENATAL AND POSTNATAL PERIOD

Throughout this document, there are illustrations of women's experiences of mental health problems, treatment and services in the antenatal and postnatal periods; these are in the form of short vignettes or longer testimonies. The intention behind the use of these extracts is to add to the understanding of individual experience described in this guideline.

The writers of the testimonies and vignettes were contacted primarily through service user and carer stakeholder organisations. They were asked to consider the following questions:

● If you had experienced mental health problems at some time before you became pregnant, did you discuss this at any point with healthcare professionals (GP, midwife and so on)? What information were you given about either starting or continuing treatment for this problem through your pregnancy and after birth?

● If your first experience of mental health problems occurred during pregnancy or within a year after giving birth, when and how did you first become aware that you had a mental health problem?

● What possible treatments were discussed with you and what treatments did you receive? Did the treatment help you feel better? (Please describe what worked for you and what didn't work for you).

● Did you attend a support group and was this helpful?

● How would you describe your relationship with your healthcare professional(s) (GP/midwife/health visitor/CPN/psychiatrist, obstetrician and so on)?

● How do you feel now?

● In what ways has your experience of mental health problems during the antenatal and postnatal period affected your life and the lives of those close to you?

Each writer of a testimony or vignette was also asked to sign a consent form to allow use of the material in the guideline.

3.9   VALIDATION OF THIS GUIDELINE

Registered stakeholders had two opportunities to comment on the draft guideline, which was posted on the NICE website during the consultation period. The GRP also reviewed the guideline and checked that stakeholders' comments had been addressed.

Following the consultation period, the GDG finalised the recommendations and the NCCMH produced the final documents. These were then submitted to NICE. NICE then formally approved the guideline and issued its guidance to the NHS in England and Wales.

4. ANTENATAL AND POSTNATAL MENTAL HEALTH: POPULATION, DISORDERS AND SERVICES

4.1   SCOPE OF THE GUIDELINE

This guideline covers the mental healthcare of women with mental disorders who are pregnant or in their first postnatal year. The latter period was determined after a review of the literature and research in this field but aspects of the guidance may be considered appropriate to the mental healthcare of mothers of children over 1 year old. The guideline is concerned with the broad range of mental disorders seen in adults, including both common mental disorders, such as anxiety, and severe and enduring disorders, such as schizophrenia. However, it focuses on the aspects of their expression, risks and management that are of special relevance in the antenatal and postnatal periods. Thus, the guidelines should be used in conjunction with other NICE guidance specific to disorders or interventions (see www.nice.org.uk).

The guideline also makes recommendations about the services required to support the delivery of effective detection and treatment of most mental disorders in the antenatal and postnatal periods in primary and secondary care. It will also be relevant to (but not make specific recommendations for) non-NHS services such as social services and the independent sector.

The optimisation of psychological well-being, as opposed to the management of mental disorders, is not covered in this guideline. However, the importance of this to the healthcare of women antenatally and postnatally is implicit and the guideline should be applied in conjunction with those NICE guidelines relating to antenatal and postnatal healthcare.

The mental health needs of fathers, partners, other carers and children, whose health and functioning will inevitably be affected by mental disorders in women, are also important and should not be neglected, and their needs have been considered in developing the recommendations in this guideline. In relevant places, the phrase 'fathers/partners and carers' has been used to remind readers of the continued importance of thinking about mental illness within the context of the family. There are currently NICE guidelines covering the treatment of several mental health problems, including depression and a number of anxiety disorders, which should be followed when considering the treatment needs of families. The GDG considered carefully the population covered by the guideline and common terminologies such as 'users', 'sufferers', 'survivors' and 'patients'. For convenience, the guideline refers to the target population being considered throughout as 'women', with a specifier as necessary, such as 'women with pre-existing schizophrenic illness'.

As can be seen from the above, it is mainly the context of care, namely during pregnancy and the postnatal period, that is the primary focus of the guideline, rather than significant differences in the nature of the particular disorders. In particular, the biological, physiological, psychological and social changes that occur at this time influence the nature of both detection and treatment of mental disorders. Much of the guideline is concerned with the balancing of the risks and benefits of treatment and not treating illness at a particularly critical time in the lives of women, the fetus, siblings and families.

Case vignettes are used throughout the text to illustrate women's experiences of mental illness, health and services in the antenatal and postnatal periods; the intention behind the use of these vignettes is to add to the understanding of individual experience described in this guideline.

4.2 MENTAL DISORDERS DURING PREGNANCY AND THE POSTNATAL PERIOD

4.2.1 Introduction

Women in the antenatal and postnatal period are vulnerable to having or developing the same range of mental disorders as other adults, and the nature and the course of the large majority of these disorders is common to all adults (Brockington, 1996). However, the nature and treatment of mental disorders occurring in the antenatal and postnatal period differ in a number of important respects:

- There is a risk of pregnant women with an existing disorder stopping medication, often abruptly and without the benefit of an informed discussion, which can precipitate or worsen an episode.
- In women with an existing disorder (for example, bipolar disorder), there may be an increased risk of developing an episode.
- The impact of any disorder may often require more urgent intervention than would usually be the case because of its effect on the fetus and on the woman's physical health and care, and her ability to function and care for her family.
- Postnatal-onset psychotic disorders may have a more rapid onset with more severe symptoms than psychoses occurring at other times (Wisner & Wheeler, 1994) and demand an urgent response.
- The effects of disorders at this time demand that not only the needs of the woman but also those of the fetus/infant, siblings and other family members are considered (including the physical needs of the woman or fetus/infant) – for example, when considering admission to an inpatient bed.
- The shifting risk/benefit ratio in the use of psychotropic drugs in pregnancy and breastfeeding requires review of the thresholds for treatment for both pharmacological and psychological treatments. This may result in a greater prioritisation of prompt and effective psychological interventions.

4.2.2 Course and prognosis of mental disorders in the perinatal period

There is little evidence that the underlying course of most pre-existing mental disorders is significantly altered during this time, with the exception of bipolar disorder, which shows an increased rate of relapse and first presentation (see Section 4.3.4). Similarly, there is little evidence that the prognosis of disorders that develop during pregnancy or postnatally are significantly different from those developing at other times (Brockington, 1996). However, there is evidence of possible adverse outcomes for infants and siblings of many disorders at this time. Maternal mental illness at this time may negatively affect the woman's relationship with her partner and increase the partner's risk of mental illness (Lovestone & Kumar, 1993). As with other mental disorders, the concept of prognosis must therefore be extended to consideration of not only the future course of the disorder and its impact on the woman, but also its impact on the other family members. Healthcare professionals should also consider that many women may have considerable anxiety about disclosing a mental disorder and may fear that their baby may be taken away. The focus of both the mother and of services on the needs of the infant should not obscure the needs of the mother.

4.2.3 Pregnancy and birth in England and Wales

In 2004 there were 639,721 live births. The average age of women giving birth was 29, with the average age of primiparous women being 27 and with 7% of births being to women under the age of 20 years. Of women giving birth in England, 85% were married or cohabiting and 15% were lone parents. Sixteen percent of children were born into low-income households. In 2000 there were 0.13 maternal deaths per 1,000 live births (this compares with figures of 0.24 per 1,000 for the whole of Europe and 0.17 per 1,000 for the USA). In England and Wales in 2002, there were 2,101 neonatal deaths (3.52 per 1,000 live births); this compares with figures of 4.7 per 1,000 live births in the USA in 2002 and 2.8 per 1,000 in Australia in 2004.

Social factors can play an important role in both the aetiology and maintenance of mental disorders. The above figures, showing significant numbers of women bringing children up alone, in poverty or in suboptimal accommodation, serve to emphasise the vulnerability of some women and their children. Such adversity may play an important role in maintenance of mental disorder in adults (Brown & Harris, 1978). In addition, the increased psychological vulnerability of children whose parents have a mental disorder (Beardslee *et al.*, 1983; Rubovits, 1996) argues strongly for the effective and prompt treatment of mental disorder in pregnancy and the postnatal period.

4.2.4 Special considerations for adolescents

The UK has a high rate of pregnancy amongst adolescents, and this raises the issue of consent for this group. For example, when admitting an adolescent to inpatient care, it is desirable to do so with the informed consent of both the adolescent and her parents, not least because the success of any treatment approach significantly depends on the development of a positive therapeutic alliance involving the adolescent, the family and the inpatient team. However, there will be times when the professionals consider admission to be necessary but either the adolescent or her family do not consent.

If an adolescent younger than 18 years refuses treatment, but the parent (or guardian) believes strongly that treatment is desirable, then the adolescent's wishes may be over-ruled. However, an adolescent has the right to consent to treatment without involving the consent of parents after his or her 16th birthday. A child under the age of 16 has a right to consent to treatment if he or she is assessed as being mentally competent (known as 'Gillick competence' after Victoria Gillick who brought a case against a health authority after a health department circular advised that doctors could prescribe contraception to under sixteens without parental consent [see Gillick, 1985]. Since the subsequent decision on the case by the House of Lords went against Mrs Gillick, this is also known as 'Fraser' competence after the judge presiding over the original case). Healthcare professionals need to be mindful of whether a child or adolescent is subject to an order under the Children Act (1989). In most cases, the use of the Mental Health Act (1983) should be considered as it includes safeguards such as involvement of other professionals, a time limit and a straightforward procedure for appeals and regular reviews.

Those professionals involved in assessing children or adolescents for possible inpatient admission (tier 4 child and adolescent mental health services [CAMHS] staff) should be specifically trained in issues of consent and capacity, the use of current mental health legislation and the use of childcare legislation as it applies to this group of patients. They should seek specialist perinatal advice if necessary.

4.2.5 Critical practice recommendation

4.2.5.1   Healthcare professionals working with adolescents experiencing a mental disorder during pregnancy or the postnatal period should:
- be familiar with local and national guidelines on confidentiality and the rights of the child
- obtain appropriate consent, bearing in mind the adolescent's understanding (including Gillick competence), parental consent and responsibilities, child protection issues, and the use of the Mental Health Act and of the Children Act (1989).

4.3   INCIDENCE AND PREVALENCE OF PERINATAL DISORDERS

The purpose of this section is not to provide an exhaustive overview of the epidemiology of perinatal disorders but to highlight important issues about the incidence and prevalence of perinatal disorders, particularly if they are different from that found in general adult disorders. The commentary below is also limited as a result of the paucity of research in this area. Most studies to date have focused principally on depression and psychotic illness, mainly in the postnatal period, and studies of depression have generally relied on the use of self-report measures applied at isolated time points. Therefore, caution must be applied to the interpretation of the data. In particular, caution is needed in the use of the term 'postnatal depression' as there is concern that its misuse is widespread, with potentially serious negative consequences. These include its use in clinical situations as a label for any mental illness occurring postnatally and has been pointed to in the Confidential Enquiry into Maternal and Child Health as a major concern because other serious illnesses fail to be identified as a consequence (Lewis & Drife, 2004). It also reinforces the view that postnatal depression is somehow different from depression at other times. Common false beliefs include the idea that its symptoms and effects are less severe, that it goes away by itself, that it is somehow associated with whether or not the woman is breastfeeding, that it is all due to hormones, that it has no risk of non-puerperal recurrence, that it carries an inevitable risk of future postnatal recurrence, that depression is less common antenatally or that depression that is already present before birth is not the same thing. All of these assumptions are misleading and can lead to disadvantageous and inappropriate responses by clinicians and women themselves. In addition, they can lead to policy and service development focused on depression postnatally, to the exclusion of the full range of mental disorders occurring antenatally and postnatally, all of which can potentially have serious effects on woman, infant and the family.

It is therefore recommended that, for the purpose of diagnosis, usual diagnostic guidelines for each condition, such as those contained in *The ICD-10 Classification of Mental and Behavioural Disorders* (ICD-10) (World Health Organization [WHO], 1992) and the *Diagnostic and Statistical Manual of Mental Disorders* of the American Psychiatric Association (DSM-IV) (APA, 2000) be followed. Clinicians should bear in mind that some changes in mental state and functioning are a normal part of the antenatal and postnatal experience and should, therefore, be cautious about basing any diagnosis largely on such features without careful consideration of the context. Such features include, for example, sleep disturbance, tiredness, loss of libido and anxious thoughts about the infant.

4.3.1   Anxiety disorders

Anxiety disorders are often comorbid with depressive disorders (NCCMH, 2004) and this link seems also to be true for pregnant women (Heron *et al.*, 2004). This has implications for the identification and management of anxiety disorders in pregnancy.

Panic disorder
Little systematic research has been undertaken on panic disorder in pregnancy and the postnatal period. A review of studies examining the occurrence of panic disorder (without concurrent affective disorder) during pregnancy and/or the postnatal period found ten studies, all except one of which were retrospective and uncontrolled (Hertzberg & Wahlbeck, 1999). One study was concerned with onset of panic disorder in the postnatal period (Sholomskas *et al.*, 1993), and the rest documented the course of existing panic disorder. Overall, the review found that symptoms improved in 41% of pregnancies

(89 of 215), and 38% had postnatal onset (105 of 278), although in most studies (n = 8), the postnatal period was defined as up to 3 months after delivery. There is no suggestion of a raised prevalence of panic disorder in pregnancy.

Generalised anxiety disorder (GAD) and symptoms of anxiety
While in a small American study (n = 68) 4.4% met criteria for GAD (based on the Structured Clinical Interview for DSM-IV [SCID-IV]), with nearly 28% having subsyndromal symptoms (Wenzel *et al.*, 2003), the prevalence of anxiety symptoms is much higher. For example, a large-scale community prospective study of around 8,300 women (based on the Avon Longitudinal Study of Parents and Children (ALSPAC)), which measured anxiety symptoms during pregnancy and the postnatal period (from 18 weeks' gestation to 8 months postnatally), found while 14.6% scored above threshold at 18 weeks' gestation (a score of 9 or more on the anxiety items of the Crown-Crisp Experiential Index (CCEI) [Crisp *et al.*, 1978]), 8% scored above threshold at 8 weeks postnatally, with 2.4% *de novo* presentations (Heron *et al.*, 2004). Two-thirds of women reporting anxiety during pregnancy reported anxiety postnatally. The study was based on a self-report questionnaire. Despite the view that anxiety disorders only constitute mild mental health problems, they contribute to significant disability to sufferers and this combined with the emerging evidence of possible negative effects on the fetus, demonstrable in infancy, reinforces the view that more attention needs to be paid to these disorders.

Obsessive-compulsive disorder (OCD)
A review of symptoms of OCD in pregnancy and the postnatal period found some evidence for onset of OCD associated with pregnancy and childbirth, although studies were of OCD populations and relied on retrospective self-report (Abramowitz *et al.*, 2003). The authors could find no studies examining prevalence of pregnancy-related OCD in the general population. The review also found no difference in levels of OCD symptomatology in women with depression in the postnatal period compared with women with depression at other times, although a large proportion of both groups had symptoms. In common with the general population, OCD symptoms were much more common amongst women who were depressed postnatally than amongst those who were not (41% versus 6%). The studies did not report on the potential impact of OCD on the mother-infant relationship.

Post-traumatic stress disorder (PTSD)
Symptoms of PTSD following childbirth have been reported in a number of women. A review of links between childbirth and PTSD in women following a live birth found prevalence figures for a 'PTSD-profile' (that is, symptom criteria of DSM-IV B, C and D) of between 2.8% and 5.6% at around 6 weeks postnatally, which reduced to 1.5% by 6 months postnatally (Olde *et al.*, 2006). This is consistent with the usual course of PTSD, which appears to have a high remittance rate following the index traumatic event (NCCMH, 2005). The rate in studies using DSM-IV criteria was between 1.7% (1 to 13 months postnatally) and 2.8% (6 months postnatally). Czarnocka and Slade (2000), in a self-report questionnaire study, found that 3% of their sample of 264

women showed clinically significant levels on all three PTSD dimensions and 24% on at least one dimension. The estimates for PTSD in non-childbearing community samples report 12-month prevalence rates between 1.3% (Creamer *et al.*, 2001) and 3.6% (Narrow *et al.*, 2002). Estimates for the 1-month prevalence rate range between 1.5% and 1.8% using DSM-IV criteria (Stein *et al.*, 1997; Andrews *et al.*, 1999), and 3.4% using the less strict ICD-10 criteria (Andrews *et al.*, 1999), suggesting that rates for postnatal women are broadly in the range for the rest of the general population. PTSD experienced by some women at this time may not be induced by traumatic delivery but will be pre-existing PTSD connected with traumatic events unrelated to the current context, though it may still have a significant impact on the woman, infant and family. Stillbirth has also been identified as a stressor for PTSD symptoms during the subsequent pregnancy (Turton *et al.*, 2001).

4.3.2   Eating disorders

Anorexia nervosa in pregnant women is less common than in the general population, due to the reduced fertility and fecundity associated with this disorder and its usual onset in adolescence. In a follow-up study of people with anorexia nervosa (n = 140), fertility was reduced to one third of the expected rate (Brinch *et al.*, 1988). However, pregnancy in women with bulimia nervosa is less rare since this disorder is less likely to cause infertility, although as many as 50% may suffer from amenorrhoea or oligo-amenorrhoea (Fahy & Morrison, 1993) at some point in the course of the illness. However, oligoamenorrhoea or vomiting oral contraceptives may increase the risk of unplanned pregnancy amongst women with bulimia nervosa (Morgan *et al.*, 1999). Turton and colleagues (1999) found an apparent improvement in eating disorder symptoms during pregnancy, with 4.9% of women (n = 410) scoring below threshold on the Eating Attitudes Test (Garner & Garfinkel, 1979) during pregnancy, but 10% scoring above threshold for the 2 years before conception. There was an overlap of about 33% between the two groups. Three per cent (of 370 complete datasets) reported symptoms during pregnancy, 6.8% scored below threshold during pregnancy but above in the 2 years before and 1.4% did not score above threshold during the 2 previous years, but scored above threshold during pregnancy. However, it should be noted that the 2-year data were collected retrospectively so are likely to be subject to bias. Factors associated with higher scores in pregnancy included younger age (less than 29 years), previous symptomatology, lower educational attainment, poorer housing, employment status and previous miscarriage. Women with eating disorders during pregnancy are also more likely to have obstetric problems, such as miscarriage, delivery by caesarean section and premature or small infants (Brinch *et al.*, 1988; Bulik *et al.*, 1999).

4.3.3   Depression

Depression is a common disorder and is associated with major disability when following a chronic course (WHO, 1992), but it is not the only mental disorder of the antenatal or postnatal period, despite its dominance in the perinatal mental health literature. The estimated point prevalence for major depression among 16 to 65 year olds in the UK is 21/1,000 (males 17, females 25), but, if the less specific and broader category of 'mixed depression and anxiety' (F41.2, ICD-10, WHO, 1992) is included, these figures rise dramatically to 98/1,000 (males 71, females 124). In mixed depression and anxiety, it can be seen that the gender ratio is more skewed to females (Meltzer *et al.*, 1995a & 1995b). Differential rates of prevalence of depression are identified in the same study, being highest among the separated (56/1,000 female, 111/1,000 male), next highest among widowed males (70/1,000) and divorced females (46/1,000), with the lowest prevalence among the married (17/1,000 and 14/1,000 respectively). Lone parents have higher rates than couples, and couples with children higher rates than those without children (Meltzer *et al.*, 1995a & 1995b). However, these studies do not report prevalence rates among pregnant women or women in the postnatal period. Epidemiological studies have also established that, for most, depression is a chronic disorder. In a WHO study, 66% of those identified as suffering from depression were still found to satisfy criteria for a mental disorder a year later, and for 50% the diagnosis was depression. It is probable that widely differing rates between the clinics studied in the countries in which the data were collected reflect true differences in prevalence in these clinics rather than differing concepts of depression between countries (Simon *et al.*, 2002).

Although research and clinical care has generally placed the greatest emphasis on the postnatal period, depression during pregnancy is still of considerable importance. A high-quality review of depression in the perinatal period, which used meta-analysis to combine point prevalence estimates from large-scale studies, estimated the point prevalence of major depression (that is, the rate at a particular point in time) as 3.8% at the end of the first trimester, 4.9% at the end of the second and 3.1% at the end of the third trimester (Gavin *et al.*, 2005). The same review estimated the postnatal point prevalence at between 1% and 5.7% in the first 12 months postnatally, with the highest rates at 2 months (5.7%) and 6 months (5.6%). Gavin and colleagues calculated the period prevalence (that is, the rate over a period of time) as 12.7% during pregnancy, 5.7% from birth to 2 months postnatally, 6.5% at 6 months and 21.9% at 12 months. However, for most of these estimates, only a single study was found. The estimates contrast with a large-scale community prospective study of around 8,300 women (based on the ALSPAC), which measured depressive symptoms during pregnancy and the postnatal period (from 18 weeks' gestation to 8 months postnatally) and found that depression scores were higher at 32 weeks' gestation than at 8 weeks postnatally, with 13.5% scoring above threshold for probable depression at 32 weeks and 9.1% at 8 weeks postnatally (Evans *et al.*, 2001). The study used self-report measures (Edinburgh Postnatal Depression Scale [EPDS] and CCEI) and did not confirm diagnoses of depression.

The variation in rates found is probably a result of different populations studied. It should be noted that Gavin and colleagues (2005) used only studies where depression had been diagnosed according to recognised criteria rather than self-report measures. These authors concluded that it was not possible, given the currently available research, to state with any certainty whether there is a difference in rates between pregnancy trimesters or between months postnatally.

Postnatal women do report higher levels of depressive symptoms and interpersonal problems, particularly marital adjustment (O'Hara *et al.*, 1990). Although this prevalence rate is no greater than that expected in the general female population, one study, which provides data on postnatal incidence (number of new cases with postnatal onset), indicates that this may be raised approximately threefold in the first 5 weeks postnatally, although it has been suggested that this higher rate may be largely the result of the higher rates in mothers of young children; this difference disappears by 6 months postnatally (Cox *et al.*, 1993). Gavin and colleagues (2005), although noting this study, concluded that there was no evidence that prevalence was higher for women in the perinatal period compared with other times. There is also no increased risk for depression in the postnatal period following an emergency caesarean (Patel *et al.*, 2005).

The Confidential Enquiry into Maternal Deaths (Lewis & Drife, 2004) has found that, for the last 9 years, psychiatric disorders have been the leading cause of maternal death in the UK, with over half of these deaths being due to suicide. For the period 1997 to 1999, depression is the mental disorder associated with the greatest number of suicides, although the rates for lifetime risk of suicide are significantly lower than those for some other less common disorders such as bipolar disorder (Lewis & Drife, 2004; NCCMH, 2006). The majority of suicides in pregnant and postnatal women (about 60%) occur in the 6 weeks before delivery and the 12 weeks after delivery. Although suicide is the most common cause of death in the perinatal period and women with severe mental illnesses have high rates of suicide postnatally, the rates of suicide for women in the antenatal and postnatal periods are lower than that for the whole female population (Appleby, 1992; Appleby *et al.*, 1998;), although there is some suggestion that rates are higher in younger women who have recently experienced a termination (Gissler *et al.*, 2005).

Vignette: A woman with pre-existing depression and depression after birth of both of her children

Before I first became pregnant in February 1998 at the age of 33, I had been taking an antidepressant for around 3 years for what a consultant psychiatrist termed 'classic diurnal depression', which included debilitating symptoms of claustrophobia and agoraphobia. Although in a long-term relationship since 1987, I had previously dismissed the notion of having children – being able to look after them and build a loving relationship – because of my depression. I had been back and forth to my GP with depression for years. I'd never discussed with anyone my anxieties about having children, but I believe some form of cognitive behavioural therapy (CBT) with the right person would have been hugely helpful if it had been suggested or on offer years earlier.

The pregnancy was an extremely happy time. Although I came off the antidepressant as soon as I discovered I was pregnant (this was my own

Continued

Vignette: (*Continued*)

decision), apart from some short-term, unpleasant physical symptoms (dizziness and so on) my mood was positive and I coped well with work and the new demands on my body. Already aware that there was a good chance of becoming depressed once my baby was born, I emphasised my worries on this score right at the beginning of my antenatal care at the GP practice. But, although I raised it time and again, and it was written clearly in my notes, it was never referred to by any healthcare professional.

Two weeks after my due date, in November 1998, I went into labour following two doses of prostaglandin gel/pessaries. After a day and a half, during which time there were oxytocin drips, cranial scrapes, constant monitoring, and so on, the doctors decided on an emergency caesarean section as there was some concern about the baby's safety. By the time my daughter was born, I was extremely distressed and unable to feel any joy or sense of 'achievement'. But she latched onto my breast as soon as we were back in the ward, and we were able to begin to bond, although my feelings for her were very confused. There was no discussion of the likelihood of postnatal depression before my discharge from hospital or during the postnatal care from the midwives.

Fourteen days after my daughter's birth I began experiencing familiar, but much more dramatic, feelings of despair, panic and inability to cope. I tried to just 'get through it' as I believed I could not ask for treatment with antidepressants, but it was nightmarish both for me and my partner; we had no family support, apart from my sister, who has a family of her own, and lives 200 miles away.

At my 6-week check, the SHO at the hospital was extremely unsympathetic about my very strong desire to continue breastfeeding. Both she, and a female GP, told me it was breastfeeding OR antidepressants. I think I remember that I did begin taking antidepressants then, but after doing some very basic searches on the internet, made the unilateral decision to continue to breastfeed: I felt my recovery and my relationship with my child depended on it. The depression began to lift after another 6 weeks or so, but not before my partner had almost resigned his job to look after us and I had thoughts of suicide and putting my daughter up for adoption. I was terrified of being on my own with the baby: rationally I knew I could cope and that nothing would happen to her, but I would beg my partner not to leave and thought no one else would want to spend time with me. I made one visit to the hospital's psychiatric emergency clinic but was strongly advised not to seek admission. I think I started feeling optimistic, and that I could cope on my own for hours at a time, in around April or May 1999. I continued taking the antidepressant for around 2 years.

For the next 3 years, we struggled with parenthood but developed a strong relationship with and love for our daughter. I wanted her to have a sibling,

Continued

Vignette: (*Continued*)

but felt I wouldn't be able to cope and that I might not recover from another bout of postnatal depression. But after going back on antidepressants in 2002, we decided to try for a second baby and, in February 2003, I conceived. The pregnancy progressed much as the first; I stopped taking antidepressants at once and felt happy and well for most of the time, although I was much more tired, working 4 days a week and having a lively 4 year old. At almost every antenatal appointment I talked about my worries about postnatal depression, but it was only at my 38-week check that the consultant took these on board and made an 'emergency' appointment with a consultant psychiatrist. When we met, I was 39 weeks pregnant and, after discussing my medical history, she suggested that I had around a 65% chance of becoming postnatally depressed again. So I agreed that I would begin to take a 50 mg daily dose of an antidepressant 2 days after the baby's birth and arrange to see my psychiatrist regularly. There was a lot of stress about getting the antidepressant medication from the pharmacy at the hospital where I gave birth, with several comments along the lines of 'Well, you'll have to stop breastfeeding now'. If I hadn't been able to argue for them, I would not have got them.

My second child, a son, was also born by emergency caesarean section, following placental abruption when I was around 5 cm dilated. I was disappointed not to have a 'normal' delivery but, unlike the first time, accepted quickly that a safe delivery and a healthy baby were the main priorities. Like his sister, my son breastfed well immediately and, when I went home, I felt quite rested and optimistic. However, my daughter immediately stopped wanting to sleep on her own in her room, so night-times became exhausting very quickly. After about 2 weeks, I started feeling extremely anxious, became unable to sleep and was worried that if I became seriously depressed again I might not recover; perhaps this time the drugs wouldn't help.

At around 3 weeks, after having the dose of my antidepressants increased to 100 mg, I had developed severe panic attacks in which I experienced tingling across my chest and down both arms. I couldn't sleep at all, even though my son was a 'good sleeper'. I stopped eating. I really felt I could not cope with the baby and dreaded hearing his cries; I ended up in Accident and Emergency, where I saw an extremely helpful psychiatric duty nurse who encouraged me to get home visits from the psychiatric nurse team. This was helpful or extremely unhelpful depending on the nurses who visited! One told me to just ping a rubber band when I felt a panic attack coming on, but two others were sympathetic, practical and kept reassuring me that I would get better, which my psychiatrist also emphasised, but which I could hardly believe.

Continued

Vignette: (*Continued*)

Over Christmas, the pattern continued, although by late afternoon every day I would feel a bit better and would eat something. Writing about it now, 2 years on, is still painful: I felt I was going to end up in a secure unit and that the family would be better off without me (but I didn't self-harm). What I could do was breastfeed and cuddle my son – I did feel a bond with him immediately. It was my daughter's behaviour and needs that I found almost impossible to cope with or address; the need to run away was intense.

As with my previous postnatal depression 5 years earlier, memories of my recovery are very blurred. Being able to see my psychiatrist made a huge difference, as did her reassurance that I was being a 'good enough' mother, who had made an informed choice to take antidepressants while breastfeeding. Although I felt hopeless for a long time, particularly in the mornings, I kept going and was very frank about how I was feeling (too frank for a lot of people). I think having to care for my mother on a regular basis forced me to go out and to drive: as the small achievements built up and the medication began to work, I started to feel better. Another factor in my recovery this time was that, after an 18-month wait, I began CBT about 2 months after my son's birth. This has been hugely helpful, especially in helping to stop the almost constant self-criticism that became all-pervasive during my illness. I went back to the gym and made the effort to socialise with other mums. By early summer 2004, I was beginning to enjoy both children and was able to plan for the future. The summer holidays, with my daughter off school, my son nearly walking and me not due back at work until mid-September, were happy.

4.3.4 Psychosis

Psychosis in the early postnatal period (up to 3 months after delivery) is often termed puerperal psychosis. However, whether it is a distinct diagnosis is unclear. DSM-IV does not categorise puerperal psychosis as a separate entity and uses a postnatal onset specifier, while ICD-10 has a special category (though advises against its use). However, there appears to be an increase in rates of psychosis in the first 90 days after delivery. A study of admissions for psychosis within 90 days of delivery found 21-fold higher rates in this period compared with other times, with figures of around 1 per 1,000 (Kendell *et al.*, 1987), which were supported by a more recent study (Munk-Olsen *et al.*, 2006).

The incidence of puerperal psychosis is also unclear, partly because many studies included episodes of bipolar disorder that may not have been psychotic (Harlow *et al.*, 2007).

The incidence rate commonly quoted is 1 to 2 per 1,000 deliveries, although it has been suggested that if more stringent criteria are applied, such as admission with definite psychotic symptoms within 2 weeks of delivery, the rate is between 0.5 and 1 per 1,000 deliveries (Kumar, 1989; Terp & Mortensen, 1998). A later study of 502,767 first-time mothers found an average rate of 0.68 per 1,000 (Nager *et al.*, 2005). This study excluded those with an admission for psychotic disorder within 2 years before delivery. This would have removed those with existing serious mental disorder liable to relapse and thus indicates that childbirth is a risk factor for the onset of psychosis, albeit a very small one. These studies illustrate how the search for 'pure postnatal' conditions has complicated and hampered research into the course and characteristics of antenatal and postnatal mental illness.

Many women admitted with psychosis in the postnatal period have a pre-existing mental disorder, including bipolar disorder and schizophrenia. Indeed, some have suggested that new-onset psychosis of the postnatal period is essentially synonymous with bipolar disorder but, although bipolar disorder confers a much higher risk of puerperal psychosis, this does not seem to be the case (Dean *et al.*, 1989). However, a number of puerperal psychoses do appear to be episodes of existing disorder (see Chapter 5).

Vignette: A woman with no history of mental health problems who went on to develop psychosis after the birth of her three children

Prior to the birth of my children, I had no experience of mental health difficulties, apart from the great shock and grief I experienced at the sudden death of my mother, when I had to be put under sedation. I positively 'bloomed' throughout my three pregnancies and was totally unprepared for what was to hit me when I experienced psychosis for the first time.

My mental distress began in hospital after the birth of my first child. I had an emergency caesarean section following a long labour. An attack of breathlessness within 48 hours of the birth led to me being put on a course of heparin, which soon caused profuse bleeding as the result of a small artery not being tied during surgery. I lost a lot of blood, and my deathly paleness and inability to move very far, or care for my baby without feeling as if I was going to collapse, caused me great anxiety. I was worried that I was going to die and leave my son motherless. No one explained the extent of my anaemia; I was simply told that I'd feel better when I'd had a transfusion, which could not be done until I had come off the heparin. My anxiety increased as the days went by, a situation that was exacerbated by some nurses mocking me because I could not 'cope'. I felt that I was a hopeless mother and I slipped further and further into depression. Not being able to relax or sleep, and feeling continually anxious, the days seemed like weeks.

Continued

Vignette: (*Continued*)

Left alone in a side ward for much of the day, I sought comfort in my thoughts. I began to think of my mother and imagined that I could hear her talking to me. The imagined gradually became 'real'. Soon I could 'hear' more voices. I thought that doctors and nurses were talking about my condition and that I was probably going to die.

After the transfusion, the anxiety and depression remained. I woke on two successive nights having wet the bed, something which raised my anxiety levels still further. A lovely night nurse told me that I had been given largactil, and this had caused me to wet the bed – I had no idea. I refused to take the 'white tablets' when attempts were made to administer them the next day; my mistrust heightened. All I wanted to do was go home with my baby. My anxiety turned to frustration and anger, such that I was unable to relax or sleep. I was visited by two psychiatrists and was eventually allowed home.

At last I had escaped, but, on arriving home, I entered a manic phase. I was very relieved to be home and could not control my excitement. I talked non-stop about my experiences in 'that place' and was unable to sleep or keep still for more than a few minutes. Normally quite a modest person, I was now full of my own importance. The 'voices' returned and I began to think I had super powers. My husband called our GP, who in turn called in a psychiatrist. I was put on an antipsychotic and became 'zombified', neither my husband nor I having any idea of the side effects. I shuffled around the house, unable to stand upright or lift my feet properly. Within a few days, I was admitted to a general ward of a local psychiatric hospital. My son was sent off to be cared for by my sister-in-law, as my husband had to return to work and he had been told that I would be in hospital for 2 months.

On arrival at the hospital, I became very confused. I did not know why I was there and thought that perhaps I was going to help with the patients (I had worked as a ward orderly/cleaner on a psychiatric ward whilst I was at college). I kept asking for my baby and, after a few days, I was allowed to have him with me in a side ward. He slept in his pram; however, I found it very difficult to look after him due to the effects of the antipsychotic. Even lifting him from his pram and trying to feed him demanded a lot of effort. The psychiatrists told my husband that I was suffering from manic puerperal psychosis and that I should be given electroconvulsive therapy (ECT), but my husband refused to let them administer it. He had witnessed the dire after effects of the treatment in a colleague with whom he'd worked closely.

I told a psychiatrist that I felt weak and was experiencing difficulty in lifting my son, let alone holding him to feed him. It was then that I was told that this was

Continued

Vignette: (*Continued*)

one of the effects of the drug. Over the next few days, my dosage was rapidly reduced, and I began to feel much more in control of myself, trying to keep myself busy by doing things for my son and helping on the ward. I had been on the ward for about a week when a new patient arrived who kept pestering me, wanting to pick up my son and do things for him. I was frightened that she would harm him, so I rang my husband and asked him to take our baby away from the hospital. I was rapidly discharged and went home with both of them. At home, my husband stayed with me for the first week. My GP and midwife visited me every day and friends gave terrific support. I battled with my mind and my restless body and was off medication after about 6 weeks.

4.3.5   Clinical practice recommendations

4.3.5.1   Women with an existing mental disorder who are pregnant or planning a pregnancy, and women who develop a mental disorder during pregnancy or the postnatal period, should be given culturally sensitive information at each stage of assessment, diagnosis, course and treatment about the impact of the disorder and its treatment on their health and the health of their fetus or child. This information should cover the proper use and likely side effects of medication.

4.3.5.2   Healthcare professionals should ensure that adequate systems are in place to ensure continuity of care and effective transfer of information, to reduce the need for multiple assessments.

4.3.5.3   Healthcare professionals should assess and, where appropriate address, the needs of the partner, family members and carers of a woman with a mental disorder during pregnancy and the postnatal period, including:

- the welfare of the infant, and other dependent children and adults
- the impact of any mental disorder on relationships with her partner, family members and carers.

4.4   AETIOLOGY OF ANTENATAL AND POSTNATAL MENTAL DISORDERS

The variation in the presentation, course and outcomes of mental disorders in the perinatal period is reflected in the breadth of theoretical explanations for their aetiology, including genetic, biochemical and endocrine, psychological and social factors. This reflects the complex aetiologies of these disorders and the social, psychological and biological changes occurring during this period. A review of the influences of these perinatal factors on mental illness is beyond the scope of this document. Much research has been undertaken to try to identify the aetiological factors that have a significant influence, but at present this research has yielded little that has a significant impact on the treatment of mental illness at this time. As for specific factors connected to the perinatal period, the predominant specific hypothesis has been that hormonal changes in pregnancy and the postnatal period may be important (including thyroid and pituitary hormones, cortisol and gonadal hormones) but no clear aetiological association has emerged (Hendrick *et al.*, 1998).

4.5   CONSEQUENCES OF MENTAL DISORDER DURING PREGNANCY AND THE POSTNATAL PERIOD

All pregnancies carry risk, in particular to the fetus, with a base rate of obstetric risk and risks of congenital malformation of between 2 and 4% (that is, between 20 and 40 in 1,000) for the general population (Brockington, 1996). These risks increase where the woman has a mental disorder and there is evidence that mental disorder during this period can have a significant detrimental impact on the well-being of the woman, the fetus and the infant. For example, severe depression is associated with an increased rate of obstetric complications, still birth, suicide attempts, postnatal specialist care for the infant and low birthweight infants (Bonari *et al.*, 2004; Lobel *et al.*, 1992; Lou *et al.*, 1994; Wadhwa *et al.*, 1993). In schizophrenia and bipolar disorder, there is an increased rate of suicide and potentially significant exacerbation of the disorder if not treated, and poorer obstetric outcomes, including increased preterm delivery (Lewis & Drife, 2004; Hedegaard *et al.*, 1993; Nordentoft *et al.*, 1996), low-birthweight infants and infants who are small for gestational age (Howard, 2005; Jablensky *et al.*, 2005). Similarly, poor fetal outcomes have been associated with maternal eating disorders during pregnancy (Kouba *et al.*, 2005).

Maternal psychoses, including schizophrenia, appear to increase the risk of infant mortality (for example, Howard, 2005) and stillbirth (Webb *et al.*, 2005), although some research studies found no significant difference in rates between offspring of mothers with schizophrenia or bipolar disorder and those of other mothers (Jablensky *et al.*, 2005). Elevated risks of sudden infant death syndrome have also been reported in relation to postnatal depression (Mitchell *et al.*, 1992; Sanderson *et al.*, 2002) and to maternal schizophrenia (Bennedsen *et al.*, 2001).

There is also emerging evidence that untreated mental disorder in pregnancy may be associated with poorer long-term outcomes for children beyond the immediate postnatal period (Nulman *et al.*, 2002). For example, maternal depression postnatally may be associated with cognitive delay, as well as a range of emotional and behavioural difficulties in young children. Maternal schizophrenia is associated with significant parenting difficulties, with a high proportion of women losing care of their infant and poor outcomes for the mental health of offspring (Beardslee *et al.*, 1983; Rubovits, 1996). Schizophrenia may also affect a woman's ability to care adequately for her children more than other severe disorders (Hipwell & Kumar, 1996). Coupled with the direct effects of maternal mental illness on the infant, there are important indirect effects such as the social isolation and other disadvantages known to be associated with severe mental illness. All of these factors point to the importance of appropriate treatment of the woman during pregnancy and the woman and the infant in the postnatal period.

Both psychological and pharmacological treatments are effective in the treatment of most major mental disorders (NICE, 2002, 2004a, 2004b, 2004c, 2005a). For a proportion of women, pharmacological treatments may be the treatment both advocated by a healthcare professional and chosen by the woman herself, but this can itself carry a potential risk to the infant. However, the risks associated with most psychotropic drug exposure in pregnancy and breastfeeding are not well understood (Patton *et al.*, 2002). For women and clinicians, the assessment of drug treatment risk is therefore highly complex and further complicated by the need to balance this against the harm of untreated disorder. The processes, and the skills needed for communicating and discussing these risks and benefits to patients, are also not well developed (Epstein *et al.*, 2004; Scialli, 2005). Furthermore, individual variation in the assessment and perception of risk are rarely acknowledged or measured. In addition to possible teratogenic and other risks to the fetus, the altered physical state of the woman over the course of a pregnancy means that increased physical monitoring, for example blood glucose during pregnancy, the impact of analgesic drugs during delivery and the impact on breastfeeding, all need to be considered in decisions about pharmacological treatment. These issues are discussed more fully in Chapter 7.

4.5.1   Consequences for the woman

For a woman who develops a mental disorder, either antenatally or postnatally, there is an additional burden to the suffering arising specifically from the disorder. The woman is very often concerned that her mental health problems may prevent her from actively caring for herself, the unborn child or the infant. This can exacerbate an already troubling and disabling disorder. Mental disorder, particularly in its more severe form, is also associated with significant impairment in social and personal functioning. The extent of this impairment may have a significant effect on the woman's ability to care effectively for herself and her children. The impact of this can most obviously and tragically be seen in the significant number of women with schizophrenia who lose custody of their children (Howard, 2005). The long-term effects of this on the woman are considerable.

4.5.2   Consequences for the infant and sibling

The impact of a maternal mental disorder can affect the social and cognitive development of children (for example, Murray *et al.*, 1996; Hay *et al.*, 2001) and can also have long-term consequences on their mental health (Beardslee *et al.*, 1983; Rubovits, 1996). Problems can be long term; for example, both behavioural problems and impaired cognitive outcome up to 7 years of age have been reported (Huizink *et al.*, 2003; O'Conner *et al.*, 2003; Van den Bergh *et al.*, 2005). Reduced IQ in children (particularly boys) aged 11 years whose mothers had depression early in the postnatal period has also been demonstrated (Hay *et al.*, 2001). The negative impact on mental health, however, is not the only area of concern and children of women with significant mental health problems may also be at risk of physical health problems. In a very small number of cases, this can lead to considerable neglect of the child and active physical abuse, with occasionally tragic consequences.

4.5.3   Consequences for the wider family

Mental health problems in pregnancy also present a burden to the wider family, not just the children and siblings. This can be seen in the difficulties faced by partners (Lovestone & Kumar, 1993), which have implications not just for the physical health and well-being of individuals but may also have a significant impact on their socioeconomic situation.

Vignette: A woman with depression and self-harming behaviour in the postnatal period

I think I have always suffered from depressive tendencies, especially during my teenage years and around my menstrual cycle. When I was 15, my mum found out that I was self-harming and she took me to see a doctor. I was living with my father at the time and when we moved it was not followed up by another doctor because my father thought I was doing it for attention.

But what I suffered was nothing compared with how low I got after my son was born in December 2003. During my pregnancy, I was very sick and extremely tired and I had to take a lot of time off work. There were days when I could not even make it out of bed. The more time I had off work, the more time I had to think and worry. I began to get very low.

My midwife was great. I broke down on her and was able to tell her how I was feeling. I was so scared about being a mum and how I thought I wouldn't be able to cope. I would have appointments with her regularly to keep a check on my emotional state and I was referred to the psychiatric assessment unit at my local hospital.

I had the assessment while I was still pregnant; it was horrible. Two men asked me all sorts of questions that were not related to how I was feeling. I felt very tense and uncomfortable and like a fake who was wasting their time. Then, after 45 minutes, they said that there was nothing wrong with me, that it was just in my personality and that I would have to live with it. I was devastated because I knew that something wasn't right, but no one listened. I tried to ignore my feelings because, after all, they were professionals, had studied for years and

Continued

Vignette: (*Continued*)

had to be right. They did, however, set me up with a floating support worker to help me once the baby was born.

I had a normal delivery and my baby was very healthy. I remember constantly crying in hospital, but everyone said it was normal baby blues that would soon wear off in a few days. My son was born a week before Christmas, so the first few weeks of his life were very hectic with people visiting. I think I went into over-drive at this point. I was breastfeeding every 3 to 4 hours on demand and through the night, which was very physically draining. A health visitor and my family told me to introduce formula milk but I refused to stop breastfeeding; it was the only thing I could offer my son that no one else could. I was struggling to bond with my son, and I felt that if I gave up breastfeeding then I would have failed him. I had to do what I thought was right. During this period, I could not sleep and when my son slept I couldn't relax – there was so much to do. I had to be a good mum. I had to get everything just right. If I did sit down I would panic that my baby was ill or that he would wake up and need something that I couldn't offer him.

I was seeing my support worker once a week and she tried to put my mind at rest, but I was very afraid to express how bad I really felt in case Social Services were called. I covered up how I truly felt because if I did mention my feelings to anyone or asked for help they just told me to give it time, that it takes a while to adjust and that it was just baby blues and would go away in a few days.

Once life settled down again, cracks in my relationship with my son's father started to show. We were arguing all the time. I began to get very low. My support worker and my health visitor started to notice, but I didn't want to admit anything, so I covered my feelings up. I was worried that if I told anyone exactly how I felt my son would be taken into care. I did see the doctor and he prescribed antidepressants (including a tricyclic antidepressant [TCA] and a selective serotonin reuptake inhibitor [SSRI]) to lift my mood. I was also given a hypnotic and a benzodiazepine.

When my son was about 3 months old, his father left; he could no longer cope with me constantly crying. He said some awful things about how I had made him miser-able and that I was failing as a mother, which just fed into my guilt and finally tipped me over the edge. I began self-harming, which was something I hadn't done since I was 15. It felt like I was in a black hole and couldn't get out. I even had suicidal thoughts and I believed that everyone would be better off without me. But I couldn't act on the thoughts – all I could think about was my son and how I couldn't put him through that. It wasn't his fault that I felt this way, but every time I looked at him he reminded me of his father and how much he had hurt me. I cared about my son but didn't feel like he was mine. I felt that I couldn't be a mum – I

Continued

Vignette: (*Continued*)

was young (23) and didn't want the responsibility. I couldn't connect with the fact he had been in my tummy and I would have flashbacks of his birth. Now he looked to me for everything – he was totally dependent on me and I could hardly look after myself. I was forgetting to eat and struggling to do anything. How could I love someone who caused this? If I hadn't accidentally fallen pregnant, I wouldn't be depressed. I hated myself for feeling, let alone thinking, those things.

I went to the doctor and he sent me to Accident and Emergency straight away for another psychiatric assessment. I had to wait 6 hours to see the on-call psychiatrist. It was very scary and upsetting: I thought I was mad and they were going to section me. They said I was suffering severe sleep deprivation and post-natal depression. I was given sleeping tablets and referred to a crisis team. The crisis team was not much help; in fact, one lady who came to visit me was terrible. She talked to me as if I was stupid, told me to pull myself together and laughed at the fact I self-harmed. My mum, who had come to look after me, nearly threw her out of the house. We asked not to see the team again. I stayed at my auntie's house – my family were too scared to leave me alone as my self-harming started to reach desperate levels.

Finally, my cousin, who came with me to another psychiatric assessment, told the doctors that no one could cope with me and that everyone was so worried I would harm my son or commit suicide. She had to beg for help before someone would do something. I was admitted to the mother and baby unit (MBU) of a psychiatric hospital, where I stayed for over 6 weeks. My son was by my side the whole time. My medication was changed because I was breastfeeding and finally the migraines that I had been suffering from stopped.

Having people around really helped, especially meeting other sufferers. I had been beginning to think I was going insane and I was the only one who had ever felt like this, so it was good to know I wasn't the only one. The nurses were very sympathetic and helpful; they explained what was happening to me and ways to cope without self-harming. The occupational therapist suggested hobbies that kept my mind busy and used my hands, like knitting and art work. The physio-therapist suggested relaxation techniques like meditation and visualisations, and the nurses suggested distraction such as having a bath and reading. Best of all, I found writing down my feelings helped. I was able to express myself without upsetting any one and it cleared my head.

As my son was older than the other children (he was about 7 months old at this time), he slept in my room at night unlike the younger babies that slept in the nursery, but someone was always around if you had a problem. I do believe I would not be here today if I had not been admitted.

4.6   TREATMENT IN THE NHS

In common with mental disorders at other stages in people's lives, detection by different professionals is variable, and this inevitably results in reduced treatment for perinatal disorders. Stigma and concerns about potential statutory involvement in the care of the infant may add to the reluctance to seek help, even where it is recognised by the woman herself. The detection of mental disorders in the perinatal period is the subject of Chapter 5 and will not be discussed in detail here. However, an idea of the consequences of under-detection can be obtained from the detection of depression in the general population. Of the 130 cases of depression per 1,000 population, only 80 will consult their GP. Of the 80 depressed people per 1,000 population who do consult their GP, 49 are not recognised as depressed, mainly because most such patients are consulting for a somatic symptom and do not consider themselves mentally unwell, despite the presence of symptoms of depression (Kisely *et al.*, 1995). This group also has milder illnesses (Goldberg *et al.*, 1998; Thompson *et al.*, 2001). GPs and other non-mental-health specialists are immensely variable in their ability to recognise depressive illnesses, with some recognising virtually all the patients found to be depressed at independent research interview and others recognising very few (Goldberg & Huxley, 1992; Üstün & Sartorius, 1995).

The communication skills of healthcare professionals make a vital contribution to determining their ability to detect emotional distress, and those with superior skills allow their patients to show more evidence of distress during their interviews, thus making detection easy. Those with poor communication skills are more likely to collude with their patients, who may not themselves wish to complain of their distress unless they are asked directly about it (Goldberg & Bridges, 1988; Goldberg *et al.*, 1993).

In summary, those with more severe disorders, and those presenting psychological symptoms, are especially likely to be recognised, while those presenting with somatic symptoms for which no cause can be found are less likely to be recognised. It is probable that the position described above for depression holds for most, if not all, mental disorders. Antenatally and postnatally, women are in frequent contact with healthcare professionals, which provides opportunities for increasing healthcare professionals'awareness of mental health problems and improving their detection skills.

4.6.1   The provision of care for perinatal disorders in the NHS
          in England and Wales

As with most common mental health problems, the large majority of women (over 90%) with perinatal disorders are treated in primary care. The remainder receive care from specialist mental health services, including general adult services, liaison services and specialist perinatal services. The current provision of specialised antenatal and postnatal mental health services in primary and secondary care is covered in Chapter 8.

4.6.2   Pharmacological treatments

There is little evidence to suggest that pharmacological treatments (the mainstay of treatment of mental disorders in the NHS) have any differential benefit in pregnancy or the postnatal period from their use in other adult populations. The major difference in the perinatal period (and for some women pre-conceptually) is in the shifting risk-benefit ratio in pregnancy and the postnatal period. This relates to the increased risk to the fetus (and subsequently the infant when breastfeeding) arising from the possible teratogenic and neurodevelopmental risks associated with the use of psychotropic medication. The risks are relative and need to be balanced carefully in the case of each woman and set against the baseline risks of malformation, the likely benefits of any treatment and the risks of untreated mental disorder that increase the baseline risk of malformations. Clinicians also need to be aware of potential changes in the pharmacokinetics of drugs in pregnant women due to increased fluid balance, particularly in the third trimester. Women may also be less able to tolerate some side effects during pregnancy or the postnatal period.

4.6.3   Psychological treatments

As with pharmacological treatments, there is little evidence, other than in the treatment of depression, on the differential effectiveness of psychological treatments during pregnancy and the postnatal period. Again, it is the changing risk–benefit ratio, in particular the cost–benefit ratio, that influences the use of treatments. For example, in the NICE depression guideline (NICE, 2004a) antidepressants were recommended before psychological treatments (on cost-effectiveness grounds) for the treatment of moderate depression, but this position may change when the possible harms associated with the issue of antidepressants are taken into account (see Chapter 7). In addition, many women are reluctant to take drugs during pregnancy. Given the limited availability of psychological treatments, this may present a considerable challenge for perinatal services (DH, 2004).

4.6.4   The organisation of perinatal mental health services

The organisation of perinatal services does not follow any consistent pattern across England and Wales; provision is variable, recommendations from various sources are often not coordinated (DH 2004, 2002; Mann, 1999), and none provides recommendations for the full range of services across primary and secondary care. The service structures required to support effective antenatal and postnatal mental healthcare are discussed in Chapter 8.

One challenge faced by those involved in the care of women with antenatal and postnatal mental health problems is the wide range of services that women use at this time. This requires close communication and agreed plans of care at the level of the individual woman and for effective collaborative working arrangements at a service level between primary care (GP, health visitor and counsellor), maternity services (midwife and obstetrician) and, where appropriate, secondary care mental health services and also social services and the independent and voluntary sectors. This network of care must not only consider the needs of the woman and her child but also other family member and carers. Poor communication has often been identified as the reason for poor-quality care and was behind the development of the care programme approach in the UK healthcare system (DH 1999).

In addition to providing effective communication, services need to be organised in ways that promote the development of cost-effective treatments and provide clear pathways, which are understandable to both providers and recipients of care. The experience for the individual woman of the involvement of multiple professionals can be bewildering and overwhelming. If not properly coordinated to prevent duplication, overlaps and gaps in service, this may also be counter-therapeutic. Despite the involvement of multiple services, it can be women's experience that their needs for practical help at this critical time are neglected because services tend to emphasise processes of assessment, monitoring, psychotherapeutic intervention and medication but rarely address the practical demands of looking after one or more young children day and night while mentally unwell.

In a number of the NICE guidelines, a 'stepped' or 'tiered care' model of service delivery has been developed, which draws attention to the different needs that women with antenatal and postnatal mental health problems have, depending on the characteristics of their problem and their personal and social circumstances, and the responses that are required from services. This stepped/tiered model is a hybrid of two ideas. At one end, is 'pure' stepped care where people are offered the least intrusive and lowest intensity intervention likely to be effective in helping them. They would only receive a more intensive, or complex, intervention if they failed to improve at an earlier step. At the other end, there is stratified care where often the intervention is linked to a particular diagnosis or service provider. Patients are directed to the service or professional who is seen to provide the optimum intervention for that person. Both these models are sometimes 'overlaid' onto a service model that identifies various tiers of services often provided by different organisations. The model also assumes effective working relationships across the system; for example, a specialist mental health or perinatal service may provide advice, training or consultation on the management of patients at levels one and two.

There are advantages and disadvantages to each of these models. The following is a model that attempts to outline the relationship between severity of illness and the most appropriate professional skill set in the corresponding organisational structure (see Figure 4). It should be used, as all models should, as an aid to thinking rather than a concrete set of proposals for who does what.

Figure 4: The stepped/tiered care model

Who is responsible for care?	What is the focus?	What do they do?

Step 5: Inpatient care, crisis teams	Risk to life, severe self-neglect	Medication, combined treatments, ECT
Step 4: Mental health specialists including perinatal and crisis teams	Psychosis, severe disorder	Medication, complex assessment and complex psychological interventions, combined treatments
Step 3: Primary care team, primary care mental health worker, clinical psychologists/therapists	Moderate or severe disorder	Medication, psychological interventions, social support
Step 2: Primary care team, primary care mental health worker, therapists	Mild disorder	Watchful waiting, guided self-help, computerised CBT, exercise, brief psychological interventions
Step 1: GP, practice nurse, midwife, obstetrician, health visitors	Recognition	Assessment

4.7   THE ECONOMIC BURDEN OF MENTAL DISORDERS IN THE ANTENATAL AND POSTNATAL PERIOD

Existing evidence on the financial implications of the presence of mental disorders in women who are pregnant or in their first postnatal year is very limited. A systematic review of the literature identified three studies that explored the additional healthcare resource use and/or financial costs associated with care of women with postnatal depression and their infants. No studies examining the economic burden imposed by women with other mental health disorders during the antenatal and postnatal period were found in the literature.

Petrou and colleagues (2002) estimated the health and social service costs of post-natal depression in a cohort of 206 women at high risk of developing the condition. The study was conducted in Reading from May 1997 to April 1999. Women were identified as being at high risk using a predictive index for postnatal depression. Costs were estimated for participating women and their infants over 18 months postnatally and included costs of inpatient, outpatient, day care and community services. Paediatric and childcare services were recorded separately.

The mean mother-infant dyad costs over 18 months were found to be £2,419 when women developed postnatal depression (according to SCID-II) and £2,027 when no postnatal depression was diagnosed (2000 prices). The overall cost difference between the two groups was non-significant (ΔC = £392, p = 0.17); however, the community care costs for women with postnatal depression were significantly higher compared with respective costs for women without postnatal depression (p = 0.01). The authors estimated that, with approximately 700,000 women giving birth in the UK annually and a 13% incidence of postnatal depression, the economic burden of this condition to the health and social services in the UK amounted to roughly £35.7 million annually (range £34.4 to £43.3 million, 2000 prices). It was acknowl-edged that this value might in reality be a conservative estimate, given that the condition was likely to have longer-term consequences in terms of health status and health service utilisation over the woman's and infant's lifetime and in terms of the child's educational requirements. Moreover, with evidence that women not at high risk for postnatal depression had fewer antenatal and postnatal contacts than the study population, the additional costs associated with care of women developing postnatal depression might be even higher in comparison to respective costs associated with care of the population of women giving birth as a whole.

Another study conducted in Canada estimated the average costs of care (health and social services) for women and infants in the first 4 weeks postnatally (Roberts *et al.*, 2001). The analysis was based on a cross-sectional survey of 1,250 mothers of normal newborn infants. Women were assessed for depression using the EPDS. Cases of depression were defined by an EPDS score ≥ 12. The total cost of health and social care over 4 weeks postnatally was $845 for women with depressive symptomatology and their infants versus $413 for those not depressed (Canadian dollars, $p < 0.01$). The total mother-infant dyad cost was $2,137 when women had very high scores (EPDS > 19) versus $434 when women were depressed but with an EPDS score of ≤ 19. Medical costs were similar for depressed and non-depressed women; however, paediatrician, community nursing and social work costs were significantly higher per mother-infant dyad when women were diagnosed with depression.

Comparable findings were reported in an Australian study by Webster and colleagues (2001). The objective of the study was to compare health and social care use and satisfaction with services between depressed (EPDS ≥ 12) and non-depressed women in the first 4 months postnatally. Data on 574 mother-infant dyads demonstrated that depressed women were more likely to visit a psychiatrist, postnatal depression group, social worker, paediatrician or GP than non-depressed women. Overall, depression led to an increased use of health and social care services and had a negative effect on satisfaction with some of the services provided.

Besides the costs reported in the above studies, one also needs to consider the long-term costs of care for infants born to mothers with mental disorders, including costs associated with management of the cognitive and behavioural problems these infants face in the future (Huizink *et al.*, 2003; O'Connor *et al.*, 2003b; Van den Bergh *et al.*, 2005), as well as costs of care for children neglected or abused because of their mothers' psychological condition. In addition to the financial cost to health and social services, there is some preliminary evidence that postnatal depression places substantial extra burdens on fathers/partners and close family members, causing financial problems within the family (Boath *et al.*, 1998). Although the available evidence is very limited and focuses on postnatal depression, it demonstrates that mental disorders during the antenatal and postnatal period, besides the established psychological and social implications for the women, their infants, and the wider family, also place a considerable financial burden to health and social services and to society as a whole.

4.8 EXPLAINING RISK TO WOMEN: HELPING PATIENTS TO MAKE DECISIONS ABOUT TREATMENT

Women may feel disempowered by being pregnant or caring for a newborn infant at the same time as requiring treatment for a mental illness. Therefore, enabling them to express their views and make choices is important. In order to help women make informed decisions about their treatment, it is vital that healthcare professionals explain the risks of different treatment options accurately, balanced against the risk of not treating mental disorder. The risks that must be taken into account include:

1) **Existing risk to the fetus:** the background risk in the general population of a fetus developing a minor or major malformation is around 2% to 4% (that is, 20 to 40 in 1,000) (Brent & Beckman, 1990; Brockington, 1996).

2) **Risk of not treating mental disorder:** the risks of not treating mental disorder depend on the disorder in question and the woman's psychiatric history. However, not treating the disorder poses a risk both to the woman's physical health as well as her ongoing mental health and well-being. There is also risk to the fetus and infant from untreated disorders and there may be risks to family, fathers/partners and carers.

3) **Risk of treating the disorder:** the risks of treating the woman's mental health problem with psychotropic medication include side effects for the woman and possible malformation or developmental problems for the fetus, such as neurobehavioural teratogenicity. This varies between different drugs and, in some cases, is dose dependent. There are also risks for the infant immediately after delivery, including withdrawal effects and toxicity.

These factors need to be considered within the context of the woman's current situation, including an appraisal of her coping resources, past illness and pregnancy experiences, and current lifestyle and family situation, such as having other children to care for. This section discusses patient participation in the decision-making process and methods for explaining risks to patients.

4.8.1   Patient preference in decision making

Given the potential risks involved during pregnancy and the postnatal period for women with mental health problems, it is vitally important that women are fully involved in treatment decisions, since even accurate individual risks have a different subjective significance to different women. For example, a high risk of becoming ill may be less important to a woman than a very small risk of a fetal malformation, whereas for another woman even a small risk of an episode of what has been a very severe illness in the past may be unacceptable. However, some patients may not want to be involved to the same degree as others. A narrative review of studies examining factors affecting patient preference for involvement in medical decisions reported that preference was affected not only by factors such as age and education level (younger patients preferred a more active role, as did those with higher education), but also factors such as experience of being a patient, with some studies reporting that increased patient experience reduced the desire to be involved (Say *et al.*, 2006). However, the authors point out that it is not clear which is more important: experience of care or experience of illness. The review also reports that clinician behaviour may play a part in patient preference for involvement in decision making, with patients being more motivated to be involved depending on factors including doctors' use of their first name and discussion of test or treatment results. Say and colleagues (2006) also reviewed qualitative studies that supported these findings, with patients who experienced good relationships with clinicians finding it easier to be involved in the decision-making process. However, the review of qualitative studies also found that patients may not understand information about risk and may find it hard to make choices when they have no experience of the potential consequences. Say and colleagues (2006) also report studies that found a fear of making the 'wrong' decision may discourage patients from participating. It should be noted that no study in this review (quantitative or qualitative) solely involved mental health patients, so these findings may not be generalisable to mental health settings.

Explaining risk is not easy. Few professionals are trained in how to understand and communicate risk effectively and few patients find it easy to fully understand or participate in risk conversations. A review by Thomson and colleagues (2005) considers the major issues involved and the current state of research in this area, an overview of which is described below.

4.8.2   Use of language

Use standardised language to convey the magnitude of risk, such as 'high/medium/low' or 'probable/unlikely/rare', may be helpful, particularly where the precise risk is unknown (Thomson *et al.*, 2005 reporting on Fox & Irwin, 1998). However, the interpretation of these terms is likely to vary between individuals (Thomson *et al.*, 2005), and approaches such as quantifying terms – for example, 'high' for risks greater than 1 in 100 – have also been suggested (Calman & Royston, 1997), although there appears to be no evidence that this is helpful to patients. Similarly, putting the risk faced by the patient into the context of everyday life, for example, expressing a risk in terms such as 'this is equivalent to one person per family/street/town/country, and so on' has been suggested (Calman & Royston, 1997) or in terms of everyday examples, such as the likelihood of being struck by lightening. Although these approaches have some intuitive appeal, none has been tested empirically.

Unfortunately, the nature of most risks related to the harm of psychotropic medication is inherently uncertain, and it is important when discussing risks with patients to help them understand this. Using terms such as 'our best guess is …' may be helpful (Thomson *et al.*, 2005), as well as the other suggestions in this section.

4.8.3   Discussing rates and the reference class

Use the natural frequency – avoid percentages
The natural frequency of an event (that is, the actual number likely to be at risk per appropriate denominator) is less likely to be misinterpreted than percentages. For example, Gigerenzer and Edwards (2003) describe a doctor who explained to his patients that taking fluoxetine resulted in a 30% to 50% chance of sexual problems. His patients thought he meant that 30% to 50% of sexual encounters would go awry,

whereas in fact the doctor meant that, of 10 patients taking fluoxetine, 3 to 5 would have a sexual problem. Similarly, clinicians also find it hard to understand how to interpret data correctly. In a study, the number of physicians correctly calculating the correct number of people with cancer given data as probabilities (as a percentage) was far lower than those given the data as natural frequencies (numbers out of 10,000) (Hoffrage & Gigerenzer, 1998). See Box 1 for an example problem.

Use absolute rather than relative risks
Percentages are also misleading because they reflect relative statistics; for example, a 25% reduction in breast cancer survival rate, may actually reflect reduction from 4 in 1,000 to 3 in 1,000.

Natural frequencies are easier to understand because they carry implicit information about base rates and reduce the number of computations required to do the calculation.

Make the baseline clear
Similarly, when describing an event such as the possibility of having a stroke, using a clear reference group makes the statistics easier to understand – for example, 'Of 100 people like you, five will have a stroke in the next year' is easier to understand than 'you have a 5% chance of having a stroke in the next year' (Thomson *et al.*, 2005).

Avoid mixing denominators
It is less confusing to say '89 in 100 will get better but 4 in 100 will experience a serious side effect' than '89 in very 100 will get better but one in 25 will experience a serious side effect' (Thomson *et al.*, 2005; Grimes & Snively, 1999).

Box 1: Examples of clinical problems with probabilities and with natural frequencies [reproduced without permission]

A blood test that can be carried out in a GP's surgery has been devised to help diagnose a disease that has few early symptoms, but can be fatal. The disease most commonly occurs in people over the age of 55. Patients who test positive are sent for further tests. You are a GP and you want to know how likely it is that a patient who has tested positive actually has the disease. The following information is available:

Probabilities
The probability that people over the age of 55 have the disease is 0.3%. If one of these people has the disease, the probability is 50% that he or she will have a positive test. If one of these people does not have the disease, the probability is 3% that he or she will still have a positive test. Imagine a person (aged over 55, no symptoms) who has a positive test in your screening. What is the probability that this person actually has the disease? _____ %

Natural frequencies
Thirty out of every 10,000 people over the age of 55 have the disease. Of these 30 people with the disease, 15 will have a positive test. Of the remaining 9,970

Continued

Box 1: (*Continued*)

> people <u>without</u> the disease, 300 will still have a positive test. Imagine a sample of people (aged over 55, no symptoms) who have positive tests in your screening. How many of these people actually do have the disease? ____ of ____
>
> The correct answer is that 5% or 1 out of 21 of those with a positive test result will have the disease.

4.8.4 Framing

How risks are presented can also affect how they are interpreted. Another review found four studies (three RCTs and a quasi-experimental study) comparing positive framing (for example, chance of a good outcome) with negative framing (for example, chance of a bad outcome) in a clinical milieu (Edwards *et al.*, 2001). Rather than support the prediction that positively framed treatment options would be more favourably viewed than negatively framed options, no clear effect was found. However, the same review also found seven papers (six RCTs and one quasi-experimental study) comparing 'loss' framing with 'gain' framing (that is, information about the risks and disadvantages of a treatment option compared with information about the benefits). Only the RCTs reported clinical behaviour outcomes, one of which was concerned with prevention of illness (skin cancer) whereas the others (including the non-randomised controlled trial) were concerned with detecting disease. Edwards and colleagues (2001) found an effect for loss framing on increasing uptake of screening (odds ratio [OR] = 1.18 [95% CI 1.01, 1.38]).

4.8.5 Visual presentation

Various visual aids have been developed to present risks in a way that can be easily assimilated; however, these do not appear to have been tested empirically. Some are computer based, such as Chris Cates' Visual Rx program (available at www.nntonline.net), which converts user-input risk rates to 100 faces to illustrate the risks involved, including smiley faces for good outcomes and unhappy faces for poor outcomes. This can help put risks into perspective.

4.8.6 Individualised risk presentation: tailored probabilities

Many risks relevant to women taking psychotropic medication during pregnancy or breastfeeding are not only not accurately established, but also often expressed in terms of population rates rather than in terms of the risk for the individual. It is, however, helpful to personalise the risks involved for the individual patient (Thomson *et al.*, 2005), although the success of this depends on good quality data. A good example of how this approach can work is available on the Harvard Center for Cancer Prevention (www.yourdiseaserisk.harvard.edu), which covers several cancers, osteoporosis and stroke. However, such a system does not appear to be available in the area of antenatal and postnatal mental health.

4.8.7 Decision aids

A Cochrane review of decision aids (O'Connor *et al.*, 2003a), which attempted to draw up a comprehensive inventory of available aids in addition to reviewing RCTs evaluating decision aids, found 221 decision aids and 35 RCTs. The review found that decision aids helped to improve knowledge of options and outcomes and to generate more realistic expectations of the benefits and harms of outcomes. The decision aids found covered many areas of clinical practice, including treatment options for cancer, hypertension and osteoporosis, birth options post-caesarean, and screening for cancer. The review did not find any decision aids specifically designed for women making choices about psychotropic medication during pregnancy and breastfeeding.

4.8.8 Issues for research

There is little empirical work evaluating strategies for understanding and explaining risks to patients and none in the area of perinatal mental health. Of particular issue in research in this area is the definition of appropriate outcome variables. These could include behavioural or physical outcomes, such as relapse rate, adherence, cognitive outcomes such as knowledge and accuracy of risk perception, and affective outcomes such as satisfaction with communication or with the decision made (Thomson *et al.*, 2005).

4.8.9 Clinical summary

Full discussion involving up-to-date information and joint decision making about all aspects of care is important, and professionals involved in such discussions must have appropriate skills in the communication, assessment and management of clinical risk. In particular:

- Clinicians need to display competence and care, and work to develop a trusting relationship with women. They need to have a willingness to explore the ideas, concerns and expectations of women and the ability to develop a partnership with them; understanding should be checked regularly.
- Clinicians need to discuss with women how much information they want about the risks and benefits of different treatment options and should enable women to feel as involved as they want to be with the right level of information and active decision making for them.
- Where possible, absolute risk values, natural frequencies and common denominators should be used.
- Decisions aids in a variety of formats, verbal and visual, including figures and images such as 'smiley faces', may be useful.
- Clinicians should aim to personalise the risks as far as possible, taking into account particular factors relating to the person to whom they are talking.
- Written material summarising the risk (individualised if possible) or, where possible, audiotaped records of the consultation should be made available to the women.

- Clinicians need to acknowledge the limits of both their knowledge and of what is known in the literature and explain the uncertainty surrounding an assessment of risk.

4.8.10   Clinical practice recommendations

4.8.10.1   Healthcare professionals should work to develop a trusting relationship with the woman, and where appropriate and acceptable to the woman, her partner and family members and carers. In particular, they should:
- explore the woman's ideas, concerns and expectations and regularly check her understanding of the issues
- discuss the level of involvement of the woman's partner, family members and carers, and their potential role in supporting the woman
- be sensitive to the issues of stigma and shame in relation to mental illness.

4.8.10.2   Before treatment decisions are made, healthcare professionals should discuss with the woman the absolute and relative risks associated with treating and not treating the mental disorder during pregnancy and the postnatal period. They should:
- acknowledge the uncertainty surrounding the risks
- explain the background risk of fetal malformations for pregnant women without a mental disorder
- describe risks using natural frequencies rather than percentages (for example, 1 in 10 rather than 10%) and common denominators (for example, 1 in 100 and 25 in 100, rather than 1 in 100 and 1 in 4)
- if possible use decision aids in a variety of verbal and visual formats that focus on an individualised view of the risks
- provide written material to explain the risks (preferably individualised) and, if possible, audio-taped records of the consultation.

4.8.11   Research recommendation

Decision aids for helping pregnant and breastfeeding women
make decisions about their care
An RCT should be conducted to compare usual care with usual care plus the use of decision aids designed to enable pregnant and breastfeeding women with mental disorders to make informed decisions about their care. Outcomes should include the development of agreed care plans, the successful implementation of the agreed care plans, and satisfaction with the care plan and the communication about the planning.

Why this is important
Psychotropic drugs carry teratogenic risk during pregnancy and are often present in breast milk. It is therefore important that women are enabled to make informed decisions about treatment choices.

5. THE PREDICTION AND DETECTION OF MENTAL ILLNESS DURING PREGNANCY AND THE POSTNATAL PERIOD

5.1 INTRODUCTION

Pregnancy and the postnatal period are critical times of psychological adjustment for women, and there is increasing evidence that a woman's mental state during this time influences both obstetric outcomes and the future development of the infant (for example, Jablensky *et al.*, 2005; Nulman *et al.*, 2002). Mental ill health in the antenatal and postnatal periods can also affect other children in the family, as well as the woman's partner and their relationship. Severe mental illness, such as psychosis, bipolar disorder or severe depression, may be particularly detrimental, both during pregnancy and subsequently, given the dependence of an infant on its mother and the rapid adjustment to motherhood faced by first-time mothers. Therefore, accurate identification of both those at risk of developing, and those currently suffering from, mental illness during this time is highly desirable.

Although mental disorders experienced during the antenatal and postnatal periods, with the possible exception of puerperal psychosis, are broadly no different in terms of aetiology and diagnostic characteristics to disorders occurring at other times, women typically have frequent contact with a range of healthcare professionals during pregnancy, childbirth and the postnatal period. Such routine contact provides an important opportunity to identify those at risk of developing, or currently suffering from, mental disorders.

This chapter addresses whether it is possible to predict postnatal mental illness during pregnancy and how to detect current illness.

Vignette: A woman with a history of depression and abuse who had anxiety postnatally but did not go on to develop depression in the postnatal period

I am 40 years old and had my first child 11 months ago. My husband and I planned to have a baby and I became pregnant right away. I enjoyed being pregnant and kept well. My son was born in March 2005, 10 days overdue. I coped with labour using gas and air, but needed a ventouse delivery and stitches for a third-degree tear.

I experienced clinical depression in my twenties. I was sexually assaulted by a boyfriend and this triggered memories and flashbacks of sexual abuse from my

Continued

Vignette: (*Continued*)

father when I was a child. I went to my GP and received counselling and a psychiatric assessment. I was prescribed an antidepressant, which I took for about 6 months. I also contacted the Scottish Society for the Prevention of Cruelty to Children who ran a counselling service for adult survivors of child sexual abuse and I got a lot of support individually and in a group.

When I considered starting a family, I was scared that I would develop postnatal depression. I read about it and spoke to my midwife about the risk factors and ways to help avoid postnatal depression. I talked about being depressed before, but I did not go into details about the reasons. My health visitor gave me good advice about postnatal depression and kept a good check on me after my son was born.

I was also scared about how I would cope with labour. I was worried that I would panic because I would feel very exposed and vulnerable. I talked to my husband about this and we discussed ways that he could reassure me and support me during labour. But I did not discuss this with the doctor or midwife. I reckoned that everyone in labour probably feels scared and vulnerable and I hoped that the staff would be reassuring no matter what the circumstances. Also, there never seemed to be an appropriate time to talk about emotional concerns. The emphasis at the antenatal clinic was on physical aspects of pregnancy. In the event, I felt able to cope in labour up until I needed a ventouse. At that point, a lot of staff came into the room, both for me and for my son, and I became very upset. My husband asked some people to leave and so only the very necessary staff stayed and the consultant dimmed the lights for me and reassured me and calmed me down.

After my son was born, I experienced a lot of emotional ups and downs, but my health visitor reassured me that these feelings were all very normal after having a baby. She encouraged me, telling me that I was doing very well. I attended a breastfeeding support group where I got lots of advice and support from staff and other mums. I am still friendly with some of the girls I met there. Talking to them really helps when I am worried or feel down.

The hardest thing I have found to deal with since my son's birth is anxiety about being separated from him. I was very anxious about returning to work because of leaving him in a nursery. My GP reassured me that this was a normal feeling. I attended a talk given by STEPS, an NHS self-referral psychological service, which gave general advice on coping with stress after having a baby. I saw a STEPS counsellor for just one session to talk about my worries. I told her about how I had been abused as a child and how this made me scared about leaving my son with anyone else in case something happened to him. She reassured me that my feelings were valid and she gave me good information about how to minimise the chances of such things happening to him and what signs there

Continued

Vignette: (*Continued*)

would be to look out for. She gave me more confidence in being able to keep my son safe.

I returned to work part-time when my son was 9 months old. I still don't enjoy leaving him at nursery, but I am enjoying being back at work and am better able to leave him with a trusted babysitter so that I can get a break.

At this moment in time, I am mostly enjoying being a mum. I find it very tiring and I worry a lot, but from talking to other mums I realise that they all feel the same too! Being depressed in the past made me very aware of the risks of becoming depressed again, so I tried my best to prepare for that and to get advice and support to help avoid illness. I am also aware that I might be overprotective of my son, so I am trying to avoid that. I want him to grow up feeling safe and secure and confident.

I feel that I have had appropriate support from my GP, psychiatrist, counsellor, midwife and especially my health visitor. I also got good support from my husband and friends from the breastfeeding support group.

5.1.1   Shifting the emphasis from screening to prediction and detection

Screening has been defined as the systematic application of a test or enquiry to identify individuals at high risk of developing a specific disorder who may benefit from further investigation or preventative action (Peckham & Dezateux, 1998). Screening programmes detect people at risk of having the condition or at risk of developing the condition in the future. They do not establish a diagnosis but give some indication of any action that may be required, such as further diagnostic investigation, closer monitoring or even preventative action. Screening is not necessarily a benign process (Marteau, 1989). Since screening tools are never 100% accurate, people who are incorrectly identified as being at risk of developing a condition (false positives) can be subject to further possibly intrusive, harmful or inappropriate investigations, management or treatment. Those falsely identified as not being at risk of developing a condition (false negatives) will also suffer by not being given the further investigation they need.

The National Screening Committee (NSC), in its criteria for determining whether a national screening programme should be undertaken for any disorder, has set 22 criteria for appraising the viability, effectiveness and appropriateness of a programme for large population screening. These include: the need for a simple, safe, precise and validated screening test; an agreed policy on the further evaluation of individuals with a positive test result; the availability of an effective treatment for those identified through early detection, with evidence of early treatment leading to better outcomes than later treatment; adequate resources available prior to commencement; and acceptability to the population. It is important that the majority of these criteria are satisfied before a screening programme is adopted, not least because screening can cause adverse effects, including distress secondary to asking specific questions, raising concerns and expectations of care[7].

Existing NICE mental health guidelines have considered the case for general population screening for a number of mental health disorders and concluded that screening should only occur for specific high-risk populations where benefits outweigh risks (for example, NICE, 2004a, 2005a). Whether women have a higher prevalence of mental disorder during pregnancy and the postnatal year than at other times is unclear (with the exception of puerperal psychosis) (Brockington, 1996; Gavin *et al.*, 2005). However, mental disorders occurring during pregnancy and the postnatal period may have greater adverse consequences for all concerned than they do at other times (for example, Sharp *et al.*, 1995). There is therefore a need to try to discover whether it is possible to predict which women are likely to develop a disorder, as well as to ensure that existing illness is detected in order to initiate appropriate treatment as quickly as possible.

The guideline uses the terms prediction and detection instead of screening in order to distinguish between the two functions involved in screening. **Prediction** is used to refer to the identification of risk factors, either current or past, which increase the probability of developing mental disorder or the probability of relapse of a previous mental disorder at some point in the future. These can include hereditary or congenital factors, psychiatric history, early life experiences and current circumstances, as well as current mood and functioning. **Detection** is used to refer to the identification of current disorder.

Since accurate prediction might lead to treatments to prevent the onset of, or ameliorate the course of, mental disorder, and accurate detection leads to treatments to treat disorder, prediction and detection require different systems and tools. This chapter will therefore attempt to answer two questions: can we successfully predict who may become ill, and can we improve the detection of women who have become ill?

Vignette: A woman with a history of mental health problems diagnosed with depression in the postnatal period

In 2004 when my son was about 5 months old, I knew that I didn't feel right; I didn't think I was feeling enough. I was looking after him quite well, I think, keeping the house tidy, cooking dinner and so on, but I felt so flat.

I had experienced a similar health problem many years before, but this was never brought up or discussed by me or my healthcare professionals when I became pregnant. I didn't think it would be an issue as previously it had been related to my

Continued

---

[7]The full NSC criteria can be found at: http://www.nsc.nhs.uk/pdfs/criteria.pdf

Vignette: (*Continued*)

personal circumstances, which were totally different from how they were when I was pregnant. The only thing I did was complete the form that they ask all pregnant women to fill in – a form on which you could easily lie. My 'score' suggested that it was highly unlikely that I would suffer from postnatal depression.

5.1.2   Sensitivity and specificity

The terms sensitivity and specificity are used in relation to prediction and detection methods discussed in this chapter.

The **sensitivity** of an instrument refers to the proportion of those with the condition who test positive. An instrument that detects a low percentage of cases will not be very helpful in determining the numbers of patients who should receive a known effective treatment, as many individuals who should receive the treatment will not do so. This would make for poor planning and underestimating the prevalence of the disorder and the costs of treatments to the community. As the sensitivity of an instrument increases, the number of false negatives it detects will decrease.

The **specificity** of an instrument refers to the proportion of those without the condition who test negative. This is important so that well individuals are not given treatments they do not need. As the specificity of an instrument increases, the number of false positives will decrease.

To illustrate this: from a population in which the point prevalence rate of depression is 10% (that is, 10% of the population has depression at any one time), 1,000 women are given a test which has 90% sensitivity and 85% specificity. It is known that 100 women in this population have depression, but the test detects only 90 (true positives), leaving 10 undetected (false negatives). It is also known that 900 women do not have depression, and the test correctly identifies 765 of these (true negatives), but classifies 135 incorrectly as having depression (false positives). The positive predictive value of the test (the number correctly identified as having depression as a proportion of positive tests) is 40% (90/90 + 135), and the negative predictive value (the number correctly identified as not having depression as a proportion of negative tests) is 98% (765/765 + 10). Therefore, in this example, a positive test result is correct in only 40% of cases, whilst a negative result can be relied upon in 98% of cases.

5.2   PREDICTION – RISK FACTORS FOR THE ONSET OF MENTAL DISORDER DURING PREGNANCY AND THE POSTNATAL PERIOD

5.2.1   Introduction

The mental disorders most associated with pregnancy and the postnatal period are depression and puerperal psychosis, although the point prevalence of the latter is relatively low (around 1 to 2 per 1000 compared with 100 to 150 per 1000 with depression). However, any mental disorder can occur during this time, including eating disorders and anxiety disorders such as PTSD.

Prediction tools are based on the use of risk factors. In order to predict future disorder accurately, it is necessary to know which factors are associated with development of future illness. These can include psychosocial and physical factors, as well as past illness and family history. Once the factors with the highest predictive value are known, a reliable prediction tool needs to be developed, which is usable by busy healthcare professionals in the clinical milieu. This is particularly important with regard to mental health during pregnancy and the postnatal period, since those caring for women during this time need robust skills in looking after the mental health as well as the physical health of women and their infants.

Vignette: A woman with pre-existing depression and depression after the birth of both of her children

Before I first became pregnant, I had been taking an antidepressant for around 3 years for what a consultant psychiatrist termed 'classic diurnal depression', which included debilitating symptoms of claustrophobia and agoraphobia. Although in a long-term relationship, I had previously dismissed the notion of having children – being able to look after them and build a loving relationship – because of my depression.

The pregnancy was an extremely happy time. Although I came off the antidepressant as soon as I discovered I was pregnant, apart from some short-term, unpleasant physical symptoms (dizziness and so on) my mood was positive and I coped well with work and the new demands on my body. Already aware that there was a good chance of becoming depressed once my baby was born, I emphasised my worries on this score right at the beginning of my antenatal care at the GP practice. But, although I raised it time and again, and it was written clearly in my notes, it was never referred to by any healthcare professional.

Vignette: A woman with depression diagnosed 1 year after the birth of her first child and with suspected PTSD from traumatic birth

I began to experience a decline in my mental health from week 8 of my pregnancy. This was due to extreme nausea, insomnia, anxiety attacks and exhaustion. I was unable to work and became increasingly isolated, while receiving poor antenatal midwifery care via my GP's surgery. I was simply told that, as my family had no history of mental illness, I was in no danger from either antenatal or postnatal depression.

5.2.2 Evidence search

In order to determine whether a particular factor accurately predicts future mental disorder, large-scale prospective studies are required which clearly define the risk factor under question and assess mental health status at an appropriate time point using a well-validated diagnostic tool. It is important to note that studies that use a simple correlational design simply show that there is a link between factor and outcome but can not establish whether the factor plays any causal role in the onset or maintenance of disorder.

The evidence search aimed to identify longitudinal prospective studies of risk factors for depression in the postnatal period, puerperal psychosis, eating disorders and anxiety disorders. High-quality reviews of such studies were also found in the general search for systematic reviews relevant to the guideline (see Chapter 3). Inclusion criteria for individual studies included diagnosis being established by diagnostic interview rather than by self-report tests such as the EPDS. Further details of the search process are in Appendix 6.

Very little data was found for conditions other than depression in the postnatal period. For depression in the postnatal period, three existing reviews were identified (see below), but for other disorders similar rigorous systematic reviews were not identified. Therefore, a search of the literature for primary research studies from 1996 to 2005 was undertaken for depression and from database inception to 2005 for anxiety disorders and eating disorders. Inclusion criteria were widened for the latter search to include studies in which diagnosis was not established by diagnostic interview. A search was also undertaken to identify prediction tools for depression in the antenatal and postnatal period from 2001 onwards. Update searches were undertaken during the remainder of the guideline development process. Table 2 shows the databases searched.

Table 2: Databases searched and inclusion/exclusion criteria for studies of risk factors for mental disorder during pregnancy and the postnatal period

Electronic databases	MEDLINE, EMBASE, CINAHL, PsycINFO
Date searched	Risk factors for depression in the postnatal period: 1 January 1996 to 4 April 2005 Risk factors for other disorders: database inception to 7 July 2005
Update searches	January 2006; May 2006; September 2006
Study design	Systematic reviews; prospective studies
Patient population	Pregnant women and women up to 1 year postnatally

5.2.3 Risk factors for depression in the postnatal period

Existing reviews
Three reviews of risk factors for depression in the postnatal period were identified: Beck (2001), O'Hara and Swain (1996) and Robertson and colleagues (2004). A brief description of each is provided in Table 3.

The reviews are difficult to reconcile since there is little overlap between included studies. O'Hara and Swain (1996) and Beck (2001) have only 18 studies in common (out of 59 and 84 respectively). In addition, neither list excluded studies or describe reasons for exclusion. Of the 26 additional studies reviewed by Robertson and colleagues (2004) (which used both the O'Hara and Swain [1996] and Beck [2001] reviews and added new studies), four were already in Beck (2001) and three in O'Hara and Swain (1996). Weaknesses of Beck (2001) are the inclusion of cross-sectional designs and studies not assessing depression according to a diagnostic interview. Similar weaknesses apply to O'Hara and Swain (1996), although a higher proportion of included studies used a clinical interview to assess depression compared with those in Beck (2001) (approximately 50%, compared with 36%). It is not clear whether Robertson and colleagues (2004) excluded studies included by the two previous reviews if they did not meet inclusion criteria, for example, the cross-sectional studies in Beck (2001). Table 4 lists the risk factors identified by each review.

Of the identified risk factors, depressed mood or anxiety during pregnancy are the strongest factors associated with developing depression in the postnatal period. Other potentially important risk factors are the level of social support, life events and psychiatric history, including previous experience of depression. With psychiatric history, the level of increased risk appears to be related to the severity and duration of the previous depression. For example, women reporting depression in the postnatal period after their first child that resolved in less than 2 months in the absence of any other risk factors were not at increased risk of depression after their second child (Elliott *et al.*, 2000).

Social support can be defined in various ways. For example, it can be defined in terms of sources of support, such as spouse, friends and relatives, or in terms of the type of support received. This includes informational support, instrumental support (such as practical help) and emotional support (Robertson *et al.*, 2004). Robertson and colleagues (2004) found that both emotional and instrumental support was negatively correlated with depression in the postnatal period, and that perceived social isolation was strongly predictive of depression in the postnatal period.

New studies
Eight additional studies were found that were published since these reviews. Study characteristics are in Table 5. These largely support the findings of earlier studies, with vulnerable personality, past history of depression, dissatisfaction with partner relationship, recent life events and poor social support associated with higher depression symptoms. In addition, a systematic review found no link between caesarean section and depression in the postnatal period (Carter *et al.*, 2006).

Table 3: Reviews of risk factors for depression in the postnatal period

Review	Method	Study inclusion criteria	Method of identifying depression
Beck, 2001	Meta-analysis, systematic search of nine electronic databases for 1990 to 2000 plus other methods (for example, contacts at conferences) (Located 107 studies; 84 met inclusion criteria; n = 16,863 combining participants across all risk factors)	Assessed relationship between postnatal depression and predictors Mood disorder assessed ≥2 weeks postnatal Adequate statistics present in result section to allow meta-analysis If an F or chi-square used, a degree of freedom (=1) was necessary to avoid unfocused, general comparisons between several means Allowed both longitudinal (80%) and cross-sectional designs (20%)	EPDS (n = 30), BDI (n = 24), CES-D (n = 16), also Zung Depression Scale, HRSD, formal diagnosis (a handful of studies used each method)
O'Hara & Swain, 1996	Meta-analysis of relationship between postnatal depression and risk factors – not clear where studies were sourced from (59 studies; n = 12,810)	Reported statistical relationship between variable of interest and postnatal depression Variable of interest assessed during either pregnancy or delivery Subjects recruited through random or quasi-random sampling techniques Depression assessed ≥2 weeks postnatally Postnatal depression assessed using a validated or standardised measure	Self-report (BDI ≥ 10; EPDS ≥ 13), clinical interview (Zung Depression Scale ≥ 48; CES-D ≥ 16) (roughly 50% each)

Continued

Table 3: (*Continued*)

Review	Method	Study inclusion criteria	Method of identifying depression
Robertson *et al.*, 2004	Meta-analysis, systematic search of 19 databases for studies published between 1990 and 2002 Used the two reviews above plus 26 additional study searches (added 10,000 participants to existing reviews)	Published between 1990 and 2002 in English Had to state diagnostic and temporal criteria of postnatal depression used Assessment method clearly stated and proven reliability Diagnoses made using standardised operational criteria Postnatal depression assessed ≥2 weeks postnatally Risk factors explicitly defined and measured Statistical relationship between the variable and postnatal depression clearly stated Prospective data collection only	Method of assessing depression in the included studies had to have 'proven reliability' (not defined) Diagnoses made using standardised operational criteria

Table 4: Risk factors for depression in the postnatal period identified by existing reviews

Factor	Effect size d; 95% CI	No. studies (no. participants where given)	Effect size R; 95% CI	No. studies (no. participants where given)
Depressed mood during pregnancy	d = 0.75; 0.67, 0.83 (1)	13	R = 0.44; 0.435, 0.519 (2)	21
Depression during pregnancy	d = 0.75 (3)	5 (n > 3,000)		
Prenatal anxiety	d = 0.68 (3)	5 (n > 1,100)	R = 0.41; 0.331, 0.531 (2)	4
Social support	d = −0.63; −0.75, −0.51 (1)	5	R = 0.36; 0.362, 0.442 (2)	27
	d = −0.64 (3)	5 (n > 3,100)		
Recent life events	d = 0.6; 0.54, 0.67 (1)	15	R = 0.38; 0.352 (2)	16
	d = 0.61 (3)	3 (n ≥ 2,500)		
History of depression	R = 0.39 (2)	11	d = 0.58 (3)	4 (n > 3,700)
Psychiatric history	d = 0.57; 0.49, 0.65 (1)	12		12
Self-esteem			R = 0.47; 0.403, 0.571 (2)	6
Childcare stress			R = 0.46; 0.42, 0.566 (2)	7

Continued

Table 4: (*Continued*)

Factor	Effect size d; 95% CI	No. studies (no. participants where given)	Effect size R; 95% CI	No. studies (no. participants where given)
Marital relationship	d = 0.39 (3)	3 (n > 1,700)		
Neuroticism	d = 0.39 (3)	3 (n > 600)		
Birth complications	d = 0.26; 0.19, 0.34 (1)	13	R = 0.39; 0.358, 0.46 (2)	14
Marital discord	d = −0.24; −0.39, −0.1 (1)	Unclear		
Obstetric factors	d = 0.26 (3)	7 (n > 9,500)		
Socioeconomic status	d = −0.14 (3)	6 (n > 1,700)		
Family history of depression	d = 0.05; −0.06, 0.16 (1)	6		

Notes: (1) O'Hara & Swain, 1996; (2) Beck, 2001; (3) Robertson *et al.*, 2004

R values use the value weighted by sample size; R = 0.1 small, 0.3 medium, 0.5 large

d = 0.2 small, 0.5 medium, 0.8 large

Table 5: Characteristics of studies of risk factors for depression published since existing reviews

Study	Description/method	Population studied	Measures	Results	Limitations
Boyce & Hickey, 2005	Prospective longitudinal cohort study; 6-month follow-up with measures taken at 6, 12, 18 and 24 weeks; calculated ORs for categorical variables comparing cases with non-cases; setting: public hospital in Australia	Women with a healthy infant recruited in first 2 days postnatally (excluded if psychotic or insufficient English); n = 425 followed up (plus 97 for whom there was insufficient data due to dropping out); mean age 26.9 (±5); 86.7% married/de facto relationship; 56.7% multiparous	Baseline interview: demographic information, pregnancy and delivery experiences; present intimate relationship, existing social support (adapted from Mannheim Interview on Social Support [Veiel, 1990]); obstetric history; vulnerable personality-style	42 (9.9%) met criteria for depression; 5 met criteria for panic disorder (4 of these included in 9.9% depression); 14 met criteria for GAD (11 included in 9.9%) (NB focus of study was depression) ORs (95% CI) meeting statistical significance for (comparing 9.9% with depression with those without): Younger age (<16 years) OR = 14.65 (2.38, 90.38) Past personal psychiatric history OR = 5.4 (2.15, 13.52) One or more life events OR = 3.14 (1.35, 7.30) **Intimate relationship:** Global dissatisfaction OR = 3.25 (1, 10.55) Communication problems OR = 5.34 (1.53, 18.71)	Convenience sample rather than consecutive sample; did not measure morbidity during pregnancy and information on past psychiatric history collected retrospectively; relied on EPDS to identify potential cases for further investigation

Continued

97

Table 5: (*Continued*)

Study	Description/method	Population studied	Measures	Results	Limitations
			questionnaire (Boyce *et al.*, 2001) At baseline, 6, 12, 18 and 24 weeks: EPDS, self-report questionnaires about infant feeding, changes in relationships, ability to cope with infant. At 12 weeks questionnaire about life events in past year Diagnosis of depression: caseness identified by EPDS > 12 on two consecutive occasions, confirmed with SCID-III-R	Deficient emotional support OR = 11.62 (1.57, 85.55) **Social support:** Unsatisfactory support OR = 2.23 (1.15, 4.32) Dissatisfaction with psychological crisis support OR = 2.51 (1.29, 4.86) **Personality variable:** Low organised/responsive OR = 3.53 (1.67, 7.45) Vulnerable personality style OR = 5.63 (2.79, 11.36) **Infant factors:** Not the desired sex of the baby OR = 3.07 (1.56, 6.04) Colic or reflux OR = 2.05 (1.05, 3.99) Hierarchical logistic regression analysis found baseline EPDS, vulnerable personality and low organised/responsive personality predictive of depression	

Chee et al., 2005	Prospective cohort study; interviews antenatally and 6 weeks postnatally; calculated ORs; setting: teaching hospital in Singapore	Pregnant women available for 6-week postnatal interview; 724 approached, 128 declined, 37 excluded as not available for second interview. 559 recruited and 278 available for second interview; mean age 31 (±4.7); 99% married; 47% Chinese, 35% Malay, 19% Indian, 9% other	Screening questionnaire including EPDS and diagnostic interview (SCID-IV) for those scoring above 7 on EPDS at both interviews (antenatal and 6 weeks postnatally); risk factors – demographic and socioeconomic factors, medical history/past psychiatric history, interpersonal relationships, sociocultural factors	Antenatal: 12% clinically significant mood disorder (4% MDD, 7.9% minor depression) Postnatal: 6.8% clinically significant mood disorder (4% MDD, 2.8% minor depression) **Antenatal interview – significant factors:** Living with husband and own parents OR = 2.1 (1.08, 4.09) Unplanned pregnancy OR = 2.22 (1.32, 3.71) Marital dissatisfaction OR = 4.95 (2.63, 9.31) Low emotional support OR = 2.83 (1.54, 5.21) Conflicts over childcare OR = 2.26 (1.34, 3.84) Depression during previous pregnancy OR = 2.26 (1.23, 4.17) Past history of depression OR = 5.47 (3.15, 9.5)	Culturally specific, especially finding about confinement practices may have missed some women with mental disorder as using the EPDS to screen. However, took low cut-off so unlikely

Continued

Table 5: (*Continued*)

Study	Description/method	Population studied	Measures	Results	Limitations
				Family history of mental disorder OR = 4.21 (1.51, 11.80) **Postnatal interview – significant factors:** Marital dissatisfaction adjusted OR = 9.42 (2.19, 40.52) Confinement adjusted OR = 9.42 (2.19, 40.52) Low instrumental support adjusted OR = 22.43 (3.68, 149.16) Past history of depression adjusted OR = 4.91 (1.08, 22.28)	
Church et al., 2005	Cross-sectional study; setting: community sample in Australia	Postnatal women who had given birth in previous 5–14 weeks; 1,100 randomly chosen from birth register invited to participate; 406 returned questionnaires and	EPDS to measure depression Dysfunctional maternal cognitions – Maternal Attitudes Questionnaire Dysfunctional general cognitions – Dysfunctional	EPDS > 12, 8.1%–10.3% significant level of postnatal depressive symptomatology 15% previous depression Used path analysis to examine relationship between risk factors and depression with cognitions as mediators	Sample may not be representative as only 37% of those invited to take part did so; not clear whether dysfunctional

Continued

		met inclusion criteria (excluded if suffering from severe puerperal psychosis or if infant required neonatal intensive care, had congenital abnormality or significant physical illness); mean age 29 ($\pm$5.07); 94% living with baby's father	Attitude Scale Risk factors: depression-prone personality, baby problems (for example, colic), educational level, unplanned pregnancy, previous diagnosis of depression	Found that depression linked to baby problems which was mediated by dysfunctional maternal cognitions; relationship between previous depression and depression in the postnatal period mediated by general dysfunctional cognitions; vulnerable personality and depression mediated by both general and maternal dysfunctional cognitions	cognitions pre- or post-date depression since cross-sectional design
Heron *et al.*, 2004	Prospective cohort study; setting: community; based on ALSPAC study	Pregnant women in Avon with due date between 1 April 1991 and 31 December 1992. Final sample with full data = 8,323	Questionnaire design. Anxiety measured on CCEI (used top 15% as threshold); depression measured on EPDS (>12 threshold); measures at 18 and 32 weeks' gestation and 8 weeks and 8 months postnatally	Depression: 76% not above threshold during study; 3.5% new cases of depression at 8 weeks postnatally, but 8.9% total depression at 8 weeks postnatally; 13% scored above cut-off in at least one assessment; 11% showed elevated depression only antenatally	Self-report measures including EPDS; those with highest levels of symptoms in early assessments most likely to drop out;

Table 5: (*Continued*)

Study	Description/method	Population studied	Measures	Results	Limitations
				Anxiety: 74% no elevated symptoms; 8.1% above threshold at 8 weeks postnatally, with 2.4% 'new' cases. Of those reporting anxiety postnatally, 2/3 experienced anxiety in pregnancy. Both anxiety and depression antenatally predicted depression in the postnatal period.	use of categorical variables not always robust
Hickey *et al.*, 1997	Prospective cohort study; setting: tertiary referral hospital in Australia	All women delivering at a hospital invited to take part (excluded if baby stillborn, had congenital abnormality, adopted, transferred to another hospital, or if mother had puerperal psychosis); 749 women gave birth, 522 agreed	Risk factor – early discharge (<72 hours postnatally) Measures: social and demographic circumstances, personality scale, obstetric history, satisfaction with labour, social support, personal and family psychiatric history,	9.9% (n = 42) had major depression; 36% discharged <72 hours (early discharge group). Some differences between groups – early discharge group more likely to be multiparous, fewer years of formal education, bottle fed in first week, poor relationship with parents. More likely to have history of depression (not significant).	Women not randomly assigned to early or late discharge

		with full data for 425. Mean age 26.9; 86.4% married or de facto relationship	quality of intimate relationships, EPDS, Tennant and Andrews Life Events Scale, SCID-III-R for those scoring >13 on EPDS	More women developed postnatal depression in early discharge group (14.4% versus 7.4%) Used hierarchical logistic regression – dissatisfaction with partner relationship, reporting ≥3 life events in past 12 months and vulnerable personality predicted depression in the postnatal period	
Howell et al., 2006	Telephone survey/medical chart review; setting: tertiary care academic medical centre, Singapore; participants given monetary incentive to participate; interviews between 35 and 45 mins	Uncomplicated postnatal mothers, English or Spanish speaking between 2 and 6 weeks postnatally; n = 720; 1,166 mothers approached; most under 35 years; 44% primiparous; 19% previous history of depression; 50% white	Collected data on demographics, physical symptoms, emotional symptoms, daily function, social support, personal competence and perceptions of their healthcare providers. Asked to think back to first 2 weeks postnatally; depressive symptoms measured using Whooley et al. (1997) questions	39% screened positive for depression; factors associated with depression were lower income, non-white race, more physical symptoms, more infant colic, lower social support and lower self-efficacy	Retrospective, although only a few weeks

Continued

Table 5: (*Continued*)

Study	Description/method	Population studied	Measures	Results	Limitations
Jesse *et al.*, 2005	Survey based on interviews; setting: urban prenatal clinical in US; assesses antenatal depression	Low-income African American and Caucasian women 16 to 28 weeks' gestation; 140 approached, 130 took part; data for 128; 58% married or de facto relationship	Collected data on sociodemographics, stress, abuse, health-risk behaviours, social support, self-esteem, spiritual perspective, religiosity, depressive symptoms (measured by BDI-II)	Mean BDI 13.6 (SD 9.9; range 2.059). 27% scored >16; logistic regression showed BDI-II scores >16 predicted by higher religiosity, higher levels of stress, lower self-esteem	Part US ethnic population – may be hard to generalise to UK
Surkan *et al.*, 2006	Cross-sectional study; setting: community health centres in urban areas in US	Women delivering live, single baby randomly selected from patient lists, stratified by race/ethnicity and postnatal interval (6 weeks to 6 months, 6 months to 12 months, 12 to 18 months, 18 to 24 months); excluded if current pregnancy, major physical disability, severe chronic mental illness, current chemotherapy treatment, severe medical condition for baby, baby not living with biological mother; 1,330 women identified, 145 ineligible plus others not available, final n = 415; mean age 29 (±6.2); 18.9%	Questionnaire including SF-36, postnatal specific measures and social support and social network measures; depression measured with CES-D	Social support and social networks independently related to depression scores with poorer social support and social networks associated with higher depression scores. African Americans and Hispanics had higher depression scores than whites (14.2 ± 10.8; 15.2 ± 10.3; 11.4 ± 9.2 respectively)	Cross-sectional; US ethnic population – may be hard to generalise to UK

Summary of risk factors for the development of depression in the postnatal period
Compared with other disorders, depression in the postnatal period is relatively well studied, and a wide variety of risk factors have been investigated. Those factors consistently associated with the onset of depressive symptoms during the postnatal period include depressed mood and depression during pregnancy, anxiety during pregnancy, poor social support (although this is defined in a number of different ways), recent life events and a history of depression or other psychiatric history.

5.2.4 Risk factors for puerperal psychosis

Puerperal psychosis is a rare event particularly compared with depression in the post-natal period (see Chapter 4). Many commentators consider much puerperal psychosis to be a variant of an episode of bipolar disorder, with a third of episodes meeting criteria for mania or schizoaffective mania (Gelder *et al.*, 2000). In an epidemiological study following 470,000 women over an 8-year period, 21.4% of those with bipolar disorder whose last episode was manic and 13.3% of those with bipolar disorder whose last episode was depressed had a psychiatric admission (a proxy for psychosis) within 3 months of delivery. These proportions were much higher than in those with other psychiatric diagnoses, for example, 3.4% of those with schizophrenia and 1.9% of those with depressive neurosis (all ICD-9 diagnostic categories) (Kendell *et al.*, 1987). In a later study, episodes (defined as a DSM-IV episode of mania or psychotic episode within 6 weeks of delivery) followed 26% of deliveries in women with a diagnosis of bipolar I disorder or schizoaffective disorder (313 deliveries in 152 women) (Jones & Craddock, 2001). It is important to note that these figures do not represent the natural history of the untreated disorder postnatally as the populations studied will have included an unknown proportion of women receiving treatment. Thus these proportions should not be quoted as the relapse risk without preventative treatment, which is likely to be higher and can only be derived from untreated samples. Small control samples of women with bipolar disorder on no medication postnatally indicate that the natural postnatal relapse risk for bipolar disorder may be considerably higher, at up to 70% (that is 700 in 1,000) postnatally (Viguera *et al.*, 2000) and 50% (that is 500 in 1,000) antenatally. Nevertheless, there appears to be a substantial number of women who experience an episode of psychosis in the early postnatal period who do not have an existing bipolar diagnosis and/or who never experience a non-puerperal episode (Dean *et al.*, 1989). In the relatively small study by Dean and colleagues (1989), these women had better overall outcomes than women with a bipolar diagnosis.

A study of the relationship between obstetric factors and onset of puerperal psychosis found 60% of women with puerperal psychosis had a diagnosis of bipolar disorder or schizoaffective disorders (Sharma *et al.*, 2004). However, the risk of recurrence of illness at any time (defined as readmission) after a puerperal psychosis appears to be much greater in women with a diagnosis of schizophrenia, with half of women with this diagnosis followed in a Danish sample relapsing within a year of discharge, compared with half with other diagnoses being readmitted within 2 years (Terp *et al.*, 1999). In all, 98% of women with schizophrenia who had a puerperal psychosis relapsed. Women who had had a puerperal psychosis but who did not have a diagnosis of schizophrenia were also at risk of relapse (*ibid.*). Within 10 years, 65% of those with no previous admission were readmitted, and 85% of those with a previous admission were readmitted. Specific risk factors for readmission in women with a functional psychosis other than schizophrenia were not being married and preterm delivery (*ibid.*). A Swedish cohort study of over 600,000 women concluded that most episodes of puerperal psychosis occurred in women with a previous psychotic or bipolar illness, and that the majority of these episodes were of a psychotic disorder rather than an episode of bipolar disorder (Harlow *et al.*, 2007).

Social and obstetric risk factors associated with psychiatric admission (used as a proxy for puerperal psychosis) include not being married, not having living children and perinatal death (index delivery) (Kendell *et al.*, 1987). Family history of puerperal illness may also be a risk factor (for example, Jones & Craddock, 2001), although family history of non-puerperal illness does not appear to be a risk factor (for example, Robertson *et al.*, 2005). Older age at delivery also appears to be a risk factor, with those aged 40 to 44 having five times the risk of those in the general female population compared with around twice the risk in younger women (Nager *et al.*, 2005). This study also found that not living with the infant's father was a risk factor. In women with bipolar disorder or schizophrenia (that is, those at high risk of puerperal psychosis), links with factors such as increased sensitivity of dopamine receptors in the hypothalamus and sleep loss have also been suggested (Sharma *et al.*, 2004; Wieck *et al.*, 1991), as have primiparity, difficult labour, genetic predisposition and hormonal changes (Brockington, 1996).

Summary of risk factors for the development of psychosis in the postnatal period
Risk factors for the development of puerperal psychosis are a history of previous serious mental disorder, particularly bipolar disorder, and previous puerperal psychosis, schizoaffective disorder and schizophrenia.

5.2.5 Risk factors for developing other disorders

While the amount of literature on risk factors predicting the development of depression in the postnatal period is relatively large, literature for risk factors predicting the development of other mental disorders during this time is lacking. However, there are a few studies and reviews describing risk factors for disorders including PTSD, panic disorder and eating disorders.

Post-traumatic stress disorder
Some work has been done looking at risk factors for symptoms of PTSD following childbirth; for example, a study by Czarnocka and Slade (2000) identified perceptions of low levels of support from partners and staff, patterns of blame and perceived low control in labour as predictive of symptoms. Personal vulnerability factors, such as

previous mental health difficulties and trait anxiety, were also related to symptoms. These factors were supported by a review of available studies (Olde *et al.*, 2006). The review found two small studies of PTSD symptoms in women following emergency caesareans, which reported high levels of symptoms.

Panic disorder

There is little systematic research on panic disorder during pregnancy, particularly on risk factors for developing panic disorder during the postnatal period. A review of studies looking at its occurrence (without concurrent affective disorder) during pregnancy and/or the postnatal period found ten studies, all except one of which were retrospective and uncontrolled (Hertzberg & Wahlbeck, 1999). Only one study was solely concerned with onset of panic disorder and the postnatal period (Sholomskas *et al.*, 1993). Overall, a collation of all the studies found that 6% of pregnancies had postnatal onset (278 pregnancies), although in most studies (n = 8) the postnatal period was defined as up to 3 months after delivery. No specific risk factors were identified that predicted the onset of panic disorder.

Generalised anxiety disorder

There appears to be little research on the predictive factors of GAD in pregnancy or the postnatal period, although anxiety itself has been shown to be predictive of depression in the postnatal period (Heron *et al.*, 2004).

Eating disorders

It is uncommon for women to develop an eating disorder *de novo* during pregnancy and the postnatal period, and women with severe eating disorders tend to have reduced fertility and therefore are less likely to become pregnant. There are also data suggesting that symptoms of existing disorders improve during pregnancy, with 68% of women in a study of 530 women attending an antenatal clinic reporting symptoms above threshold in the 2 years before conception reporting symptoms below threshold in pregnancy (Turton *et al.*, 1999). However, some women continue to experience symptoms during pregnancy, and factors associated with higher symptomatology in pregnancy include younger age (less than 30 years), previous high levels of symptoms, lower educational attainment, poorer housing, employment status and previous miscarriage (*ibid.*). Women with a history of bulimia nervosa or binge eating disorder may be at increased risk of depression in the postnatal period (Mazzeo *et al.*, 2006).

Obsessive-compulsive disorder

A review of OCD symptoms in pregnancy and the postnatal period found some evidence for onset of OCD associated with pregnancy and childbirth, although studies were of OCD populations and relied on retrospective self-report (Abramowitz *et al.*, 2003). The authors could find no evidence for predictive factors for the development or exacerbation of OCD in the postnatal period. Similarly, they found no data on the possible causal link between OCD and depression in this period, which commonly co-occur.

*Summary of risk factors for the development of other mental disorders
in the postnatal period*

Disorders other than depression and psychosis are much less well studied in pregnancy and the postnatal period. Symptoms of PTSD in the postnatal period may be associated with perceptions of low levels of support from partners and staff, patterns of blame and perceived low control in labour. Exacerbation of eating disorders during pregnancy was associated with younger age (less than 30 years), previous high levels of symptoms, lower educational attainment, poorer housing, employment status and previous miscarriage. It is not clear whether specific risk factors can predict onset of panic disorder or OCD.

5.2.6 Clinical summary of risk factors for the development of mental disorders in the postnatal period

There are a large number of studies looking at risk factors for depression in the postnatal period and some data on risk factors for psychosis and other disorders. The risk factors that consistently show reasonable predictive value, particularly for the development of depression, psychosis and recurrence of bipolar disorder, are past psychiatric history, including previous puerperal episodes, and current disorder or symptomatology. There is also some suggestion that family history of psychosis in the postnatal period is predictive.

5.3 METHODS FOR PREDICTING MENTAL DISORDER DURING PREGNANCY AND THE POSTNATAL PERIOD

5.3.1 Evidence search

In the search for formal prediction tools, the GDG decided to concentrate on methods for predicting depression, as preliminary searches established that little, if any, work has been done on other disorders. The evidence search for studies looking at methods for predicting depression during pregnancy and the postnatal period looked for studies published within the 5 years preceding the end of the guideline development process. In addition, the search for all systematic reviews relevant to the guideline published since 1994 (see Chapter 3) was used. Further details of the search process are in Appendix 6. Table 6 shows the databases searched.

5.3.2 Prediction methods

Effective prediction tools are predicated on the existence of reliable risk factors, individually or in a combination, which have been prospectively tested. Other than for psychosis and depression in the postnatal period, no reliable risk factors have

Table 6: Databases searched for reviews of tools predicting depression in the postnatal period

Electronic databases	MEDLINE, EMBASE, CINAHL, PsycINFO
Date searched	1 January 2001 to 11 April 2005
Update searches	January 2006; May 2006; September 2006
Study design	No specific design sought
Patient population	Pregnant women and women up to 1 year postnatally with depression

emerged for predicting the onset of mental disorders during pregnancy and the postnatal period.

Depression

Since a high-quality review was available looking at antenatal prediction of depression in the postnatal period (Austin & Lumley, 2003), additional individual studies were not used. This review examined methods for determining in the antenatal period whether women were at risk of depression in the postnatal period. Austin and Lumley found 16 studies in total that met their inclusion criteria (pregnant women in any care setting; any instrument, or combination of instruments, applied during pregnancy to classify women as at risk or not at risk of depression postnatally; relevant outcome measures, including sensitivity, specificity, positive predictive value and negative predictive value; positive and negative likelihood ratios; and proportion of the population defined as at risk and proportion having depression postnatally who had been classified as not at risk).

The 16 included studies used a variety of antenatal assessment methods, including both study-specific measures and established scales. Of the 10 that used study-specific measures, 5 also used additional tools (one used the General Health Questionnaire [GHQ-12], one the General Health Questionnaire – Depression Scale [GHQ-D], two the EPDS, and another the Beck Depression Inventory [BDI], Spielberger State/Trait Anxiety Scale [SAS], Eysenck Personality Inventory – neuroticism scale [EPI], Sarason Social Support Scale [SSS], and Spanier Dyadic Adjustment Scale [short form] [SDA]). Of those that used established tools, two used the EPDS alone, one used the BDI, one used the Schedule for Affective Disorders and Schizophrenia (SADS) plus Research Diagnostic Criteria (RDC)/DSM-III and one the EPDS and SADS together. To assess depression postnatally, 12 used the EPDS (four with other instruments, including the Structured Clinical Interview for DSM III [SCID-III] [n = 1], GHQ-D and Schedules for Clinical Assessment in Neuropsychiatry [SCAN] [n = 1], BDI and SAS [n = 1], and SADS [n = 1]). Other tools included the BDI (n = 2), Present State Examination (PSE) (n = 1) and SADS/RDC/DSM-III (n = 1). Few studies made a diagnosis of depression using a validated diagnostic instrument. For example, the EPDS includes anxiety and depressive symptomatology, with a higher score indicating probable depression, and the GHQ measures general distress. In addition, in the studies using the EPDS, a variety of cut-off points was used including >9 and >11, which reduces specificity, and >14, which reduces sensitivity relative to the recommended cut-off of >12 (13+).

Timing of assessments also varied between 10 and 36 weeks' gestation and between 5 weeks and 1 year postnatally. The number assessed in the studies ranged from 37 to 5,091, with only six studies having close to the number calculated by Austin and Lumley required to identify depression at a prevalence of 13%, given a 100% success rate (n = 1,300). Larger studies still (n > 2,100) would be required for a sensitivity of 40%. Three studies also used different samples for the antenatal and postnatal assessments, two of which were the larger studies.

The two biggest studies provided very different results, with one classifying 21% of those who went on to have depression postnatally as not at risk and the other 65% of those who went on to have depression postnatally as not at risk. The first study used the GHQ12 and a study-specific questionnaire antenatally and the EPDS postnatally. The second study used a study-specific questionnaire antenatally and the EPDS, SCID-III postnatally. Not surprisingly, the review concluded that no screening instruments reviewed have sufficient sensitivity or positive predictive value to form the basis of a routine screening programme.

Clinical summary for prediction methods
Epidemiological studies demonstrate that a previous history of severe mental illness, including schizophrenia, bipolar disorder, previous puerperal psychosis or severe prolonged depression in the postnatal period, can all increase the likelihood of further episodes of mental illness after the current pregnancy. So, enquiry about a previous severe mental illness, perhaps using psychiatric admission or contact with a specialist mental health service as indicators of severity (although the reliability of this may depend on local services), is important to identify women with an increased risk of puerperal psychosis or relapse of severe mental illness.

Therefore, although several risk factors have been identified that may be associated with the development of depression in the postnatal period, and some larger studies have included many of these, a validated reliable prediction tool for routine clinical assessment has not yet been developed. This does not mean that healthcare practitioners seeing women and families in the antenatal period should take no interest in levels of social support or current symptoms of anxiety, for example, but that these factors should not be used to predict future illness.

5.3.3 Clinical practice recommendations

5.3.3.1 At a woman's first contact with services in both the antenatal and the postnatal periods, healthcare professionals (including midwives, obstetricians, health visitors and GPs) should ask about:
- past or present severe mental illness including schizophrenia, bipolar disorder, psychosis in the postnatal period and severe depression

- previous treatment by a psychiatrist/specialist mental health team including inpatient care
- a family history of perinatal mental illness.

Other specific predictors, such as poor relationships with her partner, should not be used for the routine prediction of the development of a mental disorder.

5.4 METHODS FOR DETECTING MENTAL DISORDER DURING PREGNANCY AND THE POSTNATAL PERIOD

5.4.1 Detection methods

The evidence considered in Chapter 4 indicates that psychiatric disorders during the postnatal period may carry considerable risk to both the woman and the infant. In light of this, it is important that reliable methods of detection of current mental disorders in the postnatal period are available, as most mental disorders experienced during the antenatal and postnatal period respond to appropriate and timely treatments.

Detection of depression in the antenatal period
There is one study validating the EPDS in pregnancy (Murray & Cox, 1990). This validated the EPDS against RDC diagnoses of depression using a standardised psychiatric interview (Goldberg *et al.*, 1970) in 100 women of between 28 and 34 weeks' gestation. Six per cent had a diagnosis of major depression and 8% minor depression. At the 12/13 cut-off rate, the EPDS had a sensitivity of 100% for major depression but a specificity of only 87%. Specificity improved at the higher cut-off of 14/15 (96%). For minor depression, the sensitivity was 71% and the specificity 72% at the 10/11 cut-off. Therefore, a higher cut-off may be required to use the EPDS to detect depression in pregnancy.

Detection of depression in the postnatal period
Again, depression in the postnatal period is the area where most work has been done to develop detection methods, including both self-report and clinician-completed measures.

Eight self-report measures that had been assessed in mothers in the first postnatal year were reviewed by Boyd and colleagues (2005), including the BDI and BDI-II (Beck *et al.*, 1961, 1996), the Bromley Postnatal Depression Scale (BPDS; Stein & Van den Akker, 1992), the Center for Epidemiological Studies Depression Scale (CES-D; Radloff, 1977), the EPDS (Cox *et al.*, 1987), the GHQ (Goldberg, 1972), the Inventory of Depressive Symptomatology (IDS; Rush *et al.*, 1986), the Postnatal Depression Screening Scale (PDSS; Beck & Gable, 2000, 2001a) and the Zung Self-Rating Depression Scale (Zung SDS; Zung, 1965).

When describing the sensitivity, specificity and positive predictive value of the different instruments, the review defined 'excellent' as values above 0.9, 'good' as 0.8 to 0.9, 'moderate' as 0.5 to 0.7, 'low' as 0.3 to 0.5, and 'poor' as less than 0.3. Based on these categorisations, it calculated that the BDI had good specificity, variable sensitivity, depending on the sample used, and low positive predictive value. The BDI-II had excellent specificity, moderate sensitivity and excellent positive predictive value, although this reduces to moderate for minor depression if a prevalence rate of 13% is assumed (based on O'Hara & Swain, 1996).

The review found only a single study of the BPDS that showed moderate sensitivity and positive predictive value and excellent specificity. However, a self-report diagnostic tool was used. The CES-D had moderate sensitivity and positive predictive value and excellent specificity. However, the review concludes that the CES-D may miss 40% of depressed women. The review found that the positive predictive value for the EPDS varied depending on the sample used. In a population with the 'standard' prevalence rate of 13%, the positive predictive value was low to moderate, with low specificity. Sensitivity and positive predictive values were low in studies using it to detect minor and/or major depression, rather than just major depression. The review included several studies of non-English language versions of the scale.

Boyd and colleagues (2005) found studies validating the GHQ (various versions) in depression in the postnatal period, although the GHQ does not measure solely depression but rather general psychiatric morbidity. The 12-item version was found to have the highest sensitivity and positive predictive value. The review found that the IDS had excellent sensitivity, good specificity and moderate positive predictive value. The PDSS was found to have excellent sensitivity and specificity, and good positive predictive value.

For most scales, there were only between one and four studies, with the EPDS being the most studied (22 studies, with 11 being used to calculate sensitivity, specificity and positive predictive value). Only three were specifically designed to measure depression in the postnatal period (the BPDS, EPDS and PDSS). Boyd and colleagues (2005) concluded that, while more research was needed, the EPDS had been most widely studied but only had moderate psychometric properties. Other instruments such as the PDSS and the BDI may have value as methods for the detection of depression but further research is needed. The EPDS is considered below in more detail, since this is currently the most widely-used scale.

Another self-report scale in use in primary care is the Patient Health Questionnaire (PHQ; Spitzer *et al.*, 1999). Although it does not appear to have been validated in postnatal women, it seems to have good sensitivity and specificity in detecting depression in primary care populations (Spitzer *et al.*, 1999). A nine-item depression module (PHQ-9) is often used in isolation, for example by GPs, and a two-item version has also been tested and found to have good sensitivity and specificity (Kroenke *et al.*, 2003). This is discussed in more detail below.

Also in use in primary care to assess both depression and anxiety symptoms is the clinician-completed Hospital Anxiety and Depression Scale (Zigmond & Snaith, 1983). Although this does not appear to have been validated in postnatal populations, it appears to have good case-finding properties (Bjelland *et al.*, 2002). However, it was not designed as a detection tool.

5.4.2   The Edinburgh Postnatal Depression Scale (EPDS)

The EPDS (Cox *et al.*, 1987) is a ten-item self-report questionnaire developed to assist healthcare professionals to identify depression in the postnatal period. It was developed in an attempt to address the problem of the pregnancy or postnatal status *per se* affecting experiences typically taken as indicators of depression, such as disturbances of appetite. It was piloted on childbearing women in Edinburgh. Although the EPDS was originally designed as a screening tool, its use has extended well beyond this in studies of the effectiveness of treatments for depression in the postnatal period. In research settings, the EPDS has at times been applied as though it were a tool to identify those who fall within the diagnostic category of depression and distinguish them from those that do not. The EPDS is strongly correlated with anxiety (Brouwers *et al.*, 2001; Jomeen & Martin, 2005) and, for an unselected sample, the distribution of scores is continuous: it is simply not possible to determine the clear cut-offs that use as a diagnostic instrument would require because depressed mood lies on a continuum of severity (Murray & Carothers, 1990). It has been argued that the EPDS may be conceptualised as a continuous measure of emotional well-being (Green, 2005), although further studies would be required to assess its value as a continuous measure of severity or probability of clinical depression.

In order to assess the psychometric properties of the EPDS, a search was undertaken of validation papers of the English-language version, in which the validation was against diagnosis as established by diagnostic interview and for a sample of women from developed countries. Eight such studies were identified (see Table 7)[8]. In addition, another high-quality review was used to support this review (Gaynes *et al.*, 2005).

As can be seen from Table 7, the psychometric properties of the EPDS (sensitivity, specificity, positive predictive value and negative predictive value) vary considerably across the studies, particularly sensitivity and the positive predictive value, which varies from 33% to 93%. This variability probably reflects differences in the populations sampled and how the EPDS was administered in the studies, with most being research based. Also, the prevalence of depression differed between the studies, ranging from 8.7% (Boyce *et al.*, 1993) to 25% (Cox *et al.*, 1987). This is higher than the 6.8% calculated by Gaynes and colleagues (2005) in their systematic review (for the period up to 6 weeks postnatally, which is the most common time point used to assess depression in the included studies).

Gaynes and colleagues undertook a meta-analysis of three studies detecting major depression in the postnatal period using the EPDS at the ≥13 cut-off point. They removed a further study in order to calculate a meaningful standard error since this study estimated sensitivity of the EPDS at 100%, which is unlikely. They calculated a pooled sensitivity of 91% (95% CI = 0.84 to 0.99) but did not calculate a pooled specificity because of significant heterogeneity. However, when summing up, they report a specificity of 95%, although it is not clear how they calculated this.

Nevertheless, based on these figures, together with a prevalence rate for major depression of 6.8% (which they calculate based on a review of prevalence studies), Gaynes and colleagues (2005) calculate an overall positive predictive value for the

---

[8]Prediction and detection tools for depression (antenatal screening for depression) based on search within the Austin and Lumley (2003) review, amended to include detection tools. The search strategy is available on request.

Table 7: Summary of validation studies of EPDS as a detection tool for depression in the postnatal period

Study	EPDS cut-off/ comparator	Sensitivity		Specificity		Positive predictive value		Negative predictive value		No. of women/ country	Type of sample	Time of presentation administration	Method of presentation
		12/13	9/10	12/13	9/10	12/13	9/10	12/13	9/10				
Beck & Gable 2001b	Clinical interview (SCID-IV)	78	59	99	86	93	64	96	82	150 USA	Recruited by media advertisement and through antenatal classes	4–8 weeks postnatally approximately	Research nurse, psychotherapist, not clear if in clinic or at home
Boyce *et al.*, 1993	Clinical interview (Diagnostic Interview Schedule)	100	100	95	89	50	47	n/a	n/a	103 (not clear if any of those requested to participate refused) Australia	Mixed; recruited from postnatal clinic and women referred to hospital with depression postnatally	2–29 weeks postnatally	Psychologist in woman's home
Cox *et al.*, 1987	Clinical interview (RDC criteria)	86	94	78	51	73	58	n/a	n/a	84 (not clear if any of those requested to participate refused) Scotland	Identified by health visitors as high risk at 6 weeks postnatally	3 months postnatally	Researcher in woman's home

Study	Detection tool									Sample (n/country)	Recruitment	Timing	Validation
Harris et al., 1989	Clinical interview	95	n/a	93	n/a	75	n/a	n/a		126 (not clear if any of those requested to participate refused) Wales	Recruited from antenatal booking clinic	6–8 weeks postnatally	Research psychiatrist at clinic
Leverton & Elliott, 2000	Clinical interview (taken data for Catego)	70	90	93	84	33	23	n/a		199 (selected women eligible for prevention trial) England	Attendees at antenatal clinic	3 months postnatally	Research psychiatrist in woman's home
Matthey et al., 2001	Clinical interview	38	54	95	84	56	39	89	90	230 (not clear if any of those requested to participate refused) Australia	Women participating with their partners in a fee-paid parenthood class	6–9 weeks postnatally	Researcher in the woman's home
Murray & Carothers, 1990	Clinical interview (RDC criteria)	68	89	96	82	67	39	n/a		646 England	Community – recruited from postnatal wards	6 weeks postnatally	Research (study of infant development); administered by post
Zelkowitz & Milet, 1995	SCID-III	67	91	94	76	91	78	n/a		1,559/2,087 Canada	Community	6 weeks postnatally	By telephone

NB Only validation studies where the specific prediction or detection tool was completed against a standardised diagnostic interview were included. Further, the validation was of the English-language version of the EPDS and sufficient data reported

n/a = not available

Sensitivity – proportion of those with depression who test positive; specificity – proportion of those without depression who test negative; positive predictive value – those correctly identified as having depression as a proportion of all positive test results; negative predictive value – those correctly identified as not having depression as proportion of all negative test results

EPDS of 57% and a negative predictive value of 99%. The corresponding values for both major and minor depression (using a cut-off point of >10) are a positive predictive value of 30% and negative predictive value of 95%.

These data are difficult to translate into clinical practice. Specific difficulties identified with current practice in some areas are the use of cut-offs outside of the range of 13+ (>12) recommended for probable depression and 10+ (>9) for possible depression, such as use of cut-offs in the 15 to 20 range to indicate urgency of treatment or need to refer to mental health services without other information gathered by interview. Published reports of clinical practice with other cut-offs within the recommended range, typically 12+ (>11), fail to explain the rationale for the choice, usually trading off the risk of false positives and false negatives in the above two cut-offs.

Early research studies of acceptability suggested a very high degree of acceptability to the population in the context of research protocols and pre-selected populations (Murray & Carothers, 1990). Subsequent qualitative studies suggest that acceptability ratings are in fact much lower for some current clinical practices using the EPDS or variants of it: women feel compelled to complete the questionnaire but, owing to fears as to the possible consequences of being identified as symptomatic, may distort their responses accordingly (Shakespeare *et al.*, 2003; Cubison & Munro, 2005).

5.4.3   Case finding with interview questions

Detection for depression in adult populations has moved away from the use of paper-and-pencil multi-item questionnaires (for example, NICE, 2004a). Studies indicate that two brief focused questions that address mood and interest are as likely to be effective as more elaborate methods and are more compatible with routine use in busy primary and secondary care settings (Whooley *et al.*, 1997) ('During the last month, have you often been bothered by feeling down, depressed or hopeless?' and 'During the last month have you often been bothered by having little interest or pleasure in doing things?'). The questions are based on the 2-item PHQ-9 (see above), although in the study by Whooley and colleagues (1997) the questions were not scored but simply required a yes or no answer.

Whooley and colleagues (1997) found that the two questions have a sensitivity of 96% (95% CI 90% to 99%) and a specificity of 57% (95% CI 53% to 62%), giving a positive likelihood ratio of 2.2. Arroll and colleagues (2005) have developed an extension to these two questions by adding the following question: 'Is this something with which you would like help?', with three possible responses: 'No', 'Yes, but not today' and 'Yes'. The two Whooley questions plus the help question have been validated against a standardised psychiatric interview and the addition of the help question resulted in a sensitivity of 96% (95% CI 86% to 99%) and an improved specificity of 89% (95% CI 87% to 91%), with a positive likelihood ratio for the help question of 9.1. Based on calculations using data given in the paper, the three questions have a positive predictive value of 32% and a negative predictive value of 99%. It is not clear in the paper whether the diagnostic criteria used to validate the three questions (and the other instruments tested) included both minor and major depression or major depression alone.

5.4.4 Clinical summary for methods for detecting mental disorder in the postnatal period

Although a number of tools (essentially self-report questionnaires) have been developed for the detection of depression, only eight have been found with studies assessing their use in the postnatal period. Only one of these, the EPDS, has been the subject of a sufficient number studies to make a judgement of its usefulness. However, this dataset has a number of problems, including relatively high prevalence of depression amongst the included studies compared with that calculated by a high-quality review of prevalence studies, relatively small studies (the majority had fewer than 250 women, although one assessed around 1,500 women) and many studies undertaken in a research rather than a clinical setting. Given this, although the sensitivity of the test is reasonably high, the lower specificity means that the positive predictive value is poor and that, although the reliability of a negative test result is good, that for a positive test is poor, and would mean that nearly half of all women referred for further assessment would be referred unnecessarily, placing an increased and wasteful burden on resources. Similarly, the two Whooley questions plus the additional Arrol question have poor positive predictive value.

The NSC in its review of screening for depression in the postnatal period also found insufficient evidence to support a national screening programme based on any of the existing screening tools, including the EPDS (Shakespeare, 2001). It should be noted that the review's criteria are much broader than an assessment of psychometric properties as they attempt to validate screening tools for use within a healthcare system rather than just whether the tool is effective in detecting a disorder; for example, 'there must be evidence from high-quality RCTs that the screening programme is effective in reducing mortality or morbidity'. The two Whooley questions were not included in this review, although they probably would not meet the criteria either.

Current NICE guidelines for depression (NICE, 2004a) recommend the two questions and, although little specific evidence exists for their use in the perinatal period, their ease of use and reasonable sensitivity and specificity, particularly if combined with the additional help question from Arrol and colleagues (2005), suggest that their use in routine care may be practical and acceptable; for example, they do not require additional resources (such as copies of a questionnaire). The value of the questions lies in part in their brevity and the fact that they lend themselves to use both in the antenatal and postnatal periods.

5.4.5 Clinical practice recommendations

5.4.5.1 At a woman's first contact with primary care, at her booking visit and postnatally (usually at 4 to 6 weeks and 3 to 4 months), healthcare professionals (including midwives, obstetricians, health visitors and GPs) should ask two questions to identify possible depression.

- During the past month have you often been bothered by feeling down, depressed or hopeless?

- During the past month, have you often been bothered by having little interest or pleasure in doing things?

A third question should be considered if the woman answers 'yes' to either of the initial questions:

- Is this something you feel you need or want help with?

5.4.5.2 Healthcare professionals may consider the use of self-report measures such as the EPDS, HADS or PHQ-9 as part of subsequent assessment or for the routine monitoring of outcomes.

5.4.5.3 If a woman has a current mental disorder or a history of severe mental illness, she should be asked about her mental health at all subsequent contacts.

5.4.6   Research recommendation

Case finding for depression
A validation study should be undertaken of the 'Whooley questions' ('During the past month, have you often been bothered by feeling down, depressed or hopeless?' 'During the past month, have you often been bothered by having little interest or pleasure in doing things?') in women in the first postnatal year, examining the questions' effectiveness when used by midwives and health visitors compared with a psychiatric interview.

Why this is important
Depression in the first postnatal year is relatively common and may have a lasting impact on the woman, her baby and other family members. Case finding is most conveniently undertaken by healthcare professionals in regular contact with women, but they do not traditionally have training in mental health. The Whooley questions appear to offer a relatively quick and convenient way of case finding for healthcare professionals who are not specialists in mental health.

5.5   REFERRAL PATHWAYS

If initial detection of a disorder is to be useful, clear referral pathways supported by effective treatment options need to be available. All healthcare professionals involved in detecting mental illness in women in the antenatal and postnatal periods must be aware of the appropriate care and referral options, so that effective assessment and treatment is available to those who are identified as requiring further assessment. The nature of the assessment and any subsequent treatment will vary between primary and secondary care services and will reflect the nature of the potential disorder identified.

For the large majority of women with identified or suspected mental disorder, the major source of effective assessment and treatment will take place in primary care, coordinated by the GP. Where a women is identified within primary care as suffering from a common mental disorder, the further treatment and assessment of the disorder will be managed and coordinated in primary care according to the protocols in that practice. As a minimum, it is expected that a record of the disorder should be entered in the woman's notes and further appropriate assessment or monitoring undertaken. The extent of this assessment and monitoring will vary with the severity of the disorder and the presence of any potential risk factors.

If the initial detection of a common mental disorder occurs in secondary care maternity services, again the minimum should be an entry in the notes and a communication with the GP of the initial outcome of the assessment. Depending on the severity of the disorder, healthcare professionals should consider further assessment of the woman's psychological state, where appropriate seeking advice from colleagues on the details of the further assessment to be undertaken. Where the methods for the detection of mental disorder identify a history of, or the presence of a severe mental disorder, healthcare professionals in primary care or maternity services should refer the woman for a specialist mental health assessment, given the high risk of relapse or exacerbation of symptoms for some women with a history of severe mental illness and the risks associated with the presence of these conditions.

5.5.1   Clinical practice recommendations

5.5.1.1   A written care plan covering pregnancy, delivery and the postnatal period should be developed for pregnant women with a current or past history of severe mental illness, usually in the first trimester. It should:
- be developed in collaboration with the woman and her partner, family and carers, and relevant healthcare professionals
- include increased contact with specialist mental health services (including, if appropriate, specialist perinatal mental health services)
- be recorded in all versions of the woman's notes (her own records and maternity, primary care and mental health notes) and communicated to the woman and all relevant healthcare professionals.

5.5.1.2   In all communications (including initial referral) with maternity services, healthcare professionals should include information on any relevant history of mental disorder.

5.5.1.3   After identifying a possible mental disorder in a woman during pregnancy or the postnatal period, further assessment should be considered, in consultation with colleagues if necessary.
- If the healthcare professional or the woman has significant concerns, the woman should normally be referred for further assessment to her GP.
- If the woman has, or is suspected to have, a severe mental illness (for example, bipolar disorder or schizophrenia), she should be referred to a specialist mental health service, including, if appropriate, a specialist perinatal mental health service. This should be discussed with the woman and preferably with her GP.
- The woman's GP should be informed in all cases in which a possible current mental disorder or a history of significant mental disorder is detected, even if no further assessment or referral is made.

5.5.1.4   Managers and senior healthcare professionals responsible for perinatal mental health services (including those working in maternity and primary care services) should ensure that:
   ● there are clearly specified care pathways so that all primary and secondary healthcare professionals involved in the care of women during pregnancy and the postnatal period know how to access assessment and treatment
   ● staff have supervision and training, covering mental disorders, assessment methods and referral routes, to allow them to follow the care pathways.

6. PSYCHOLOGICAL AND PSYCHOSOCIAL INTERVENTIONS

6.1   INTRODUCTION

Pregnancy and childbirth is a unique period of change for women that may have a profound effect on their biological, psychological and social functioning. The changes at this time interact with the woman's genetic, psychological, and social vulnerabilities, which may lead to overt psychological difficulty. The effects of any such psychological disturbance are also intimately linked to the development of the fetus, the newborn infant and the rest of the family, as well as with the woman's developing relationship with her newborn child.

Psychological difficulties in the antenatal and postnatal period range from minor transient disturbance with rapid unaided adjustment through common mental disorders to severe psychiatric disturbance. Women with the whole range of mental disorders become pregnant and have children. Pregnancy, childbirth and the demands of a child may precipitate psychological problems or lead a woman to seek help for her long-standing difficulties at this time.

The bulk of this chapter is concerned with reviewing psychological and psychosocial interventions for the treatment or prevention of mental disorders in the antenatal and postnatal period, together with health economics evidence where appropriate. It also includes studies of treatments focused on the mother-infant interaction and studies of broader psychosocial interventions, such as timing of postnatal appointments. It also considers mothers whose babies are stillborn.

6.2   ISSUES IN RESEARCH INTO PSYCHOLOGICAL TREATMENTS

6.2.1   Efficacy of psychological treatments in general

There is good evidence of efficacy for psychological treatments in a range of psychological disorders, including depression (NICE 2002, 2004a, 2005a; Roth & Fonagy, 2004), and this has been widely acknowledged. Many reviews have found that psychological treatments specifically designed for depression, for example, CBT and IPT are equivalent to drugs in terms of their efficacy (NCCMH, 2005). This evidence will not be reviewed here. Given that the nature of most mental disorders in pregnancy is little different from that of disorders of non-pregnant women in both their presentation and course, it is reasonable to assume, in the absence of evidence to the contrary, that treatment developed for non-pregnant women is likely to be effective.

However, a number of factors specific to pregnancy may alter the view of the efficacy of psychological treatments in pregnancy. These include access, both in terms of the availability of the treatments and the women's capacity (relative to increased physical demands and childcare demand) during pregnancy, the relative cost effectiveness of the treatments and, in particular, the need to consider the relative benefits of drug and psychological treatments in light of the increased risk of harm to the fetus associated with pharmacological treatment in pregnancy.

There are many drivers encouraging the resourcing and provision of psychological treatments in general settings, such as primary care (Clinical Standards Advisory Group, 1999; DH, 2001), and their effectiveness has been widely accepted in many countries (Beutler *et al.*, 2000; Segal *et al.*, 2001a, 2001b).

6.2.2 Factors to consider in the evaluation of psychological treatment

Determining whether a particular psychological treatment is of clinical benefit or not, and making recommendations for its general availability and use, is a complex issue that has been much debated (Roth & Fonagy, 2004). Many factors need to be taken into account when assessing treatment outcome studies.

6.2.3 The RCT in psychological treatments

The RCT is often seen as the 'gold standard' in treatment outcome research. It is widely used in drug studies but its use in psychological treatment outcome research can be problematic (Elliot, 1998; Roth & Fonagy, 2004). The RCT assumes the existence of well-defined clinical problems and disorders as well as an equally tightly defined treatment. In mental health, most disorders are not so well defined and psychological treatments can be difficult to deliver uniformly.

A common criticism of the RCT is that the patient population is often unrepresentative of clinical populations. This can arise because of the need to include patients who are likely to complete the study protocol and to include patients happy to accept that they may be allocated to the control group. This means that patients with more unstable or more severe illness may not be included in clinical trials, thus reducing the generalisability of the results. Although this is not a problem limited to psychological treatments, it presents a particular challenge for women in the postnatal period. Other problems for psychological treatments include the design and development of measures that are clinically meaningful and manage to encapsulate all treatment-related outcomes, particularly patient quality-of-life variables. In addition, it is impossible to blind participants to treatment allocation and often difficult to blind assessors as well. More general problems with the interpretation of the findings of RCTs and other clinical trials include the issue of generalisability to 'real world' and 'real patient' settings from frequently quite small-scale research studies, often conducted by enthusiastic researchers in specialist centres with highly motivated patients with 'pure' or less complex disorders.

Despite this, the RCT occupies a key role in psychological treatment research but is best seen as one step in a process that involves other methods of evaluation, from initial case series through controlled trials (development studies) and RCTs (efficacy studies) to application in routine care (effectiveness studies) (NCCMH, 2005).

6.2.4   Evaluation of the evidence

It is difficult to determine which aspects of a psychological treatment are effective. In addition, there are many other variables relating to the therapist, the patient and her context, the adherence to the treatment model and the disorder being treated. All these factors need to be considered when judging the value of evidence provided by a study.

Non-specific factors in therapy
It is well recognised that, although many therapies have been operationalised and 'manualised' into 'pure forms', many factors that may contribute to efficacy and effectiveness are in fact common to all forms and therefore 'non-specific'. There has been much debate about the relative potency of specific versus non-specific factors (Karasu, 1986). Elements such as focusing on the problem, the conveyed belief that a solution is possible and the development of a positive relationship between thera-pist and patient are considered to be 'non-specific'. There is no consensus on the 'necessary and sufficient ingredients' of the therapeutic process.

Therapist variables
Therapists differ in their personality, values and beliefs about causes of psychologi-cal distress and these may affect the outcome of treatment (Blatt *et al.*, 1996a). The quality of the relationship between therapist and patient may account for a significant variance in outcome (Norcross, 2002; Roth & Fonagy, 2004). Therapists who take part in research studies vary in their level of training and experience, the therapeutic approach may be atypical of routine practice and the approach may vary dramatically in the degree of structure imposed. Even within well-conducted clinical trials (for example, Hollon *et al.*, 2006), considerable differences in outcome can be attributed to differences in therapist competence.

Variation in treatment delivery
Therapies can be undertaken in different settings (group, home, individual or telephone) and this may influence outcome. In addition, therapists may vary in their adherence to a particular treatment model in experimental and controlled conditions. Non-adherence to treatment models is associated with a significant attenuation in treatment effects (Roth & Fonagy, 2004) and efforts should be made, through effective supervision and process-and-outcome monitoring, to ensure that treatments are delivered effectively.

Disorder variations
The symptom-focused diagnostic approach adopted in current classificatory systems uses the presence, clustering and duration of symptoms as its primary means of

determining a diagnosis. There are problems with this approach, not least being that a number of personality, biological and social factors not only affect an individual's vulnerability to illness in the first instance but also the course of the illness (Brown & Harris, 1978) and the response to treatment (Rector *et al.*, 2000). In addition, for many mental disorders, comorbidity is the norm and this may also have an impact on treatment outcomes (Brown *et al.*, 2001).

Therapy length
A key issue in the provision of a psychological treatment is the number of sessions to be offered. There are many conflicting aims that need to be taken into account such as cost and therapist availability as well as outcome. There is reasonable evidence that inadequate 'doses' of treatment are associated with less positive outcomes, particularly in moderate to severe disorders (Hollon *et al.*, 2006). Barkham and colleagues (1996) found that eight sessions of two different therapies generated faster change than 16 sessions. Other factors, such as the ability to form a therapeutic relationship and a history of sexual abuse, will also influence course of the disorder and response to treatment (Hardy *et al.*, 2001) and, in the case of personality disorder, may require increased duration of treatment (Arntz, 1994).

Patient variables
There is evidence that the effectiveness of psychotherapy designed for depression can vary extensively across individuals, with some patients doing well quickly and others improving more slowly (Hardy *et al.*, 2001; Roth & Fonagy, 2004). Any patient group will vary widely and extensively in terms of personality, cultural background, psychological mindedness, current relationships and social problems, all of which influence outcome (Sotsky *et al.*, 1991). Patients who are perfectionistic (Blatt *et al.*, 1996b) and self-critical (Rector *et al.*, 2000) do less well with standardised therapies.

6.2.5   Psychological treatment in the antenatal and postnatal periods

In common with other treatments in the postnatal period, in terms of treating mental health disorder, psychological treatments have focused almost exclusively on the treatment of depression, despite the evidence (see Chapter 4) that anxiety disorders and depression antenatally are as common in the postnatal period as at any other time in a woman's life. There is also some research focusing on mother-infant interaction during this period. In addition, psychotic disorders outside of the postnatal period can also benefit from psychological treatments. As indicated at the beginning of this chapter, effective and prompt treatment is a major challenge in the delivery of psychological treatments.

Despite the evidence illustrating that mental health problems are common, debilitating and have a broader direct effect on the woman's fetus and newborn infant (see Chapter 4), and that medication is less acceptable in the antenatal and postnatal periods than at other times, the efficacy and acceptability of psychological treatments in pregnancy and the postnatal period has not been extensively researched and is not routinely available. There are several reasons to explain this. Historically, there has been an emphasis on postnatal depression and most research has been carried out in this field. Treatment in the antenatal period has been aimed at preventing the development of postnatal illness, making such studies difficult to interpret.

There seem to be widely held but poorly substantiated beliefs that neither pregnancy nor the early postnatal period are times to make life changes and that psychological treatment may be harmful and should be avoided. This, in combination with the fact that being pregnant or having a newborn infant clearly leads to difficulties in accessing standard psychological treatments in general services that may have long waiting lists and inflexible clinic times, has exacerbated the problems of access to psychological treatment for this group. A number of attempts have been made to modify psychological treatments for pregnancy and the postnatal period, involving a broad range of healthcare professionals delivering treatments at home or in groups. Research comparing these modified treatments with standardised therapies such as CBT and IPT has not been undertaken and the advantage in the modification remains unclear.

6.2.6 Evaluation of evidence in antenatal and postnatal psychological treatment outcome research

The evidence base for psychological treatments in the postnatal period is limited and is further constrained by a number of methodological problems. These include the difficulties in recruitment to trials, the relatively high attrition rates in some studies (see Table 10, Table 11, Table 12 and Table 13 below), the use of certain non-standard outcome measures such as the EPDS and the difficulties in characterising the comparator treatments, particularly when they are drawn from a number of different healthcare systems across the world, where maternity practices, not just the delivery of psychological treatments, may be very different. The studies described below also include a limited number of studies that compare psychological and pharmacological treatments.

6.3 DEFINITIONS OF PSYCHOLOGICAL AND PSYCHOSOCIAL INTERVENTIONS

This chapter considers non-pharmacological treatments, including psychological therapies such as CBT and IPT, psychosocial interventions such as social support, including intrapartum support (for example, having a 'doula' [a non-medical assistant] present during childbirth), and non-pharmacological physical treatments including acupuncture. Treatments focusing on mother-infant interaction beyond the first postnatal year are outside the scope of this guideline. Most of the treatments described below have been adapted from treatments developed in patient populations.

The definitions of the main psychological treatments covered in this guideline are listed below.

6.3.1 Cognitive behavioural therapy

CBT for depression was developed by Aaron Beck during the 1950s. One of the assumptions underlying this form of therapy is that psychological distress is strongly influenced by patterns of thinking, beliefs and behaviour. Depressed patients have patterns of thinking and reasoning that focus on a negative view of the world (including themselves and other people) and what they can expect from it. Psychological distress may be alleviated by altering these thought patterns and behaviours without the need to understand how earlier life events or circumstances may have contributed to how those patterns arose. A key aspect of the therapy is an educative approach, where the patient learns to recognise their negative thinking patterns and how to re-evaluate them. The new approach needs to be practised outside of the sessions in the form of homework.

CBT is a discrete, time-limited, structured psychological treatment. The patient and therapist work collaboratively to identify the types of thoughts, beliefs and interpretations and their effects on current symptoms, feeling states and problem areas. The patient then develops the skills to identify, monitor and counteract problematic thoughts, beliefs and interpretations related to the target symptoms. The patient also learns a repertoire of coping skills appropriate to targeting thoughts, beliefs or problem areas.

6.3.2 Debriefing

Debriefing is the term used to describe one or two brief session treatments based on the work of Mitchell (1983). Mitchell developed critical-incident stress debriefing (CISD), which was intended for those suffering from a range of traumatic experiences. In the antenatal and postnatal mental health setting, the term refers to treatments targeted at women who have reported the experience of a distressing or traumatic birth. The mother is encouraged to articulate her reactions to distressing, traumatic aspects of the birth, and the treatment facilitates some normalisation of the reactions to traumatic stimuli. Debriefing in this setting could occur at home or in hospital and is usually offered by a midwife. It is offered to individuals and usually within 72 hours of birth.

6.3.3 Non–directive counselling (listening visits)

Counselling was developed by Rogers (1957) who believed that people had the means for self-healing, problem resolution and growth if the right conditions could be created. These include the provision of positive regard, genuineness and empathy. Rogers' original model was developed into structured counselling approaches by both Truax and Carkhuff (1967) and Egan (1990). Voluntary sector counselling training tends to draw on these models. Counsellors are trained to listen and reflect patient feelings and meaning (Rogers, 1957). Many other therapies use these basic ingredients of client-centred counselling, but there are differences in how they are used. Holden and colleagues (1989) developed the concept of 'listening visits' based on these Rogerian, non-directive counselling skills and this has been taken up by a number of healthcare professionals working in the postnatal area, in particular health visitors. The healthcare professional is trained to help clients to gain better understanding of their circumstances and themselves. The therapist adopts an empathic and non-judgemental approach, listening rather than directing but offering non-verbal encouragement, reflecting back to assist the person in making decisions. This approach is usually offered by briefly trained healthcare professionals rather than mental health professionals and often takes place in the client's home.

6.3.4 Interpersonal psychotherapy

IPT was developed by Klerman and Weissman (Klerman *et al.*, 1984) initially for depression, although its use has been extended to other areas (Weissman *et al.*, 2000). It may be defined as a discrete, time-limited, structured psychological treatment derived from an interpersonal model of affective disorders that focuses on interpersonal issues. The patient and therapist work collaboratively to identify effects of key problem areas related to interpersonal conflicts, role transitions, grief and loss, and social skills, and their effect on current symptoms, feeling states and/or problems. The treatment seeks to reduce symptoms by learning to cope with or resolve these interpersonal issues.

IPT focuses on current relationships and interpersonal processes and on the difficulties that arise in the daily experience of maintaining relationships and resolving difficulties. The main tasks are to help patients to link their mood with their interpersonal contacts, recognising that, by appropriately addressing interpersonal problems, they may improve both relationship and mood. There is usually an agreed focus for treatment, such as interpersonal role transitions. Therapy sessions concentrate on facilitating understanding of recent events in interpersonal terms and exploring alternative ways of handling interpersonal situations. IPT is usually delivered as an individually focused therapy but has also been developed as a group treatment.

6.3.5 Psychodynamic psychotherapy

Psychodynamic psychotherapy is a derivative of psychoanalysis. There are many variations of the original model (Roth & Fonagy, 2004). It is usually offered in weekly sessions over a time-limited period, with the number of sessions usually varying between 10 and 40. The therapist and patient explore and gain insight into conflicts and how these are represented in current situations and relationships, including the therapy relationship (transference and countertransference). This leads to the patient being given the opportunity to explore feelings and conscious and unconscious conflicts originating in the past, with a focus on interpreting and working through them.

6.3.6 Support and education

Support and education comprises a range of treatments that offer a mix of practical and emotional support, often focusing on practical issues in relation to the care of the infant or on tasks indirectly related to the care of the infant. The treatment is not underpinned by a robust psychological model and limited training is usually required. Some of these treatments may be described as 'multi-modal' and can be offered by a range of health-care professionals.

6.3.7 Psychoeducation

Psychoeducation is a structured educational treatment (often offered in groups), which may focus on preparation for childbirth (antenatal) or practical aspects of childcare (postnatal). The programmes may have a specific mental health component only, although more often they offer an integrated approach to pregnancy, delivery and the mental and physical health and well-being of the woman and the infant. Often they take as a focus the social and personal adjustment to the role of a parent following the birth of a child (Gagnon, 2000).

6.3.8 Broader psychosocial interventions

This category includes treatments where there is no specific psychological treatment, but where aspects of standard perinatal care are manipulated to assess their effect on mental health outcomes in general perinatal populations. They include continuity of midwife care, timing of appointments and hospital discharge following delivery, and source of care (community based or primary-care based). More information on the treatments is given in the analyses below.

**Vignette: A women with depression and self-harming behaviour
in the postnatal period**

After discharge from hospital, the community psychiatric team sent me for counselling. I also needed some intensive therapy and learnt a lot about CBT. This was extremely useful. I began to understand who I really was as a person and understand the reason behind why I self-harmed. Slowly I began to recover.

**Vignette: A woman with pre-existing depression and depression
after birth of both of her children**

A factor in my recovery from postnatal depression after the birth of my second child was that, after an 18-month wait, I began CBT about 2 months after my son's birth. This has been hugely helpful, especially in helping to stop the almost constant self-criticism that became all pervasive during my illness.

Vignette: A woman with a history of depression and abuse who had anxiety postnatally but did not go on to develop depression in the postnatal period

After my son was born, I experienced a lot of emotional ups and downs, but my health visitor reassured me that these feelings were all very normal after having a baby. She encouraged me, telling me that I was doing very well. I attended a breastfeeding support group where I got lots of advice and support from staff and other mums. I am still friendly with some of the girls I met there. Talking to them really helps when I am worried or feel down.

The hardest thing I have found to deal with since my son's birth is anxiety about being separated from him. I was very anxious about returning to work because of leaving him in a nursery. My GP reassured me that this was a normal feeling. I attended a talk given by STEPS, an NHS self-referral psychological service, which gave general advice on coping with stress after having a baby. I saw a STEPS counsellor for just one session to talk about my worries. I told her about how I had been abused as a child and how this made me scared about leaving my son with anyone else in case something happened to him. She reassured me that my feelings were valid and she gave me good information about how to minimise the chances of such things happening to him and what signs there would be to look out for. She gave me more confidence in being able to keep my son safe.

Vignette: A woman with a history of depression diagnosed with depression in the postnatal period

In conjunction with an antidepressant, I was given the support of a CPN, psychiatrist and a clinical psychologist. I also had CBT, which helped me feel better, put things into perspective and meet my goal, which was to learn coping techniques to help me manage in future life-changing situations. There was discussion of seeing a forensic psychologist because I was self-harming, but this scared me. As I had been depressed before, I felt I knew what I wanted and that CBT was the best option for me.

6.4 OVERVIEW OF CLINICAL REVIEW

6.4.1 Evidence search

The databases searched for studies of psychological and psychosocial treatments and interventions for women during pregnancy and the postnatal period are shown in Table 8, regardless of diagnosis. Fuller details of the search strategy used are in Appendix 6.

Table 8: Databases searched for clinical effectiveness of psychological, psychosocial or non-pharmacological physical treatments

Electronic databases	MEDLINE, EMBASE, PsycINFO
Date searched	Database inception to December 2004
Update searches	January 2006; May 2006; September 2006
Study design	RCT
Patient population	Pregnant women and women up to 1 year postnatally
Treatments	Any psychological, psychosocial or non-pharmacological physical treatments
Outcomes	See below

6.4.2   Outcomes

Primary outcomes were the number depressed at endpoint as defined by the study (based on EPDS, Hamilton Rating Scale for Depression [HRSD], or BDI scores, or on presence of depression according to a diagnostic tool) and leaving the study early for any reason. Continuous scores on depression rating scales were also extracted, although fewer studies reported this outcome, particularly those of treatments for the prevention of illness. Therefore, since the majority of studies reported dichotomous efficacy outcomes (for example, EPDS $> = 12$, BDI > 9 or the number of participants with a diagnosis of depression), these outcomes were used in the main analyses in all reviews, although in that of the treatment of depression, continuous data are also reported.

6.4.3   Presentation of evidence

The data are presented in evidence profiles in Appendix 18, with summary evidence tables presented below. See Chapter 2 for an explanation of the ratings for the likelihood of clinically important effect and quality. Graphical presentation of the analyses are available in forest plots in Appendix 20, with specific forest plots referenced in the text as 'RM' followed by the identifier of the plot in Appendix 20. Characteristics of the included studies are available in Appendix 18, which also includes information on excluded studies with reasons for exclusion. Summary study characteristics tables are also presented below.

6.4.4   Review strategy

The following reviews are presented in this chapter: psychological and psychosocial treatments aimed at preventing mental disorder in women with existing risk factors; psychological and psychosocial treatments aimed at preventing mental disorder in all women; non-pharmacological treatment of identified mental disorder; interventions targeting the mother-infant interaction; and broader psychosocial interventions and other treatments. There is some overlap between some of the sections; for example, prevention studies where risk factors included existing depression symptoms could be classed as treatment studies. However, these were classified as prevention studies where the trialists' intention was prevention rather than treatment.

Please note that recommendations for psychological treatments in disorders covered by existing NICE guidelines are included in the clinical recommendations in Chapter 6.

6.5 REVIEW OF TREATMENTS AIMED AT PREVENTING THE DEVELOPMENT OF MENTAL DISORDERS DURING THE ANTENATAL AND POSTNATAL PERIODS FOR WOMEN WITH EXISTING RISK FACTORS

6.5.1 Introduction

Since the subsequent morbidity of mental illness during pregnancy and the postnatal period can be serious, researchers have sought to design treatments aimed at preventing the development of disorder, most commonly depression in the postnatal period. A few have looked at treatments aimed at preventing the development of PTSD. This section considers treatments aimed at preventing mental disorder in women with existing risk factors for future depressive episodes.

6.5.2 Treatments in populations with identified risk factors: studies considered

Sixteen studies met inclusion criteria, five of which did not report dichotomous outcomes. All studies were aimed at preventing depression in the postnatal period, although one also aimed to reduce symptoms of other disorders, including those of trauma and stress (GAMBLE2005). Important characteristics of the included studies are in Table 9.

Studies were included in this section if the treatment was aimed at preventing future disorder in a population with specific risk factors. As can be seen from Table 9, a wide range of risk factors was used, including factors related to delivery, such as traumatic birth or caesarean section, and psychosocial factors, such as childhood abuse and relationship difficulties. In addition, existing symptoms as measured by a raised EPDS score were also used. Since the EPDS is not a diagnostic tool and only levels higher than those used in the studies considered here indicate probable depression (usually a score over 12), these studies are included in this section rather than that on the treatment of depression. However, they could be classified as treatment studies for subthreshold symptoms.

131

Table 9: Summary of study characteristics for trials of treatments for prevention of mental disorder versus standard care (risk factors identified)

Study ID (n = no. participants)	Treatment (length of treatment)	When?	Risk factor	Baseline (treatment/control); % possible depression	Mean age
ARMSTRONG1999[9] (n = 181)	Multi-modal treatment (12 months)	PN	Psychosocial risk factors: one or more of: physical domestic violence, childhood abuse, sole parenthood, ambivalence to the pregnancy; or three or more of: <18 years, unstable housing, financial stress, <10 years' education, low income, social isolation, history of mental health disorder (either parent), alcohol or drug misuse, non-physical domestic violence	Mean (SD) EPDS 8.18 (4.95)/9.17 (5.57) 22% (EPDS > 12)	Not given
BRUGHA2000 (n = 209)	Group psychoeducation (6 weeks)	AN/PN	(Subthreshold) symptoms (presence of one of six depression items that indicated antenatal depression on modified GHQ)	22%–23% scored 'high' on GHQ-D	19

Study	Intervention	Timing	Inclusion criteria	Baseline severity	Ref
DENNIS2003 (n = 42)	Social support (8 weeks)	PN	(Subthreshold) symptoms: EPDS > 9	100% EPDS > 9; 20%/18% history of postnatal depression 100% (EPDS > 9)	30
GAMBLE2005 (n = 103)	Debriefing (one session)	PN	PTSD criterion A	Not given	28
GORMAN unpublished (n = 45)	IPT (5 sessions)	AN/PN	Psychosocial risk factors or subthreshold symptoms: one or more of: history of treatment for depression, history of sustained period of depression or having a loss of interest or pleasure in activities, BDI > 12, first-degree relative with history of psychiatric treatment, marital/ partner relationship difficulties, 2 or more major life events occurring since beginning of pregnancy	BDI > 12: 45.8%/47.6% 45.8%– 47.6% (BDI > 12)	28
HAGAN2004 (n = 199)	CBT (6 weeks)	PN	Preterm or low birthweight baby	Mean (range) EPDS: 8 (4–12)/8 (4–11) Not given, but excluded if depressed	29

Continued

Table 9: (*Continued*)

Study ID (n = no. participants)	Treatment (length of treatment)	When?	Risk factor	Baseline (treatment/ control); % possible depression	Mean age
HEINICKE1999* (n = 70)	Multi-modal treatment	AN	Psychosocial risk factors (termed infant at risk of inadequate parenting by the study): 4+ needed: economic status, lack of support, unwanted pregnancy, childhood abuse, previous suicidal thoughts, previous mental health counselling/substance abuse treatment, homelessness	Not available	24
HISCOCK2002* (n = 156)	Infant sleep behavioural treatment	PN	Severe infant sleep problems	EPDS mean (SD): treatment group 9.0 (0.44); control group 8.8 (0.49) 44%–45% (EPDS $\geq$ 10)	34
HOROWITZ2001* (n = 122)	Relationship/ attachment-based therapy	PN	(Subthreshold) symptoms: EPDS > 10	100% EPDS > 10	31

Continued

Study	Intervention	AN/PN	Population		
MARCENKO1994* (n = 225)	Multi-modal treatment	AN	Psychosocial risk factors (termed infant at risk of inadequate parenting by the study): substance abuse, homelessness, domestic violence, psychiatric illness, incarceration, HIV infection, low social support	Not available	23
MEYER1994 (n = 34)	Multi-modal treatment (2–8 weeks)	PN	Preterm or low birthweight baby	BDI $\geq$ 9: 31%–39%	28
MIDDLEMISS1989* (n = 60)	Home visiting	AN	High risk of hospital admission due to obstetric problems; routinely treated by hospital admission: small-for-date foetus, previous perinatal loss, isolated small antenatal bleeds. None were thought to require immediate treatment	Not available	28

Table 9: (*Continued*)

Study ID (n = no. participants)	Treatment (length of treatment)	When?	Risk factor	Baseline (treatment/ control); % possible depression	Mean age
RYDING2004 (n = 162)	Debriefing (two sessions)	PN	Emergency caesarean	Not available	32
SMALL2000 (n = 1,041)	Debriefing (one session)	PN	Operative delivery	Not available	Not given
STAMP1995 (n = 144)	Social support (three sessions)	AN/PN	Vulnerable to postnatal depression (modified antenatal screening questionnaire – unclear in paper which factors questionnaire focuses on)	'High' on screening test: 18%/20%	27
WEBSTER2003 (n = 600)	Psychoeducation (unclear)	AN	Psychosocial risk factors: one or more of: low social or partner support, history of mental illness, family psychiatric history, previous postnatal depression, having a mother who had postnatal depression	EPDS > 12: 27.5%	27

| ZLOTNICK2001 (n = 37) | IPT (4 weeks) | AN | Psychosocial risk factors or (subthreshold) symptoms: one or more of: previous episode of depression or postnatal depression, mild to moderate levels of depressive symptoms, poor social support, life stressor within last 6 months | Mean (SD) BDI: 11.06 (6.84); BDI > 10: 57% | 37 |
| ZLOTNICK2006 (n = 99) | IPT (4 weeks) | AN | Psychosocial risk factors or (subthreshold) symptoms: one or more of: previous episode of depression or postnatal depression, mild to moderate levels of depressive symptoms, poor social support, life stressor within last 6 months | Mean (SD) BDI: 15.3 (6.96)–% over threshold not given, allocated to >45% group based on mean (SD) | 22 |

[9]Reviewed studies, which are referred to by a study identifier consisting of primary author in capital letters and date of study publication
*Studies not used because dichotomous outcomes not reported, although data from these studies are reported in the evidence profile (Appendix 19)

A range of treatments are included in this section, such as social support and psychological therapy. Timing of treatment also varies, with some studies intervening during the antenatal period and some during the postnatal period. In a few, the treatment period spans pregnancy and the postnatal period. Given the heterogeneous nature of the dataset, it was examined in several ways: by treatment, by risk factor and by treatment timing (antenatal or postnatal). In addition, those studies where the risk factor was a psychosocial risk factor or where populations had symptoms of depression (most of which were subthreshold symptoms but could have met criteria for a diagnosis of depression) were analysed separately by treatment and by percentage of the study population with a possible diagnosis of depression.

Most studies compared psychological therapy with standard care. The content of standard care varied, based on the setting of the study (including Australia, Canada and the UK).

6.5.3   Analyses

The studies in this section were analysed in Review Manager file *APMH Non-Pharmacological Treatments – Prevention (Risk Factors Present)* – see Appendix 20 for forest plots, identified as 'RMnppr'. Since most studies reported dichotomous data (number scoring above threshold for depressive symptoms, including BDI $\geq$ 9, EPDS $\geq$ 11 or 12 and DSM diagnosis), only these studies are used in the meta-analyses. Studies therefore not used include HEINICKE1999, HISCOCK2002, HOROWITZ2001, MARCENKO1994 and MIDDLEMISS1989. Efficacy data were not extracted on an intention-to-treat basis since the included populations did not have the extracted outcomes (possible depression) at baseline. For this reason, the number of participants in the summary evidence profiles and evidence profile in Appendix 19 are different for efficacy and tolerability outcomes.

6.5.4   Analysis of all studies of populations with specific
factors for depression

Studies of treatments to prevent depression in populations with a risk factor for the development of depression showed that, overall, there is benefit in providing treatments for this group. However, when the risk factors are examined separately, there appears to be no benefit in providing treatments for women with risk factors such as traumatic birth, PTSD criterion A or preterm/low birthweight baby, but there may be some benefit for those with psychosocial risk factors or existing depressive symptoms. Table 10 summarises the evidence profile.

When the dataset is examined by treatment, only the multi-modal treatments (for example, child health nurse visits providing practical and emotional parenting support at home) provided by MEYER1994 and ARMSTRONG1999 showed a strong effect, although social support showed some effect. Debriefing showed no effect, and the

Table 10: Summary evidence profile for psychological treatments versus standard care for the prevention of depression (risk factors present): by risk factor

	Overall result (all studies)	Psychosocial risk factors or (subthreshold) symptoms	Traumatic birth/emergency caesarean/ operative delivery	Preterm/low birthweight baby	PTSD criterion A
Study IDs	ARMSTRONG1999 BRUGHA2000 DENNIS2003 GAMBLE2005 GORMANunpublished HAGAN2004 MEYER1994 RYDING2004 SMALL2000 STAMP1995 WEBSTER2003 ZLOTNICK2001 ZLOTNICK2006	ARMSTRONG1999 BRUGHA2000 DENNIS2003 GORMANunpublished STAMP1995 WEBSTER2003 ZLOTNICK2001 ZLOTNICK2006	SMALL2000 RYDING2004	HAGAN2004 MEYER1994	GAMBLE2005
Overall quality of evidence	Moderate	Moderate	Low	Low	Low

Continued

Table 10: (*Continued*)

	Overall result (all studies)	Psychosocial risk factors or (subthreshold) symptoms	Traumatic birth/emergency caesarean/ operative delivery	Preterm/low birthweight baby	PTSD criterion A
Depression above threshold	RR (random effects) = 0.75 (0.57, 0.97) (K = 13; n = 2,395) RMnppr 01.01	RR = 0.63 (0.44, 0.91) (K = 8; n = 1,019) RMnppr 01.01	RR = 1 (0.56, 1.79) (K = 2; n = 1,064) RMnppr 01.01	RR (random effects) = 0.55 (0.17, 1.75) (K = 2; n = 210) RMnppr 01.01	RR = 0.96 (0.55, 1.67) (K = 1; n = 103) RMnppr 01.01
% attrition rate, treatment group versus standard care	16% versus 17% (K = 12*; n = 2,896) RMnppr 02.01	23% versus 25% (K = 8; n = 1,357) RMnppr 02.01	10% versus 13% (K = 2; n = 1,203) RMnppr 02.01	8% versus 2% (K = 1; n = 233) RMnppr 02.01	2% versus 0% (K = 1; n = 103) RMnppr 02.01

Notes: RR = relative risk (95% CI); K = number of trials contributing to the summary statistic; n = number of participants; 'RMnppr *nn.nn*' refers to the relevant forest plot in Appendix 20

*The attrition rate in MEYER1994 was 0% in both groups and therefore this study has not been counted in the meta-analysis

effect sizes for structured psychological treatments and psychoeducation were inconclusive, see Table 11.

The dataset was also examined by treatment timing (antenatal, postnatal, and antenatal and/or postnatal), which showed some advantages for treatment in the postnatal period, although most studies fell into this category.

6.5.5 Separate analyses of studies with psychosocial risk factors or subthreshold depressive symptoms

Since the risk factor 'psychosocial risk factors of (subthreshold) depressive symptoms' showed some effect compared with standard care, these studies were examined separately in two additional sub-analyses. The first divided the dataset by treatment. All treatments apart from psychoeducation (booklet or group) showed an effect, although there was some heterogeneity in the datasets and results were not statistically significant. The other sub-analysis divided the dataset by the percentage of participants with possible depression at baseline (based on EPDS > 12 or > 9, BDI > 10 or similar); those studies with more than 45% of participants in this category showed a clinically significant effect. (The 45% cut-off was chosen to reflect the available data; the forest plot shows the studies ordered by approximate percentage with possible depression.) The treatments provided in these studies (DENNIS2003, GORMANunpublished, ZLOTNICK2001 and ZLOTNICK2006) were social support and IPT. A summary of these results can be seen in Table 12.

6.5.6 PTSD symptoms at follow-up

The three studies that also focused on reducing PTSD symptoms (RYDING2004, GAMBLE2005 and HAGAN2004) showed inconclusive results, although there was some evidence of an effect for debriefing (see Table 13).

6.5.7 Clinical summary for prevention of mental disorder in groups with identified risks in the postnatal period

Providing treatments for women with risk factors for developing depression may have some benefit, particularly for those with existing subthreshold symptoms, in the postnatal period. Most benefit is apparent in women with symptoms of depression at baseline; social support and structured psychological short-term treatments such as IPT are appropriate choices of treatment.

Table 11: Summary evidence profile for psychological treatments versus standard care for the prevention of depression: by treatment

	Debriefing	Structured psychological treatments (CBT/IPT)	Social support (individual or group)	Multi-modal	Psycho-education (booklet or group)
Study IDs	SMALL2000 RYDING2004 GAMBLE2005	GORMAN unpublished ZLOTNICK2001 HAGAN2004 ZLOTNICK2006	DENNIS2003 STAMP1995	ARMSTRONG 1999 MEYER1994	BRUGHA2000 WEBSTER2003
Overall quality of evidence	Moderate	Moderate	Moderate	Moderate	Moderate
Depression above threshold at endpoint or first available measure	RR = 1.09 (0.85, 1.41) (K = 3; n = 1,166) RMnppr 01.02	RR = 0.52 (0.3, 0.9) (K = 4; n = 336) RMnppr 01.02	RR (random effects) = 0.51 (0.26, 0.98) (K = 2; n = 169) RMnppr 01.03	RR = 0.36 (0.15, 0.87) (K = 2; n = 165) RMnppr 01.02	RR = 0.85 (0.63, 1.15) (K = 2; n = 559) RMnppr 01.02
% attrition rate, treatment group versus standard care	9% versus 12% (K = 3; n = 1,306) RMnppr 02.02	11% versus 4% (K = 4; n = 380) RMnppr 02.02	8% versus 5% (K = 2; n = 186) RMnppr 02.02	20% versus 20% (K = 1; n = 215) RMnppr 02.02	29% versus 32% (K = 2; n = 809) RMnppr 02.02

Notes: RR = relative risk (95% CI); K = number of trials contributing to the summary statistic; n = number of participants; 'RMnppr *nn.nn*' refers to the relevant forest plot in Appendix 20

Table 12: Summary evidence profile for psychological treatments versus standard care for the prevention of depression (psychosocial risk factors or (subthreshold) symptom studies only): by treatment and by percentage of participants with depression

	Structured psychological treatments	Multi-modal treatment	Psycho-education (booklet or group)	Social support (individual or group)	<c. 45% possible depression	>c. 45% possible depression
Study IDs	GORMAN unpublished ZLOTNICK2001 ZLOTNICK2006	ARMSTRONG 1999	BRUGHA2000 WEBSTER2003	DENNIS2003 STAMP1995	ARMSTRONG 1999 BRUGHA2000 STAMP1995 WEBSTER 2003	DENNIS 2003 GORMAN unpublished ZLOTNICK 2001 ZLOTNICK 2006
Overall quality of evidence	Low	Low	Moderate	Moderate	Moderate	High
Depression above threshold at endpoint or first available measure	RR (random effects) = 0.32 (0.1, 1.01) (K = 3; n = 160) RMnppr 01.06	RR (random effects) = 0.45 (0.15, 1.39) (K = 1; n = 131) RMnppr 01.06	RR = 0.85 (0.63, 1.15) (K = 2; n = 559) RMnppr 01.06	RR (random effects) = 0.49 (0.2, 1.21) (K = 1; n = 103) RMnppr 01.06	RR = 0.79 (0.6, 1.05) (K = 4; n = 818) RMnppr 01.07	RR = 0.28 (0.14, 0.57) (K = 4; n = 201) RMnppr 01.07
% attrition rate, treatment group versus standard care	13% versus 9% (K = 3; n = 181) RMnppr 02.04	24% versus 23% (K = 1; n = 181) RMnppr 02.04	29% versus 32% (K = 2; n = 809) RMnppr 02.04	8% versus 5% (K = 2; n = 186) RMnppr 02.04	26% versus 28% (K = 4; n = 1,134) RMnppr 02.05	10% versus 8% (K = 4; n = 223) RMnppr 02.05

Notes: RR = relative risk (95% CI); K = number of trials contributing to the summary statistic; n = number of participants; 'RMnppr *nn.nn*' refers to the relevant forest plot in Appendix 20

Table 13: Summary evidence profile for studies focusing on reducing PTSD symptoms

	Debriefing (self-report) (emergency caesarean) 6-month follow-up	Debriefing (clinician rated) (traumatic birth) follow-up 3 months postnatally	CBT (preterm weight baby) follow-up 6 months postnatally
Study IDs	RYDING2004	GAMBLE2005	HAGAN2004
Overall quality of evidence	Low	Low	Low
Depression above threshold at endpoint or first available measure	RR = 0.53 (0.25, 1.1) (K = 1; n = 147) RMnppr 01.07	RR = 0.35 (0.1, 1.23) (K = 1; n = 103) RMnppr 01.07	RR = 5.1 (0.25, 104.94) (K = 1; n = 192) RMnppr 01.07
% attrition rate, treatment group versus standard care	8% versus 11% (K = 1; n = 162) RMnppr 02.06	2% versus 0% (K = 1; n = 103) RMnppr 02.06	9% versus 2% (K = 1; n = 199) RMnppr 02.06

Notes: RR = relative risk (95% CI); K = number of trials contributing to the summary statistic; n = number of participants; 'RMnppr *nn.nn*' refers to the relevant forest plot in Appendix 20

6.6 HEALTH ECONOMICS EVIDENCE ON PSYCHOLOGICAL AND PSYCHOSOCIAL INTERVENTIONS AIMED AT PREVENTING THE DEVELOPMENT OF DEPRESSION DURING THE ANTENATAL AND POSTNATAL PERIODS IN WOMEN WITH IDENTIFIED PSYCHOSOCIAL RISK FACTORS AND/OR SUBTHRESHOLD DEPRESSIVE SYMPTOMS

6.6.1 Economic evidence from the systematic literature review

No evidence on the cost effectiveness of any psychological or psychosocial interventions aimed at preventing the development of depression during the antenatal and postnatal period in women with identified psychosocial risk factors and/or subthreshold depressive symptoms was found.

6.6.2 Economic modelling

Introduction – rationale for economic modelling

The provision of psychological and psychosocial interventions aimed at preventing the development of depression during the antenatal and postnatal periods in women with identified psychosocial risk factors and/or subthreshold depressive symptoms was identified by the GDG and the health economist as an area with potentially significant resource implications. Since there was no existing economic evidence to support decision making, a decision-analytic model was developed in order to assess the cost effectiveness of different types of psychological and psychosocial interventions added to standard antenatal/postnatal care, relative to standard antenatal/postnatal care alone, for the prevention of depression in this population of women.

Study population
The study population consisted of women with identified psychosocial risk factors and/or subthreshold depressive symptoms in the antenatal period.

Interventions examined
Two different types of treatments were considered:
● psychological group therapy (IPT) added to standard antenatal/postnatal care
● social support added to standard antenatal/postnatal care.

In addition, standard antenatal/postnatal care alone was considered as an alternative option, in order for the active value of the preventive treatments to be assessed.

Model structure
The economic model was developed in the form of a decision tree using Microsoft Excel XP. According to the model structure, hypothetical cohorts of 1,000 women with identified psychosocial risk factors and/or subthreshold depressive symptoms received one of the treatments assessed. At the end of treatment, women either developed major depression or not. Women who received any of the preventive treatments were assumed to continue or discontinue treatment; those receiving standard antenatal/postnatal care were assumed to continue treatment. Women who discontinued any of the preventive treatments developed major depression at the same rate as women who received standard antenatal/postnatal care only. A schematic diagram of the decision-analytic model is provided in Figure 5.

Costs and health benefit measures included in the analysis
The analysis adopted the perspective of the NHS. Health service costs consisted of preventive treatment costs (either psychological therapy or social support) plus costs of treating those women who developed major depression. Standard antenatal/postnatal care costs were omitted from the analysis, because they were common to all therapeutic options assessed. Costs associated with care of infants born to mothers developing major depression were not considered, owing to lack of relevant data. Health benefits were expressed as the number of additional women prevented from developing major depression relative to standard care alone. Total costs and health benefits associated with each option were estimated and combined in order to assess the relative cost effectiveness of the treatment options evaluated.

Figure 5: Schematic diagram of the structure of the economic model

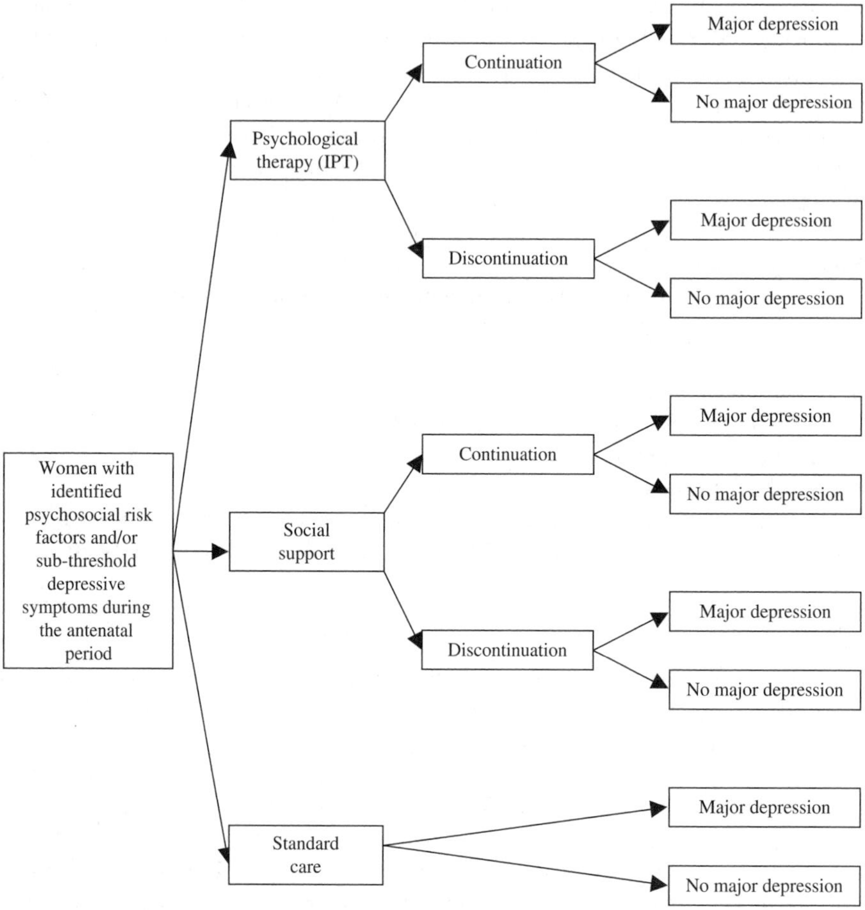

Cost data

Since no patient-level data in terms of resource use were available, the economic analysis was based on deterministic costing of the treatment options. Relevant health-care resource use was estimated and subsequently combined with UK unit prices to provide costs associated with each treatment strategy assessed. Estimated resource use associated with the two preventive treatments was based on definitions of the treatments in the studies that provided the efficacy data and further GDG opinion. Healthcare resource use for the treatment of major depression was based on the GDG expert opinion. It was estimated that 80% of women developing major depression would be treated by health visitors, GPs and CPNs in a primary care setting, while 20% would require antidepressant medication and more intensive treatment in a secondary care setting. Unit prices were taken from *Unit Costs for Health and Social Care 2005*, excluding qualification costs (Curtis & Netten, 2005), and the *British*

National Formulary (BNF) 52 (British Medical Association & Royal Pharmaceutical Society of Great Britain, 2006). All costs utilised in the analysis reflect 2005 prices. Discounting of costs was not applied, as costs were incurred within a period that was shorter than one year. Table 14 shows the unit costs utilised in the economic model; estimated resource use and total costs associated with each treatment option assessed are presented in Table 15.

Table 14: Unit costs utilised in the economic model of psychosocial interventions for prevention of depression in the antenatal and postnatal periods (Curtis & Netten, 2005)

Cost element	Unit price* (2005)
Clinical psychologist per hour of patient contact	£77
Primary care counselling by British Association for Counselling and Psychotherapy-accredited counsellor per hour	£39
Consultant psychiatrist per hour of patient contact	£216
Specialist registrar per hour worked	£33
GP per hour of patient contact	£120
CPN per hour of home visiting including travel costs	£79
Health visitor per hour spent on home visiting including travel costs	£89
Sertraline 50 mg daily, per week	£3.53

*Unit prices of healthcare professionals do not include qualification costs

Costs associated with discontinuation
Women who discontinued one of the preventive treatments assessed were assumed to incur 25% of the treatment costs.

Effectiveness data and other input parameters of the economic model
Effectiveness data used in the economic model were derived from the guideline meta-analyses. All studies providing dichotomous efficacy data on psychological therapy or social support aiming at prevention of major depression in the study population were considered in the economic analysis. The studies considered are presented in Table 16.

All studies compared one of the preventive treatments assessed added to standard antenatal/postnatal care versus standard care alone. Since there were no direct comparisons between the treatments under assessment, it was decided to perform an indirect comparison between them. In order to do this, relative risks of a) development of

Table 15: Resource use and total costs associated with prevention and treatment of depression in the antenatal and postnatal periods

Resource use	Cost
Preventive psychological therapy (IPT) Five group sessions (three women) with clinical psychologist × 60 min each	£128
Social support Three group sessions (five women) + three telephone contacts by British Association for Counselling and Psychotherapy accredited counsellor × 30 min each	£70
Treatment of major depression – 80% of women 12 home visits by health visitors × 45 min each Three GP visits × 10 min each One CPN visit lasting 1 hour Total cost *Treatment of major depression – 20% of women*	£807 £60 £79 £946
Two contacts with consultant psychiatrist × 60 min (first) and 30 min (second) Six contacts with specialist registrar × 30 min each Six CPN home visits × 60 min each Eight home visits by health visitors × 45 min each Six GP visits × 10 min each Sertraline 50 mg/day × 26 weeks Total cost Treatment of major depression Total average cost	£324 £99 £476 £538 £120 £95 £1,652 £1,087

major depression (efficacy) at the endpoint of analysis and b) discontinuation of each of the two treatments versus standard care alone were used, with standard care serving as the baseline common comparator. The absolute rates of development of major depression and discontinuation of standard care were based on the whole dataset of studies evaluating relevant treatments included in the guideline systematic review, all of which had a 'standard care' arm (that is, studies reported in Table 16 plus ARMSTRONG1999, which evaluated a multi-modal treatment, and BRUGHA2000 and WEBSTER2003, which assessed psychoeducation).

The absolute rates of development of major depression for each treatment were estimated by multiplying the respective relative risks for each treatment, derived from the meta-analysis, by the absolute rate of development of major depression obtained for women in the study population receiving standard care, using the formula:

$$MDAR_{int(i)} = MDRR_{int(i)} \times MDAR_{st\ care}$$

Table 16: Types of treatments for prevention of depression in the antenatal and postnatal periods examined in the clinical studies considered in the economic analysis

Study	Treatments assessed (in addition to standard care)
GORMANunpublished	Five individual sessions of IPT
ZLOTNICK2001	Four group sessions of IPT (number of women = 4–6)
ZLOTNICK2006	Four group sessions of IPT (number of women = 3–5)
STAMP1995	Three group sessions for social support (max number of women = 10)
DENNIS2003	Social support received via telephone (average 5.4 contacts)

where:

$MDAR_{int(i)}$ = absolute rate of development of major depression for each treatment

$MDRR_{int(i)}$ = relative risk of development of major depression of each treatment versus standard care

$MDAR_{st\,care}$ = absolute rate of development of major depression for standard care

In order to calculate the absolute discontinuation rates of each treatment, the respective discontinuation relative risks for each treatment, derived from the meta-analysis, were first multiplied by the absolute discontinuation rate of standard care to get an initial absolute rate for each treatment. However, discontinuation rates of standard care as described in the clinical trials were deemed to reflect mainly the conditions of conduct of each trial, and not women's acceptability of the treatment (since standard care represented routine antenatal/postnatal care in the trials). For this reason, the absolute discontinuation rate of standard care was subtracted from the initial multiplication product, in order to estimate the discontinuation rate for each treatment, expressing acceptability on top of discontinuation reflecting the trial conduct conditions. Thus, the final absolute discontinuation rate of each treatment was calculated using the following formula:

$$DAR_{int(i)} = (DRR_{int(i)} \times DAR_{st\,care}) - DAR_{st\,care}$$

where:

$DAR_{int(i)}$ = absolute discontinuation rate of each treatment

$DRR_{int(i)}$ = relative risk of discontinuation of each treatment versus standard care

$DAR_{st\,care}$ = absolute discontinuation rate of standard care

It is acknowledged that the indirect comparison between treatments may have introduced bias in the analysis, as there were differences between the studies in terms

149

of criteria of identification of psychosocial risk factors and/or subthreshold depressive symptoms in study samples, diagnostic measures used, content of treatments and comparators, and some other aspects of protocol design. Nevertheless, due to the limited availability of data, indirect comparison was considered necessary in order to populate the economic model.

All effectiveness rates and other input parameters included in the economic model are provided in Table 17.

Table 17: Effectiveness rates and other input parameters included in the model of psychosocial interventions for prevention of depression in the antenatal and postnatal periods

Input parameter	Baseline value (95% CI)	Source – comments
Relative risk of development of major depression Psychological therapy (IPT) Social support	0.28 (0.11–0.69) 0.49 (0.20–1.21)	Guideline meta-analysis
Relative risk of discontinuation Psychological therapy (IPT) Social support	1.33 (0.57–3.10) 1.35 (0.46–3.95)	Guideline meta-analysis
Absolute risk of development of major depression Standard care	23.35%	Guideline meta-analysis
Absolute risk of discontinuation Standard care	24.52%	Guideline meta-analysis

Sensitivity analysis

Apart from the base-case analysis, which utilised the most accurate data available, additional sensitivity analyses were also undertaken to investigate the robustness of the results under the great uncertainty characterising the model input parameters. One-way sensitivity analysis was carried out to explore the impact on the base-case results of:

- changes in relative risks of development of major depression
- employing alternative methods for the calculation of discontinuation rates of each treatment; alternative values of discontinuation rates examined in the sensitivity analysis included:
  - average absolute discontinuation rates of each treatment, directly used as reported in the trials (this method broke the indirect comparison between the two treatments, since no common comparator was used)
  - values resulting from simply multiplying relative risks of discontinuation for each treatment (versus standard care) by the absolute discontinuation rate of standard care, without subsequently subtracting the absolute discontinuation

rate of standard care from the multiplication product (as was done for the base-case analysis)
- changes in the absolute rate of development of major depression in women receiving only standard care
- changes in treatment costs.

Results

The results of the economic analysis are presented in the form of incremental cost-effectiveness ratios (ICERs), expressing additional cost per additional unit of benefit associated with one treatment option compared with another.

ICER = difference in costs between two treatment options/difference in benefit between two treatment options

ICER = additional cost of one treatment option versus another/additional benefit of one treatment option versus another

The estimation of such a ratio allows consideration of whether the additional benefit is worth the additional cost when choosing one treatment option over another.

In the case of a treatment option being more effective (that is providing greater benefit) and less costly than its comparator, the calculation of such a ratio is not required; the treatment option in question, characterised as the dominant option, is clearly more cost effective than its comparator.

All treatment options under assessment have been ranked from the most to the least effective. Cases of dominance have been identified and excluded from further analysis. ICERs between the non-dominated treatment options remaining in the analysis have been subsequently calculated.

Results of the base-case analysis are provided first, followed by the results of the sensitivity analysis.

Base-case analysis

Both preventive treatments dominated standard care alone (that is, they were less costly overall and prevented a higher number of cases of major depression compared with standard care). Treatment costs were offset by great savings owing to the large number of cases of major depression prevented, thus not requiring treatment or further healthcare resource use. Psychological therapy was overall more effective and more costly than social support, with an ICER of £114 per additional case of major depression prevented.

Full results of the base-case analysis are presented in Table 18.

Sensitivity analysis

Changes in relative risks of development of major depression

Increasing the relative risks of developing major depression of each preventive treatment versus standard care reduced their health benefits (as expected) and increased their overall costs. When the relative risk of developing major depression versus standard care became 0.48 for psychological therapy and 0.72 for social support, the two treatments incurred the same overall costs as standard care (but they were still more effective). Above these points, preventive treatments became more costly and more

Table 18: Results of the base-case analysis referring to a hypothetical cohort of 1,000 women with identified psychosocial risk factors for depression and/or subthreshold depressive symptoms in the antenatal and postnatal periods

Treatment option	Cases of major depression prevented (relative to standard care)	Costs (£)	Cost effectiveness
Psychological therapy	155	206,435	
			ICER of psychological therapy versus social support: £114 per additional case of major depression prevented
Social support	109	201,214	
Standard care	0	254,916	Dominated by both preventive treatments

effective than standard care; at a relative risk of 0.90, the ICERs of psychological therapy and social support versus standard care became £4,530 and £1,991 per case of major depression prevented respectively. A graph showing the changes in the ICERs of preventive treatments versus standard care following increases in relative risks of developing major depression is provided in Figure 6.

Employing alternative methods for the calculation of discontinuation rates of each treatment

Using different ways to estimate absolute discontinuation rates for each treatment had no impact on the cost effectiveness of the two treatments relative to standard care. The ICER of psychological therapy versus social support became £226 per additional case of depression prevented when discontinuation rates were estimated by multiplying relative risks of discontinuation for each treatment by the absolute discontinuation rate of standard care, and £271 per additional case of depression prevented when absolute discontinuation rates reported in the clinical trials were used (consequently breaking the indirect comparison between treatments).

Changes in the absolute rate of development of major depression in women with identified psychosocial risk factors and/or subthreshold depressive symptoms receiving standard care alone

Reducing the absolute rates of development of major depression in women in the study population receiving standard care alone resulted in decreases in benefits and increases in overall costs associated with the two preventive treatments. However, both treatments remained dominant over standard care alone until the rate of developing major

Figure 6: Changes in the ICER of preventive treatments versus standard care following increases in the respective relative risk of developing major depression in women with identified risk factors or subthreshold depressive symptoms

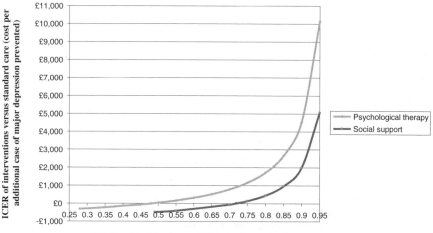

depression under standard care became 0.17. Below this point, psychological therapy was more expensive than standard care. Social support became more costly than standard care below an absolute rate of 0.13. A graph demonstrating the changes in the cost effectiveness of preventive treatments versus standard care following changes in the absolute rate of developing major depression under standard care is presented in Figure 7.

Changes in treatment costs

Increasing the treatment costs by 40% resulted in psychological therapy becoming roughly as expensive as standard care (regarding overall associated costs). Social support incurred the same cost as standard care alone when the treatment cost increased by 95%.

Limitations of the economic analysis

The economic analysis was undertaken using the most accurate effectiveness and cost data available. However, evidence on clinical effectiveness was based on indirect comparisons between treatments, derived from a very limited number of studies. Cost estimates were based on the description of relevant healthcare resource use as provided in the clinical studies, further supported by the GDG opinion. Costs of care for infants born to mothers developing major depression in the postnatal period were not included in the analysis, owing to lack of relevant data. The quality of life of women and their infants, as well as the well-being of the wider family, associated with development of major depression or prevention of a depressive episode by providing one of the treatments assessed in the study population was not addressed in the analysis, as relevant data were not available. It is recognised that, overall, results of the analysis are subject to considerable uncertainty and potential bias.

Figure 7: Changes in the ICER of preventive treatments versus standard care following changes in the absolute risk of developing major depression in women with identified risk factors or subthreshold depressive symptoms receiving standard care alone

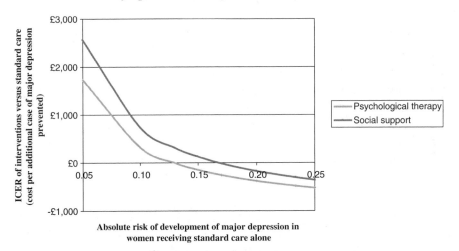

Discussion – overall conclusions from economic analysis
The economic analysis demonstrated that both preventive treatments examined (psychological therapy and social support) prevented a significant number of women with identified risk factors or subthreshold depressive symptoms from developing major depression in the antenatal and postnatal periods and at the same time resulted in cost savings compared with standard care alone. Treatment costs were offset by substantial savings from cases of major depression averted. It must be noted that if costs of care for infants born to mothers developing major depression in the postnatal period were included in the analysis, the cost savings achieved by preventive treatments would significantly increase. Moreover, prevention of major depressive episodes, apart from affecting the health-related quality of life (HRQoL) of the women, has also a significant positive impact on the well-being of the infants and the wider family.

Psychological therapy was more effective than social support, at an additional cost of £114 per additional case of major depression prevented. This cost is deemed to be low, considering the benefits to the women, their infants and their family from preventing the development of a major depressive episode. It must be noted that, when interpreting the above result, one needs to bear in mind that the *financial* cost of treating a major depressive episode has already been included in the analysis; therefore, one needs to consider whether the outcome measure used in the analysis (that is, a case of major depression prevented) is worth the additional cost of £114 *on top of* the financial cost of treating this episode.

The conclusions from the economic analysis are subject to the considerable uncertainty underlying the input parameters. Further research is needed on the effectiveness of treatments aiming at preventing the development of mental disorders during the antenatal and postnatal periods in women with identified risk factors, in order to determine the cost effectiveness of such approaches. Nevertheless, the economic analysis suggests that inexpensive, effective preventive treatments could lead to substantial cost savings from preventing major depression in women with psychosocial risk factors for developing this condition, as the treatment of major depression is likely to be significantly more costly than its prevention.

6.7 CLINICAL PRACTICE AND RESEARCH RECOMMENDATIONS

Since the available data, including both the efficacy data and the data underlying the health economic model, are limited, recommending interventions for women with specific psychosocial risk factors is not supported by the current evidence. However, given that there was a strong effect for treatment in those with more depression symptoms, intervening here may be worthwhile.

6.7.1.1 For pregnant women who have symptoms of depression and/or anxiety that do not meet diagnostic criteria but significantly interfere with personal and social functioning, healthcare professionals should consider:

● for women who have had a previous episode of depression or anxiety, offering individual brief psychological treatment (four to six sessions), such as IPT or CBT

● for women who have not had a previous episode of depression or anxiety, offering social support during pregnancy and the postnatal period; such support may consist of regular informal individual or group-based support.

6.7.1.2 Single-session formal debriefing focused on the birth should not be routinely offered to women who have experienced a traumatic birth. However, maternity staff and other healthcare professionals should support women who wish to talk about their experience, encourage them to make use of natural support systems available from family and friends, and take into account the effect of the birth on the partner.

6.7.2 Research recommendation

Interventions for women with subthreshold symptoms of depression and/or anxiety
An RCT should be conducted to compare the efficacy and cost effectiveness of an intervention for women with chronic subthreshold symptoms of depression and anxiety with usual maternity and primary care. The intervention should be a brief psychoeducational intervention. Primary outcome measures may include symptoms of depression and anxiety, and there should be a 1-year follow-up period.

Why this is important
Depression and anxiety in the postnatal period can have a serious impact on a woman's ability to cope with day-to-day life, including looking after her infant and

other children in the family. Even subthreshold symptoms can affect a woman's general functioning and the development of her infant. Treating subthreshold symptoms may prevent escalation of symptoms into a diagnosis of depression or anxiety, and also improve a woman's ability to cope.

6.8 REVIEW OF TREATMENTS AIMED AT PREVENTING THE DEVELOPMENT OF MENTAL DISORDERS DURING THE ANTENATAL AND POSTNATAL PERIODS FOR WOMEN WITH NO IDENTIFIED RISK FACTORS

6.8.1 Studies considered

Sixteen studies met inclusion criteria. Excluded studies with reasons for exclusion can be seen in Appendix 18. Important characteristics of the included studies are in Table 19, with fuller details of studies in Appendix 18.

6.8.2 Analyses

The studies in this section were analysed in Review Manager file *APMH Non-Pharmacological Interventions – Prevention* (*No Risk Factors*); see Appendix 20 for forest plots (identifier 'RMnppa'). Since most studies reported dichotomous data (number scoring above threshold for depressive symptoms, including $BDI \geq 9$, $EPDS \geq 11$ or 12 and DSM diagnosis), only these studies are used in the meta-analyses. Studies that therefore did not contribute efficacy data include HAYES2001 and HOFMEYER2001. Efficacy data were not extracted on an intention-to-treat basis since the included populations did not have the extracted outcomes (possible depression) at baseline. For this reason, the number of participants in the summary evidence profiles and evidence profile in Appendix 19 are different for efficacy and tolerability outcomes.

6.8.3 Evidence profile

There was some heterogeneity in the dataset, which was removed in a sensitivity analysis that omitted LAVENDER1998 from the analysis. There was no difference between treatments aimed at preventing depression in the postnatal period and standard care in women with no identified risk factors for future onset of depression. See Table 20 for a summary of the evidence profile.

No individual treatment reduced subsequent depression symptoms, with two treatments (social support and psychoeducation) producing an effect size that favoured control, although neither was statistically significant. See Table 21 for a summary of the evidence profile.

Table 19: Summary of study characteristics for trials of treatments for prevention of mental disorder versus standard care (no risk factor identified)

	Debriefing	Social support	Multi-modal support	Psycho-education	Home visiting/ home supportive listening	Intrapartum support
No. trials (No. participants)	2 RCTs (1,865)	1 RCT (84)	1 RCT (731)	2 RCTs (1,208)	2 RCTs (1,354)	1 RCT (6,915)
Study IDs	(1) LAVENDER 1998 (2) PRIEST2003	REID2002*	WIGGINS2005*	(1) HAYES 2001** (2) REID2002*	(1) MORELL 2000 (2) WIGGINS 2005*	HODNETT 2002
Mean age (or range if not given)	(1) 24 (2) not given	27	30	(1) 26 (2) 27	(1) 28 (2) 30	30
Timing of treatment	(1) PN (first few days after birth) (2) PN (within 72 hrs of birth)	PN (starting 2 weeks PN)	2 MPN	(1) AN (2) PN	(1) PN (first month) (2) 2 MPN	Intrapartum

Continued

157

Table 19: *(Continued)*

	Debriefing	Social support	Multi-modal support	Psycho-education	Home visiting/home supportive listening	Intrapartum support
Content of treatment	(1) Discussion about labour (untrained research midwife) (2) CISD (CISD-trained midwife)	PN support group (trained midwives)	Home visiting, phone support, drop-in sessions	(1) Booklet and audiotape on PN mood change, coping plan and info for partner/family (2) Postnatal support manual with supportive information on sleep, health etc	(1) Community PN support worker (in addition to standard midwife visits) (2) Support health visitor – listening, responding to needs, practical support and info as required	Continuous labour support
Length of treatment	(1) 1 session (2) 1 session	Weekly sessions	1 year	N/A	(1) Up to 10 visits over 4 weeks (2) Monthly for a year	N/A
Length of follow-up	(1) 3 weeks (2) 12 months	6 months	6 months	(1) 16–24 weeks PN (2) 6 months	6 months	6 weeks PN

Notes:

*REID2002 is a four-arm trial, including social support and psychoeducation, plus a combination arm (data not extracted); WIGGINS2005 is a three-arm trial, including multi-modal support and home supportive visiting

**Not used in efficacy analyses as does not report dichotomous data

Table 20: Summary evidence profile for studies of treatments versus standard care to prevent depression in the postnatal period (no risk factors)

	All therapies
Study IDs	LAVENDER1998 PRIEST2003 REID2002* WIGGINS2005* HAYES2001 MORELL2000 HODNETT2002
Overall quality of evidence	Moderate
Depression above threshold at endpoint or first available measure	RR = 0.94 (0.84, 1.04) (K = 5; n = 8,886) RMnppa 01.02
% attrition rate, treatment group versus standard care	11% versus 10% 0 (K = 6; n = 4,176) RMnppa 02.01

*Data entered for REID2002 to calculate the overall effect size includes data from the support group and psychoeducation group since the results from each group were similar; data entered for WIGGINS2005 is for the health visiting group only
Notes: RR = relative risk (95% CI); K = number of trials contributing to the summary statistic; n = number of participants; 'RMnppa nn.nn' refers to the relevant forest plot in Appendix 20

6.8.4 Clinical summary for treatments for the prevention of depression in the postnatal period for women with no identified risk factors

Treatments aimed at preventing depression in the postnatal period that are not targeted at high-risk populations do not have any effect on future depression. In subanalyses by treatment, there was no difference between treatment and control except for psychoeducation and social support, which showed a benefit (not statistically significant) favouring control treatment.

6.8.5 Clinical practice recommendation

6.8.5.1 Psychosocial interventions (for example, group psychoeducation) designed specifically to reduce the likelihood of developing a mental health disorder

Table 21: Summary evidence profile for studies of treatments versus standard care to prevent depression in the postnatal period (no risk factors): by treatment

	Debriefing	Social support	Multi-modal support	Psycho-education	Home visiting	Intrapartum support
Study IDs	LAVENDER 1998 PRIEST2003	REID2002	WIGGINS2005	HAYES2001 REID2002	MORELL2000 WIGGINS2005	HODNETT2002
Overall quality of evidence	Moderate	Moderate	Moderate	Moderate	Moderate	Moderate
Depression above threshold at endpoint or first available measure	RR = 0.98 (0.8, 1.2) (K = 1; n = 1,745) RMnppa 01.03	RR = 1.58 (0.9, 2.77) (K = 1; n = 366) RMnppa 01.03	RR = 0.93 (0.69, 1.27) (K = 1; n = 458) RMnppa 01.03	RR = 1.6 (0.92, 2.79) (K = 1; n = 371) RMnppa 01.03	RR = 0.92 (0.72, 1.17) (K = 2; n = 994) RMnppa 01.03	RR = 0.86 (0.73, 1.02) (K = 1; n = 5,601) RMnppa 01.03
% attrition rate, treatment group versus standard care	1% versus 1% (K = 2; n = 1,865) RMnppa 02.02	29% versus 25% (K = 1; n = 501) RMnppa 02.02	14% versus 18% (K = 1; n = 548) RMnppa 02.02	22% versus 21% (K = 2; n = 707) RMnppa 02.02	14% versus 16% (K = 1; n = 1,170) RMnppa 02.02	N/A

Notes: RR = relative risk (95% CI); K = number of trials contributing to the summary statistic; n = number of participants; 'RMnppa *nn.nn*' refers to the relevant forest plot in Appendix 20

during pregnancy or the postnatal period should not be part of routine antenatal and postnatal care.

6.9 REVIEW OF NON-PHARMACOLOGICAL TREATMENTS FOR DEPRESSION IN THE POSTNATAL PERIOD

6.9.1 Introduction

Compared with treatment for other mental disorders in the postnatal period, there is a relatively large literature on non-pharmacological interventions for the treatment of depression in the postnatal period, including psychosocial, psychological and physical treatments. These are reviewed in two sections: treatments compared with standard care or waitlist control and treatments compared with other treatments.

For most comparisons, studies contributed data for both dichotomous and continuous outcomes.

6.9.2 Treatments compared with standard care or waitlist control: studies considered

Eight studies met inclusion criteria, four of psychological treatments (including psychodynamic psychotherapy, CBT and IPT), three of non-directive counselling (listening visits) and two of social support, one of which also included exercise. One four-arm study included two psychological treatments and non-directive counselling (listening visits) (COOPER2003). Excluded studies with reasons for exclusion can be seen in Appendix 18. Important characteristics of the included studies are in Table 22, with fuller details of studies in Appendix 18.

Note that some treatments were adapted for this client group, for example, focusing on the woman's interaction with her infant rather than on specifically depression-related issues.

Evidence profile
(The studies were analysed in Review Manager file *APMH Non-Pharmacological Interventions – Treatment* [RMnpta].) There is an effect for treatments compared with standard care on reducing depression symptoms. However, there was some heterogeneity in the dataset, which was only partly explained by a sub-analysis by treatment, with heterogeneity remaining in the studies of psychological treatments. There was nevertheless benefit for all treatments except group exercise. See Table 23 for a summary of the evidence profile. Table 24 shows sub-analyses by treatment.

A further sub-analysis by baseline diagnosis method was also undertaken (see Table 24). This showed that, while the effect of treatment over standard care was evident in both those with a formal diagnosis of depression and those with a

Table 22: Summary of study characteristics for trials of non-pharmacological treatments for depression versus standard care or waitlist control

	Psychological treatments	Non-directive counselling (listening visits)	Social support	Group exercise
No. trials (no. participants)	4 RCTs (415)	3 RCTs (296)	2 RCTs (84)	1 RCT (20)
Study IDs	(1) COOPER2003 (2) HONEY2002 (3) OHARA2000 (4) PRENDERGAST2001	(1) COOPER2003 (2) HOLDEN1989 (3) WICKBERG1996	(1) ARMSTRONG2003 (2) CHEN2000	ARMSTRONG2003
Diagnosis	(1) Depression, DSM-III-R (2) EPDS > 12 (3) Depression, DSM-IV (4) Depression, DSM-IV	(1) Depression, DSM-III-R (2) Depression, Goldberg's psychiatric interview (3) EPDS ≥ 12	(1) EPDS ≥ 12 (2) BDI ≥ 10	EPDS ≥ 12
Mean age (or range if not given)	(1) 28 (2) 28 (3) 30 (4) 32	(1) 28 (2) 26 (3) 28	(1) 21–30 (2) 29	21–30

Timing of treatment	(1) From 8 weeks PN (2) Up to 12 months PN (3) Average 6 months PN (4) Up to 12 months PN	(1) From 8 weeks PN (2) 12–18 weeks PN (3) 3–4 months PN	(1) 6 weeks to 18 months PN (2) 3 weeks PN	6 weeks to 18 months PN
Concomitant treatments	(1) Not reported (2) Some antidepressant use – no details (3) Not reported (4) 1 in each group on medication	(1) Not reported (2) 12 took antidepressants (only 6 at therapeutic dose) (3) None took antidepressants	(1) 50% taking medication, some having counselling (2) Not reported	50% taking medication, some having counselling
Treatment	(1) Psychodynamic psychotherapy (used in most comparisons), CBT, non-directive counselling (listening visits) (2) CBT (3) IPT (4) CBT	(1) Psychodynamic psychotherapy (used in most comparisons), CBT, non-directive counselling (listening visits) (2) Non-directive counselling (listening visits) (3) Non-directive counselling (listening visits)	(1) Group exercise with social support (2) Social support	Group exercise with social support

Continued

163

Table 22: (*Continued*)

	Psychological treatments	Non-directive counselling (listening visits)	Social support	Group exercise
Length of treatment	(1) 10 weeks (2) 8 weeks (3) 12 weeks (4) 6 weeks	(1) 10 weeks (2) 8 weeks (3) 6 weeks	(1) 12 weeks (2) 4 weeks	12 weeks
Length of follow-up	(1) 9 months PN, 18 months PN, 5 years PN (2) 6 months after endpoint (3) None (4) 6 months after endpoint	(1) 9 months PN, 18 months PN, 5 years PN (2) 9 months PN (3) 6 weeks after endpoint	(1) None (2) None	None

high depression-scale score, treatment was more effective in those with a formal diagnosis.

In a sub-analysis of the psychological therapies, all therapies (CBT, psycho-dynamic psychotherapy and IPT) showed an effect on depression symptoms. See Table 25.

Clinical summary for non-pharmacological treatments compared with standard care for depression in the postnatal period
There is an effect on depression symptoms in the postnatal period of targeted treatments compared with standard care, particularly in those with a formal diagnosis of depression. Treatments with at least moderate-quality evidence that show an effect include CBT, IPT, psychodynamic psychotherapy and non-directive counselling.

Table 23: Summary evidence profile for studies of non-pharmacological treatments versus standard care

	Non-pharmacological treatments versus standard care
Study IDs	ARMSTRONG2003 CHEN2000 COOPER2003 HOLDEN1989 HONEY2002 OHARA2000 PRENDERGAST2001 WICKBERG1996
Overall quality of evidence	Moderate
Depression above threshold at endpoint or first available measure	RR (random effects) = 0.57 (0.43, 0.76) (K = 8; n = 486) RMnpta 01.01
Depression symptoms at endpoint	SMD (random effects) = − 0.61 (−1.07, −0.14) (K = 6; n = 345) RMnpta 01.02
% attrition rate, treatment group versus standard care	17% versus 7% (K = 6; n = 586) RMnpta 05.01

Notes: RR = relative risk (95% CI); K = number of trials contributing to the summary statistic; n = number of participants; 'RMnpta *nn.nn*' refers to the relevant forest plot in Appendix 20

Table 24: Summary evidence profile for studies of non-pharmacological treatments versus standard care (sub-analyses)

	Psychological treatments	Sub-analysis by treatment			Sub-analysis by method of baseline depression diagnosis	
		Non-directive counselling (listening visits)	Social support	Group exercise	DSM or similar	EPDS ≥ 12, BDI ≥ 10 or similar
Study IDs	COOPER2003 HONEY2002 OHARA2000 PRENDERGAST 2001	COOPER2003 HOLDEN1989 WICKBERG 1996	ARMSTRONG 2003 CHEN2000	ARMSTRONG 2003	ARMSTRONG 2003 COOPER2003 HOLDEN1989 OHARA2000 PRENDERGAST 2001	CHEN2000 HONEY2002 WICKBERG 1996
Overall quality of evidence	Moderate	High	Low	Low	Moderate	Moderate
Depression above threshold at endpoint or first available measure	RR (random effects) = 0.61 (0.4, 0.92) (K = 4; n = 304) RMnpta 01.04	RR = 0.61 (0.45, 0.83) (K = 3; n = 198) RMnpta 01.05	RR = 0.69 (0.42, 1.13) (K = 1; n = 64) RMnpta 01.04	RR = 0.07 (0, 1.03) (K = 1; n = 20) RMnpta 01.04	RR = 0.46 (0.36, 0.60) (K = 5; n = 329) RMnpta 01.08	RR (random effects) = 0.72 (0.49, 1.05) (K = 3; n = 157) RMnpta 01.08
Depression symptoms at endpoint	SMD (random effects) = −0.49 (−0.95, −0.02) (K = 5; n = 325) RMnpta 01.06	SMD = −0.26 (−0.66, 0.14) (K = 1; n = 97) RMnpta 01.06	SMD = −0.71 (−1.23, −0.19) (K = 1; n = 60) RMnpta 01.07	SMD = −1.64 (−2.68, −0.59) (K = 1; n = 20) RMnpta 01.06	SMD (random effects) = −0.66 (−1.21, −0.11) (K = 5; n = 300) RMnpta 01.010	SMD = −0.71 (−1.23, −0.19) (K = 1; n = 60) RMnpta 01.011
% attrition rate treatment group versus standard care	19% versus 7% (K = 4; n = 426) RMnpta 05.02	14% versus 9% (K = 2; n = 148) RMnpta 05.02	12% versus 0% (K = 1; n = 64) RMnpta 05.02	No data	18% versus 8% (K = 3; n = 429) RMnpta 05.03	15% versus 4% (K = 3; n = 157) RMnpta 05.03

Table 25: Summary evidence profile for psychological therapies for the treatment of depression (by therapy)

	CBT	Psychodynamic psychotherapy	IPT
Study IDs	COOPER2003 HONEY2002 PRENDERGAST 2001	COOPER2003	OHARA2000
Overall quality of evidence	Moderate	Moderate	Moderate
Depression above threshold at endpoint or first available measure	RR = 0.78 (0.58, 1.03) (K = 3; n = 177) RMnpta 01.011	RR = 0.59 (0.38, 0.9) (K = 1; n = 102) RMnpta 01.011	RR = 0.41 (0.27, 0.62) (K = 1; n = 120) RMnpta 01.011
Depression symptoms at endpoint	WMD (random effects) = −0.99 (−3.31, n = 174) RMnpta 01.012	WMD = −2.4 (−4.21, −0.59) 1.33) (K = 3; (K = 1; n = 95) RMnpta 01.012	WMD = −8.5 (−11.25, −5.75) (K = 1; n = 99) RMnpta 01.012
% attrition rate, treatment group versus standard care	19% versus 7% (K = 4; n = 426) RMnpta 05.02	14% versus 9% (K = 2; n = 148) RMnpta 05.02	12% versus 0% (K = 1; n = 64) RMnpta 05.02

Notes: RR = relative risk (95% CI); K = number of trials contributing to the summary statistic; n = number of participants; 'RMnpta $nn.nn$' refers to the relevant forest plot in Appendix 20

6.9.3 Psychological and psychosocial interventions compared with other treatments: studies considered

Four studies met inclusion criteria. Excluded studies with reasons for exclusion can be seen in Appendix 18. Important characteristics of the included studies are in Table 26, with fuller details of studies in Appendix 18.

Evidence profile
(The studies were analysed in Review Manager file *APMH Non-Pharmacological Interventions – Treatment*.) There is some evidence that IPT more effectively reduces depression symptoms compared with psychoeducation, although this was not the case on all outcomes (see evidence profile in Appendix 19). There was also some evidence that six sessions of counselling are more effective than a single session, and that psychoeducation with the partner was more effective than psychoeducation for the woman alone. Individual counselling was more effective than group-based counselling, but it was not clear whether CBT or either individual or group-based counselling was more effective. See Table 27 for a summary of the evidence profile in Appendix 19.

Table 26: Summary of study characteristics for trials of psychological or psychosocial interventions compared with other treatments

	Psychosocial interventions
No. trials (No. participants)	4 RCTs (358)
Study IDs	(1) APPLEBY1997 (2) MILGROM2005 (3) MISRI2000 (4) SPINELLI2003
Diagnosis	(1) Depression, CIS-R (2) Depression, DSM-IV (3) Depression, DSM-IV (4) Depression, DSM-IV
Mean age	(1) 25 (2) 30 (3) 33 (4) 29
Timing of treatment	(1) 6–8 weeks PN (2) PN – mean 18 weeks (3) 5 months PN (4) Antenatal – mean 21 weeks gestation
Concomitant treatments	(1) None (all on placebo) (2) Unclear (3) Some use (no details) (4) None took antidepressants
Treatments	(1) Counselling single session; counselling 6 sessions (both + placebo)* (2) CBT; group counselling; individual counselling; standard care (3) Psychoeducation with partner; psychoeducation without partner (4) IPT; psychoeducation
Length of treatment	(1) 12 weeks (2) 12 weeks (3) 6 weeks + follow-up session after 1 month (4) 16 weeks
Length of follow-up	(1) None (responders only; not extracted) (2) None (3) None (4) None

*This study has two further arms – fluoxetine + single-session counselling; fluoxetine + 6 sessions of counselling

Table 27: Summary evidence profile for studies of psychological or psychosocial interventions for depression versus other treatments

	IPT versus psycho-education	Counselling (single session versus six sessions)	Psychoeducation (with partner) versus psychoeducation (mother only)	Counselling (individual versus group)	CBT versus individual counselling	CBT versus group counselling
Study IDs	SPINELLI 2003	APPLEBY 1997	MISRI2000	MILGROM 2005	MILGROM 2005	MILGROM 2005
Overall quality of evidence	Moderate	Moderate	Moderate	Low	Low	Low
Depression above threshold at endpoint	RR = 0.84 (0.71, 1) (K = 1; n = 50) RMnpta 019.02	N/A	RR = 0.51 (0.22, 1.18) (K = 1; n = 29) RMnpta 022.02	N/A	N/A	N/A
Depression above threshold at follow-up	N/A	N/A	1 month post-natally RR = 0.3 (0.1, 0.92) (K = 1; n = 29) RMnpta 022.02	N/A	N/A	N/A

Continued

169

Table 27: (*Continued*)

IPT versus	Counselling psycho-education	Psycho-education (single session versus six sessions)	Counselling (with partner) versus psychoeducation (mother only)	CBT versus (individual versus group)	CBT versus individual counselling	group counselling
Depression symptoms at endpoint	WMD = -4.52 (-9.14, 0.1) (K = 1; n = 38) RMnpta 019.05	WMD = 3.2 (-1.57, 7.97) (K = 1; n = 44) RMnpta 020.02	WMD = -3.2 (-8.22, 1.82) (K = 1; n = 28) RMnpta 022.03	WMD = -5.42 (-10.35, -0.49) (K = 1; n = 72) RMnpta 028.01	WMD = 1.87 (-2.28, 6.02) (K = 1; n = 69) RMnpta 029.01	D = -3.55 (-8.68, 1.58) (K = 1; n = 65) RMnpta 030.01
Depression symptoms at follow-up	N/A	N/A	1 month postnatally WMD = -6.1 (-10.77, -1.43) (K = 1; n = 29) RMnpta 022.03	12 months postnatally WMD = -3.98 (-9.96, 2) (K = 1; n = 37) RMnpta 028.01	12 months postnatally WMD = 2.38 (-3.28, 8.04) (K = 1; n = 36) RMnpta 029.01	12 months postnatally WMD = -1.6 (-9.13, 5.93) (K = 1; n = 25) RMnpta 030.01
% attrition rate, treatment group versus comparison	16% versus 32% (K = 1; n = 50) RMnpta 019.01	26% versus 29% (K = 1; n = 44) RMnpta 020.01	N/A	N/A	N/A	N/A

Notes: RR = relative risk (95% CI); K = number of trials contributing to the summary statistic; n = number of participants; 'RMnpta *nn.nn*' refers to the relevant forest plot in Appendix 20

Clinical summary for trials of psychological or psychosocial interventions compared with other treatments

There are few studies comparing one non-pharmacological treatment with another in the treatment of depression in the postnatal period, and each comparison involved only a single study. However, in these studies, IPT was more effective than psycho-education, six sessions of counselling were more effective than one session, group exercise was more effective than social support, psychoeducation with the woman's partner was more effective than psychoeducation with the woman alone, and individual counselling was more effective than group counselling.

6.9.4 Physical non-pharmacological treatments compared with other treatments: studies considered

Three studies met inclusion criteria. Excluded studies with reasons for exclusion can be seen in Appendix 18. Important characteristics of the included studies are in Table 28, with fuller details of studies in Appendix 18.

Evidence profile

(The studies were analysed in Review Manager file *APMH Non-Pharmacological Interventions – Treatment.*) There is some evidence that both group exercise (pram pushing) and infant massage more effectively reduce depression symptoms compared with social support. Acupuncture for depression does not appear to be more effective than standard acupuncture or massage. See Table 29 for a summary of the evidence profile in Appendix 19.

Clinical summary for trials of physical non-pharmacological treatments

There are also few studies of non-pharmacological physical treatments and all studies involved small numbers. The evidence for a structured exercise programme confirmed the view from the NICE depression guideline (NICE, 2004a; NCCMH, 2005) that exercise may be of some benefit in depression but the limited evidence for massage and acupuncture is not supported by evidence for such treatments in non-postnatal populations.

6.9.5 Overall clinical summary for the non-pharmacological treatment of depression

There is some evidence that psychological treatments have some benefit in reducing depression symptoms compared with treatment as usual, although very little evidence on differential effectiveness. However, the evidence is not high quality and there are few studies overall. Evidence from the treatment of depression in non-perinatal populations suggests that structured psychological therapies focused on depression, such as short-term CBT, are beneficial (NCCMH, 2005). Similarly, the benefit of

Table 28: Study characteristics for studies of physical non-pharmacological treatments for depression versus other treatments

	Physical non-pharmacological treatments
No. trials (no. participants)	3 RCTs (119)
Study IDs	(1) ARMSTRONG2004 (2) MANBER2004 (3) ONOZAWA2001
Diagnosis	(1) EPDS ≥ 12 (2) Depression DSM-IV (3) EPDS > 12
Mean age	(1) 30 (2) 33 (3) 32
Timing of treatment	(1) 6 weeks – 18 months PN (2) Antenatal – mean 20 weeks' gestation (3) 9 weeks PN
Concomitant treatments	(1) 55% taking antidepressants and/or having counselling (2) None (3) 1 massage participant taking antidepressants
Treatments	(1) Group exercise; social support (2) Acupuncture for depression; non-depression acupuncture; massage (3) Infant massage; social support
Length of treatment	(1) 12 weeks (2) 8 weeks (3) 5 weeks
Length of follow-up	(1) 3 months after endpoint (data not reported) (2) 2 weeks after endpoint (3) None

Table 29: Summary evidence profile for studies of physical non-pharmacological treatments for depression versus other treatments

	Group exercise versus social support	Infant massage (group) versus social support (group)	Acupuncture for depression versus non-depression acupuncture	Acupuncture for depression versus massage
Study IDs	ARMSTRONG2004	ONAZAWA2001	MANBER2004	MANBER2004
Overall quality of evidence	Moderate	Moderate	Low	Low
Depression above threshold at endpoint	N/A	N/A	RR = 0.9 (0.37, 2.22) (K = 1; n = 41)	RR = 1.2 (0.44, 3.3) (K = 1; n = 40)
Depression symptoms at endpoint	WMD = −7 (−12.32, −1.68) (K = 1; n = 19)	WMD = −4.7 (−7.63, −1.77) (K = 1; n = 25)	WMD = −3 (−8.1, 2.1) (K = 1; n = 35)	WMD = −0.7 (−5.28, 3.88) (K = 1; n = 35)
% attrition rate treatment group versus comparison	25% versus 17% (K = 1; n = 24)	37% versus 14% (K = 1; n = 34)	20% versus 10% (K = 1; n = 41)	20% versus 5% (K = 1; n = 40)

Notes: RR = relative risk (95% CI); K = number of trials contributing to the summary statistic; n = number of participants; 'RMnpta $nn.nn$' refers to the relevant forest plot in Appendix 20

173

exercise in the treatment of depression is supported by a reasonable evidence base in non-perinatal populations.

6.10   HEALTH ECONOMICS EVIDENCE ON PSYCHOSOCIAL INTERVENTIONS FOR TREATMENT OF DEPRESSION IN THE POSTNATAL PERIOD

6.10.1   Economic evidence from the systematic literature review

The NICE guideline on depression included a primary economic analysis examining the relative cost effectiveness between antidepressant therapy and the combination of antidepressant therapy and CBT for the treatment of moderate/severe depression (NICE, 2004a). CBT alone was excluded from the analysis, as it was demonstrated to have similar efficacy to antidepressant therapy at a significantly higher cost, and therefore it was not cost effective. The economic analysis showed that combination of antidepressant therapy and CBT was a cost-effective option, especially for severe depression. Based on the clinical and economic evidence, the guideline recommended use of antidepressant medication for moderate depression, and the combination of antidepressant therapy and CBT for severe or treatment-resistant depression.

6.10.2   Economic modelling

Introduction – rationale for economic modelling
Although antidepressant treatment has been shown to be a cost-effective option for the treatment of moderate depression (NICE, 2004a), the willingness of women to take medication in the postnatal period is likely to be low. Reduced willingness to take medication may lead to refusal to start antidepressant treatment or to higher rates of treatment discontinuation. Increased discontinuation of antidepressant medication in the postnatal period is expected to reduce its overall effectiveness as well as its relative cost effectiveness. Moreover, some antidepressants (notably citalopram and fluoxetine) have been detected in high levels inbreast milk and their use during breast-feeding should be avoided (see Chapter 7).

Taking the above issues into account, the GDG considered psychological therapy as first-line treatment in the postnatal period, in particular for women with mild to moderate depression. The choice of psychological therapy was identified by the GDG and the health economist as an area with potential major resource implications. Since there was no existing economic evidence to support decision making, a decision-analytic model was developed in order to assess the relative cost effectiveness of different types of psychological treatments for women with mild to moderate depression in the postnatal period.

Study population
The study population consisted of women with mild to moderate depression in the postnatal period.

Psychological treatments examined
Two different types of psychological treatments were considered:
- structured psychological therapy (CBT, IPT or psychodynamic psychotherapy)
- listening home visits (non-directive counselling delivered at home).

Model structure
The economic model was developed in the form of a decision tree using Microsoft Excel XP. According to the model structure, hypothetical cohorts of 1,000 women with depression in the postnatal period received one of the treatment options assessed. Women were assumed to continue or discontinue treatment. Those who discontinued might improve by receiving the clinical benefits of standard care (defined as routine postnatal care for women with depression without any specialised psychological treatment). Women were followed for 1 year since initiation of treatment. Over this period, women who responded to treatment or improved under standard care, that is the severity of their clinical symptoms fell below the threshold of a depression diagnosis ('non-depressed'), either remained in this state or relapsed. A schematic diagram of the decision-analytic model is provided in Figure 8.

Costs and health benefit measures included in the analysis
The analysis adopted the perspective of the NHS. Health service costs consisted of treatment costs, either structured psychological therapy or listening home visits, plus standard postnatal care for women with depression in the postnatal period. Costs associated with infant care were not included in the estimation of costs, owing to lack of relevant data. Other costs to women and family, such as personal expenses and productivity losses were also excluded as they were beyond the scope of the analysis. Intangible costs (negative impact of the woman's depression on infants' cognitive and emotional development as well as distress to the family) were also not estimated, but they should be taken into account when interpreting the results.

Two different measures of health benefit were used in the economic analysis:
1. Number of women who responded to treatment or improved after standard care at endpoint (non-depressed)
2. Number of quality adjusted life years (QALYs) gained at the end of 1-year follow-up. QALYs are considered to be the most appropriate generic measure of health benefit that incorporates both gains from reduced mortality and improvements in HRQoL. An analysis using QALYs as a measure of outcome is called cost–utility analysis.

Total costs and health benefits associated with each treatment were estimated and combined in order to assess the relative cost effectiveness of the treatment options evaluated.

Figure 8: Schematic diagram of the structure of the economic model of psychological treatments for mild to moderate depression in the postnatal period

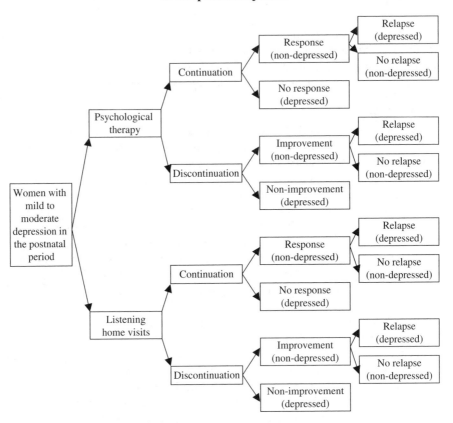

Cost data

Since no patient-level data in terms of resource use were available, the economic analysis was based on deterministic costing of the treatment options. Relevant healthcare resource use was estimated and subsequently combined with unit prices to provide costs associated with each treatment strategy assessed. Estimated resource use associated with the two treatments evaluated (structured psychological therapy and listening home visits) was based on definitions of the treatments in the studies that provided the efficacy data. Further healthcare resource use required was based on the GDG expert opinion, owing to lack of research-based evidence. Unit prices were taken from the *Unit Costs for Health and Social Care 2005*, excluding qualification costs (Curtis & Netten, 2005). All costs utilised in the analysis reflect 2005 prices. Discounting of costs was not applied, as costs were incurred over a short period of time (8 to 9 weeks). Table 30 shows the unit costs utilised in the economic model; estimated resource use and total costs associated with each treatment option assessed are presented in Table 31.

Table 30: Unit costs utilised in the economic model of psychological treatments for mild to moderate depression in the postnatal period (Curtis & Netten, 2005)

Cost element	Unit price* (2005)
Clinical psychologist per hour of client contact	£77
Health visitor per hour spent on home visiting, including travel costs	£89
GP per hour of patient contact	£120
CPN per hour of home visiting, including travel costs	£79

*Unit prices of healthcare professionals do not include qualification costs

Table 31: Resource use and total costs associated with treatment of women with mild to moderate depression in the postnatal period

Resource use	Cost	
Structured psychological therapy (CBT, IPT or psychodynamic psychotherapy)		
Eight sessions × 50 min each, provided at a clinic by a clinical psychologist		£513
Plus additional care:		
One CPN visit lasting 1 hour		£79
Three GP visits × 10 min each		£60
Four health visitor home visits × 45 min each		£269
	Total cost:	£921
Listening home visits		
Eight home visits × 45 min each by health visitors		£538
Plus additional care:		
One CPN visit lasting 1 hour		£79
Three GP visits × 10 min each		£60
Four health visitor home visits × 45 min each		£269
	Total cost:	£946

Psychological and psychosocial interventions

Costs associated with discontinuation
Women who discontinued one of the treatments assessed were assumed to incur 25% of the treatment costs and 100% of the additional care costs.

Effectiveness data and other input parameters of the economic model
Effectiveness data used in the economic model were derived from the guideline meta-analyses. All studies providing dichotomous efficacy data on structured psychological therapy or non-directive counselling (listening home visits) were considered in the economic analysis. The types of treatments examined in each of the studies considered are presented in Table 32.

Since the only direct comparison between structured psychological therapy and non-directive counselling (listening home visits) was made in COOPER2003, it was decided to perform an indirect comparison between the two treatments examined. In order to do this, relative risks of a) no improvement (efficacy) and b) discontinuation of each of the two treatments versus standard care/waitlist were used, with standard care serving as the baseline common comparator. The absolute rates of no improvement and

Table 32: Types of treatments examined in the clinical studies considered in the economic analysis of psychological treatments for mild to moderate depression in the postnatal period

Study	Treatment	Comparator
O'HARA2000	12 sessions of IPT	Waitlist
PRENDERGAST2001	Six sessions of CBT	Standard care
HONEY2002	Eight sessions of group CBT	Standard care
MILGROM2005*	12 sessions of group CBT	Standard care
COOPER2003	Ten sessions of CBT (aimed at improving mother-infant interaction rather than focused on depression) Ten sessions of psychodynamic psychotherapy Ten sessions of non-directive counselling (listening home visits)	Standard care
HOLDEN1989	Eight sessions of non-directive counselling (listening home visits)	Standard care
WICKBERG1996B	Six sessions of non-directive counselling (listening home visits)	Standard care

*Only data on discontinuation were used as efficacy was measured using continuous data

discontinuation of standard care were based on the whole dataset of studies evaluating treatments for depression in the postnatal period, included in the guideline systematic review, that had a 'standard care' arm (that is, studies reported in Table 32 plus ARMSTRONG2003 and CHEN2000).

The absolute rates of no improvement of each treatment were estimated by multiplying the respective relative risks for each treatment, derived from the meta-analysis, by the absolute rate of no improvement as calculated for standard care, using the formula:

$$NIAR_{int(i)} = NIRR_{int(i)} \times NIAR_{st\ care}$$

where:

$NIAR_{int(i)}$ = absolute rate of no improvement of each treatment

$NIRR_{int(i)}$ = relative risk of no improvement of each treatment versus standard care

$NIAR_{st\ care}$ = absolute rate of no improvement of standard care

In order to calculate the absolute discontinuation rates of each treatment, the respective discontinuation relative risks for each treatment, derived from the meta-analysis, were first multiplied by the absolute discontinuation rate of standard care. However, discontinuation rates of standard care as described in the clinical trials were deemed to reflect mainly the conditions of conduct of each trial and not women's acceptability of the treatment (since standard care represented basic care in the trials). For this reason, the absolute discontinuation rate of standard care was subtracted from the initial multiplication product, in order to estimate the discontinuation rate for each treatment, expressing acceptability on top of discontinuation reflecting the trial conduct conditions. Thus, the final absolute discontinuation rate of each treatment was calculated using the following formula:

$$DAR_{int(i)} = (DRR_{int(i)} \times DAR_{st\ care}) - DAR_{st\ care}$$

where:

$DAR_{int(i)}$ = absolute discontinuation rate of each treatment

$DRR_{int(i)}$ = relative risk of discontinuation of each treatment versus standard care

$DAR_{st\ care}$ = absolute discontinuation rate of standard care

It is acknowledged that the indirect comparison between treatments may have introduced bias in the analysis, as there were differences between the studies in terms of severity of depression in study samples, diagnostic measures used, content of treatments and comparators, and some other aspects of protocol design. Nevertheless, due to the limited availability of data, indirect comparison was considered necessary in order to populate the economic model.

Estimation of relapse rates

Relapse rates over 12 months were assumed to be common to both women having responded to any treatment and those having improved under standard care. Data were taken from a relevant meta-analysis performed in the NICE clinical guideline on depression (NICE, 2004a). The meta-analysis included studies that examined the relapse rates within up to 12 months of patients with depression receiving CBT but no continuation treatment. These data were used as a proxy for relapse rates of women with depression in the postnatal period due to lack of more appropriate available data. Relapse rates were utilised in the model only for the estimation of benefits in the form of QALYs and were not taken into account in the estimation of additional costs due to relapse.

Estimation of QALYs
In order to express clinical outcomes in the form of QALYs for the cost–utility analysis, utility weights for health states relating to depression were required. Utility weights represent the HRQoL associated with defined health states; they are estimated based on people's preferences and perceptions of quality of life, which characterise the health states under consideration.

No studies that reported utility weights for women with depression in the postnatal period were identified. In order to populate the economic model, utility weights from Revicki and Wood (1998), referring to health states experienced by the general population of patients with depression treated with antidepressant medication, were used as a proxy. However, the use of these data in the cost-utility analysis performed for this guideline is characterised by a number of limitations:

● Data express the HRQoL of the general population of patients with depression and are not specific to women with depression in the postnatal period. However, this period is associated with wide physical and emotional events in women's lives, which are likely to further affect their HRQoL.

● Data refer to utility weights of patients under antidepressant medication, and therefore incorporate aspects of treatment, such as the presence of side effects, that are not relevant to the treatments examined in this analysis. In order to reduce the impact of this limitation, the highest utility weight for moderate depression was chosen among utilities provided separately for three medications (nefazodone, fluoxetine and imipramine), which apparently expressed HRQoL associated with a lower prevalence and severity of side effects of medication and thus reflected more accurately the HRQoL related to psychological treatment.

● Data refer to *women's* HRQoL and they do not take into account that of the *infants*, which is substantially affected by their mothers' psychological condition. Although it would be very difficult to actually measure the infants' HRQoL and express it in utility weights, this parameter should be considered in the interpretation of the results.

Utility weights were used to express HRQoL of two different health states: moderate depression and remission without continuation treatment. Women who responded to treatment or improved under standard care (non-depressed) were assumed to experience a linear improvement in HRQoL (expressed in QALYs) from initiation of treatment to week 8. Women who were non-depressed at 8 weeks but relapsed within the first year were assumed to experience a linear deterioration in QALYs from 8 weeks to 1 year.

All effectiveness rates and other input parameters included in the economic model are provided in Table 33.

**Table 33: Effectiveness rates and other input parameters included
in the economic model of psychological treatments for mild
to moderate depression in the postnatal period**

Input parameter	Baseline value (95% CI)	Source – comments
Relative risk of no response (no improvement) Structured psychological therapy Non-directive counselling (listening visits)	0.63 (0.43–0.92) 0.61 (0.45–0.83)	Guideline meta-analysis
Relative risk of discontinuation Structured psychological therapy Non-directive counselling (listening visits) Absolute risk of no improvement – standard care Absolute risk of discontinuation – standard care	2.66 (0.84–8.44) 1.49 (0.60–3.71) 61.57% 6.64%	Guideline meta-analysis Guideline meta-analysis Guideline meta-analysis
Utility weights Moderate depression Remission without maintenance treatment	0.63 0.86	Revicki and Wood, 1998; data refer to the general patient population with depression under antidepressant medication – the value for moderate depression reflects HRQoL of patients treated with nefazodone or fluoxetine

Sensitivity analysis

Apart from the base-case analysis, which utilised the most accurate data available, additional sensitivity analyses were undertaken to investigate the robustness of the results under the great uncertainty characterising the model input parameters. One-way sensitivity analyses were carried out to investigate whether alternative methods for the calculation of discontinuation rates of each treatment had an impact on the base-case results. Alternative values of discontinuation rates examined in the sensitivity analysis included:

● Average absolute discontinuation rates of each treatment, directly used as reported in the trials. This method broke the indirect comparison between the two treatments, since no common comparator was used as baseline.

● Values resulting from simply multiplying relative risks of discontinuation for each treatment (versus standard care) by the absolute discontinuation rate of standard care, without subsequently subtracting the absolute discontinuation rate of standard care from the multiplication product (as was done for the base-case analysis).

Moreover, threshold sensitivity analyses were conducted to explore the magnitude of change in base-case values of all the remaining input parameters required for the conclusions from the cost-utility analysis to be reversed.

Results
The results of the economic analysis are presented in the form of ICERs, expressing additional cost per additional unit of benefit associated with one treatment option compared with another. Results of the base-case analysis are provided first, followed by the results of the sensitivity analysis.

Base-case analysis
Non-directive counselling (listening home visits) was more effective than structured psychological therapy as it resulted in more women recovering from depression (non-depressed) at the end of treatment (8 weeks) and in greater gains in QALYs. At the same time, it was more expensive. The ICER of non-directive counselling (listening home visits) versus structured psychological therapy was £1,824 per additional woman recovering from depression, or £9,435 per additional QALY gained. This latter value is within the cost-effectiveness threshold of £20,000/QALY set by NICE in its technology appraisal (NICE, 2004d). Full results of the base-case analysis are presented in Table 34.

Table 34: Results of the base-case analysis referring to a hypothetical cohort of 1,000 women with mild to moderate depression in the postnatal period

Treatment option	Costs (£)	Number of women non-depressed	Total gain in QALYs	ICERs of non-directive counselling (listening visits) versus structured psychological therapy
Non-directive counselling (listening visits)	932,856	616	119	£1,824/woman non-depressed
Structured psychological therapy	879,153	587	113	£9,435/QALY gained

Sensitivity analysis
One-way sensitivity analysis showed that using different ways of estimating discontinuation rates for each treatment had no impact on the base-case results. When absolute discontinuation rates reported in the clinical trials were used, the ICERs of non-directive counselling versus psychological therapy became £1,873 per woman non-depressed at endpoint and £9,692/QALY gained. These figures fell to £1,833 and £9,483 respectively when the rates were derived from multiplying relative risks of discontinuation for each treatment by the absolute discontinuation rate of standard care.

Threshold analysis showed that the results were very sensitive to the relative risk of no response of each of the two treatments. Results were also sensitive to moderate changes in treatment costs; conclusions were reversed following changes in costs roughly ±10% of their base-case values. Full results of threshold sensitivity analyses are provided in Table 35.

Limitations of the economic analysis
The economic analysis was undertaken using the most accurate effectiveness and cost data available. However, evidence on clinical effectiveness was based on indirect comparisons between treatments, derived from a limited number of studies. Cost estimates were based on the description of relevant healthcare resource use as provided in the clinical studies, further supported by GDG opinion. Costs of care for infants born to mothers with depression in the postnatal period were not included in the analysis, owing to lack of relevant data; this is acknowledged as a limitation of the analysis. It is recognised that, overall, results of the analysis are subject to considerable uncertainty and possible bias.

Utility weights used in the model referred to HRQoL of the general population of patients with depression and not to women with depression in the postnatal period. Moreover, they incorporated a likely decrement in HRQoL due to side effects of antidepressant medication since they were specific to pharmacological treatment, which is not applicable to the health states included in the model. Finally, they did not take into account the HRQoL of the infants, which is highly affected by mothers' psychological mood. This parameter should always be considered when evaluating treatments for this patient population.

Discussion – overall conclusions from the economic analysis
Based on the results of the economic analysis, it can be concluded that non-directive counselling (listening home visits) are likely to be a cost-effective treatment option for women with mild to moderate depression in the postnatal period. Results were mainly driven by the substantially higher discontinuation rate of structured psychological therapy compared with that of non-directive counselling (listening home visits), since the two treatments were practically equal in terms of efficacy (expressed by the relative risk of no improvement). The additional cost of providing listening home visits to women with depression postnatally was shown to be offset by the additional clinical benefits achieved, as women seem to accept this kind of therapy more than paying clinic visits for structured psychological therapy. Clinical benefits from treatment are higher than those estimated in the analysis, since improvement in women's

Table 35: Results of threshold sensitivity analyses

Parameter	Values that resulted in:		
	Non-directive counselling (listening home visits) becoming dominant*	**ICER exceeding the threshold of £20,000/QALY**	**Psychological therapy becoming dominant***
Relative risk of no improvement Psychological therapy Non-directive counselling (listening home visits)	– –	0.60 0.64	0.57 0.66
Absolute risk of no improvement Standard care	–	29%	–
Utility weights Moderate depression Remission	– –	0.76 0.73	Weights needed to approximate each other – not realistic
Treatment costs (without additional care) Psychological therapy Non-directive counselling (listening home visits)	12% increase 11% reduction	13% reduction 12% increase	– –

*An option becomes dominant when it is both more effective and less costly than its comparator

psychological condition has a significant positive impact on infants' cognitive and emotional development, as well as on the well-being of their wider family.

However, the above conclusions are subject to the great uncertainty characterising the input parameters. Further research is needed on the efficacy and acceptability of psychological treatments for the treatment of women with depression in the postnatal period, on the HRQoL of women with this condition and their infants, and on the long-term costs of health and social care of those infants, in order to determine more accurately the relative cost effectiveness of psychological treatments and assist decision making.

6.11 FOCUSING ON THE INFANT: INTERVENING IN THE MOTHER-INFANT INTERACTION OR MEASURING CHILD-RELATED OUTCOMES

6.11.1 Introduction

Research has shown that a child's development may be affected by maternal mental illness (for example, Hay *et al.*, 2001), and some researchers have studied whether intervening in the relationship with an intervention designed to improve the quality of the interaction may help to improve maternal symptoms and to aid the child's development (Brockington, 1996). There is a small evidence base of controlled trials comparing mother-infant interaction interventions with other interventions and standard care, mostly in mothers with depression.

6.11.2 Studies considered

This review considers controlled studies reporting maternal mental health outcomes plus either infant behavioural or development outcomes, or mother-infant interaction outcomes, regardless of whether the intervention(s) offered were specifically designed to improve infant-related outcomes or were focused on mental health symptoms. In addition, since the scope of the present guideline is up to the end of the first postnatal year, studies where infants are older than 1 year have been excluded (n = 10). Studies of interventions that were designed to improve the mother-infant interaction are considered first.

6.11.3 Intervening in the mother-infant interaction

Six studies were found that used interventions that had been designed to improve the mother-infant interaction. Since both the interventions used and the outcomes reported are heterogeneous, a meta-analytic synthesis of outcomes was not attempted and the study results are instead described. Study characteristics of the studies reviewed, together with an overview of the results found, are in Table 36.

In a non-randomised controlled trial, Clark and colleagues (2003) compared a mother-infant therapy intervention consisting of 12 weekly 1.5-hour sessions with an IPT group and waitlist control in women with a diagnosis of depression. Both interventions included a mother-infant 'element'. The mother-infant therapy included a peer-support element for the mothers, an infant development component and a dyadic group element including activities designed to improve the responsiveness and sensitivity of the mother-infant interactions. IPT, although it did not focus on the mother-infant interaction, emphasised helping the mother to develop improved ways of interacting with her infant and partner. As can be seen from the table, there was no difference in BDI scores between any of the groups, although mothers in the two therapy groups scored significantly lower on the CES-D than mothers in the

185

waitlist control group. These women also verbalised more with their children and displayed more positive affective involvement with their infants following the interventions.

Field and colleagues (2000) undertook an RCT comparing a multifaceted rehabilitation programme with a no-intervention group and non-depressed control group, targeting low-income, adolescent mothers with a BDI score greater than 12 (mean BDI score at baseline = 18.1). The intervention included mood-induction activities, such as massage, relaxation therapy and infant massage, social and vocational activities for the mothers, and coaching to help improve mother-infant interactions, primarily focused on asking mothers to imitate their infants. At endpoint, the intervention group had lower depression scores than the no-intervention group (mean BDI: 10.9 versus 13.0) and the non-depressed control group (mean BDI: 6.5). Mother-infant interaction scores (as measured by ratings of 3-minute video tapes of face-to-face interaction for each dyad) were better in the intervention group than the no-intervention group, comparable with those of the non-depressed control group. Patterns of depression scores for the groups remained the same at follow-up (6 months after the completion of the intervention), and at this time infants in the intervention group had higher development scores than the infants in the no-intervention group (measured using the Bayley Mental and Motor scales), which were similar to those of infants in the non-depressed control group. The authors noted that with such a multifaceted intervention it is difficult to pinpoint any important key components.

Ammaniti and colleagues (2006) undertook an RCT of women with CES-D scores greater than or equal to 20 at 8 months pregnant comparing a home-visiting intervention group with a control. The home-visiting intervention ran for the first postnatal year and included weekly visits (by a psychologist or social worker) throughout the first 6 months postnatally, and visits every 2 weeks for 6 to 12 months postnatally. The aim of the home-visiting intervention was to help the mother interpret her infant's signals and behaviours and to encourage sensitive interactions with the infant. At 6 months postnatally, assessments of the mother-infant relationship (based on rating of a face-to-face interaction of the dyad and a semi-structured interview with the mother) revealed that depressed mothers who received home visits showed more sensitivity towards their infants than control-group mothers ($p < 0.08$) and their interaction with their infants was more cooperative ($p < 0.07$). The authors describe that mothers in the intervention group were more able to respond appropriately to their infants' cues and developed ways of encouraging the infant to engage in the interaction. These improvements in the mother-infant relationship were also observed at the 12-month assessment. The authors state that there was no change in depressive symptoms throughout the trial but did not present relevant data.

Stein and colleagues (2006) compared a mother-infant-focused intervention and a mother-focused intervention in reducing psychopathology related to eating disorders and improving mother-infant interaction patterns in women with an eating disorder diagnosis. The mother-infant intervention used video feedback to aid the mother in recognising her infant's cues and to be more responsive to them, and to be more aware

Table 36: Study characteristics for trials of mother-infant interactions

Study reference/ study design	Population (number/diagnosis/ other information)	Intervention(s)	Benefit to mother-infant relationship or infant?	Benefit to maternal mental health?	Additional information
Clark et al., 2003[10] /non-randomised controlled trial	39/depression (DSM-IV diagnosis and BDI ≥ 16)/infant age range 1–24 months (mean 8.9 months)	1) Mother-infant therapy (12 weekly 1.5-hour sessions) 2) IPT for mother (12 weeks) 3) Waitlist control (waiting for mother-infant therapy)	Both (1) and (2) led to better communication with infant, more positive affective involvement	No affect on BDI scores, but participants in (1) and (2) had reduced CES-D scores compared with (3) (no difference between 1 and 2)	(1) Fathers sometimes included in intervention
Field et al., 2000/RCT	100 low income, adolescent mothers/ depression (BDI > 12) versus non-depressed (BDI < 9)	1) Multifaceted rehab programme including relaxation, infant massage, coaching, etc. (depressed) (3 months – began at 3 months postnatally) 2) Control group (depressed) 3) Control group (non-depressed)	Better mother-infant interaction scores in (1) versus (2) (scores for (1) similar to those of (3) after treatment) At 6 months follow-up: mother-infant interaction same pattern, and children in (1) showed better development on Bayley scale	(1) Significantly lower depression scores than (2) (mean BDI: 10.9 versus 13.0); however still significantly higher depression scores than (3) (mean BDI: 6.5)	

[10]Excluded from the meta-analysis of psychological intervention studies as not fully randomised.

Continued

Table 36: *(Continued)*

Study reference/ study design	Population (number/diagnosis/ other information)	Intervention(s)	Benefit to mother-infant relationship or infant?	Benefit to maternal mental health?	Additional information
Ammaniti, 2006/RCT	30/depression (CES-D ≥ 20/recruited during 8 months of pregnancy, although intervention postnatally	1) Home-visiting group focused on mother-infant interaction 2) Control group	(1) More maternal sensitivity towards infants and more cooperative interaction *p-values reported for these findings are not significant*	No data reported, although authors describe that there was no change in depressive symptomatology	
Cooper *et al.*, 2003[11]/RCT	193/depression (DSM-III criteria)	1) CBT focused on mother-infant interaction 2) Psychodynamic therapy focused on mother-infant interaction	Of women who reported relationship problems at recruitment, % still reporting difficulties: (1) 41%, (2) 50%, (3) 72%, (4) 83%.	Significant reductions in EPDS scores for those women in (1), (2) and (3) compared with (4). More in (1), (2) and 3) remitted also	Follow-up assessments (18 months and 5 years) reveal no benefit of any therapy on mother-infant interaction, maternal depression or Ainsworth

[11]Included in meta-analysis of psychological intervention studies.

Author/Design	Sample/diagnosis	Intervention	Outcome (interaction)	Outcome (EPDS)	Comments
		3) Non-directive counselling (all: 10 weekly sessions; 8–18 weeks postnatally) 4) Routine primary care	No difference (between any group) in ratings of mother-infant interaction via video tape when maternal sensitivity at baseline controlled for		Strange Situation Assessment (at 18 months only)
Onozawa *et al.*, 2001/RCT	34/depression (EPDS ≥ 13 at 4 weeks postnatally)	1) Infant massage including support-group element (5 weekly 1-hour sessions) 2) Support group only (5 weekly half-hour sessions)	(1) Improved on every dimension of the mother-infant interaction scale (2) Did not improve	(1) Lower EPDS scores from pretreatment (2) No reduction in EPDS scores	Improvements in EPDS in both groups between recruitment and immediately pre-treatment Small sample and high attrition rate for (1)
Stein *et al.*, 2006/RCT	77/eating disorders (DSM-IV)/infants aged 4–6 months at baseline	1) Video-feedback interactional treatment 2) Non-specific supportive counselling Both 13 1-hour sessions (weekly, in the home); both given self-help materials to help with eating-disorder symptoms	Typical mealtime feeding of infant: (1) displayed lower levels of conflict during mealtimes than (2). Also (1): infant had more autonomy, mother showed better responses to infant cues	No differences between groups on EPDS or eating disorder scale but both groups improved from baseline on both outcomes	No control (no treatment) group

of her infant's skills as they developed. The mother-focused intervention was a supportive counselling intervention. Following treatment, mother-infant dyads who had participated in the video-feedback intervention displayed significantly lower levels of conflict during mealtimes (23.7% exhibited marked or severe conflict) than in dyads where the mother received counselling (53.8% exhibited marked or severe conflict). Infants in the video-feedback group also demonstrated more autonomy during mealtimes, and their mothers responded to their cues more often with appropriate non-verbal techniques. Post treatment, there were no differences between the two intervention groups in either Eating Disorder Examination scores or EPDS scores, although both groups had improved from baseline.

Onozawa and colleagues (2001), whose study is described elsewhere in this chapter, compared infant massage plus support group with support group only. Following the intervention, mother-infant dyads in the massage group improved on every dimension of the interaction rating scale from their first session scores to the endpoint scores, while the support group only interaction scores did not change. The infant massage group's EPDS scores were significantly reduced from their baseline levels following the intervention (baseline: 15.0; endpoint: 5.0), while there was no difference in the EPDS scores from pre- to post-intervention for the support group only participants (baseline: 16.0; endpoint: 10.0). Limitations of this study include a high attrition rate, particularly for the infant-massage group (7/19 dropouts in the infant-massage group versus 2/15 dropouts in the control group).

Cooper and colleagues (2003), whose study is also described elsewhere in this chapter, compared CBT, psychodynamic psychotherapy, non-directive counselling and routine care in women with depression (both CBT and psychodynamic psychotherapy focused on the mother-infant relationship). The interventions focused on the mother-infant interaction rather than on depression. Immediately after treatment, the EPDS scores of women who had received any one of the therapy interventions were lower than those of women in the routine-care group (mean difference: −1.9, 95% CI −3.5 to −0.3). At this time, 61% of women who had participated in a therapy intervention had remitted and 40% of controls had remitted (percentage difference: 21%, 95% CI 5 to 37%). Of the mothers in the control group who reported relationship problems at the start of the trial, 83% were still reporting these problems at 4 months; for the counselling, psychotherapy and CBT groups respectively, 72%, 50% and 41% were still reporting relationship problems. Mother-infant interaction was assessed via independent rating of 5-minute video recordings of face-to-face play. The assessors were looking for engagement between the mother and her infant, the mother's responsiveness to the infant and the mother's warmth towards and acceptance of the infant during the interaction. Immediately following treatment, there were no differences in mother-infant interaction between any of the groups after controlling for maternal sensitivity at baseline. At follow-up assessments (9 months, 18 months and 5 years), there were no differences in scores on the EPDS between any of the groups, and remittance rates were comparable. Similarly, there were no long-term benefits of these treatments in improving the mother-infant interaction and infant attachment security (as measured by the Ainsworth Strange Situation Assessment at 18 months).

Clinical summary
There appears to be some benefit in providing interventions that specifically aim to improve mother-infant interactions although, given the different interventions studied and the range of outcomes measures used, it is difficult to evaluate precisely which elements of the mother-infant interaction are amenable to intervention. It is also not clear whether improvement in the mother's mental health symptoms leads to improvement in the mother-infant interaction, or whether improving aspects of the quality of the interaction improves infant-related outcomes.

6.11.4   Trials with interventions not focused on mother-infant relationship but which report mother-infant outcomes

A small number of trials reviewed elsewhere in this chapter, which provided interventions focused on the mother's mental health disorder, also reported mother-infant interaction outcomes (ARMSTRONG1999; MARCENKO1994; HEINICKE1999; MEYER1994). As with trials of interventions focused on the mother and infant, a range of outcome variables was used.

Studies of interventions for depression
ARMSTRONG1999 reported the Home Observation for Measurement of the Environment (HOME) Inventory, which included an assessment of the quality of mother-child interactions based on observation of the natural behaviour between mother and infant. For maternal involvement with the child (scored from 0 to 4), the intervention group scored more highly than the control group (mean, standard deviation [SD]: 3.62 [0.78] versus 2.77 [1.24] [$p < 0.001$]).

Studies of interventions for the prevention of depression (risk factors present)
HEINICKE1999, which included women with psychosocial risk factors, reported a range of outcome measures for assessing maternal responsiveness to the infant and infant attachment, including the Attachment Q-Set, Bayley Scales of Infant Development, Ainsworth Strange Situation Assessment (at 14 months), the HOME subscale of avoidance of restricting and punishing the child (encouraging autonomy) and two subscales of the Steps Toward Effective, Enjoyable Parenting (STEEP) mother-child free-play assessment: intrusiveness of the mother, and child non-compliance. At 6 months, responsiveness of mothers in both groups was similar, although by 12 months the intervention-group mothers were more responsive to their infants. By 12 months also, analysis of play-time observations revealed that the intervention-group mothers were less intrusive, and their infants less noncompliant, than the dyads in the control group, and both mothers and infants in the intervention group were more involved with the task at hand when interacting at 12 months. Mothers

who received the intervention used restriction and punishment less often than mothers in the control group.

MARCENKO1994, which included women with psychosocial risk factors, also used the HOME Inventory, in particular the maternal emotional and verbal responsivity, avoidance of restriction and punishment, and maternal-involvement-with-infant subscales. No significant differences were found on the HOME Inventory between the intervention and control groups.

MEYER1994, which included women with pre-term of low-weight babies, assessed interaction in 15 of 18 intervention pairs and 15 of 16 control pairs by videoing bottle-feeding. Infants in the intervention group grimaced and gagged less during feeding (that is, had fewer feeding problems), and mothers in this group also interrupted the infants' feeding less and attempted to stimulate their infants' suckling less often. These mothers also smiled more and more frequently vocalised with their infants than mothers in the control group. Intervention-group mothers also displayed more positive affect and were more sensitive to their infants' behaviour.

HOROWITZ2001, which included women with psychosocial risk factors, used the Dyadic Mutuality Code (DMC) to measure the level of responsiveness in the relationship between mother and infant. At visit two and endpoint, the intervention group had significantly higher DMC scores than the control group. Therefore women in this group showed more responsiveness towards their infants following the intervention.

Clinical summary

There appears to be some benefit from interventions aimed at improving or preventing depression symptoms, with amelioration of some aspects of the mother-infant interaction, even though these interventions do not specifically target this. It therefore appears that both therapies aimed specifically at improving the mother's mental health and those aimed at improving the mother-infant interaction have some efficacy, although the range of outcomes used makes it hard to be specific about what elements can be improved. There are also no data directly comparing 'standard' disease-specific interventions with those aimed at intervening in the mother-infant relationship. More research should be undertaken to assess these interventions.

6.12 BROADER PSYCHOSOCIAL INTERVENTIONS AND OTHER TREATMENTS

6.12.1 Introduction

This section covers broader psychosocial interventions where the focus is not on providing a specific psychological treatment, but on improving outcomes by ameliorating some aspects of care.

6.12.2 Continuity of midwife care

The aim of continuity of midwife care is to provide stability of service to women in the hope that this will improve mental health outcomes, for example, by improving uptake of services. Four studies met inclusion criteria and no study was excluded. Two provided continuity of midwife care throughout the antenatal and postnatal periods, and two during just the postnatal period. Continuity of care was provided within different service configurations in different studies – for example, MACARTHUR2002 developed a guideline-driven protocol for delivering care. Other than MARKS2003, which included only women with a history of depression, studies included all women presenting for maternity care. One study was cluster randomised and was analysed separately (MACARTHUR2002). Important characteristics of the included studies are in Table 37, with fuller details of studies in Appendix 18. A summary of the evidence profile is in Table 38, with the full profile in Appendix 19. (The studies were analysed in Review Manager file *APMH Service Delivery* [RMs].)

Continuity of midwifery care throughout the antenatal and early postnatal periods does not seem to have a differential effect on depression symptoms, even in women with a history of depression. However, continuity in the postnatal period seemed to result in fewer women with probable depression at 7 weeks postnatally compared with standard care.

6.12.3 Strategies based in primary care or the community to improve depression outcomes

Another way to improve outcomes for women with depression in the postnatal period is to configure services so that care is delivered from within primary care or based in the community. One study met inclusion criteria (LUMLEY2006), and there were no excluded studies. The study included training for healthcare professionals in primary care to help improve recognition of depression and response when depression is recognised. Community-based strategies included increasing the support available for mothers, providing better information about services, improving baby friendliness of local environments (such as pram-friendly car parking at shopping facilities) and increasing inter-organisational collaboration and advocacy for parents. Other characteristics of the included study are in Table 39, with more details in Appendix 18. A summary of the evidence profile is in Table 40, with the full profile in Appendix 19. (The studies were analysed in Review Manager file *APMH Service Delivery* [RMs].)

There was no difference in depression scores between women receiving the enhanced services and those receiving standard care, and therefore there does not appear to be any benefit in terms of improving depression outcomes in providing additional services.

Table 37: Summary of study characteristics for studies comparing continuity of midwife care with standard care

	Antenatal and postnatal	Postnatal only
No. trials (no. participants)	2 RCTs (1,098)	2 RCTs (3,363)
Study IDs	(1) MARKS2003 (2) WALDENSTROM 2000	(1) MACARTHUR 2002 (2) SHIELDS1997
Setting	(1) UK (2) Australia	UK
Timing	Antenatal booking (12–16 weeks) to 1 month postnatally	Postnatal (1) Up to 3 months (2) Unspecified
Treatment	(1) Named midwife, weekly drop-in groups (2) Team midwifery care with continuity	(1) Individualised midwife-led community care (2) Care provided by midwives (same midwife providing hospital and home care)
Comparison	(1) Standard maternity care (2) Standard care (mostly by doctors)	(1) Standard community care (2) Standard care (different midwives provide hospital and home care)
Outcomes	(1) 1 and 3 months postnatally (2) 2 months postnatally	(1) Day 28 postnatally (2) 7 weeks postnatally
Other	(1) Inclusion criteria: women with ≥1 episode of major depression	(1) Cluster randomised by GP practice

Table 38: Summary evidence profile for comparing continuity of midwife care with standard care

	Antenatal and postnatal	**Postnatal only**
Study IDs	(1) MARKS2003 (2) WALDENSTROM2000	(1) MACARTHUR 2002* (2) SHIELDS1997
Overall quality of evidence	Moderate	Moderate
Probable depression (first measure)	(1) N/A (2) RR = 1.33 (0.91, 1.94) (K = 1; n = 684) RMs 01.01	(1) RR = 0.68 (0.54, 0.85) (K = 1; n = 1,485) RMs 03.01 (2) RR = 0.72 (0.54, 0.95) (K = 1; n = 788) RMs 02.01
Probable depression (second measure)	N/A	N/A
Depression symptoms at first measure	(1) WMD = 1.62 (−0.72, 3.96) (K = 1; n = 72) RMs 01.02 (2) N/A	(1) N/A (2) WMD = −0.9 (−1.59, −0.21) (K = 1; n = 788) RMs 02.02
Depression symptoms at second measure	(1) WMD = −0.01 (−2.55, 2.53) (K = 1; n = 85) RMs 01.03 (2) N/A	N/A
% attrition rate, treatment group versus standard care	7% versus 7% (K = 2; n = 1,098) RMs 01.04	(1) 4% versus 3% (K = 1; n = 2,064) RMs 03.02 (2) N/A

Notes: RR = relative risk (95% CI); K = number of trials contributing to the summary statistic; n = number of participants; N/A = not available; 'RMs *nn.nn*' refers to the relevant forest plot in Appendix 20
*Cluster randomised so analysed separately

Table 39: Summary of study characteristics for studies comparing community-based and primary care strategies with standard care

No. trials (no. participants)	1 RCT (18,555); cluster randomised
Study IDs	LUMLEY2006
Setting	Australia
Treatment	Community group services (PRISM – Program of Resources, Information and Support for Mothers)
Outcomes	6 months postnatally

Table 40: Summary evidence profile for comparing community-based and primary care strategies with standard care

Study ID	LUMLEY2006
Overall quality of evidence	High
Probably depression (EPDS $\geq$ 13) at 3 months postnatally	RR = 1.05 (0.96, 1.15) (K = 1; n = 11,248) RMs 04.01
Depression scores at 3 months postnatally	WMD = 0.08 (-0.23, 0.39) (K = 1; n = 10,932) RMs 04.02

Notes: RR = relative risk (95% CI); K = number of trials contributing to the summary statistic; n = number of participants; 'RMs *nn.nn*' refers to the relevant forest plot in Appendix 20

6.12.4   Protocols for women following stillbirth

Outcomes for women whose baby is stillborn or dies soon after birth can include depression and PTSD (for example, Turton *et al.*, 2001; Turton *et al.*, 2006). A matched case-control study found that women who had been encouraged to have continued contact with their dead baby, for example, holding the baby, had increased rates of depression, anxiety and PTSD symptoms than women who had either not seen the baby at all or who had not held the baby (Hughes *et al.*, 2002). This study also found that having a funeral or keeping mementoes was not associated with increased rates in morbidity, although since many of these women also held their baby, this is not straightforward to interpret. However, the findings of this suggest that women should not be encouraged to hold their dead baby if they do not wish to.

6.12.5   Varying timing of postnatal GP appointment

Another strategy that has been suggested to help improve outcomes is to move the timing of a routine postnatal GP appointment from 6 weeks postnatally to 1 week postnatally. This is based on the Australian healthcare system. One study met inclusion criteria, and there were no excluded studies. Important characteristics of the included study are in Table 41, with fuller details in Appendix 18.

A summary of the evidence profile is in Table 42, with the full profile in Appendix 19. (The studies were analysed in Review Manager file *APMH Service Delivery* [RMs].)

Table 41: Summary of study characteristics for studies comparing timing of postnatal GP appointment

	Timing of postnatal GP appointment
No. of trials (no. participants)	1 RCT (683)
Study IDs	GUNN1998
Setting	Australia
Treatments	GP appointment 1 week postnatally GP appointment 6 weeks postnatally (standard care)
Outcomes	3 months postnatally

Table 42: Summary evidence profile for studies comparing timing of postnatal GP appointment

	Timing of postnatal GP appointment (1 week postnatally versus 6 weeks postnatally)
Study ID	GUNN1998
Overall quality of evidence	Low
Probably depression (EPDS $\geq$13) at 3 months postnatally	RR = 1.24 (0.81, 1.9) (K = 1; n = 475) RMs 05.01
Depression scores at 3 months postnatally	WMD = -0.1 (-1.06, 0.86) (K = 1; n = 475) RMs 05.02

Notes: RR = relative risk (95% CI); K = number of trials contributing to the summary statistic; n = number of participants; 'RMs *nn.nn*' refers to the relevant forest plot in Appendix 20

There was no difference in depression scores between women receiving their postnatal GP appointment at 1 week postnatally and those receiving an appointment at 6 weeks.

6.12.6 Timing of hospital discharge

The timing of hospital discharge for women delivering in hospital could affect outcomes. One study met inclusion criteria. There was one excluded study – see Appendix 18. Important characteristics of the included studies are in Table 43, with fuller details of studies in Appendix 18. A summary of the evidence profile is in Table 44, with the full profile in Appendix 19. (The studies were analysed in Review Manager file *APMH Service Delivery* [RMs].) There is no evidence that the timing of hospital discharge following giving birth by vaginal delivery had any effect on depression symptoms.

Table 43: Summary of study characteristics for studies comparing timing of hospital discharge

	Timing of hospital discharge
No. trials (no. participants)	1 RCT (186)
Study IDs	CARTY1990
Setting	Canada
Treatments	Hospital discharge 12–24 hours postnatally Hospital discharge 25–48 hours postnatally Hospital discharge 4 days postnatally (standard care)
Outcomes	1 week and 1 month postnatally
Other	Excluded those having non-vaginal birth post-randomisation

6.12.7 Clinical summary for broader psychosocial interventions

There does not appear to be any effect for broader psychosocial interventions on depression symptoms in women who do not have any specified risk factor for depression (other than women whose babies are stillborn). Similarly, the one study in women with previous depression did not show any benefit. This largely supports the

Table 44: Summary evidence profile for studies comparing timing of hospital discharge

	Hospital discharge 25–48 hours postnatally versus discharge 4 days postnatally	Hospital discharge 12–24 hours postnatally versus hospital discharge 25–48 hours postnatally	Hospital discharge 12–24 hours postnatally versus hospital discharge 4 days postnatally (standard care)
Study ID	CARTY1990	CARTY1990	CARTY1990
Overall quality of evidence	Low	Low	Low
Depression symptoms 1 month postnatally	WMD = −2.48 (−4.87, −0.09) (K = 1; n = 87) RMs 06.01	WMD = −0.85 (−2.28, 0.58) (K = 1; n = 93) RMs 07.01	WMD = −3.33 (−5.52, −1.14) (K = 1; n = 82) RMs 08.01
State anxiety (STAI)	WMD = −0.47 (−5.67, 4.73) (K = 1; n = 87) RMs 06.02	WMD = −2.39 (−7.06, 2.28) (K = 1; n = 93) RMs 07.02	WMD = −2.86 (−8.59, 2.87) (K = 1; n = 82) RMs 08.02
Trait anxiety (STAI)	WMD = −2.93 (−7.83, 1.97) WMD = −2.93 (−7.83, 1.97) RMs 06.02	WMD = −1.36 (−5.76, 3.04) (K = 1; n = 93) RMs 07.02	WMD = −4.29 (−9.05, 0.47) (K = 1; n = 82) RMs 08.02

Notes: RR = relative risk (95% CI); K = number of trials contributing to the summary statistic; n = number of participants; 'RMs *nn.nn*' refers to the relevant forest plot in Appendix 20

findings of the studies of psychological treatments aimed at preventing depression, where treatments were effective mainly in women with identified risk factors for the development of depression rather than in all women.

6.12.8   Clinical practice recommendation

6.12.8.1   Mothers whose infants are stillborn or die soon after birth should not be routinely encouraged to see and hold the dead infant. These women should be offered an appropriate follow-up appointment in primary or secondary care.

6.13 PSYCHOLOGICAL AND PSYCHOSOCIAL TREATMENTS FOR WOMEN WITH DISORDERS OTHER THAN DEPRESSION

The evidence covered in this guideline has, with few exceptions (for example, PTSD and related symptoms), concentrated on the treatment of depression. This is unfortunate and represents not only a limitation of the evidence base but also a skewing of healthcare professionals' priorities to a narrow focus on depression. As has been made clear in Chapter 4, women in the antenatal and postnatal period suffer from a broad range of psychological disorders. There is no evidence focusing on treatments for the range of anxiety disorders, psychosis or other mental disorders in the postnatal period to provide evidence for the necessary adaptations and developments of these treatments. There is some suggestion in the data on home visiting that such an approach is an acceptable means to provide psychological treatments for women, particularly in the late antenatal and postnatal periods, for depression and it may be reasonable to suppose that such benefits could be obtained for anxiety and other disorders. However, in the absence of specific evidence, the view of the GDG is that the broad range of treatments identified in other NICE guidance (NICE, 2002, 2004a, 2004b & 2005a) should be made available to women as appropriate. Adapting existing NICE guidance is considered in Section 7.5 below.

7. THE PHARMACOLOGICAL TREATMENT OF MENTAL DISORDERS IN PREGNANT AND BREASTFEEDING WOMEN

7.1 INTRODUCTION

Women may be prescribed psychotropic medication during pregnancy and when breastfeeding for a variety of mental problems, including prophylaxis of a pre-existing disorder, such as bipolar disorder, or treatment of a new episode of mental disorder, such as an episode of mania, psychosis, anxiety or depression. All women, whether already taking medication or with untreated or new disorders, require a review of indications for treatment, the treatment options and the associated risks. It should not be assumed that it is always better to avoid medication as there is important evidence that untreated mental disorders during this period can have a significant detrimental impact on the physical and/or mental well-being of the woman, the fetus/ infant, partners, carers and family. For example, depressive illness is associated with an increased rate of obstetric complications, stillbirth, suicide attempts, postnatal specialist care for the infant and low birthweight infants (Bonari *et al.*, 2004). In women with schizophrenia or bipolar disorder, there is also an increased rate of suicide and potentially significant exacerbation of the disorder if not treated and poorer obstetric outcomes, including increased preterm delivery, low birthweight infants and infants who are small for gestational age (Howard, 2005; Jablensky *et al.*, 2005). Similarly, poor fetal outcomes have been associated with maternal eating disorders during pregnancy (Kouba *et al.*, 2005). There is also emerging evidence that mental disorders in pregnancy may be associated with poorer long-term outcomes for children beyond the immediate postnatal period (Nulman *et al.*, 2002). All of these factors point to the need for prompt and effective treatment of mental illness during pregnancy and the postnatal period. In some cases, effective interventions may be non-pharmacological but, for a significant proportion of women with severe mental illness, medication may be an appropriate treatment. There is good evidence in the treatment of most major mental disorders that pharmacological interventions can have significant benefits in promoting remission, reducing the severity of symptomatology and maintaining mental well-being (NICE, 2002; 2004a; 2004b; 2004c; 2005a).

However, there is also evidence that many psychotropic drugs carry risk of harm in pregnancy, in particular to the fetus. This risk is in addition to the background risk of congenital malformation (structural abnormalities with surgical, medical or cosmetic importance) of between 2% and 4% in the general population (that is, between 20 and 40 in 1,000) (Brent & Beckman, 1990; Nelson & Holmes, 1989). Unfortunately, the magnitude of such risks associated with most psychotropic medications is not reliably established (for example, Patton *et al.*, 2002). Also, the systems, tools and necessary skills for communicating these risks to patients, together with the information on risk of not treating mental disorder, are not well developed (Epstein *et al.*, 2004; Scialli, 2005). The lack of information on the risks of treating arises in significant part from the difficulty in conducting appropriate clinical studies with pregnant women. It is also difficult to predict the effects of drugs on the woman's physiology because of her altered physical state during pregnancy, which means that increased monitoring, for example of liver function, blood pressure and blood glucose, may be required. For instance, the interaction between analgesic drugs used during delivery with psychotropic medication should be considered, together with the rapid changes in body fluid levels postnatally.

Thus the potential harm of treatment must continually be balanced against the risks posed to the woman and infant by the illness. In such circumstances it is the clinician's responsibility to support women in reaching decisions. In circumstances where this is not possible, the clinician will have to take responsibility for guiding the woman, taking full account of the circumstances and any existing advance directives (renamed advance decisions in the Mental Capacity Act, 2005 [DCA, 2005]) she may have made. As discussed in Chapter 4, it is important that women not only understand the risks involved in taking psychotropic medication during pregnancy and when breastfeeding, but also the risks of inadequately or untreated disorder as these relate to their particular circumstances.

This chapter considers the safety of psychotropic medication during pregnancy and breastfeeding, and the pharmacological treatment of mental disorders in pregnant and breastfeeding women. It covers the drugs most commonly prescribed in the treatment of mental disorder, including antidepressants (SSRIs, TCAs, monamine-oxidase inhibitors (MAOIs) and novel antidepressants), anticonvulsants (sodium valproate, lamotrigine and carbamazepine), lithium, antipsychotics (including both typical and atypical antipsychotics) and benzodiazepines, as well as the various indications for their use. It also considers how existing NICE guidance on the pharmacological treatment of mental disorders can be adapted for women during pregnancy and the postnatal period.

Vignette: A woman with no history of mental health problems prior to diagnosis of depression in the postnatal period with her first child

The antidepressants I tried were all suitable for use whilst breastfeeding which, although everyone was bullying me to stop ('get him on a bottle, you'll feel much better'), I was determined to continue. It was the only thing I felt I could do right and clung on to it for dear life.

Vignette: A woman with depression and self-harming behaviour in the postnatal period

I was breastfeeding every 3 to 4 hours on demand and through the night, which was very physically draining. A health visitor and my family told me to introduce formula milk, but I refused to stop breastfeeding; it was the only thing I

Continued

Vignette: (*Continued*)

could offer my son that no one else could. I was struggling to bond with him, and I felt that if I gave up breastfeeding then I would have failed him. I had to do what I thought was right.

When I was admitted to the MBU, a nurse told me that if I stopped breastfeeding the range of antidepressants available to me would be much wider and my recovery would be quicker.

Vignette: A woman with pre-existing depression and depression after birth of both of her children

At my 6-week check, the SHO at the hospital was extremely unsympathetic about my very strong desire to continue breastfeeding. Both she, and a female GP, told me it was breastfeeding OR antidepressants. I think I remember that I did begin taking antidepressants then, but after doing some very basic searches on the internet, made the unilateral decision to continue to breastfeed: I felt my recovery and my relationship with my child depended on it.

There was a lot of stress about getting the antidepressant medication from the pharmacy at the hospital where I gave birth, with several comments along the lines of 'Well, you'll have to stop breastfeeding now'. If I hadn't been able to argue for them, I would not have got them.

My psychiatrist's reassurance that I was being a 'good enough' mother, who had made an informed choice to take antidepressants while breastfeeding, helped in my recovery.

7.2   RISK ASSOCIATED WITH SPECIFIC DRUGS IN PREGNANCY AND THE POSTNATAL PERIOD

7.2.1   Methodology

There is scant evidence about the safety of most psychotropic medication in pregnancy and breastfeeding, partly because distinguishing problems such as fetal abnormalities due to medication from the relatively high background rate of congenital abnormalities is difficult, and partly because many drugs are relatively new (for example, some antidepressants), so insufficient data have been collected. In addition, there are ethical issues with undertaking experimental controlled trials in this population, so only naturalistic trials, which may be prone to biases from confounding factors, are available. This means that information is rarely available before a drug is licensed and must be collected naturalistically. Few studies have sufficient power to detect relatively low event rates accurately, since a great deal of the limited published evidence comprises case studies with very low numbers of subjects, particularly those studies looking at psychotropic medication while breastfeeding.

The safety of drugs in breastfeeding is also difficult to establish because the long-term effects on the developing infant of early exposure to antidepressants via breast milk are largely unknown, although side effects have been reported. However, infants over 10 weeks of age may have a lower risk of adverse effects compared with younger infants (Wisner *et al.*, 1996). Studies report the amount of drug present in breast milk, with the assumption that any amount is unsafe since young infants are not able to excrete drugs as efficiently as older children and adults.

In order to develop recommendations in this area, the GDG drew on expert advice on the specific issue of the risk of psychotropic medication in the postnatal period. In conjunction with the NICE bipolar disorder GDG, a consensus conference was held, to which relevant experts were invited. During the day-long conference, invited experts gave presentations and answered questions. (Invited speakers are in Appendix 2.)

7.2.2   Antidepressants

For antidepressants as an overall group, there is no indication of an increase in major malformations, but there is some suggestion of low birthweight in the infant (Oberlander *et al.*, 2006), particularly with fluoxetine (Hendrick *et al.*, 2003), and respiratory distress at birth (Oberlander *et al.*, 2006). An increased rate of spontaneous abortion has also been suggested, with similar rates between classes, although the rates for trazodone/nefazodone[12] and venlafaxine were higher than those for SSRIs and TCAs (Hemels *et al.*, 2005). This review of controlled studies (9 studies, 2,699 women) also found some evidence of an increased risk of major malformations in those exposed to SSRIs compared with those not exposed, although the result was not statistically significant (RR = 1.36 [95% CI, 0.9 to 2.04]; risk difference = 0.01 [95% CI, 0.0 to 0.03][13]). Unfortunately, insufficient data are available to allow a sub-analysis by individual drug.

Some antidepressants, such as mirtazapine, are relatively new, so sufficient data to allow the risks to be assessed have not been collected. For this reason, TCAs, since they have been in use for a relatively long period of time, are considered to have the lowest *known* risk in pregnancy and breastfeeding. However, individual TCAs may carry some risk, including imipramine (Food and Drug Administration [FDA] category D [positive evidence of human fetal risk]). Other than lofepramine, TCAs are more dangerous in overdose than most other antidepressants (Buckley & McManus, 2002).

For SSRIs as a class, there is no reported increase in risk over other classes of antidepressants, although in September 2005 the FDA in the US and the pharmaceutical company GlaxoSmithKline issued a warning concerning the use of paroxetine in

---

[12]Drug no longer available.
[13]The original review reports ORs but gives raw data from which the RR and risk difference could be calculated.

pregnancy based on retrospective, uncontrolled data (NTIS, 2005). In particular, it warned that exposure to paroxetine in the first trimester of pregnancy may increase the risk of congenital malformations, especially cardiac malformations, such as atrial and ventricular septal defects (hole in the heart). Other than this, there are no data to privilege one SSRI above another in pregnancy; for example, a study by Ericson and colleagues (1999), based on the Swedish Medical Birth Registry, found no increase in malformations above the background rate for any SSRI. Fluoxetine is generally considered the safest SSRI in pregnancy since the known risks are lower than with other drugs in this class. However, levels in breast milk are relatively high compared with other drugs (see below).

For MAOIs, there is limited evidence of an increased risk of congenital malformation. For novel antidepressants, there is no evidence of increased risk, although caution is recommended in the use of venlafaxine, which the manufacturer does not advise during either pregnancy or breastfeeding.

There is also concern about neonatal complications with some antidepressants. A study by Chambers and colleagues (2006) suggests that the use of antidepressants in pregnancy may be associated with the development of persistent pulmonary hypertension of the neonate. Most of the women in the study whose babies developed persistent pulmonary hypertension had taken SSRIs (sertraline, paroxetine and fluoxetine), although a few had taken TCAs, so problems with all these drugs cannot be ruled out. With antidepressants, particularly SSRIs, a range of neonatal symptoms have been reported, including jitteriness, convulsions, crying, poor feeding and hypertonia (Laine *et al.*, 2003). Whether these symptoms represent serotonin toxicity, a withdrawal effect or a combination of both mechanisms remains unclear (Haddad *et al.*, 2005). Other problems include preterm delivery (Kallen, 2004).

With regard to breastfeeding, case studies have shown levels of citalopram and fluoxetine in breast milk to be higher than for other SSRIs (Altshuler *et al.*, 1995; Burch & Wells, 1992; Isenberg, 1990; Lester *et al.*, 1993; Spigset *et al.*, 1996; Spigset *et al.*, 1997; Taddio *et al.*, 1996; Wright *et al.*, 1991). A review of antidepressants in breastfeeding also found adverse effects in infants of women breastfeeding while taking fluoxetine, but found studies that showed that levels of sertraline and some TCAs (amitriptyline, nortriptyline, clomipramine and dosulepin) were low or unquantifiable (Wisner *et al.*, 1996). A later review concluded that nortriptyline, sertraline and paroxetine resulted in the lowest (undetectable) levels in breast milk compared with other antidepressants for which data are available (Weissman *et al.*, 2004). It should be noted that the results of these studies depend on the sensitivity of the assay used to detect the presence of antidepressants in breast milk, which may vary from test to test.

Symptoms (including irritability, constant crying, shivering, tremor, restlessness, increased tone, feeding and sleeping difficulties and, rarely, seizures) have been reported in children born to mothers taking SSRIs at delivery. Many of these symptoms are mild and self-limiting. In many cases they appear casually related to antidepressant exposure, though there is debate as to the extent to which they represent serotonergic toxicity or a withdrawal reaction. Neonates of mothers taking psychotropic drugs during pregnancy should be carefully monitored.

7.2.3   Anxiolytics and hypnotics

Benzodiazepines and related sedatives
It is not entirely clear whether benzodiazepines are associated in the first trimester with an increased risk of malformations, for example, cleft palate (Eros *et al.*, 2002; Dolovich *et al.*, 1998; McElhatton, 1994). Later in pregnancy they may be associated with floppy baby syndrome and the possibility of withdrawal symptoms and restlessness in neonates (Briggs *et al.*, 2002). Use of benzodiazepines in pregnancy should therefore be restricted to treatment of acute and severe symptoms for a maximum period of 4 weeks. For those women dependent on chronic use of benzodiazepines, pregnancy and/or the postnatal period may present an opportunity to support them through a reduction programme.

There is evidence that some benzodiazepines are excreted into breast milk but that the levels are low and therefore the concentration passed on to the infant is likely to be insignificant (McElhatton, 1994). A case series based on 35 infants of mothers referred to a perinatal psychiatry service found no detectable serum concentration of benzodiazepines in the infant of the one mother taking this class of drug (clonazepam) while breastfeeding (Birnbaum *et al.*, 1999).

'Z' hypnotics (zopiclone, zolpidem and zaleplon)
Data are scarce for the use of 'z drugs' in pregnancy. There have been no reported adverse effects of zopiclone in animal pregnancies (Medicines and Healthcare Products Regulatory Agency [MHRA], 2005), and one human study has reported that zopiclone use during pregnancy is not associated with teratogenicity, with a comparable rate of major malformations in both zopiclone-exposed neonates and non-exposed control infants (0% and 2.7% [27 per 1 000], respectively) (Diav-Citrin *et al.*, 1999). However, it has been reported that the infant may experience hypothermia and respiratory depression if zopiclone is taken by the mother in the third trimester (MHRA, 2005). There is a substantial shortage of evidence regarding the teratogenicity of zopiclone, zolpidem and zaleplon (Bazire, 2005) and the BNF recommends that they be avoided during pregnancy.

There are also very few data available regarding the effects of 'z drugs' on the infant during breastfeeding. One human study suggests that zaleplon is transferred to breast milk but that the quantities are likely to be small and unlikely to be clinically relevant (Darwish *et al.*, 1999).

7.2.4   Antipsychotics

There is some indication of an overall increased risk of malformations associated with the use of antipsychotics (2.4%, that is 24 per 1,000), although it is not clear if this may relate to the underlying illness (information on individual drugs is very limited [Altshuler *et al.*, 1996; Slone *et al.*, 1977]). However, a prospective matched-case control study (151 women exposed) found no evidence of increased risk for exposed mothers compared with non-exposed mothers (McKenna *et al.*, 2005), although, again, data on individual drugs are limited. There is little evidence to distinguish between any first- or second-generation antipsychotic, although there is some evidence that olanzapine is associated with greater and significant adverse effects on weight, lipids and glucose metabolism compared with other antipsychotics (Nasrallah, 2006), leading to a concern about increasing the risk of the development of diabetes, and some uncertainty whether the accumulation of clozapine in the fetus may increase the likelihood of floppy baby syndrome and neonatal seizures. Olanzapine appears to be associated with the onset of diabetes in patients with schizophrenia compared with both patients with schizophrenia who did not take any antipsychotic and with those taking conventional antipsychotics (Koro *et al.*, 2002). In a further study of patients with schizophrenia, atypical antipsychotics were associated with the onset of diabetes, in particular clozapine, olanzapine and quetiapine (Sernyak *et al.*, 2002).

Some antipsychotics (such as amisulpride, risperidone and sulpiride) are known to raise levels of prolactin and this can make it difficult for women to conceive. With regard to taking clozapine during pregnancy, there is a theoretical risk of agranulocytosis in the fetus, and also a risk of agranulocytosis in breastfed infants (Eberhard-Gran *et al.*, 2006). There are very few data on the safety of depot antipsychotics in pregnancy and, generally, these preparations should be avoided because of their lack of flexibility. Although symptoms are usually self-limiting, infants may show extrapyramidal symptoms several months after administration of the depot.

There is concern about the accumulation of antipsychotics in breast milk and the potential impact on children (Briggs *et al.*, 2002). A review of the published literature on atypical antipsychotics found no data on levels of the drugs in breast milk in mothers taking quetiapine, ziprasidone or aripiprazole (Gentile, 2004). It also found that, while levels of risperidone in breast milk are low, those of clozapine are relatively high and that this drug has also been subject to reports of adverse reactions in infants, including sedation, agranulocytosis and cardiovascular instability. Olanzapine is detectable in breast milk and adverse reactions have been reported, but it is unclear whether these were related to olanzapine (*ibid.*).

7.2.5   Sodium valproate

Sodium valproate is associated with the development of a range of major abnormalities, including facial dysmorphias, distal digit hypoplasia, and neural tube defects (Holmes *et al.*, 2001; Morrow *et al.*, 2006; O'Brien & Gilmour-White, 2005). Data from the UK Epilepsy and Pregnancy Register show a major malformation rate (MMR) of 2.4% (24 per 1,000) (95% CI 0.9 to 6.0) in fetuses of women with epilepsy who were not taking anti-epileptic drugs, 4% (40 per 1,000) (95% CI 2.7 to 4.4) for monotherapy and 6.5% (65 per 1,000) (95% CI 5.0 to 9.4) for polytherapy. The monotherapy MMR for valproate was 5.9% (59 per 1,000) (95% CI 4.3 to 8.2), significantly higher than that for the other commonly used mood stabilising drugs (carbamazepine 2.3% [23 per 1,000] [95% CI 1.4 to 3.7] and lamotrigine 2.1% [21 per 1,000] [95% CI 1.0 to 4.0]) (Morrow *et al.*, 2006). The risk is thought to be greater in those prescribed over 1 g of valproate per day versus lower doses (Omtzigt *et al.*, 1992). It is important to note that the neural tube closes at day 28 of gestation, which will often be before a pregnancy has been confirmed. For this reason, prevention of neural tube defects is essential. The rate of neural tube defects in the general population has been estimated at 0.06% (0.6 per 1,000) (Nakano, 1973). Valproate is estimated to increase the rate to between 1% and 2% (10 per 1,000 and 20 per 1,000) (Lindhout & Schmidt, 1986). In addition, there is evidence that the use of valproate may be associated with a significant reduction in cognitive functioning of children born to women who used valproate during pregnancy, with 22% with 'exceptionally low' verbal IQ compared with the expected 2% in the general population (Adab *et al.*, 2004a, 2004b).

There is strong evidence that folic acid supplements reduce the incidence of neural tube defects (Lumley *et al.*, 2001). As a result, all women planning pregnancy are advised to take 0.4 mg of folic acid per day before conception and during the first 12 weeks of pregnancy. Women with a neural tube defect, or a neural tube defect in a previous child, are advised to take a higher dose of 5 mg per day (British Medical Association & the Royal Pharmaceutical Society of Great Britain, 2006). Given the association of valproate and carbamazepine with neural tube defects, and the fact that both drugs interfere with folic acid metabolism, some authorities recommend that women of child-bearing potential prescribed these drugs should receive folic acid supplements. However, to date, no study has demonstrated that prescribing folic acid supplements to women taking anticonvulsants during pregnancy reduces the risk of neural tube defects, which have been reported in the offspring of such women (for example, Duncan *et al.*, 2001). There is a danger that routine folic acid prescribing in this group may incorrectly imply that getting pregnant is safe and that the risk of neural tube defect posed by the anticonvulsant has been counteracted. Given this and the lack of data, it is unclear whether prescribers should routinely prescribe additional folic acid to women of child-bearing potential prescribed valproate or carbamazepine. If a woman receiving either of these drugs presents at less than 12 weeks of pregnancy, it would seem prudent to start folic acid supplementation although, given that the neural tube closes by day 28 after fertilisation, it is debatable whether or not this provides any protection.

7.2.6   Lithium

The primary risk that has been identified with lithium occurs in the first trimester and is associated with an increase in the rate of congenital heart disease. While rates of heart defects in the general population are around 0.8% (8 in 1,000) of all live births (Wieck, 2004), the relative risk amongst neonates exposed to lithium in the first trimester is estimated at 7.7 times that in the general population (Kallen & Tandberg, 1983). Rates of Ebstein's anomaly, in particular, are estimated at between 0.1% and 0.05% (1 in 1,000 to 1 in 2,000) in neonates exposed to lithium in the first trimester, compared with 1 in 20,000 in a non-lithium treated population (Cohen *et al.*, 1994), although the need for further studies is noted (Wieck, 2004). There is no consistent evidence of increase in other congenital abnormalities. However, the use of lithium in the second to third trimester has also been associated with floppy baby syndrome, potential thyroid abnormalities and nephrogenic diabetes insipidus (Llewellyn *et al.*, 1998), and with a range of cardiovascular, central nervous system, hepatic and other complications at birth (Newport *et al.*, 2005). It appears to cross the placenta at a similar ratio, regardless of the mother's serum levels and therefore the dose should be kept at the lower end of the therapeutic range (Newport *et al.*, 2005). Withdrawing lithium treatment is associated with a high rate of relapse in the postnatal period among women with bipolar disorder, although this appears to be controllable with careful tapering (Viguera *et al.*, 2000). Lithium is present in high concentrations in breast milk and therefore is generally not recommended when breastfeeding.

7.2.7   Carbamazepine

Carbamazepine is associated with a higher rate of congenital abnormalities, including neural tube defects (0.2% [2 per 1,000] of women treated with the drug compared to a rate of 0.1% [1 per 1,000] in the general population), facial cleft (0.4% [4 per 1,000]), gastrointestinal tract problems (0.2% [2 per 1,000]) and cardiac abnormalities (0.7% [7 per 1,000]), giving an overall rate of around 2.2% (22 per 1,000) for major malformations (based on the UK Epilepsy and Pregnancy Register; Morrow *et al.*, 2006). However, a meta-analysis of worldwide prospective studies reporting major congenital anomalies (based on broad criteria) among women taking carbamazepine (1,255 children) calculated a rate of 6.7% compared with 2.34% in controls (3,756 children), with a rate of around 0.5% for neural tube defects (Matalon *et al.*, 2002). In addition, some studies have suggested an increase in minor malformations such as facial anomalies (for example, malformed ears and a high palate) and small fingernails (Wide *et al.*, 2000). The levels of carbamazepine reported in breast milk appear low in comparison with therapeutic levels in infants (Rubin *et al.*, 2004; Bar-Oz *et al.*, 2000).

7.2.8   Lamotrigine

Evidence has emerged of a relatively high rate of oral clefts in infants born to women taking lamotrigine during pregnancy, with a rate of 0.89% (8.9 per 1,000) (Holmes *et al.*, 2006). Given this and the limited evidence for its efficacy in bipolar disorder (NICE, 2006), lamotrigine should not be routinely used in pregnancy. If the drug is used in pregnancy, it should be noted that the physiological changes during pregnancy may result in decreased lamotrigine levels. These changes in lamotrigine levels can occur from early in pregnancy and progress antenatally, reverting quickly after delivery. Little is known about the effect of lamotrigine on breastfed infants, although it is present at high levels in breast milk (Rambeck *et al.*, 1996). Given the potential seriousness of dermatological problems associated with lamotrigine (including Stevens-Johnson syndrome), considerable caution should be exercised before advising breastfeeding.

7.2.9 Other drugs

Amphetamines

Amphetamine use during pregnancy has recently been linked with significantly higher rates of preterm birth, lower birthweight and significantly lower appearance, pulse, grimace, activity and respiration (APGAR) scores (Ludlow *et al.*, 2004). There is also evidence linking methamphetamine exposure in the prenatal period to significantly higher rates of small-for-gestational-age infants (Smith *et al.*, 2003) and to smaller subcortical volumes in children at follow-up between 3 and 16 years (Chang *et al.*, 2004).

Antihistamines

Of antihistamines licensed in the UK, chlorpheniramine appears to have the lowest risk in pregnancy based on data from human (for example Schatz *et al.*, 1997) and animal studies (Keles, 2004). Schatz and colleagues (1997) found no significant relationships between chlorpheniramine and major congenital malformations (rate of congenital malformations in the exposed group 3.9% [39 per 1,000] versus 5.7% [57 per 1,000] in the unexposed group, p > 0.05) or other adverse perinatal outcomes such as preterm birth and low birthweight. Exposure to doxylamine appears not to be associated with increased instances of major or minor malformations (Kutcher *et al.*, 2003; Mazzotta & Magee, 2000). Similarly, loratadine (Diav-Citrin *et al.*, 2003; Pedersen *et al.*, 2006), meclozine (Asker *et al.*, 2005; Kallen & Mottett, 2003) and dimenhydrinate[14] (Czeizel & Vargha, 2005) appear not to be a teratogenic risk.

However, data regarding the teratogenicity of antihistamines such as diphenhydramine and meclozine are not homogenous (Mazzotta & Magee, 2000). Also, a more recent review of the literature describes older studies that did find an association between antihistamines (diphenhydramine and promethazine) and teratogenicity (Keles, 2004).

There is little evidence regarding the transfer of antihistamines to the infant via breast milk, particularly the newer, non-sedating antihistamines (Spencer *et al.*, 2001). Diphenhydramine is known to be excreted into the breast milk in small quantities and has been reported to cause irritability or lethargy in infants, though this risk can be reduced by taking the antihistamine shortly after breastfeeding (Spencer *et al.*, 2001).

7.2.10 Electroconvulsive therapy (ECT)

The use of ECT during pregnancy is not well researched, although some complications for mother and fetus have been described, including transient, self-limited disturbances in fetal cardiac rhythm, suspected vaginal bleeding, uterine contractions (although these did not result in premature labour or adverse consequences, severe abdominal pain directly after ECT treatments was reported in pregnant women – though the babies were

---

[14]Not licensed in the UK.

born healthy) and premature labour (Miller, 1995). Five cases of congenital anomalies in offspring prenatally exposed to ECT have been reported, including hypertelorism, optic atrophy, anencephaly, clubbed foot and pulmonary cysts, although these were not considered the direct result of ECT (*ibid.*). The risks of ECT therefore need to be balanced against the risks of using alternative treatments, in consultation with anaesthetist and obstetrician. ECT was cautiously recommended in the NICE Technology Appraisal (NICE, 2003).

7.2.11   Clinical practice recommendations

Antidepressants

7.2.11.1   If a woman taking paroxetine is planning a pregnancy or has an unplanned pregnancy, she should be advised to stop taking the drug.

7.2.11.2   When choosing an antidepressant for pregnant or breastfeeding women, prescribers should, while bearing in mind that the safety of these drugs is not well understood, take into account that:

● TCAs, such as amitriptyline, imipramine and nortriptyline, have lower known risks during pregnancy than other antidepressants

● most TCAs have a higher fatal toxicity index than SSRIs

● fluoxetine is the SSRI with the lowest known risk during pregnancy

● imipramine, nortriptyline and sertraline are present in breast milk at relatively low levels

● citalopram and fluoxetine are present in breast milk at relatively high levels

● SSRIs taken after 20 weeks' gestation may be associated with an increased risk of persistent pulmonary hypertension in the neonate

● paroxetine taken in the first trimester may be associated with fetal heart defects

● venlafaxine may be associated with increased risk of high blood pressure at high doses, higher toxicity in overdose than SSRIs and some TCAs, and increased difficulty in withdrawal

● all antidepressants carry the risk of withdrawal or toxicity in neonates; in most cases the effects are mild and self-limiting.

Benzodiazepines

7.2.11.3   Benzodiazepines should not be routinely prescribed for pregnant women, except for the short-term treatment of extreme anxiety and agitation. This is because of the risks to the fetus (for example, cleft palate) and the neonate (for example, floppy baby syndrome). Consider gradually stopping benzodiazepines in women who are pregnant.

Antipsychotics

7.2.11.4   Women taking antipsychotics who are planning a pregnancy should be told that the raised prolactin levels associated with some antipsychotics (notably amisulpride, risperidone and sulpiride) reduce the chances of conception. If prolactin levels are raised, an alternative drug should be considered.

7.2.11.5   If a pregnant woman is taking clozapine, switching to another drug and careful monitoring should be considered. Clozapine should not be routinely prescribed for women who are pregnant (because of the theoretical risk of agranulocytosis in the fetus) or for women who are breastfeeding (because it reaches high levels in breast milk and there is a risk of agranulocytosis in the infant).

7.2.11.6   When deciding whether to prescribe olanzapine to a woman who is pregnant, risk factors for gestational diabetes and weight gain, including family history, existing weight and ethnicity, should be taken into account.

7.2.11.7   Depot antipsychotics should not be routinely prescribed to pregnant women because there is relatively little information on their safety, and their infants may show extrapyramidal symptoms several months after administration of the depot. These are usually self-limiting.

7.2.11.8   Anticholinergic drugs should not be prescribed for the extrapyramidal side effects of antipsychotic drugs except for acute short-term use. Instead, the dose and timing of the antipsychotic drug should be adjusted, or the drug changed.

Valproate

7.2.11.9   Valproate should not be routinely prescribed to women of child-bearing potential. If there is no effective alternative, the risks of taking valproate during pregnancy, and the importance of using adequate contraception, should be explained.

7.2.11.10 Valproate should not be prescribed to women younger than 18 years because of the risk of polycystic ovary syndrome and increased risk of unplanned pregnancy in this age group.

7.2.11.11 If a woman who is taking valproate is planning a pregnancy, or is pregnant, she should be advised to stop taking the drug. Where appropriate in the treatment of bipolar disorder, an alternative drug (usually an antipsychotic) should be considered.

7.2.11.12 If there is no alternative to valproate, doses should be limited to a maximum of 1 gram per day, administered in divided doses and in the slow release form, with 5 mg/day folic acid. However, it is not clear how the serum level of valproate affects the risk of abnormalities.

Lithium

7.2.11.13 Lithium should not be routinely prescribed for women, particularly in the first trimester of pregnancy (because of the risk of cardiac malformations in the fetus) or during breastfeeding (because of the high levels in breast milk).

7.2.11.14 If a woman taking lithium is planning a pregnancy, and is well and not at high risk of relapse, she should be advised to stop taking the drug because of the risk of cardiac malformations in the fetus.

7.2.11.15 If a woman who is taking lithium becomes pregnant:
- if the pregnancy is confirmed in the first trimester, and the woman is well and not at high risk of relapse, lithium should be stopped gradually over 4 weeks; it should be explained that this may not remove the risk of cardiac defects in the fetus
- if the woman is not well or is at high risk of relapse, the following should be considered:
  - switching gradually to an antipsychotic, or
  - stopping lithium and restarting it in the second trimester if the woman is not planning to breastfeed and her symptoms have responded better to lithium than to other drugs in the past, or
  - continuing with lithium if she is at high risk of relapse.

7.2.11.16 If a woman continues taking lithium during pregnancy, serum lithium levels should be checked every 4 weeks, then weekly from the 36th week, and less than 24 hours after childbirth; the dose should be adjusted to keep serum levels towards the lower end of the therapeutic range, and the woman should maintain adequate fluid intake.

7.2.11.17 Women taking lithium should deliver in hospital, and be monitored during labour by the obstetric team. Monitoring should include fluid balance, because of the risk of dehydration and lithium toxicity (in prolonged labour, it may be appropriate to check serum lithium levels).

Carbamazepine and lamotrigine

7.2.11.18 If a woman who is taking carbamazepine or lamotrigine is planning a pregnancy or has an unplanned pregnancy, healthcare professionals should advise her to stop taking these drugs because of the risk of neural tube defects and other malformations in the fetus. If appropriate an alternative drug (such as an antipsychotic) should be considered.

7.2.11.19 Carbamazepine or lamotrigine should not be routinely prescribed for women who are pregnant because of the lack of evidence of efficacy and the risk of neural tube defects in the fetus.

7.2.11.20 Lamotrigine should not be routinely prescribed for women who are breastfeeding because of the risk of dermatological problems in the infant, such as Stevens–Johnson syndrome.

Electroconvulsive therapy

7.2.11.21 A course of ECT should be considered for pregnant women with severe depression, severe mixed affective states or mania in the context of bipolar disorder, or catatonia, whose physical health or that of the fetus is at serious risk.

Rapid tranquillisation

7.2.11.22 A pregnant woman requiring rapid tranquillisation should be treated according to the NICE clinical guidelines on the short-term management of disturbed/violent behaviour, schizophrenia and bipolar disorder (NICE, 2005d, 2002, 2006), except that:

● she should not be secluded after rapid tranquillisation
● restraint procedures should be adapted to avoid possible harm to the fetus
● when choosing an agent for rapid tranquillisation in a pregnant woman, an antipsychotic or a benzodiazepine with a short half-life should be considered; if an antipsychotic is used, it should be at the minimum effective dose because of neonatal extrapyramidal symptoms; if a benzodiazepine is used, the risks of floppy baby syndrome should be taken into account
● during the perinatal period, the woman's care should be managed in close collaboration with a paediatrician and an anaesthetist.

Sleep problems

7.2.11.23 Pregnant women with a mental disorder who have sleep problems should initially be given general advice about sleep hygiene (including bedtime routines, the avoidance of caffeine, and the reduction of activity before sleep). For women with serious and chronic problems, low-dose chlorpromazine or low-dose amitriptyline may be considered.

Care of the infant

7.2.11.24 If a pregnant woman was taking drugs with known teratogenic risk (lithium, valproate, carbamazepine, lamotrigine and paroxetine) at the time of conception and/or in the first trimester, healthcare professionals should:

● confirm the pregnancy as quickly as possible
● offer appropriate screening and counselling about the continuation of the pregnancy, the need for additional monitoring and the risks to the fetus if the woman continues to take medication
● undertake a full paediatric assessment of the newborn infant
● monitor the infant in the first few weeks after delivery for adverse drug effects, drug toxicity or withdrawal (for example, floppy baby syndrome, irritability, constant crying, shivering, tremor, restlessness, increased tone, feeding and sleeping difficulties and, rarely, seizures); if the mother was prescribed antidepressants in the last trimester, these may result from serotonergic toxicity syndrome rather than withdrawal.

7.2.11.25 Infants of mothers who are breastfeeding whilst taking psychotropic medication should be monitored for adverse reactions.

7.2.12 Research recommendation

Prescription patterns

A study of the General Practice Research Database should be undertaken to assess the impact of pregnancy on changing psychotropic medication (including both switching and stopping medication). Outcomes should include relapse of mental disorders, exacerbation of symptoms, type and duration of treatment, and birth outcomes.

Why this is important
Most women with a mental disorder during pregnancy will be cared for in primary care. Knowing how pregnancy affects the pattern of psychotropic prescription would help to target educational campaigns for healthcare professionals caring for pregnant women.

7.3 THE PHARMACOLOGICAL TREATMENT OF MENTAL DISORDER DURING PREGNANCY AND THE POSTNATAL PERIOD – REVIEW OF AVAILABLE STUDIES

7.3.1 Introduction

Although there is a relatively large amount of literature on the pharmacological treatment of most mental disorders in general adult populations, the number of trials in pregnant or postnatal women is very small, largely because of the ethical issues in studying these populations. However, there is little reason to believe that efficacy data cannot be generalised from broader adult trials, although some caution must be exercised in doing so. Caveats include:

● the evidence that efficacy of some drugs is different in women compared with men (for example, in patients with chronic depression, women respond better to SSRIs than to TCAs, whereas there is some indication that men may respond better to TCAs (NCCMH, 2005). Women also have poorer tolerance to imipramine than men (NICE, 2004a)

● different subgroups of women may be having children (based on age range, fertility and functioning, for example) and factors affecting willingness to take medication at this time may also affect efficacy (for example, insight, motivation and cultural factors)

● women or their illnesses may be susceptible to different treatments at this time due to the unique biopsychosocial environment (for example, hormonal treatments)

● the indications for which medications are prescribed may be different (for example, prevention of risk known to occur at a certain time and prevention of higher than usual level of risk), and the suitability of alternatives may be altered (motivation for engaging in a psychological treatment may be enhanced by parental responsibilities).

This section reviews the trials that have been undertaken in pregnant and postnatal women. They are considered in three sections: the prevention of serious mental disorder (studies that included participants with no specific identified risk factor for the development of future illness), the treatment of depression, the treatment of depression and OCD, and the prophylaxis of severe mental disorder (studies were found for the prophylaxis of bipolar disorder, schizoaffective disorder and depression).

7.3.2   Outcomes

For studies relating to the prevention, treatment or prophylaxis of depression, primary outcomes were the number depressed at endpoint as defined by the study (based on EPDS, HRSD or BDI scores, or on presence of depression according to a diagnostic tool), depression symptoms as measured by appropriate rating scales including the HRSD and EPDS, and leaving the study early for any reason. For studies of the prophylaxis of bipolar disorder, the primary outcome was recurrence.

7.3.3   Evidence search

Databases searched are given in Table 45. Further details of the search strings used are in Appendix 6.

Table 45: Databases searched and inclusion/exclusion criteria for clinical effectiveness of pharmacological treatments

Electronic databases	MEDLINE, EMBASE, PsycINFO
Date searched	Database inception to December 2004
Update searches	January 2006; May 2006; September 2006
Study design	RCT
Patient population	Pregnant women and women up to 1 year postnatally with severe mental disorder including depression
Treatments	Any pharmacological treatment for the prevention, treatment or prophylaxis of severe mental disorder
Outcomes	See 7.3.2

7.3.4   Pharmacological treatments for the prevention of severe mental disorder for women with no specific risk factors for illness

Four studies met inclusion criteria, all aiming to prevent depression in women in whom no specific risk factors for depression were identified. One was of treatment with calcium, one with omega-3 and two with hormones. Excluded studies with reasons for exclusion can be seen in Appendix 18. Important characteristics of the included studies are in Table 46, with fuller details of studies in Appendix 18.

A summary of the evidence profile is in Table 47, with the full profile in Appendix 19.

Table 46: Summary of characteristics for pharmacological studies of prevention of depression (no risk factors)

	Calcium	Docosahexaenoic acid (omega-3)	Thyroxine	Norethisterone
No. trials (no. participants)	1 RCT (374)	1 RCT (138)	1 RCT (446)	1 RCT (180)
Study IDs	HARRISONHOHNER 2001[15]	LLORENTE 2003	HARRIS 2002	LAWRIE 1998
Mean age	22	31	29	32
Timing of treatment	Antenatal 11 to 21 weeks to delivery	Immediate/early postnatal	Postnatal 6 weeks to 6 months	Immediate postnatal (first few days)
Treatment	Calcium 2,000 mg versus placebo	Docosahexaenoic acid 200 mg versus placebo	Thyroxine 100 µg versus placebo	Norethisterone enanthate 200 mg versus placebo
Outcomes	6 and 12 weeks postnatally	3 weeks, 2 months, 4 months postnatally	12, 16, 20, 24 weeks postnatally	6 and 12 weeks postnatally

[15]Reviewed studies, which are referred to by a study identifier consisting of a primary author in captial letters and date of study publication.

Table 47: Summary evidence profile for pharmacological studies for the prevention of depression (no risk factors)

	Calcium	Docosahexaenoic acid	Thyroxine	Norethisterone
Study IDs	HARRISONHOHNER 2001	LLORENTE2003	HARRIS2002	LAWRIE1998
Overall quality of evidence	Moderate	Moderate	Low	Moderate
Depression above threshold, first measure	6 weeks postnatally RR = 0.72 (0.45, 1.16) (K = 1; n = 374) RMpprev 01.01	4 weeks postnatally WMD = 1 (−1.72, 3.72) (K = 1; n = 89) RMpprev 02.02	RR = 0.81 (0.48, 1.38) (K = 1; n = 341) RMpprev 03.02	6-week follow-up RR = 1.74 (1.08, 2.81) (K = 1; n = 163) RMpprev 04.04
Depression above threshold, second measure	12 weeks postnatally RR = 0.37 (0.16, 0.85) (K = 1; n = 247) RMpprev 01.02	18 months postnatally WMD = 0 (−2.32, 2.32) (K = 1; n = 63) RMpprev 02.03	N/A	3-month follow-up RR = 0.97 (0.6, 1.58) (K = 1; n = 168) RMpprev 04.04
Depression scores at first measure	6 weeks postnatally WMD = −0.9 (−2.05, 0.25) (K = 1; n = 247) RMpprev 01.03	WMD = 1 (−1.72, 3.72) (K = 1; n = 89) RMpprev 02.02	N/A	6-week follow-up RR = 3.4 (0.72, 6.08) (K = 1; n = 163) RMpprev 04.02

Depression scores at second measure	6 weeks postnatally WMD = − 0.9 (−2.05, 0.25) (K = 1; n = 247) RMpprev 01.03	WMD = 1 (−1.72, 3.72) (K = 1; n = 89) RMpprev 02.02	N/A	3-month follow-up RR = 0.5 (−2.14, 3.14) (K = 1; n = 168) RMpprev 04.02
% attrition rate, treatment group versus standard care	N/A	26% versus 28% (K = 1; n = 138) RMpprev 02.01	22% versus 25% (n not compliant) (K = 1; n = 446) RMpprev 03.01	6-week follow-up 4% versus 14% (K = 1; n = 180) 3-month follow-up 3% versus 10% (K = 1; n = 180) RMpprev 04.01

Notes: RR = relative risk (95% CI); K = number of trials contributing to the summary statistic; n = number of participants; N/A = not available; '*RMpprev* nn.nn' refers to the relevant forest plot in Appendix 20

(The studies were analysed in Review Manager file *APMH Pharmacological Interventions – Prevention (No Risk Factors and Risk Factors Present)* (RMpprev).)

The studies showed some effectiveness for calcium on postnatal EPDS scores, although no outcome other than the EPDS was available. However, there was no difference between docosahexaenoic acid and placebo or between thyroxine and placebo on any outcome measure. There was no effect for norethisterone on depression; indeed, at 6 weeks, placebo was more effective with regard to minor depression, although this effect was not sustained at 12-week follow-up, where there was no difference between treatment and placebo. There was no effect on major depression.

Given that only a single study met inclusion criteria for each treatment, there is insufficient evidence on which to recommend the preventative treatment of women with these agents.

7.3.5   Physical treatments for depression in the postnatal period

Eight studies met inclusion criteria. These included four uncontrolled studies. Excluded studies with reasons for exclusion can be seen in Appendix 18. Important characteristics of the included studies are in Table 48, with fuller details of studies in Appendix 18.

Evidence for the treatment of depression in the postnatal period
Summaries of the evidence profiles for physical treatments for depression in the postnatal period are in Table 49 and Table 50, with the full profile in Appendix 19.

Evidence from uncontrolled studies
Evidence from uncontrolled studies was also considered:

Bright light therapy – OREN2002 cohort study (n = 18). This small study found that half of participants completing 3 weeks' treatment had a 50% reduction in depression scores. This compares with 60% of those in the RCT in this area (EPPERSON2004), which also found a 60% reduction in the control group. Seven participants completed 5 weeks' therapy, four of whom experienced a 50% reduction in symptoms.

Omega-3 fatty acids – FREEMAN2006 uncontrolled, open-label study of omega-3 fatty acids: eicosapentaenoic acid and docosahexaenoic acid (n = 15). EPDS scores were reduced at endpoint by an average of 40.9% (SD 21.9) and HRSD scores were reduced at endpoint by an average of 34.1% (SD 27.1). The only side effect reported was a slight increase in burping after tablet ingestion.

Venlafaxine – COHEN2001 uncontrolled open-label study (n = 19). At endpoint, 12 of the 15 (63% of original number) completing the trial had remitted (HRSD, 7). This compares with 50% in the trial of paroxetine-only arm of the MISRI2004 RCT. There were some reports of side effects, including sweating (n = 7), dry mouth (n = 6) and nausea (n = 6).

Table 48: Summary of characteristics for studies of physical treatments of depression in the postnatal period

	Light therapy	Oestrogen	Antidepressants
No. trials (no. participants)	1 RCT (10), 1 uncontrolled open study (18)	1 RCT (64)	3 RCTs (232), 3 uncontrolled open studies (56)
Study IDs	(1) EPPERSON2004 (2) OREN2002	GREGOIRE1996	(1) APPLEBY1997 (2) COHEN2001 (3) NONACS2005 (4) MISRI2004 (5) STOWE1995 (6) WISNER2006
Study design	(1) RCT (2) Cohort study	RCT	(1) (4) (6) RCT (2) (3) (5) Uncontrolled open study
Baseline depression scores	(1) SIGH-SAD scores mean (SD): treatment group: 27.6 (5.6); placebo group: 28.6 (8.7) (2) None reported; graph shows mean SIGH-SAD score for group approximately 35 (no indication of SD, SE, etc)	EPDS mean (SD): Treatment group: 21.8 (3); placebo group: 21.3 (2.9) SADS mean (SD): treatment group: 66.3 (11.4); placebo group: 64.3 (10.7)	(1) Not reported (2) Mean (SD): HRSD (17-item) = 26.13 (5.15); Kellner anxiety subscale 18.8 (3.8); CGI score 4.6 (0.6) (3) HRSD (17-item) median (range): 20.5 (15–38) Kellner depression median (range): 17.5 (11–33); Kellner anxiety median (range): 15 (3–22) CGI median (range): 4 (3–6); 37% in first depressive episode (4) Paroxetine only, paroxetine + CBT (mean [SD]): HRSD 22.06 (3.38), 21.16 (2.03); HRSA 20.31 (6.58), 21.32 (8.22); EPDS 18.15 (6.45), 18.87 (4.42) (5) Not reported (6) Not reported

Continued

221

Table 48: (*Continued*)

	Light therapy	Oestrogen	Antidepressants
Treatments	(1) Bright light (7,000 lux) 60 mins daily versus placebo (500 lux) (2) Bright light 10,000 lux 60 mins daily	Oestradiol patches, mean dose 200 mcg	(1) Fluoxetine or placebo + counselling (6 or 1 session[s]) (2) Venlafaxine mean dose 162.5 mg (3) Bupropion SR 150 mg–400 mg (4) Paroxetine versus paroxetine + CBT (5) Sertraline mean dose 108 mg (6) Sertraline 50 mg versus nortriptyline 25 mg
Mean age (or range if not given)	32	31	22 (6) not reported
Study length	(1) 5 weeks (2) 2 weeks	26 weeks	(1) Average 13 weeks (2) 8 weeks (3) 8 weeks (4) 12 weeks (5) 8 weeks (6) 8 weeks + 4-month continuation phase

Table 49: Summary evidence profile for studies of light therapy and oestrogen in the treatment of depression in the postnatal period

	Light therapy	Oestrogen
Study IDs	EPPERSON2004	GREGOIRE1996
Overall quality of evidence	Low	Moderate
Depression above threshold at endpoint	RR = 1 (0.36, 2.75) (K = 1; n = 10) RMptreat 01.01	RR = 0.47 (0.3, 0.74) (K = 1; n = 64) RMptreat 02.03
Depression symptoms at endpoint	N/A	WMD = − 5.75 (−8.66, −2.84) (K = 1; n = 45) RMptreat 02.02
Anxiety symptoms at endpoint	N/A	N/A
% attrition rate, treatment group versus standard care	0% versus 40% (K = 1; n = 10) RMptreat 01.02	22% versus 39% (K = 1; n = 64) RMptreat 02.00
% attrition rate due to side effects, treatment group versus standard care	N/A	N/A
% side effects treatment group versus standard care	N/A	N/A

Notes: RR = relative risk (95% CI); K = number of trials contributing to the summary statistic; n = number of participants; N/A = not available; '*RMptreat* nn.nn' and '*RMpprev* nn.nn' refer to the relevant forest plot in Appendix 20

Buproprion – NONACS2005 uncontrolled open-label study (n = 11). At endpoint, 75% of participants had achieved a 50% reduction on depression scores, with 3 remitting.

Sertraline – STOWE1995 uncontrolled open-label study (n = 26). At endpoint, 76% of participants had achieved a 50% reduction on depression scores, with 14 remitting. There were reports of side effects including gastrointestinal upset (n = 4), decreased appetite (n = 4), night sweats (n = 3) and diarrhoea (n = 3).

Clinical summary
The studies were analysed in Review Manager file *APMH Pharmacological Interventions – Prevention (No Risk Factors and Risk Factors Present* [RMpprev] and *APMH Pharmacological Interventions – Treatment* [RMptreat].

Table 50: Summary evidence profile for studies of antidepressants in the treatment of depression in the postnatal period

	Fluoxetine versus placebo (both with six sessions of counselling)	Fluoxetine versus placebo (both with one session of counselling)	Paroxetine versus paroxetine + CBT	Sertraline versus nortriptyline
Study IDs	APPLEBY1997	APPLEBY1997	MISRI2004	WISNER2006
Overall quality of evidence	Low	Low	Low	Low
Depression above threshold at endpoint	N/A	N/A	N/A	RR = 1.05 (0.74, 1.5) (K = 1; n = 109) (RMptreat 06.03)
Depression symptoms at endpoint	WMD = 0.2 (−5.53, 5.93) (K = 1; n = 42) RMptreat 04.01	WMD = −3.7 (−7.67, 0.27) (K = 1; n = 45) RMptreat 05.01	WMD = −1.5 (−5.31, 2.31) (K = 1; n = 35) RMpprev 03.01	WMD = 0.2 (−2.34, 2.74) (K = 1; n = 83) RMptreat 06.04
Depression above threshold at end of continuation phase	N/A	N/A	N/A	RR = 1.24 (0.34, 4.6) (K = 1; n = 29) RMptreat 06.06
Depression symptoms at end of continuation phase	N/A	N/A	N/A	WMD = 1.1 (−2.79, 4.99) (K = 1; n = 29) RMptreat 06.05

224

Anxiety symptoms at endpoint	N/A	N/A	WMD = −0.62 (−5.08, 3.84) (K = 1; n = 35) RMpprev 03.02	N/A
% attrition rate, treatment group versus standard care	N/A	N/A	N/A	42% versus 24%
% attrition rate due to side effects, treatment group versus standard care	38% versus 29% (K = 1; n = 42) RMptreat 04.02	27% versus 26% (K = 1; n = 45) RMptreat 05.02	N/A	N/A
% side effects, treatment group versus standard care	5% versus 5% (K = 1; n = 42) RMptreat 04.02	0% versus 9% (K = 1; n = 45) RMptreat 05.02	N/A	N/A

Notes: RR = relative risk (95% CI); K = number of trials contributing to the summary statistic; n = number of participants; N/A = not available; 'RMptreat *nn.nn*' refers to the relevant forest plot in Appendix 20

There was no evidence for the efficacy of bright light therapy in the treatment of depression compared with placebo, although the randomised controlled study (EPPERSON2004) is very small (n = 10). There was no additional convincing evidence from the uncontrolled study (OREN2002).

One study of oestrogen found some evidence in favour of treatment compared with placebo for depression.

There is some evidence of the efficacy of antidepressants in the treatment of depression in the postnatal period, particularly fluoxetine (with a single session of counselling) (although fluoxetine with six sessions of counselling was only as effective as the counselling sessions alone), and some evidence from uncontrolled trials. There was no evidence of superior efficacy of sertraline over nortriptyline although fewer participants taking the TCA left treatment early. Although both the number of trials and number of participants is low, the findings are similar to those from research of treatment in non-postnatal populations (NCCMH, 2005). The suitability of treatment with antidepressants depends on a consideration of the risks to infants if the mother is breastfeeding.

7.3.6 Pharmacological treatments for depression and OCD

A single uncontrolled open study met inclusion criteria. Important characteristics of the included studies are in Table 51, with fuller details of studies in Appendix 18.

Evidence for the treatment of depression and OCD in the postnatal period
There was no controlled evidence for the treatment of depression and OCD.

Table 51: Summary study characteristics for treatment of depression plus OCD in the postnatal period

	Antipsychotics
No. trials (no. participants)	1
Study IDs	MISRI2004B
Study design	Uncontrolled open study
Disorder	Depression + OCD
Treatments	Quetiapine (mean dose 112.5 mg) added to existing antidepressants (participants treatment resistant to antidepressants)
Mean age (or range if not given)	33
Study length	12 weeks

Adjunctive quetiapine – MISRI2004B uncontrolled open-label study (n = 17). At endpoint, 78.6% had at least a 50% reduction in OCD symptom scores, although there were some side effects, including sedation (n = 5), grogginess (n = 3), fatigue (n = 3) and dizziness (n = 2).

7.3.7　Pharmacological treatments for the prophylaxis of severe mental disorder

Seven studies were reviewed, including two RCTs, two cohort studies, two non-randomised controlled studies and a case study. Populations included those with diagnoses of bipolar disorder, schizoaffective disorder and depression. Excluded studies with reasons for exclusion can be seen in Appendix 18. Important characteristics of the included studies are in Tables 51 to 54 inclusive, with fuller details of studies in Appendix 18.

Prophylaxis of bipolar disorder

Two studies were found for the prophylaxis of bipolar disorder, one a cohort study and one a controlled study. Summary study characteristics are in Table 52.

Table 52:　Summary of characteristics for pharmacological studies of prophylaxis of bipolar disorder

	Bipolar disorder
No. trials (no. participants)	1 cohort study (33), 1 controlled study
Study IDs	(1) COHEN1995 (2) WISNER2004A
Study design	(1) Cohort study (2) Non-randomised controlled study
Timing of treatment	Immediate/early postnatal
Treatments	(1) Antimanic medication (lithium; carbamazepine; lithium + carbamazepine; lithium + an antidepressant [unspecified]) versus standard care (2) Divalproex versus monitoring alone
Mean age (or range if not given)	33
Study length	(1) 3 months (2) 4 months

Evidence profile for the prophylaxis of bipolar disorder
A summary of the evidence profile for the prophylaxis of bipolar disorder is in Table 53, with the full profile in Appendix 19.

There is some evidence that providing prophylactic medication (lithium, carbamazepine or a combination) helps to reduce relapse in the postnatal period in women with bipolar disorder. However, the quality of the evidence is low.

Prophylaxis of schizoaffective disorder

A single case study describing the prophylaxis of schizoaffective disorder was found. Study characteristics are in Table 54.

No study of the prophylaxis of schizoaffective disorder could be found other than a case study (MALEK2001). This showed that a patient who continued on medication (antipsychotics) delivered healthy children and remained well. A brief period without

Table 53: Summary evidence profile for pharmacological studies for the prophylaxis of bipolar disorder

	Divalproex	**Antimanic medication**
Study IDs	WISNER2004A	COHEN1995
Overall quality of evidence	Low	Low
Recurrence – all episodes	RR = 0.92 (0.44, 1.91) 22% versus 24% (K = 3; n = 78) RMpproph 03.01	RR = 0.12 (0.02, 0.81) 7% versus 62% (K = 1; n = 27) RMpproph 04.01
Recurrence – hypomania/mania	RR = 0.73 (0.05, 10.49) 7% versus 9% (K = 1; n = 26) RMpproph 03.01	N/A
Recurrence – mixed states	RR = 0.37 (0.04, 3.55) 7% versus 18% (K = 1; n = 26) RMpproph 03.01	N/A
Recurrence – depression	RR = 1.17 (0.53, 2.62) 53% versus 45% (K = 1; n = 26) RMpproph 03.01	N/A

Notes: RR = relative risk (95% CI); K = number of trials contributing to the summary statistic; n = number of participants; N/A = not available; '*RMpproph* nn.nn' refers to the relevant forest plot in Appendix 20

Table 54: Summary characteristics for studies of the prophylaxis of schizoaffective disorder

	Schizoaffective disorder
No. trials (no. participants)	1 case study
Study IDs	MALEK2001
Study design	Case study
Timing of treatment	Antenatal
Treatments	Psychotropic medication
Age/gender	21 years/female

medication during the early stages of her first pregnancy resulted in relapse. Symptoms remitted when pharmacotherapy was restarted.

Prophylaxis of depression

Two RCTs and two controlled trials were found for the prophylaxis of depression in women with a history of depressive episodes. Three studies compared providing an antidepressant with placebo in women with a history of depression, and the fourth study examined women currently taking antidepressant medication and compared relapse rates in those who increased, maintained, decreased or stopped medication. Summary study characteristics are in Table 55.

Evidence profile for the prophylaxis of depression
A summary of the evidence profile for antidepressants versus placebo is in Table 56, the summary evidence profile for changing the medication schedule is in Table 57 and the full profiles are in Appendix 19.

The studies were analysed in Review Manager file *APMH Pharmacological Interventions – Prevention (No Risk Factors and Risk Factors Present)* (RMpprev) and *APMH Pharmacological Interventions – Prophylaxis* (RMpproph).

All studies included women with a history of depression, which is a strong predictor of future illness (see Chapter 4). WISNER2001 and WISNER2004 gave prophylactic antidepressants to women with a history of depression on delivery of another infant. They found that, while nortriptyline was not effective in reducing recurrence, sertraline was, although it should be noted that the recurrence rate in the placebo groups in the two trials was markedly different (24% in WISNER2001 and 50% in WISNER2004). The authors account for this by citing research showing that the placebo response is increasing across time (Walsh *et al.*, 2002.) However, given the relatively short time period between the two studies, there may be other explanations for this finding.

Table 55: Summary of characteristics for pharmacological studies of prophylaxis of depression

	Nortriptyline	Various antidepressants	Sertraline	Maintaining, increasing, decreasing or discontinuing medication
No. trials (no. participants)	1 RCT (56)	1 controlled trial (23)	1 RCT (446)	1 non-randomised controlled study (n = 201)
Study IDs	WISNER2001	WISNER1994	WISNER2004	COHEN2006
Mean age (or range if not given)	Not given	Not given	32	34
Timing of treatment	Immediate/early postnatal	Immediate/early postnatal	Immediate/early postnatal	Antenatal
Clinical history	≥1 previous episode of MDD	Recurrent depression	≥1 previous episode of MDD	History of major depression
Treatment	Nortriptyline mean dose 83 mg/ml versus placebo	Antidepressants (clomipramine, fluoxetine, nortriptyline, imipramine based on previous response) versus placebo	Sertraline mean 75 mg versus placebo	Maintaining medication; decreasing medication; increasing medication; discontinuing medication (medication = various antidepressants)
Length of study	Up to 7-month follow-up	Up to 3-month follow-up	Up to 3-month follow-up	12 weeks

Table 56: Summary evidence profile for pharmacological studies for the prophylaxis of depression (antidepressants versus placebo)

	Nortriptyline	Various antidepressants	Sertraline
Study IDs	WISNER2001	WISNER1994	WISNER2004
Overall quality of evidence	Low	Moderate	Low
Depression above threshold, first measure	17 weeks postnatally RR = 0.96 (0.36, 2.59) (K = 1; n = 51) RMpprev 05.02	Up to 3 months postnatally RR = 0.11 (0.01, 0.76) (K = 1; n = 23) RMpprev 06.01	RR = 0.14 (0.02, 1.07) (K = 1; n = 22) RMpprev 07.02
Depression above threshold, second measure	7-month follow-up RR = 1.2 (0.57, 2.55) (K = 1; n = 51) RMpprev 05.03	N/A	RR = 2.22 (0.14, 36.49) (K = 1; n = 11) RMpprev 07.03
% attrition rate, treatment group versus standard care	14% versus 19% (K = 1; n = 56) RMpprev 05.01	N/A	47% versus 13% (K = 1; n = 25) RMpprev 07.01
% attrition rate due to side effects, treatment group versus standard care	0% versus 4% (K = 1; n = 51) RMpprev 05.04	N/A	N/A
% side effects, treatment group versus standard care	N/A	N/A	Dizziness 57% versus 13% Drowsiness 100% versus 50% (K = 1; n = 22) RMpprev 07.04

Notes: RR = relative risk (95% CI); K = number of trials contributing to the summary statistic; n = number of participants; N/A = not available; 'RMpprev nn.nn' refers to the relevant forest plot in Appendix 20

Table 57: Summary evidence profile for pharmacological studies for the prophylaxis of depression (changing medication schedule)

	Maintaining medication versus decreasing medication	Maintaining medication versus discontinuing medication
Study IDs	COHEN2006	COHEN2006
Overall quality of evidence	Low	Low
Relapse	RR = 0.73 (0.4, 1.3) 26% versus 35% (K = 1; n = 116) RMpproph 01.01	RR = 0.38 (0.25, 0.57) 26% versus 68% (K = 1; n = 147) RMpproph 02.01

Notes: RR = relative risk (95% CI); K = number of trials contributing to the summary statistic; n = number of participants; N/A = not available; '*RMpproph* nn.nn' refers to the relevant forest plot in Appendix 20

The WISNER1994 study also shows a protective effect for antidepressants, although this was a patient preference trial rather than an RCT. However, women with a history of depression who choose to take an antidepressant in the immediate postnatal period may reduce future symptoms, although the decision should be weighed against the possible risks to the infant of antidepressant medication during breastfeeding.

There is also some evidence, for women taking medication, that maintaining rather than discontinuing medication reduces relapse. Similarly, for women with bipolar disorder, there is some evidence of the efficacy of maintaining medication throughout pregnancy. However, the decision to maintain medication must be weighed against the risks of medication to the developing fetus.

7.4   PRESCRIBING PSYCHOTROPIC MEDICATION TO PREGNANT AND BREASTFEEDING WOMEN

The use of psychotropic medication during pregnancy should be influenced by the stage of pregnancy in which medication is being prescribed. Some drugs have specific problems only during early pregnancy, while others may be harmful later or during breastfeeding. When determining the appropriate pharmacological treatment of women with mental health problems during pregnancy and the postnatal period, two major decisions are faced by clinicians: what medication to initiate in an unmedicated unwell woman and what changes to an existing treatment regime may be required. This can present considerable challenges, for example, the requirement to consider changing a currently effective treatment regime because of concerns about potential harm to the fetus.

The circumstances in which dilemmas about use of medication arise include:

- planning pregnancy in women taking medication for an existing disorder
- unplanned pregnancy in women taking medication for an existing disorder or with a history of mental disorder
- a new illness episode in women who are pregnant
- the intrapartum period in women taking medication or at high risk of relapse during this time
- breastfeeding.

7.4.1   PRESCRIBING PSYCHOTROPIC MEDICATION TO WOMEN OF CHILD-BEARING POTENTIAL

As can be seen above, some drugs have a high teratogenic risk during the first trimester of pregnancy, notably valproate, which is particularly risky during the first 28 days of pregnancy. Given that in many cases pregnancy may not be confirmed until it is relatively well advanced, it is important that women of child-bearing potential are given information about the risks of psychotropic medication on any future pregnancy and of the risks of untreated illness, together with appropriate information about contraception. Women should be encouraged to discuss pregnancy plans with their doctor. This means that appropriate alternative treatment can be discussed in advance.

Despite such provisions, many women have unplanned pregnancies. In these cases, it is important to establish the risk of harm to the fetus of any medication the mother is taking, together with the possible risks to the mother of the pregnancy.

7.4.2   Principles guiding the use of psychotropic medication during pregnancy and breastfeeding

A number of principles should guide the practice of clinicians treating women with psychotropic medication who are considering pregnancy, are pregnant or are in the postnatal period:

a) The individual woman's views, wishes, fears and priorities are key factors in decisions about treatment.
b) The woman's history of previous treatment response should help guide future treatment decisions.
c) The lowest effective dose should be used and an appropriate time allowed for response before titrating the dose up. This is particularly important where identified risks are potentially dose-related.
d) Monotherapy should be used in preference to combination treatment.
e) Drug interactions with non-psychotropic drugs used at this time should be considered.
f) The balance of risks and benefits of pharmacological treatment during pregnancy (particularly in the first trimester) may favour the prompt provision of a psychological treatment instead.

g) Changes in medication may be considered to reduce the risk of harm but the risks should be balanced against the disadvantages of switching.

h) Drugs with the greatest evidence of safety for mother and fetus/infant should be considered first.

i) Wherever possible, suitable treatment options should be found for women who wish to breastfeed rather than recommending avoidance of breastfeeding.

j) The most effective means of discussing risk and benefit with patients, partners and families should be adopted, coupled with skilled negotiation of care plans.

7.4.3 Clinical practice recommendations

7.4.3.1 Women requiring psychological treatment should be seen for treatment normally within 1 month of initial assessment, and no longer than 3 months afterwards. This is because of the lower threshold for access to psychological therapies during pregnancy and the postnatal period arising from the changing risk–benefit ratio for psychotropic medication at this time.

7.4.3.2 Discussions about treatment options with a woman with a mental disorder who is planning a pregnancy, pregnant or breastfeeding should cover:
- the risk of relapse or deterioration in symptoms and the woman's ability to cope with untreated or subthreshold symptoms
- severity of previous episodes, response to treatment and the woman's preference
- the possibility that stopping a drug with known teratogenic risk after pregnancy is confirmed may not remove the risk of malformations
- the risks from stopping medication abruptly
- the need for prompt treatment because of the potential impact of an untreated mental disorder on the fetus or infant
- the increased risk of harm associated with drug treatments during pregnancy and the postnatal period, including the risk in overdose
- treatment options that would enable the woman to breastfeed if she wishes, rather than recommending she does not breastfeed.

7.4.3.3 When prescribing a drug for a woman with a mental disorder who is planning a pregnancy, pregnant or breastfeeding, prescribers should:
- choose drugs with lower risk profiles for the mother and the fetus or infant
- start at the lowest effective dose, and slowly increase it; this is particularly important where the risks may be dose related
- use monotherapy in preference to combination treatment
- consider additional precautions for preterm, low birthweight or sick infants.

7.4.3.4 When stopping a drug in a woman with a mental disorder who is planning a pregnancy, pregnant or breastfeeding, take into account:
- NICE guidance on the specific disorder (see NICE, 2002, 2004a, 2004b, 2004c, 2005a, 2005c, 2006)

- the risk to the fetus or infant during the withdrawal period
- the risk from not treating the disorder.

7.4.3.5　Healthcare professionals should discuss contraception and the risks of pregnancy (including relapse, risk to the fetus and risks associated with stopping or changing medication) with all women of child-bearing potential who have an existing mental disorder and/or who are taking psychotropic medication. Such women should be encouraged to discuss pregnancy plans with their doctor.

7.5　THE PHARMACOLOGICAL TREATMENT OF SPECIFIC MENTAL DISORDERS DURING PREGNANCY AND THE POSTNATAL PERIOD – ADAPTATION OF EXISTING GUIDELINES

7.5.1　Introduction

The course of mental illness during pregnancy is generally no different to that at other times, although the postnatal period carries increased risk of relapse for women with some disorders, particularly bipolar disorder. However, the pharmacological treatment of most disorders carries some risk to the fetus in terms of teratogenicity. NICE guidelines have been published on several mental disorders, including schizophrenia, depression, bipolar disorder, OCD and PTSD. This section considers how guidance from existing NICE guidelines may be modified for women during pregnancy and the postnatal period based on the considerations above.

7.5.2　Clinical practice recommendations

Depression

　Women being treated for depression who are planning a pregnancy or have an unplanned pregnancy

7.5.2.1　If a woman being treated for mild depression is taking an antidepressant, the medication should be withdrawn gradually and monitoring ('watchful waiting') considered. If intervention is then needed the following should be considered:
- self-help approaches (guided self-help, C-CBT, exercise) or
- brief psychological treatments (including counselling, CBT and IPT).

7.5.2.2　If a woman is taking an antidepressant and her latest presentation was a moderate depressive episode, the following options should be discussed with the woman, taking into account previous response to treatment, her preference, and risk:
- switching to psychological therapy (CBT or IPT)
- switching to an antidepressant with lower risk.

7.5.2.3   If a woman is taking an antidepressant and her latest presentation was a severe depressive episode, the following options should be discussed with the woman, taking into account previous response to treatment, her preference, and risk:
- combining drug treatment with psychological treatment, but switching to an antidepressant with lower risk
- switching to psychological treatment (CBT or IPT).

Pregnant or breastfeeding women who have a new episode of depression

7.5.2.4   For a woman who develops mild or moderate depression during pregnancy or the postnatal period, the following should be considered:
- self-help strategies (guided self-help, C-CBT or exercise)
- non-directive counselling delivered at home (listening visits)
- brief CBT or IPT.

7.5.2.5   Antidepressant drugs should be considered for women with mild depression during pregnancy or the postnatal period if they have a history of severe depression and they decline, or their symptoms do not respond to, psychological treatments.

7.5.2.6   For a woman with a moderate depressive episode and a history of depression, or with a severe depressive episode during pregnancy or the postnatal period, the following should be considered:
- structured psychological treatment specifically for depression (CBT or IPT)
- antidepressant treatment if the woman has expressed a preference for it
- combination treatment if there is no response, or a limited response to psychological or drug treatment alone, provided the woman understands the risks associated with antidepressant medication.

Treatment-resistant depression

7.5.2.7   For pregnant women with treatment-resistant depression, a trial of a different single drug or ECT should be considered before combination drug treatment. Lithium augmentation should be avoided.

Generalised anxiety disorder

This section should be read in conjunction with the NICE clinical guideline on the management of anxiety in primary, secondary and community care (NICE, 2004c).

Women with GAD who are planning a pregnancy or pregnant

7.5.2.8   If a woman is planning a pregnancy or becomes pregnant while being treated with medication for GAD, the following should be considered:
- stopping medication and starting CBT if it has not already been tried
- if necessary, switching to a safer drug, if the decision is to maintain medication.

Women who have a new episode of GAD

7.5.2.9   A woman who has a new episode of GAD during pregnancy should be treated according to the NICE guideline on anxiety, and CBT should be offered.

Panic disorder

This section should be read in conjunction with the NICE clinical guideline on the management of anxiety in primary, secondary and community care (NICE, 2004c).

Women with panic disorder who are planning a pregnancy or pregnant

7.5.2.10   If a woman is planning a pregnancy or becomes pregnant while being treated for panic disorder, the following should be considered:
● stopping medication and starting CBT if it has not already been tried
● if necessary, switching to a safer drug, if the decision is to maintain medication.

Women who have a new episode of panic disorder

7.5.2.11   For women who have a new episode of panic disorder during pregnancy, psychological therapy (CBT), self-help or C-CBT should be considered before starting drug treatment.

7.5.2.12   For women who have a new episode of panic disorder during pregnancy, paroxetine should not be started and a safer drug should be considered.

Obsessive–compulsive disorder

This section should be read in conjunction with the NICE clinical guideline on the treatment and management of OCD (see NICE, 2005c).

Women with OCD who are planning a pregnancy or pregnant

7.5.2.13   A woman with OCD who is planning a pregnancy or pregnant should be treated according to the NICE clinical guideline on OCD except that:
● if she is taking medication alone, stopping the drug and starting psychological therapy should be considered
● if she is not taking medication, starting psychological therapy should be considered before drug treatment
● if she is taking paroxetine, it should be stopped and switching to a safer antidepressant considered.

7.5.2.14   A pregnant woman with OCD who is planning to breastfeed should be treated according to the NICE clinical guideline on OCD, except that the use of a combination of clomipramine and citalopram should be avoided if possible.

Women who have a new episode of OCD while breastfeeding

7.5.2.15   A woman who has a new episode of OCD while breastfeeding should be treated according to the NICE clinical guideline on OCD, except that the combination of clomipramine and citalopram should be avoided because of the high levels in breast milk.

Post-traumatic stress disorder

This section should be read in conjunction with the NICE clinical guideline on the management of PTSD (see NICE, 2005a).

Women with PTSD who are planning a pregnancy or pregnant

7.5.2.16   A woman with PTSD who is planning a pregnancy or pregnant should be treated according to the NICE clinical guideline on PTSD, except that if she is taking an antidepressant the drug should be stopped and trauma-focused psychological therapy (for example, CBT or eye movement desensitisation and reprocessing therapy) offered.

7.5.2.17   For a woman with PTSD who is planning a pregnancy or pregnant, adjunctive olanzapine should not be prescribed.

Eating disorders

This section should be read in conjunction with the NICE clinical guideline on the treatment and management of eating disorders (NICE, 2004b).

Women with anorexia nervosa

7.5.2.18   A woman with anorexia nervosa who is planning a pregnancy, has an unplanned pregnancy or is breastfeeding should be treated according to the NICE clinical guideline on eating disorders.

Women with binge eating disorder

7.5.2.19   A woman with binge eating disorder who is taking an antidepressant and is planning a pregnancy, has an unplanned pregnancy or is breastfeeding should be treated according to the section on depression in this guideline (recommendations 7.5.2.1–7.5.2.7).

Women with bulimia nervosa

7.5.2.20   If a woman who is taking medication for bulimia nervosa is planning a pregnancy or pregnant, healthcare professionals should consider gradually stopping the medication after discussion with her. If the problem persists, referral for specialist treatment should be considered.

Women who have an episode of bulimia nervosa while breastfeeding

7.5.2.21   If a woman has an episode of bulimia nervosa while breastfeeding, psychological treatment should be offered, rather than fluoxetine at 60 mg. If a woman is already taking fluoxetine at 60 mg, she should be advised not to breastfeed.

Bipolar disorder

These recommendations are from the NICE clinical guideline on the management of bipolar disorder (NICE, 2006).

Pregnant women with bipolar disorder who are stable on an antipsychotic

7.5.2.22   If a pregnant woman with bipolar disorder is stable on an antipsychotic and likely to relapse without medication, she should be maintained on the antipsychotic, and monitored for weight gain and diabetes.

Women with bipolar disorder planning a pregnancy

7.5.2.23   If a woman who needs antimanic medication plans to become pregnant, a low-dose typical or atypical antipsychotic should be the treatment of choice.

7.5.2.24   If a woman with bipolar disorder planning a pregnancy becomes depressed after stopping prophylactic medication, psychological therapy (CBT) should be offered in preference to an antidepressant because of the risk of switching to mania associated with antidepressants. If an antidepressant is used, it should usually be an SSRI (but not paroxetine) and the woman should be monitored closely.

Women with bipolar disorder who have an unplanned pregnancy

7.5.2.25   If a woman with bipolar disorder has an unplanned pregnancy and is stopping lithium as prophylactic medication, an antipsychotic should be offered.

Pregnant women with acute mania or depressive symptoms

  Acute mania

7.5.2.26   If a pregnant woman who is not taking medication develops acute mania, a typical or an atypical antipsychotic should be considered. The dose should be kept as low as possible and the woman monitored carefully.

7.5.2.27   If a pregnant woman develops acute mania while taking prophylactic medication, prescribers should:
  ● check the dose of the prophylactic agent and adherence
  ● increase the dose if the woman is taking an antipsychotic, or consider changing to an antipsychotic if she is not
  ● if there is no response to changes in dose or drug and the patient has severe mania, consider the use of ECT, lithium and, rarely, valproate.

7.5.2.28   If there is no alternative to valproate, augmenting it with antimanic medication (but not carbamazepine) should be considered.

Depressive symptoms

7.5.2.29 For mild depressive symptoms in pregnant women with bipolar disorder the following should be considered, in this order:
- self-help approaches such as guided self-help and C-CBT
- brief psychological treatments (including counselling, CBT and IPT).

7.5.2.30 For moderate to severe depressive symptoms in pregnant women with bipolar disorder the following should be considered:
- psychological treatment (CBT) for moderate depression
- combined medication and structured psychological treatments for severe depression.

7.5.2.31 If prescribing medication for moderate to severe depressive symptoms in a pregnant woman with bipolar disorder, quetiapine alone, or SSRIs (but not paroxetine) in combination with prophylactic medication should be preferred because SSRIs are less likely to be associated with switching to mania than the TCAs. Monitor closely for signs of switching and stop the SSRI if the woman starts to develop manic or hypomanic symptoms.

Care in the perinatal period

7.5.2.32 After delivery, if a woman with bipolar disorder who is not on medication is at high risk of developing an acute episode, prescribers should consider establishing or reinstating medication as soon as the woman is medically stable (once the fluid balance is established).

7.5.2.33 If a woman maintained on lithium is at high risk of a manic relapse in the immediate postnatal period, augmenting treatment with an antipsychotic should be considered.

Women with bipolar disorder who wish to breastfeed

7.5.2.34 Women with bipolar disorder who are taking psychotropic medication and wish to breastfeed should be offered a prophylactic agent that can be used when breastfeeding. The first choice should be an antipsychotic.

Schizophrenia

This section should be read in conjunction with the NICE clinical guideline on the treatment and management of schizophrenia (NICE, 2002).

Women with schizophrenia who are planning a pregnancy or pregnant

7.5.2.35 Women with schizophrenia who are planning a pregnancy or pregnant should be treated according to the NICE clinical guideline on schizophrenia, except that if the woman is taking an atypical antipsychotic consideration should be given to switching to a low-dose typical antipsychotic, such as haloperidol, chlorpromazine or trifluoperazine.

Women with schizophrenia who are breastfeeding

7.5.2.36 A woman with schizophrenia who is breastfeeding should be treated according to the NICE clinical guideline on schizophrenia, except that women receiving depot medication should be advised that their infants may show extrapyramidal symptoms several months after administration of the depot. These are usually self-limiting.

8. THE ORGANISATION OF PERINATAL MENTAL HEALTH SERVICES

8.1 INTRODUCTION

This chapter covers the organisation of services for women with mental health problems during pregnancy and the postnatal period. It also looks at services for women with existing mental disorder who are considering pregnancy. It takes as its starting point a review of the current structure of services based on two surveys commissioned by the GDG, sets out the principles that may guide the configuration of services and considers the functions that services should provide. It examines relevant aspects of the epidemiology of perinatal mental health, before making recommendations for the future organisation of services.

8.2 THE CURRENT STRUCTURE OF SERVICES

To inform the guideline development process, the GDG undertook surveys of mental health services for pregnant and postnatal women currently provided by PCTs and secondary care mental health services.

8.2.1 Survey of primary care trusts

The survey of mental health services for pregnant and postnatal women provided by PCTs targeted all PCTs in England and local health boards in Wales. A brief questionnaire was sent to all PCT chief executives in England and chief executives of National Health Trusts in Wales (a copy of the questionnaire is included in Appendix 15). The aims of this were to gain an understanding of current service provision within primary care.

Summary of results:

- 48% response rate (144 PCTs)
- 55% reported having an identified lead clinician/manager responsible for perinatal mental health
- 69% reported having a policy of asking about mental health at routine antenatal and postnatal appointments
  - 63% ask about mental health on initial contact
  - 42% ask about mental health at appointments during pregnancy
  - 71% ask about mental health at postnatal appointments
- 56% reported having a protocol for the care of women with current mental health problems (of these 90% were partially or fully implemented)

- 54% reported having a mental health training programme for health visitors (64% trained)
- 79% reported having access to specialist MBU services for women with serious mental illness
- 64% included free-text comments:
  - 46% mentioned support groups, 16% listening visits, 7% CBT and 5% counselling
  - 40% used the EPDS as an assessment tool (93% of those mentioning such tools)
  - 88% mentioned a close working relationship with other levels of care (midwifery or specialist mental health services)

The results of the survey are limited by its design, with those responding likely to be those most interested in this area. Therefore, the sample is likely to be biased and as a consequence probably gives a more favourable picture of services than is the reality. Despite this, only just over half had an identified clinical lead or manager; a similar number had a protocol for the care of women with existing disorder, although nearly 70% had a policy of asking about mental health at routine antenatal and postnatal appointments. Nearly 80% said they had access to an MBU.

The suggestion is that current specialist provision for women with mental health problems during pregnancy and the postnatal period is patchy. A reasonable estimate is that perhaps only 25% of PCTs have a fully developed and implemented policy for antenatal and postnatal mental health. It is also worth noting that the large majority of services that have established assessment systems use the EPDS. Where this tool is integrated with additional clinical assessment, this may indicate a well-developed approach, but there are doubts about reliance on the EPDS as the sole system for screening (Shakespeare et al., 2003).

8.2.2   Survey of specialist perinatal services

A survey was conducted of all potential provider trusts of specialist mental health services for women in the antenatal and postnatal period in England and Wales. Initially, all potential providers were approached via a letter to the chief executive, asking whether or not they did in fact provide specialist perinatal services. A total of 92 replies were received, 61 from mental health trusts in England, 20 from PCTs in England and 11 from specialist mental health trusts in Wales. This initial response was followed up by a more detailed questionnaire seeking information on the specific specialist services provided by trusts. A total of 91 of the original 92 applicants responded.

Inpatient facilities
Thirty one percent of respondents disclosed that they were direct providers of either a specialist MBU or had designated beds specifically for women in the antenatal or postnatal period. A further 40% made use of mother and baby (or such designated) beds outside of the trust. However, 52% reported using general beds, without a

facility for admitting infants. When these responses are totalled, they actually represent a greater number than the total number of trust that responded (123% of the 91). This indicates that a number of trusts make use of several different services, which could well imply a limited capacity to best make use of any one particular service. See Figure 9 for a geographical representation of the provision of beds for acute postnatal mental health admissions in England and Wales.

Specialist perinatal community teams
Of the 21% of responding providers who disclosed that they had a specialist perinatal mental health team, the services of 42% were provided as part of comprehensive specialist perinatal services (including MBUs). The services of 32% were provided through community mental health teams and a further 21% provided through other services, such as liaison psychiatry or CAMHS (one provider failed to provide this information).

**Figure 9: Provision of beds for acute postnatal mental health admissions
in England and Wales**

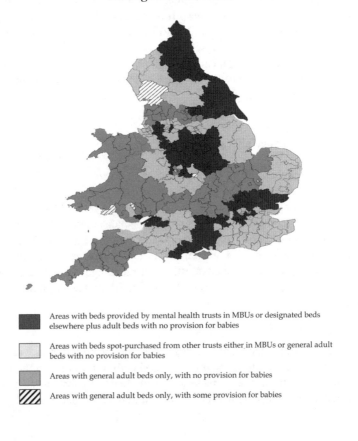

Areas with beds provided by mental health trusts in MBUs or designated beds
elsewhere plus adult beds with no provision for babies

Areas with beds spot-purchased from other trusts either in MBUs or general adult
beds with no provision for babies

Areas with general adult beds only, with no provision for babies

Areas with general adult beds only, with some provision for babies

Team sizes vary considerably, reflecting both provision of local resources and span of responsibilities of individual teams. Over 60% of the teams had a size of 7 or more team members. The composition of the teams, although multidisciplinary, varied very considerably. For example, 20% of teams had no representation either from consultant psychiatrists or CPNs, 74% had no psychologist team member and 79% had no social work membership. It is not surprising therefore to learn that over 30% had limited or no access to prompt provision of specialist psychological treatments.

The population served also varied very considerably, with populations of between 4,000 and 12,000 live births. Most services saw themselves as directly providing specialist assessment and treatment for mild, moderate and severe mental disorders. However, it is worth noting that a significant number of services (over 70%), saw themselves as having no responsibility for women (in the postnatal period) who had alcohol or drug-related problems, personality disorder or eating disorders. Most accepted direct referrals and the majority also claimed to be able to provide rapid assessment (70% within 2 days). A number also had limited capacities to offer daily visiting at homes in times of crisis. The majority (over 80%) saw their trusts continuing to provide services for up to 1 year postnatally. A smaller number (50%) saw themselves providing preconceptual counselling to women who had significant mental health problems.

Summary
There is very patchy provision of specialist perinatal services, with the expertise concentrated in one or two areas. The distribution of services and their precise location also varies considerably.

8.3   ESTIMATING THE NEED FOR SERVICES

Service functions and the structures to ensure their effective delivery should be based on an understanding of the nature of mental disorders and their epidemiology, which are summarised in Chapter 4. The number of live births in 2004 in England and Wales was 639,721 (Office for National Statistics, 2006), which is an average of 13 per 1,000, although the rate will vary considerably from area to area. A GP with an average-sized list (1,800 patients) may therefore expect somewhere between 15 and 27 live births on his or her list each year.

8.3.1   Common mental health disorders during pregnancy and the postnatal period

The epidemiology of perinatal disorder has been covered in Chapter 4; it is briefly considered again here, to give an indication of the likely need for services. As is apparent from Chapter 4, the epidemiology of antenatal and postnatal mental health disorders is not well understood and caution must be exercised in basing service structures on this data. Careful and critical analysis of this and other locally collected data must be used when developing local services.

Common mental health problems during the antenatal and postnatal period include depression and anxiety disorders, such as panic disorder, OCD and PTSD. An estimated 10% to 15% of women suffer from depression after the birth of an infant (Brockington, 1996; Nonacs & Cohen, 1998); in England and Wales this is between 64,000 and 94,000 women a year and is equivalent to between two and three women per year on the average GP list and 100 to 150 per 1,000 live births. Prevalence data for anxiety disorders during the perinatal period are not as reliable. The Office for National Statistics estimates that the prevalence of anxiety is around 4% of men and 5% of women (Office for National Statistics, 2006). This would mean that around 30,000 women giving birth per year are also likely to be suffering from anxiety, with two or three women per year on the average GP list (50 per 1,000 live births). A key role of maternity and primary care services in antenatal and postnatal mental healthcare is the identification of mental disorder. Prediction and detection of mental disorder is covered in Chapter 5.

It has been estimated that 50% of people with depression (that is, all those with depression, not just those with depression occurring in the postnatal period) are not identified (Williams *et al.*, 1995). This means that around half of the 128 to 192 pregnant or postnatal women who develop depression per 100,000 population may present to primary care mental health services each year (that is, 50 to 75 per 1,000 live births). A similar or lower figure might reasonably be expected for anxiety disorders, with fewer disorders being identified than for depression.

For the vast majority of these women, professional help will be provided solely by primary healthcare services. However, this is not always the case; for example, around 3% to 5% of women giving birth have moderate or severe depression, with about 1.7% being referred to specialist mental health services (Cox *et al.*, 1993; O'Hara & Swain, 1996). Thus, around 17 women per 1,000 live births would be referred to specialist mental health services with depression postnatally. Again, it is reasonable to expect the figures for anxiety disorders to follow the national trend, with a lower rate of referral through to specialist services.

8.3.2   Severe mental illness during pregnancy and the postnatal period

First presentations of severe mental illness, primarily schizophrenia and bipolar disorder, in the perinatal period are rare, with a rate in the region of two per thousand resulting in hospital admissions (based on admission as a proxy for psychosis) (Kendell *et al.*, 1987). These episodes are associated with a clustering of admissions in the first month after the birth (1 per 2,000 live births). More common, particularly with bipolar disorder, is the exacerbation of an existing disorder, with some studies reporting relapse rates for bipolar disorder approaching 50% in the antenatal period and 70% in the postnatal period (Viguera *et al.*, 2000). These women, along with others suffering from severe depression and other severe disorders such as severe anxiety disorders or personality disorders, will benefit from referral to specialist mental health services.

These figures, along with data obtained from a survey in the Nottingham area (Oates, 2000), give some indication of the range of presentations to specialist services, with estimates of the number of new presentations in the range of 18 to 30 per 100,000 head of population and a further 12 to 24 per 100,000 presentations of already identified disorder, giving a total estimate in the region of 30 to 54 per 100,000.

Some of these women will require inpatient care. These include those with puerperal psychosis and a number of women with severe depressive disorders. Some of these are cared for in MBUs. A recent survey, as part of a larger study of alternatives to admission in the UK, identified 19 units: MBUs and mother and baby facilities (hospitals where one or two mother and baby beds are provided in the absence of a designated unit) with 126 available beds (Johnson, S., personal communication, 30 June 2006).

Determining the need for specialist services, including where appropriate specialist perinatal teams and the number of inpatient facilities, their size and location, is difficult for a number of reasons. Firstly, the incidence of severe mental illness requiring inpatient care varies across the country, with much higher morbidity in inner city areas compared with suburban or rural areas. (For example, bed usage by PCTs reveals a bed use approximately 1.7 times higher in urban than in rural areas, although this may not simply be the result of higher urban morbidity but due to women living in rural areas being reluctant to travel long distances to the nearest inpatient facility.) Secondly, the local structure of services (for example, the presence of crisis and home treatment teams) may also impact significantly on the use of inpatient services (Killaspy *et al.*, 2006). Thirdly, the presence of specialist perinatal services that have responsibility for the coordination/delivery of care to women with severe perinatal psychiatric disorders, and the way in which they are designed, may also impact on referral rates and on bed usage. (For example, in the present Southampton/New Forest/Eastleigh Test Valley South service, with a comprehensive perinatal community team and home treatment services, and serving three PCTs, current mean bed use is approximately 110 occupied bed days per 1,000 deliveries.) There is also some evidence to suggest that the provision of specialist inpatient services without specialist community services to coordinate such care can be associated with higher inpatient bed usage. (For example, Basingstoke PCT, with no specialist perinatal community service, had a bed usage of 215 occupied bed days per 1,000 deliveries in the same period.) Fourthly, significant numbers of MBUs also use a number of their beds for parenting assessments; that is, the assessment of a woman's capacity to care for her child. These assessments, which can be extended over several weeks, may occupy up to 80% of beds in some MBUs and as such may limit the capacity of the units to care effectively for emergency admissions.

In arriving at estimates of need for inpatient services, the balance of geographical proximity and the need to develop economies of scale also need to be taken into account. Current statistics suggest an average length of stay of 33 days (DH, 2005) and, with a recommended bed occupancy of 85%, this suggests between 0.13 and 0.51 beds per 100,000. In smaller trusts, a service of only 2 to 3 beds would be needed, which may not be economically viable, and combination of resources at a supra-trust level in such cases may be required to obtain clinical and cost-effective bed use. In addition, caution is required when determining bed requirements from average bed-use data; there will be considerable variation in demand for beds and duration of use, which can seriously undermine calculations based on averages (Gallivan *et al.*, 2002). These figures would suggest that, given the current provision of approximately 110 specialist beds, between 30 and 50 additional perinatal specialist beds would be required to meet the needs for women with severe mental illness who require admission in the perinatal period. This assumes that all units would be equally accessible but, given the geography and population distribution of England and Wales, it is likely that additional beds would be required to provide reasonable access and to provide the capacity to respond appropriately to emergency admissions. This suggests that between 60 and 80 additional beds would be required.

8.4 THE FUNCTIONS OF SERVICES FOR WOMEN, THEIR PARTNERS AND CARERS IN THE ANTENATAL AND POSTNATAL PERIOD

When identifying the key functions of any healthcare system, the needs of the patient are central. Anyone with a mental health problem, regardless of other factors, should have:

- the disorder detected effectively
- effective assessment and referral to appropriate services when necessary
- timely, appropriate treatment
- accurate information about the disorder and the benefits and risks associated with treatment, including psychotropic medication
- provision of care in the most appropriate setting
- appropriate communication about their care, with other services as required and without unnecessary breaches of confidentiality or stigmatising procedures
- choice.

For women with mental disorder during pregnancy and postnatally, the clinical context is complicated by the needs of the fetus and infant, such as the safety of drugs during pregnancy and breastfeeding, and by the woman's psychological adjustment to pregnancy, motherhood or having an additional child while experiencing mental illness. Services also need to take into account the needs of fathers/partners, carers and other children in the family. Therefore, services need to be tailored to meet these needs, which may include the provision of specialist inpatient services, integration of specific mental health services and maternity services, and dedicated treatment programmes. These must be provided in a timely fashion to ensure that treatments giving relief to the woman do so before her condition has damaged the health and development of the fetus and other family members. This is particularly relevant for the provision of psychological treatment. Such services may be configured in different ways to provide the same functions to patients, dependent on local considerations, such as population density and variations in morbidity.

In meeting the mental health needs of women in the perinatal period, services should seek to provide the most effective and accessible treatments in the least intrusive and disruptive manner. This principle, of stepped care, is now helping organise services in other aspects of mental health provision (for example, NICE, 2004a). Professionals, from core primary care team members such as health visitors and GPs through to perinatal psychiatrists, and women and families themselves, are all involved in delivering an effective mental health service for women in the antenatal and postnatal periods. A key function is the development and implementation of clear care pathways and effective working between different professionals that always hold the women (and fetus/infant) at the centre of consideration. Figure 10 presents a model for the structuring of services in a stepped-care framework.

In general, early steps in the pathway will be provided by generalist primary care professionals and generalist maternity services, involving primary care. The model includes mental health professionals such as counsellors and primary care mental health workers as appropriate. When there is a requirement for more intensive treatments, more specialist professionals will need to be involved. Some women (and their fetus/infant) may need the intervention of a specialist inpatient setting. Specialist perinatal teams may provide input (including advice and consultations, as well as direct care) at a variety of points in an individual woman's care pathway.

Figure 10: Stepped-care model

Personnel	Service	Core functions
Psychiatrists, nurses, nursery nurses, clinical psychologists	Specialist perinatal mental health services	Prevention and treatment of moderate/severe mental illness; source of specialist advice, consultation and training to primary and secondary care services
Community mental health teams (psychiatrists, clinical psychologists, nurses, social workers, occupational therapists)	Specialist mental health services	Assessment and treatment; referral to specialist services and inpatient care
GPs, health visitors, midwives, psychological therapists, primary care mental health workers	Primary care mental health services	Assessment and referral; treatment of mild/moderate mental illness
GPs, obstetricians, midwives, practice nurses, health visitors	General healthcare services (including maternity and primary care)	Detection of history of and current mental illness; referral for treatments

8.4.1 General healthcare services (including primary care and maternity services)

All pregnant women have contact with general healthcare services. Maternity services may be a mix of community services, which may be midwife-led, and hospital-based services, including hospital-based midwives and obstetricians. It is these professionals who are well placed to identify women with a history of, or current, mental disorder in pregnancy. (The prediction and detection of mental disorder is covered in Chapter 5.)

Maternity services
Midwives, working in both primary care and hospital settings, are central to the planning and coordination of services for pregnant women and have a key role in identifying mental illness during the antenatal, intrapartum and postnatal periods. In addition to providing antenatal care and care during delivery, they provide care for 28 days following birth and for longer if necessary. As with GPs, they can have a role in enquiry about existing or previous mental illness, education, treatment and support, including integration into local support networks, liaison with and referral to mental health services, and liaison with GPs, health visitors and other primary care staff.

Obstetricians, paediatricians and neonatologists can also be expected to play a role in the detection of possible symptoms of new episodes of mental illness, monitoring and care of fetal and neonatal health in the context of added risks amongst women with serious mental illness, the provision of basic information and referral for advice on the safety of psychotropic medication during pregnancy and for breastfeeding, and liaison with and referral to mental health services. Complex discussions

Vignette: A woman with depression and self-harming behaviour in the postnatal period

My midwife was great. I broke down on her and was able to tell her how I was feeling. I was so scared about being a mum and how I thought I wouldn't be able to cope. I would have appointments with her regularly to keep a check on my emotional state.

Vignette: A woman with no history of mental health problems prior to depression and psychosis in the postnatal period with her first child following a traumatic birth

The midwives were fine, but there was no follow-up after the birth. Some midwives on the ward expect you to 'know it all' and do not offer advice concerning the new skills of being a mother. You feel like just 'another one on the conveyor belt' – it could be so much better if you were made to feel special.

about the risks and benefits of various treatment options will often need input from specialist perinatal mental health workers.

Primary care services

GPs often have a good overview of the women coming for maternity care and their families, and are usually in the best position to coordinate both the obstetric and mental health needs of their patients. With regard to mental health issues, GPs can provide the following roles: identification of existing or previous mental illness; provision of basic information and sourcing of additional advice on the safety of psychotropic medication during pregnancy and for breastfeeding; treatment of common mental health problems; liaison with and referral to specialist mental health services; collaboration with health visitors, midwives and practice-based mental health services in the provision of care; and coordination and sharing of information between maternity and mental health services at all levels of severity.

Health visitors have most frequent contact with women in the first 6 weeks after delivery (from some time in the second week after birth), during which time they often visit women and their infants at home. They are therefore well placed to detect early symptoms of new episodes of mental illness postnatally and to help with a woman's psychological adjustment to motherhood. Specifically, they could take on the following roles: the initial identification of existing mental illness and enquiry about previous mental illness where this has not already been done in pregnancy; involvement in the implementation of pre-birth plans for women with identified risk of relapse of severe mental illness; helping women with mental health problems to overcome the challenges they face in caring for their infant, siblings and themselves; liaison with and referral to mental health services; liaison with GPs and other primary care staff; and treatment of mild to moderate depression.

Vignette: A woman with no history of mental health problems prior to a diagnosis of depression in the postnatal period with her first child

When I got home, a pattern evolved. My husband went to work and I sat on the sofa, with my son in my arms, making sure I had phone, remote control, pillows and drinks at hand. I would feed and doze all day, to be found still on the sofa at the end of the day when my husband returned. I dared not put my son down because I knew that he would cry. I left the front door open so that my health visitor, Caroline, could just come in. During this time, Caroline was my saviour, my friend, my confidante, my counsellor, my shoulder to cry on, the reason I am still here and have come out the other side. I owe that woman everything: my sanity, my marriage, my life!

My health visitor suggested that I write a list of ten things that I wanted to achieve, which really helped. It gave me something to aim for, even if it was just having a hot bath or making a roast dinner.

Vignette: A woman with depression and self-harming behaviour in the postnatal period

The GP I am with now isn't very approachable, especially about women's problems or feelings. I did see another doctor from the practice who was great and really listened to me. Unfortunately, she has left. Now whenever I go to the doctor, no matter who I see, I am very honest and keep telling them till they listen. It would be helpful if doctors listened and showed compassion to new mums and did not just hand out prescriptions.

Fortunately, my health visitor was able to set up sponsored childcare for my son so I could get some time to myself on a regular basis. She also put me in contact with a volunteer counsellor though a church, which helped a lot. My support worker also helped me a lot at this time, giving me the confidence to help myself and arrange my own support plan. It was a long, hard struggle but with the support and help from my family, my health visitor, and especially my support worker, the bad days got fewer and fewer.

Vignette: A woman with a history of mental health problems diagnosed with depression in the postnatal period

My GP told me that the way I was feeling was quite normal, and he was actually surprised that he didn't see more new mothers for the same reasons. He thought having a baby was 'mind-blowing for a woman', so I knew I had a sensible, sympathetic ear. He told me to try and get at least 3 hours a week to myself, away from my son, my husband and the house, which I tried for a month and failed to achieve once.

8.4.2 Primary care mental health services

The vast majority of women with mental health problems during the perinatal period present to, and are treated solely by, primary care services. Primary care mental health services include GPs, practice counsellors and psychological therapists, practice nurses, health visitors, midwives and primary care mental health workers. Key functions of these services are to: provide assessment, treatment and care as necessary; liaise with and make appropriate referrals to specialist services; make appropriate use of service-user support groups; identify risk, including risk to the infant's health and well-being, or that of other children in the family; and communicate with other services.

8.4.3 Specialist mental health services including specialist perinatal mental health services

Women requiring specialist care may be treated by general mental health services, mental health liaison services or specialist perinatal mental health services, and by combinations of these services. The functions of specialist mental health services, including specialist perinatal services, are as follows:

- assessment of women with moderate and severe mental disorder (or those with milder but treatment-resistant disorder) during pregnancy and the postnatal period, including assessment of the risk of relapse of existing disorder during pregnancy, childbirth or the postnatal period
- treatment of mental disorder during pregnancy and the postnatal period
- provision of intensive services, such as crisis, home treatment and inpatient services and, in the case of some specialist perinatal services, the provision of specialist inpatient beds
- communication with primary care, maternity and obstetric services and, where appropriate, coordination and management of care pathways and service access
- provision of specialist consultation and advice to services providing treatment and care to patients with existing disorder who are planning a pregnancy or who become pregnant, and to services managing women with less severe disorders; this may include advice on care, treatment, mother-infant relationships, child protection issues and diagnosis
- liaison with primary care and maternity services concerning the care of women with moderate to severe mental disorders
- education and training for maternity and primary and secondary care mental health services.

Vignette: A woman with depression and self-harming behaviour in the postnatal period

I had an assessment while I was still pregnant; it was horrible. Two men asked me all sorts of questions that were not related to how I was feeling. I felt very tense and uncomfortable and like a fake who was wasting their time.

Then, after 45 minutes, they said that there was nothing wrong with me, that it was just in my personality and that I would have to live with it. I was devastated because I knew that something wasn't right, but no one listened. I tried to ignore my feelings because, after all, they were professionals, had studied for years and had to be right. They did, however, set me up with a floating support worker to help me once the baby was born.

The crisis team was not much help; in fact, one lady who came to visit me was terrible. She talked to me as if I was stupid, told me to pull myself together and laughed at the fact I self-harmed. My mum, who had come to look after me, nearly threw her out of the house. We asked not to see the team again.

Vignette: A woman with no history of mental health problems prior to depression and psychosis in the postnatal period with her first child following a traumatic birth

My CPN spent hours listening to me and finally I was convinced that I had been ill and was not a failure. On very bad days, it helped to be reminded of small improvements I had made rather than dwelling on the things I could not do. For example, one day I would not answer the phone, but a week later I picked it up and said 'hello'. It was a small step, maybe, but positive.

Vignette: A woman with pre-existing depression and depression after the birth of both of her children

Three weeks after the birth of my second child, I had developed severe panic attacks and I ended up in accident and emergency, where I saw an extremely helpful psychiatric duty nurse who encouraged me to get home visits from the psychiatric nurse team. This was helpful or extremely unhelpful, depending on the nurses who visited! One told me to just ping a rubber band when I felt a panic attack coming on, but two others were sympathetic, practical and kept reassuring me that I would get better, which my psychiatrist also emphasised.

Vignette: A woman with no history of mental health problems prior to PTSD and depression following a traumatic birth

After some delay, a CPN came to see me, which was great at first as he explained why I felt the way that I did and how the brain works, and so on. I did start to make some progress. My CPN worked with me, gradually enabling me to stay on my own and go out for short periods of time without anyone else. He also identified that the root cause of my problems was the birth of my baby, which was very traumatic, and not helped by the behaviour of some of the healthcare professionals I saw at that time. He said that I was suffering from a type of post-traumatic stress syndrome, as well as postnatal illness. He then began to try a technique, which he called disassociation, where he taught me to relax then run through the birth over and over again. I did not find this beneficial at all and my CPN also agreed that this seemed to be having no effect.

The consultant I eventually saw did not seem to understand my feelings at all and discarded many of the factors that my CPN and I feel are the major causes of my illness. I did not feel listened to or understood at all, especially when, despite my telling him that it was impossible for me to go out or speak to anyone without my husband or mum present, he told me that it would be a good

Continued

Vignette: (*Continued*)

idea for me to return to work in 2 weeks' time. On leaving the hospital, I felt that everything was hopeless; even the people who were supposed to be experts could not help and didn't really seem interested. That day, I tried to commit suicide by walking in front of a car – I just felt that I could no longer live like this and that no one could understand or help me.

At an appointment with a consultant psychiatrist at the local MBU, the consultant that I was supposed to see was ill, so I was seen by a medical student, who then gave the details of the assessment to another consultant. He came in to see me and again I felt a total lack of understanding. Despite telling him everything, including the self-harm, suicide attempt and suicidal feelings, he told me that I did not need individual psychological treatment, but that I may benefit from attending a group session (which I had told him twice that I already attended) and sent me away, giving me an appointment for 3 weeks' time. At this point, I felt at the end of my tether and I told him that I could not carry on like this any more. I asked him what I should do at 3 o'clock in the morning when I was feeling so ill that I was tearing the hair out of my scalp, with myself and my husband unable to cope; he simply replied that I was already on a high dose of diazepam, and that I should come back in 3 weeks.

8.4.4   Inpatient services

Women presenting to secondary care mental health services during pregnancy or the postnatal period may require inpatient care. Over the past 30 years, there has been an increasing practice to admit such women to MBUs (Brockington, 1996). These units are designed to address a number of challenges, including the need for specialist expertise in the treatment of severe perinatal illness, the need to support the development of the mother-infant relationship through a joint admission, and the provision of an environment that is safe and appropriate to the care of a young infant (for example, the presence of specialist nursery nurses and the avoidance of the severe disturbance seen on many general inpatient wards) and to the physical needs of pregnant and postnatal women. The functions of inpatient services for women with mental health problems during pregnancy and the postnatal period include:

- assessment of mental illness, including risk assessment and assessment of ability to care for the infant
- provision of expert care of women requiring admission
- in MBUs, the expert provision of safe care for the infants of women admitted
- support for the woman in caring for and developing a relationship with her baby, wherever appropriate fostering the involvement of the partner or other carers
- liaison and integrated working with other services, including maternity and obstetric services, GPs, and maternity-based and community mental health services.

A key factor in the decision to admit a woman with her infant is consideration of the welfare of the infant. That is, whether it is better for the infant to stay with his or her mother or whether he or she should be cared for by another family member while the woman receives inpatient treatment. Currently, where specialist units are available, women are usually admitted with their infants unless there is good reason not to, for example, the woman preferring not to have her child with her or the child requiring specialist medical care not available in the unit. Admission to a unit will be influenced by geographical proximity (Brockington, 1996). This is a crucial consideration at this important time for women and their families to ensure visiting and contact with family and social networks, on which support after discharge, and early discharge, will depend. The development of MBUs has been determined by balancing this against the need to establish services of sufficient size to be able to maintain necessary skills and resources. This is a challenge that should be addressed by careful planning with the involvement of key stakeholders, taking into account population needs and the influence of related services.

There are few formal evaluations of the provision of MBUs and fewer still of the cost effectiveness of this model of care provision. A systematic search of the literature identified no economic studies of inpatient units or specialist perinatal teams, and only one study that assessed the cost effectiveness of a specialised psychiatric day-hospital unit for the treatment of women with depression in the postnatal period was found (Boath *et al.*, 2003) (see Appendix 14). In this study, the economic analysis was conducted alongside a prospective cohort study carried out in the UK. The study population consisted of 60 women with an EPDS score ≥12 and a diagnosis of major or minor depressive disorder according to RDC, who had an infant aged between 6 weeks and 1 year. The comparator of the analysis was a neighbouring area providing routine primary care by GPs and health visitors with referrals into secondary care.

The primary clinical outcome used in the economic analysis was the number of women successfully treated, defined as no longer fulfilling RDC for major or minor depressive disorder. The analysis adopted a societal perspective and costs and outcomes were measured over a period of 6 months. The analysis demonstrated that the day-hospital unit resulted in a significantly higher number of women successfully treated compared with routine primary care, but at an additional cost of £1,945 per successfully treated woman (1992/93 prices). The cost per successfully treated woman in the routine primary care group was estimated at £2,710. Since the NHS was prepared to pay £2,710 for a successful outcome achieved in routine primary care, the authors concluded that the unit was a cost-effective alternative treatment approach, providing additional benefit at an incremental cost below what the NHS was already paying for the treatment of women with depression in the postnatal period.

The study had a number of limitations, such as the cohort design, which was subject to systematic bias and confounding variables, the short time horizon of the analysis and, most importantly, the selection of the comparator (that is, non-specialised primary care with only occasional referrals to specialists), which may have led to overestimation of incremental benefits associated with the unit.

Details of the study are presented in the form of evidence tables in Appendix 19.

256

**Vignette: A woman with depression and self-harming behaviour
in the postnatal period**

I was admitted to the MBU of a psychiatric hospital, where I stayed for over
6 weeks. My son was by my side the whole time. My medication was changed
because I was breastfeeding and finally the migraines that I had been suffering
from stopped. Having people around really helped, especially meeting other
sufferers. I had been beginning to think I was going insane and I was the only
one who had ever felt like this, so it was good to know I wasn't the only one.
The nurses were very sympathetic and helpful; they explained what was
happening to me and ways to cope without self-harming. The occupational therapist suggested hobbies that kept my mind busy and used my hands, like knitting
and art work. The physiotherapist suggested relaxation techniques such as
meditation and visualisations. The nurses suggested distraction like having a
bath and reading. Best of all, I found writing down my feelings helped. I was
able to express myself without upsetting any one and it cleared my head.

As my son was older than the other children (he was about 7 months old at this
time), he slept in my room at night, unlike the younger babies that slept in the
nursery, but someone was always around if you had a problem. I do believe
I would not be here today if I had not been admitted.

Vignette: A woman with a history of anxiety and anxiety postnatally

I was admitted to an MBU to have the effects of the drug I was taking (an antidepressant) monitored and to help me with relaxation techniques and anxiety
management. It was reassuring that my son was admitted with me so that we did
not have to be separated. The unit is new and provides a very warm, comfortable
environment to keep a baby. I had initially been worried about bringing my baby
into a hospital environment but the unit was like a home from home.

I attended the unit's support groups and found them extremely useful in that it
was nice meeting other people going through similar experiences and to perhaps
see that there could be light at the end of the tunnel. After two admissions to the
unit, I was eventually stabilised on my treatment.

8.5   THE STRUCTURE OF PERINATAL MENTAL HEALTH SERVICES

8.5.1   Introduction

As described in 7.2 above, services for women with mental health problems during
pregnancy and the postnatal period, are unevenly distributed across England and
Wales, and specialist perinatal services (community and inpatient) are sparse. A
central concern is that this uneven distribution of services is addressed in a way that

257

ensures not only equity of access but does so in a way that is cost effective and that promotes the collaboration of specialist and generalist services, thereby reducing the degree of disruption faced by women as they access different elements of the service.

8.5.2   Principles guiding the organisation of mental health services

Principles that guide the configuration of services include:
* reduction of cross-agency/service barriers to a minimum and, where possible, their elimination

Women with mental health problems who are pregnant or have an infant will require care from several services, including primary care, mental health and maternity services. These need to be organised so that the woman's movement between various services should not interfere with, or limit access to, services. To ensure this, all relevant agencies and stakeholders, including service users, should be involved in the organisation of services.
* accessible care (including access to expertise, the availability of relevant professionals, the provision of a prompt service and appropriate geographical location)

During pregnancy and the postnatal period, women need access to mental health services through a variety of contact points. The timeframe of pregnancy and the importance of the well-being of the child (see below) require that services should be available with a minimum delay. This improved access should also extend to partners, carers and family members who have an important role in the care and support of the woman and infant, as well as having needs in their own right.
* consideration of the well-being of the infant

While providing appropriate care for the woman, the needs of the fetus/infant (and siblings) must be a central consideration in the organisation and delivery of services. This will often be best served by prompt and effective treatment of the woman's illness, but meeting the infants' needs and the needs of the mother-infant relationship should not be deferred while this is happening.
* provision of care in a stepped-care framework so as to provide the most effective and cost-effective treatments in the least intrusive manner possible, with the best possible outcome for all concerned

For many people, this will involve the initial provision of brief low-intensity evidence-based treatments, followed by the provision of more intensive evidence-based treatments for women with greater or persistent needs. More intensive care should be provided at home in preference to hospital, whenever safe and appropriate, but women should still have access to expert advice. In some cases, it will be clear that the woman should enter the pathway at different points in order to access more intensive treatments.

8.5.3   Managed clinical networks

Since the precise structure of services will vary in different parts of the country based on local factors, including the organisation of existing mental health services, the demographic profile of the local population and geographical issues, the provision of services needs to be seen in terms of standard features that can be adopted by any service and adapted to meet local need in order to deliver integrated care. One way of conceptualising this is to use a managed network model. For the purposes of this chapter, managed clinical networks are defined as linked groups of health professionals and organisations from primary, secondary and tertiary care working in a coordinated manner, unconstrained by existing professional and service boundaries, to ensure equitable provision of high-quality clinically effective services.

Models of managed clinical networks

A number of models for the development of managed clinical networks have been developed and these have been reviewed by Goodwin and colleagues (2004). Goodwin describes three broad types of network: enclave, hierarchical and individualistic. All three have potential benefits and no one model is held to be superior to the others. In fact, in practice most networks have elements of all three models. However, in view of the potential functions of a perinatal mental health network, the hierarchical model is probably the most appropriate here. This is defined as having 'an organisational core and authority to regulate the work of members via joint provision, inspection and/or accreditation'. Such networks are held to be most successful in coordinating and controlling a pre-defined task that involves complex division of labour, and therefore would seem the most appropriate structure for a perinatal mental health network, where agreement on care pathways, thresholds for admission and allocation of resources to community and inpatient services will need to be determined. In contrast to some networks based on this model, for example cancer networks, the limitations of the current evidence base would suggest that the emphasis in a perinatal network would be on joint provision and ensuring the quality of services, as it is unlikely that the evidence base is sufficient to develop accreditation systems at this stage.

Goodwin and colleagues (2004) also described the characteristics of successful networks and these include:

- Central coordination – key for hierarchical networks and should be financed, proactive and with the possibility of a 'neutral manager or agency' where there are competing interests.
- Clear mission statement and unambiguous rules of engagement.
- Inclusivity – ensuring all agencies and individuals gain ownership of the network.
- Manageable size – large networks should be avoided due to high administrative costs and the inertia that can develop.
- Cohesion – strategies should be developed aimed at achieving network cohesion, which could include joint finance arrangements, pooled budgets, agreed care protocols and common targets. A 'boundary spanner', acting as an intermediary between organisations and agencies, allows individualistic networks to function effectively and helps hierarchical networks engage with peripheral agencies. It can be a key enabler in promoting network cohesion across all network types.
- Ownership facilitated by formalised contracts and agreements, with avoidance of over-regulation.

- Leadership – respected professional leaders who will promote the network to peers should be actively engaged.
- Avoidance of network domination by a professional elite or a particular organisational culture.
- Response to the needs of network members in such a way that the network remains relevant and worthwhile.
- Professionals in networks providing the mandate to allow managers to manage and govern their activities.

Such models have been adopted in the UK for the development of a number of medical services, including those for cancer (34 cancer networks were developed in 2001 in England), cardiovascular care, emergency care and genitourinary medicine. In addition, they have been extensively promoted in the Scottish healthcare system. Formal evaluations are underway, but as yet little has been completed.

Developing a perinatal mental health managed network

A central concern in developing a perinatal mental health managed network would be ensuring that women with mental health problems during pregnancy and the postnatal period have appropriate access to both specialist perinatal expertise and, where necessary, inpatient care. This factor is important in determining the size of a network with coordinated inpatient services. Such units and the networks that are built around them would need to be in accordance with the factors associated with success identified by Goodwin and colleagues (2004), be clinically and economically viable and be geographically located so that undue burdens are not placed on patients and their families in accessing them.

Adopting a hierarchical model for a perinatal network would require that the network has:

- an identified manager with clearly specified and delegated responsibilities, who may be independent of any one element of the network or located in the element of the network that contains the inpatient unit(s) and has responsibilities to ensure that the relationship within the network is properly developed and maintained
- a clear mission statement – in which the expectations of all parties are clearly set out
- a system – normally a management board that recognises and guarantees the ownership of the network by all agencies, including clinicians, commissioners and managers, and supports the development of a shared and reflective network culture
- a size that delivers appropriate economies of scale but which does not generate high administrative costs and inertia
- clearly specified and contracted finance arrangements, agreed referral and care protocols and information systems to support the effective operation of the network
- active professional leadership and full multidisciplinary involvement.

Advantages of perinatal mental health managed networks

Perinatal mental health managed networks may therefore bring a number of advantages. These include the effective concentration of expertise and the identification of dedicated time and explicit responsibility for the delivery of appropriate care to mentally ill women and their families. It is possible that this will lead to more favourable outcomes in terms of reduced mortality and morbidity, and increased patient satisfaction. The identification of clear care pathways, a threshold for referrals and evidence-based protocols will support healthcare professionals in identifying and managing the most serious disorders presenting around childbirth, as these episodes are infrequent and services are not organised to provide adequately for the special needs of women and their families in these circumstances.

This should lead to more timely services for those women who need treatment for their mental disorders urgently because their illnesses may have a disproportionate effect on the fetus. Clarity about treatment thresholds should also improve access to psychological therapies, which are seldom available quickly enough. Postnatally, services must be able to respond rapidly to emerging illness and link effectively with obstetricians, midwives and health visitors expressing concern. The development of clinical networks may also improve liaison with, and ensure effective monitoring and support of, maternity services where services often respond late, even for the most disabled women. A clinical network should also provide more widely available up-to-date information about the impact of psychotropic medication in pregnancy and breastfeeding and advice on how to assess and effectively communicate the risks and benefits of their use in an individual woman. Perinatal managed networks should also lead to more equitable and cost-effective use of inpatient services, with more effective evaluation of the likely risks and benefits of admission for particular women and the purpose of admission to an MBU. In particular, it must be clear whether the purpose of admission is for treatment or for evaluation of parenting capacity.

Clinical networks can also play a key role in training, education and raising awareness. The availability of specialist expertise in the network means that training and support to maternity services, general mental health services and primary care will be provided that will enable non-specialists to be as effective and confident about perinatal mental health as possible and have access to advice about where their limits lie. This may also include training in infant mental health, such as the health and development of the fetus/infant and siblings of women in their care.

The establishment of clinical networks will also support standard setting and monitoring, participation in research and the integration of learning from national schemes such as the Confidential Enquiry into Maternal and Child Health (CEMACH).

Structure of perinatal mental health managed networks
It would be expected that the broad structure of all networks would be common, but their precise composition would vary, as would the details of the protocols for movement between different levels of the network. Typically, it might be expected that services in the network would agree common structures and processes for the organisation and delivery of perinatal mental healthcare at every level of the stepped framework, wherever this is possible, and improve the quality and efficiency of care. However, the composition and detailed operation of the elements of a network may vary according to local epidemiology, geography and service composition, and the network should facilitate local determination of these to ensure ownership, empowerment and innovation amongst staff.

An outline of such a model is set out in Figure 11. This model, in line with a stepped-care approach, assumes that inpatient care in a network could be provided on behalf of the network by one or more member organisations, depending on the identified need in the network and its geographical structure.

Figure 11: Perinatal clinical network

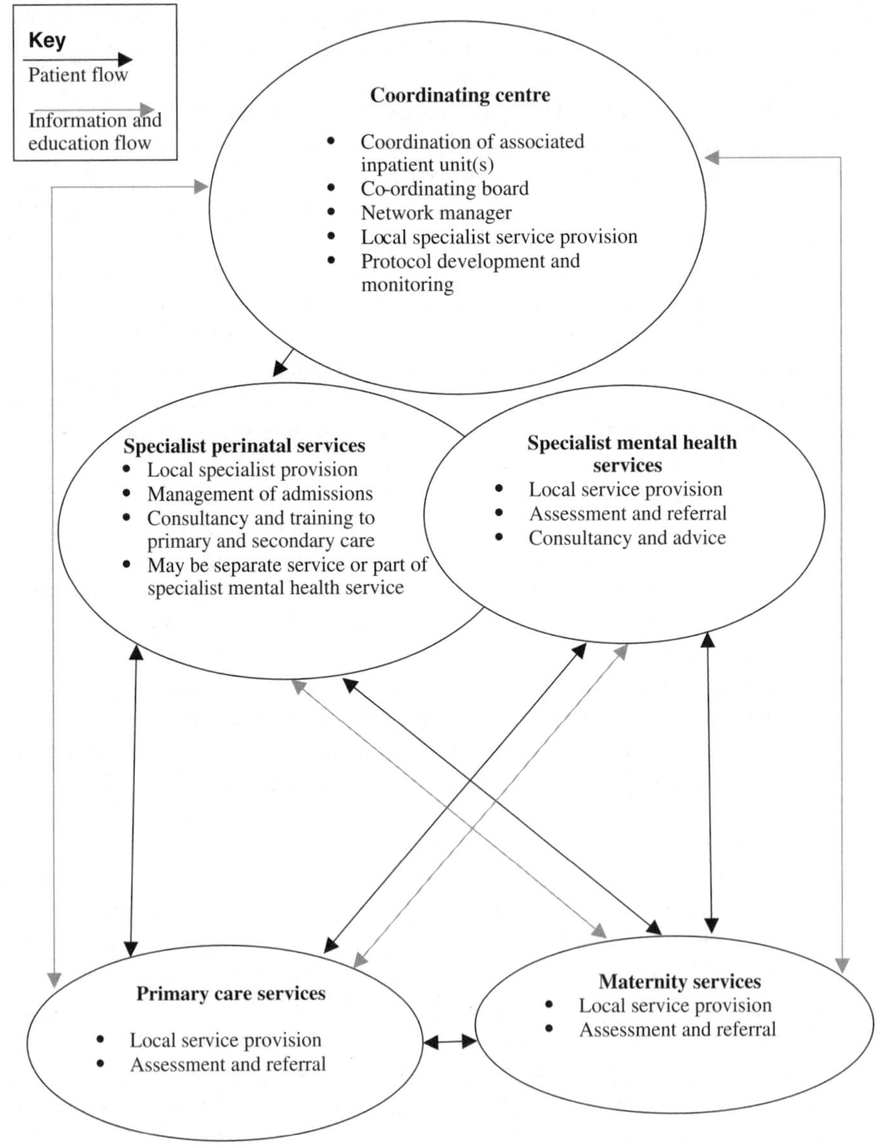

Key

Patient flow

Information and education flow

Coordinating centre

- Coordination of associated inpatient unit(s)
- Co-ordinating board
- Network manager
- Local specialist service provision
- Protocol development and monitoring

Specialist perinatal services
- Local specialist provision
- Management of admissions
- Consultancy and training to primary and secondary care
- May be separate service or part of specialist mental health service

Specialist mental health services
- Local service provision
- Assessment and referral
- Consultancy and advice

Primary care services

- Local service provision
- Assessment and referral

Maternity services
- Local service provision
- Assessment and referral

In the model set out above, the managed network would be coordinated by a network board, with a core coordinating team drawn from senior staff in relevant specialist perinatal teams, maternity services, secondary care mental health services, and primary care, as well as commissioners and service user and carer representatives. The board would have responsibility for overseeing the development of protocols and pathways for the coordination of care between services, implementing good practice, coordinating expert clinical advice, management and local strategy. It would ensure that services work together to improve quality of care and address any inequalities in provision and access in the area covered by the network.

The precise area covered by each network will be determined by local need, but one determinant will be the need for effective use of inpatient services. As set out above, it may be the function of the central coordinating element of the network to provide inpatient services, but in other networks geography or existing service provision may suggest more than one provider. However, if networks are not to be so large as to be overly bureaucratic, it is unlikely that there could be more than two such units. Data that give an indication of the factors influencing network size are set out in Section 8.5.4. In determining the need for inpatient beds, a number of factors need to be considered; these include the critical mass of expertise to ensure effective treatment of women and their infants and the trade-off of geographical proximity. Units of fewer than 8 to 10 beds may be less cost effective, and units of fewer than 4 to 6 beds may not be able to maintain sufficient staffing and expertise to be able to respond comprehensively to the needs of women and their infants; units above 12 beds are likely to present complex organisational and management problems.

In this model, local specialist perinatal services have a key role in linking specialist inpatient services with general mental health, maternity and primary care services. Such specialist services would vary in size and composition according to local circumstances. They may include 'stand-alone' specialist perinatal services providing a broad community-based service, services linked to liaison psychiatry or liaison obstetric services, or services linked to community mental health services. Indeed, given local variations in morbidity and service structures, the latter models may be the most effective way to provide services in some areas rather than stand-alone specialist perinatal mental health teams given that there is no direct evidence for the effectiveness of such teams within the UK healthcare system. Also, there is patchy evidence for the effectiveness of other functional mental health teams in the NHS, including crisis teams, assertive outreach teams (for example, Killaspy *et al.*, 2006), and early intervention services for first-episode psychosis. However, whatever the model of local service provision, their role in the provision of specialist clinical, advisory, training and gate-keeping functions will need to be clearly set out in the protocols governing the operation of the network. Typically, given expected demand for inpatient care, a network brings together a number of specialist perinatal teams (normally coterminous with a specialist mental health trust).

In a managed network, referral pathways for women requiring specialist care and sources of advice available to healthcare professionals without specialist training would be managed using protocols agreed within the network. This allows care to be provided according to the principles of a stepped-care model (see Figure 10 above). In particular, a managed network should aim to provide:

- active working relationships between healthcare professionals working in different parts of the network
- shared care protocols
- shared educational and training programmes
- shared user groups or user group networks
- explicit pathways of care following a woman's journey through care.

Women identified by general medical services, such as maternity services or through their GPs, as having a mental disorder can then either be referred directly to the part of the network that can give them the most appropriate care, or healthcare professionals in general medical services can source appropriate information and advice from colleagues in other parts of the network to provide adequate care themselves. A crucial aspect of the network should be that it will provide for women with severe mental disorder, such as schizophrenia or bipolar disorder, prompt advice and, where appropriate, treatment from specialist perinatal mental health services, where necessary facilitating prompt access to specialist inpatient services.

8.5.4   Estimating need in the managed network model

The estimation of need in this model starts with one of the building blocks of the network, the need for inpatient care. In section 8.3.2 the number of additional beds required was estimated at between 60 and 80. However, as has already been stated in this chapter, there will be considerable variation of need and provision of existing services between the areas covered by the perinatal networks. Each managed network should cover a population of between 25,000 and 50,000 live births, depending on local population morbidity. It will be a key task for the local networks to determine need for all levels of care, including inpatient care, in light of the local epidemiology and current service provision and configuration.

8.6   IMPLEMENTING THE MANAGED NETWORK MODEL: SERVICE RECOMMENDATIONS

8.6.1.1   Clinical networks should be established for perinatal mental health services, managed by a coordinating board of healthcare professionals, commissioners, managers, and service users and carers. These networks should provide:

- a specialist multidisciplinary perinatal service in each locality, which provides direct services, consultation and advice to maternity services, other mental health services and community services; in areas of high morbidity these services may be provided by separate specialist perinatal teams

- access to specialist expert advice on the risks and benefits of psychotropic medication during pregnancy and breastfeeding
- clear referral and management protocols for services across all levels of the existing stepped-care frameworks for mental disorders, to ensure effective transfer of information and continuity of care
- pathways of care for service users, with defined roles and competencies for all professional groups involved.

8.6.1.2   Each managed perinatal mental health network should have designated specialist inpatient services and cover a population where there are between 25,000 and 50,000 live births a year, depending on the local psychiatric morbidity rates.

8.6.1.3   Specialist perinatal inpatient services should:
- provide facilities designed specifically for mother and infants (typically with 6–12 beds)
- be staffed by specialist perinatal mental health staff
- be staffed to provide appropriate care for infants
- have effective liaison with general medical and mental health services
- have available the full range of therapeutic services
- be closely integrated with community-based mental health services to ensure continuity of care and minimum length of stay.

8.6.1.4   Women who need inpatient care for a mental disorder within 12 months of childbirth should normally be admitted to a specialist MBU, unless there are specific reasons for not doing so.

8.7   RESEARCH RECOMMENDATION

Assessing managed perinatal networks

An evaluation of managed perinatal networks should be undertaken to compare the effectiveness of different network models in delivering care. It should cover the degree of integration of services, the establishment of common protocols, the impact on patients' access to specified services and the quality of care, and staff views on the delivery of care.

Why this is important

Although only a relatively small number of women have serious mental disorder during pregnancy and the postnatal period, those who do may need specialist care, including access to knowledge about the risks of psychotropic medication, specialist inpatient beds and additional intrapartum care. Managed clinical perinatal networks may be a way of providing this level of care in a cost effective and clinically effective way by allowing access to specialist care for all women who need it, whether or not they live near a specialist perinatal team.

9.   APPENDICES

APPENDIX 1:

SCOPE FOR THE DEVELOPMENT OF A CLINICAL GUIDELINE ON THE MANAGEMENT AND SERVICE GUIDANCE OF ANTENATAL AND POSTNATAL MENTAL HEALTH

1.   GUIDELINE TITLE

Antenatal and postnatal mental health: clinical management and service guidance

Short title

Antenatal and postnatal mental health (APMH)

2.   BACKGROUND

a) The National Institute for Clinical Excellence ('NICE' or 'the Institute') has commissioned the National Collaborating Centre for Mental Health to develop a clinical guideline on antenatal and postnatal mental health for use in the NHS in England and Wales. This follows referral of the topic by the Department of Health and Welsh Assembly Government (see Appendix 1a). The guideline will provide recommendations for good practice that are based on the best available evidence of clinical and cost effectiveness.

b) The Institute's clinical guidelines will support the implementation of National Service Frameworks (NSFs) in those aspects of care where a Framework has been published. The statements in each NSF reflect the evidence that was used at the time the Framework was prepared. The clinical guidelines and technology appraisals published by the Institute after an NSF has been issued will have the effect of updating the Framework.

3.   CLINICAL NEED FOR THE GUIDELINE

a) At least half of women who give birth experience low mood at some point in their pregnancy and/or in the initial days or weeks following the birth. Symptoms include feeling tearful, overwhelmed and irritable, but these may pass with rest, support and reassurance.

b) If low mood persists during pregnancy, a diagnosis of antenatal depression may be applicable. Low mood is thought to affect up to 15% of pregnant women and, although prevalence is similar to that of postnatal depression, antenatal depression is often a neglected aspect of pregnancy. It has been suggested that early detection and management may prevent the development of postnatal depression. Diagnostic features include a loss of interest in oneself, anxiety, loss of appetite and feeling tearful, lonely, irritable and irrational.

c) If, following the birth of the child, marked low mood persists for a prolonged period of time, the mother may be diagnosed with postnatal depression. Diagnostic features include irritability, fatigue, sleeplessness, lack of appetite, anxiety, poor mother–infant interaction (for example, lack of interest in the child), anxieties about the child (possibly including thoughts of harming the child), lack of motivation, panic attacks, feelings of isolation, a sense of being overwhelmed and physical signs of tension, such as headaches or gastrointestinal symptoms. Thoughts of self-harm and suicide may also be present, which may or may not lead to self-harming behaviour. Postnatal depression affects 15 to 20% of new mothers within 12 months of their child's birth.

d) A more severe illness, with acute onset, is puerperal psychosis, a relatively rare disorder characterised by psychotic depression, mania or atypical psychosis. It affects between 1 in 500 and 1 in 1,000 women who have given birth. Characteristic features in those with mania include excitability, disinhibition and intense over-activity. More commonly, pregnancy, childbirth and the postnatal period can be associated with the re-emergence or exacerbation of a pre-existing psychotic illness, such as schizophrenia or bipolar disorder. For some women, there may be an increased risk of danger to themselves or others.

e) In addition to the development of depressive disorders, the onset or re-emergence of psychotic disorders during pregnancy, childbirth and the postnatal period can be associated with the re-emergence of a pre-existing or past psychotic illness, such as schizophrenia or bipolar disorder.

f) The development of mental disorders in pregnancy and postnatally may be associated with or aggravated by a number of factors. These include:

- psychological factors, such as the demands and expectations of being a mother, in addition to the psychological effects of a traumatic delivery
- social factors, including social isolation, economic status, ethnicity, cultural issues and housing
- family factors, including the relationship with the child's father and the support received from family and friends
- biological factors, including genetic factors and the hormonal changes that occur during pregnancy, childbirth and following childbirth
- personal history (including drug and alcohol use, domestic violence, and childhood sexual and physical abuse), family history, past psychiatric history and previous maternal history
- the infant's general health.

g) The UK Confidential Enquiry into Maternal Deaths (CEMD) reports that psychiatric disorders contributed to 12% of all maternal deaths (10% of which were due to suicide).

h) Mental disorders may go untreated, although response to treatment in the case of antenatal and postnatal depression tends to be good. If untreated, women may remain depressed, sometimes for many years, with consequent negative impact, not only for the mother but also for other family members. The rate of recurrence of postnatal depression after a subsequent birth is about 30%.

i) Individuals with antenatal and postnatal depression and puerperal psychosis are treated in a variety of NHS settings, including primary care services, obstetric and gynaecological services, general mental health services and specialist secondary care mental health services. The majority of cases of antenatal and postnatal depression and other disorders that arise in pregnancy and postnatally will be mild to moderate and managed in primary care.

j) All mental disorders in the antenatal and postnatal period may have a significant impact on the mother–infant relationship and, as a result, there may be longer-term consequences for all areas of the infant's development. In addition, the mother–father (partner) relationship may be affected.

k) The provision and uptake of services varies across England and Wales. In part, this reflects variation in the recognition of disorders, but also the presence or absence of specialist multidisciplinary and multi-agency services, particularly for the more severely unwell.

4.   THE GUIDELINE

a) The guideline development process is described in detail in two publications, which are available from the NICE website (see 'Further information'). *The Guideline Development Process – An Overview for Stakeholders, the Public and the NHS* describes how organisations can become involved in the development of a guideline. The *Guideline Development Methods – Information for National Collaborating Centres and Guideline Developers*[16] provides advice on the technical aspects of guideline development.

b) This document is the scope. It defines what this guideline will (and will not) examine, and what the guideline developers will consider. The scope is based on the referral from the Department of Health and Welsh Assembly Government (see Appendix 1a).

c) The areas that will be addressed by the guideline are described in the following sections.

---

[16]Since the development of this scope this has been superseded by the Guidelines Manual available on the NICE website at http://www.nice.org.uk/page.aspx?o=308639

Population

Groups that will be covered
The recommendations made in the guideline will cover the following:
a) Women who are suffering from mental disorders during pregnancy and the postnatal period, including antenatal and postnatal depression and puerperal psychosis.
b) The needs and role of families and carers in the care and support of women who have mental disorders. In addition, the role of other support systems, for example, support groups and voluntary organisations, will be considered.
c) The impact of the mother's disorder on the infant and siblings.
d) The mental health needs of the family, including the partner, and how this may have an effect on both the mother and the infant.

Groups that will not be covered
a) Although the guideline will be relevant to all women with a mental disorder during pregnancy and postnatally, whether or not the disorder is accompanied by other illnesses, it will not address separately or significantly the management of physical disorders during this period or psychiatric conditions outside of this period.
b) Women who experience transient low mood ('baby blues') during pregnancy and/or in the initial days following the birth of their child will not be covered. This is addressed in a separate NICE guideline: *Clinical Guidelines and Evidence Review for Postnatal Care: Routine Postnatal Care of Recently Delivered Women and Their Babies* (2006).

Healthcare setting and services

a) The guideline will cover the care and shared care provided in primary, secondary and tertiary healthcare services in the NHS and that provided by healthcare professionals and others working in healthcare settings who have contact with, and make decisions concerning, the mental healthcare of women in pregnancy and the postnatal period.
b) The guideline will also be relevant to the work of, but will not provide specific recommendations to, non-NHS services, for example:
   ● social services
   ● non-statutory sector.
However, it will consider the interface between healthcare services and these services.

Clinical and service management

The guideline will cover the following areas of clinical practice and, in doing so, will consider the ethnic and cultural background of women.
a) The full range of care that may be routinely made available by the NHS, including primary, secondary and tertiary services, for women with mental disorders during pregnancy and the postnatal period.

b) The prevention of mental disorders in pregnancy and the postnatal period.
c) Early identification and diagnosis for mental disorders in pregnancy and the post-natal period.
d) Psychosocial interventions, including type, format, frequency, duration and intensity.
e) Pharmacological treatments, including type, dose and duration.

   When referring to pharmacological treatments, normally guidelines will recommend use within licence indications. However, where the evidence clearly supports it, recommendations for use outside the licence indications may be made in exceptional circumstances. It is the responsibility of prescribers to be aware of circumstances where medication is contraindicated. The guideline will assume that prescribers are familiar with the side-effect profile and contraindications of medication they prescribe for patients. It will consider the implication for breastfeeding of pharmacological treatments and effects on the fetus and neonate.

f) Appropriate use of combined pharmacological and psychological treatments.
g) Electroconvulsive therapy.
h) The side effects, toxicity and other disadvantages of all treatments.
i) The needs of infants, other children and partners of women who have developed mental disorders in pregnancy and the postnatal period.
j) The role of the family and carers in the treatment and support of women with mental disorders in pregnancy and the postnatal period.
k) Consideration of the need for joint mother-baby admission.
l) Identification and management of risk to self and others.

The guideline will also address the following appropriate service configurations for the provision of effective care for women and their children:

a) Services for identification and diagnosis including:
   – general practitioners and other members of the primary care team, including health visitors
   – maternity services, including community-based midwifery services
   – general mental health services
   – specialist mental health services, including Child and Adolescent Mental Health Services (CAMHS) and Mother and Baby Units (MBUs).
b) Treatment services, to include treatment in the following settings:
   – primary care settings
   – secondary physical and mental health settings
   – tertiary care settings, including specialist treatment centres (for example, MBUs).
c) Multiprofessional working and service integration across sectors, including the place of shared care arrangements and appropriate care pathways.
d) Information resources for patients, carers and family members.

Status

Scope
This is the final scope, which has been through a 4-week period of consultation with stakeholders and has been reviewed by the Institute's independent Guidelines Review Panel (GRP).

The guideline will incorporate relevant technology appraisal guidance issued by the Institute, including: *Guidance on the Use of Electroconvulsive Therapy* (2003); *Guidance on the Use of Computerised Cognitive Behavioural Therapy for Anxiety and Depression* (2002 – updated 2005); and *Olanzapine and Valproate Semisodium in the Treatment of Acute Mania Associated with Bipolar I Disorder* (2003).

The guideline will also incorporate relevant clinical guidance issued by the Institute, including: *Schizophrenia: Core Interventions in the Treatment and Management of Schizophrenia in Primary and Secondary Care* (2002); *Depression: Management of Depression in Primary and Secondary Care* (2004); *Anxiety: Management of Anxiety (Panic Disorder, with or without Agoraphobia, and Generalised Anxiety Disorder) in Adults in Primary, Secondary and Community Care* (2004); *Caesarean Section* (2004); *Antenatal Care: Routine Care for the Healthy Pregnant Woman* (2003); *Bipolar Disorder: the Management of Bipolar Disorder in Adults, Children and Adolescents, in Primary and Secondary Care* (2006); and *Clinical Guidelines and Evidence Review for Postnatal Care: Routine Postnatal Care of Recently Delivered Women and their Babies* (2006).

Previous recommendations made in other guidelines may be updated by this guideline, based on the most up-to-date evidence for this particular population.

Guideline
The development of the guideline recommendations will begin in November 2004.

Further information

Information on the guideline development process is provided in:
- *The Guideline Development Process – An Overview for Stakeholders, the Public and the NHS*
- *Guideline Development Methods – Information for National Collaborating Centres and Guideline Developers*[17].

These booklets are available as PDF files from the NICE website (www.nice.org.uk). Information on the progress of the guideline will also be available from the website.

---

[17]Since the development of this scope this has been superseded by the Guidelines Manual available on the NICE website at http://www.nice.org.uk/page.aspx?o=308639

APPENDIX 1A:
REFERRAL FROM THE DEPARTMENT OF HEALTH AND WELSH ASSEMBLY GOVERNMENT

The Department of Health and Welsh Assembly Government asked the Institute: "to prepare a clinical and service guideline for the NHS in England and Wales for the early identification, prevention and drug and non-drug management of puerperal/perinatal mental illness. The guidance should include consideration of:
- the respective roles of primary care, secondary acute/maternity services, specialist mental health services and tertiary services, including the place of shared care arrangements
- the range of treatment to be provided by specialist mental health services, including specific drugs and ECT
- drug treatments for breast-feeding mothers
- recommendations for joint mother–baby admissions in very severe disorder and the role of health visitors in providing counselling and the provision of drug treatments by GPs in milder cases

Early recognition of women at risk should be looked at as part of the management approach, including specific inquiry about psychiatric risk factors at antenatal booking in. The guideline needs to be culturally competent so as to not exclude any groups of people."

APPENDIX 2:
ADVISORS TO THE GUIDELINE
DEVELOPMENT GROUP

Mr Stephen Bazire
Dr Roch Cantwell
Dr Margaret Oates

Speakers in consensus conference on the pharmacological management of mental disorders in pregnancy and lactating women

Professor David Chadwick
Professor Nicol Ferrier
Dr Peter Haddad
Dr Elizabeth McDonald
Dr Patricia McElhatton
Mr Patrick O'Brien

Speakers at an Infant Mental Health Day

Dr Eia Asen
Mr Robin Balbernie
Professor Vivette Glover
Dr Sebastian Kraemer
Dr Tessa Leverton
Dr Veronica O'Keane
Dr Susan Pawlby

Development of the specialist perinatal services survey

Dr Alain Gregoire

Development of the primary care trust survey

Ms Susannah Pick

APPENDIX 3:

STAKEHOLDERS WHO RESPONDED TO EARLY

REQUESTS FOR EVIDENCE

Association for Infant Mental Health
Cambridgeshire and Peterborough Mental Health Partnership NHS Trust
College of Occupational Therapists
National Perinatal Epidemiology Unit
National Mental Health Partnership
Royal College of Midwives
Royal College of Nursing
Royal College of Pathologists
Scottish Intercollegiate Guidelines Network
Sheffield Teaching Hospitals NHS Foundation Trust

APPENDIX 4:

STAKEHOLDERS AND EXPERTS WHO SUBMITTED COMMENTS IN RESPONSE TO THE CONSULTATION DRAFT OF THE GUIDELINE

STAKEHOLDERS

5 Boroughs Partnership NHS Trust
Action 16 Group, Care Services Improvement Partnership Social Inclusion Programme
The Association for Family Therapy
Association for Improvements in the Maternity Services
The Association for Infant Mental Health UK
Association for Psychoanalytic Psychotherapy in the NHS
Berkshire Healthcare NHS Trust
British Association for Psychopharmacology
British Association for Counselling and Psychotherapy
The British Dietetic Association
The British Psychological Society
CIS'ters
College of Occupational Therapists
Community Practitioners' and Health Visitors' Association
Counsellors and Psychotherapists in Primary Care
Croydon Primary Care Trust
Department of Health
Derbyshire Mental Health Services NHS Trust
Eli Lilly
Gloucestershire Partnership NHS Trust
Lambeth Primary Care Trust
London and South Thames Clinical Network in Perinatal Psychiatry
Medway NHS Trust
Midwifery Studies Research Unit, University of Central Lancashire
Mind
National Childbirth Trust
Netmums
Newcastle, North Tyneside and Northumberland Mental Health NHS Trust
North Cumbria Maternal Mental Health Alliance
North Essex Mental Health Partnership NHS Trust
North Staffordshire Combined Healthcare NHS Trust
North Tees and Hartlepool NHS Trust

Northwest London Hospitals NHS Trust
Nottinghamshire Healthcare NHS Trust
Postnatal Depression Steering Group, Camden Primary Care Trust
Rochdale Primary Care Trust
Royal College of General Practitioners
Royal College of Midwives
Royal College of Nursing
Royal College of Obstetricians and Gynaecologists
Royal College of Paediatrics and Child Health
Royal College of Psychiatrists
Salford Royal Hospitals NHS Trust
South East Essex Primary Care Trust
UK National Screening Committee
UK Psychiatric Pharmacy Group
UK and Ireland Marcé Society
University College London Hospitals NHS Foundation Trust
Victim Support

EXPERTS

Dr Kathryn Abel
Professor Ian Brockington
Dr Ian Jones
Dr Maureen Marks
Dr Susan Pawlby
Dr Judith Shakespeare

APPENDIX 5:
CLINICAL QUESTIONS

Prediction

For women in the antenatal and postnatal period, what factors predict the development or recurrence of particular mental disorders?
- Subsidiary questions: repeat for different disorders.
- Are there any tools developed (simple questions or more comprehensive tools) that reliably predict the development or recurrence of mental disorders?
- Does the benefit of using these tools outweigh the harm?

Detection/[diagnosis]

For women in the antenatal or postnatal period, are there methods (specific questions/simple tools) that can be used to detect particular mental disorders?
- Subsidiary questions: repeat for different disorders.
- Which tools/questions are best for which populations (ethnicity, whether pregnant or not, women under 18)?
- Is there evidence that use of these tools improves outcomes for women, taking full account of potential harm through the use of such tools? [Repeat question for diagnosis]

Prognosis

For women who have a mental disorder in the antenatal or postnatal period, are there differences in the aetiology, consequences, experience and/or diagnostic features that indicate that different management of the condition is required than for the disorder occurring at other times?
- Subsidiary questions: repeat for different disorders.

Prevention

For women identified as being at risk of developing depression in the antenatal or postnatal period, what interventions are most effective in reducing that risk?
- Subsidiary questions: repeat for different disorders.
- Subsidiary question: repeat for psychological/psychosocial interventions, combined psychological and drug interventions, and pharmacological interventions.
- Also consider outcomes for partners and children.

Treatment

For women with mental disorders in the antenatal or postnatal period, what interventions are associated with a reduction in symptomatology, increased remission and/or improved social and personal functioning?
- Subsidiary question: repeat for psychological/psychosocial interventions, combined psychological and drug interventions, and pharmacological interventions.
- Subsidiary question: repeat for different disorders.
- Subsidiary question: repeat for different mental health histories.
- Also consider outcomes for partners and children.

Harm

For women with mental disorders in the antenatal or postnatal period in receipt of interventions for the prevention and/or treatment of mental disorders, what strategies should be adopted to **minimise the potential harm** of these interventions?
- Subsidiary questions: consider harm to woman, fetus, breastfeeding infant and possibly also harm to other children or partners.

Service delivery

Delivery and coordination of care
What arrangement of **maternity services**, in terms of the functions performed by different services and how they are structured (including the relationship with other services), provide for the most effective delivery and coordination of care for women at risk of/or suffering from a mental disorder during the antenatal or postnatal period and their children?
- Subsidiary question: repeat for **primary care services**
- Subsidiary question: repeat for **secondary general mental health services**
- Subsidiary question: repeat for **specialist perinatal mental health services**
- Subsidiary question: repeat for **non-NHS services**
- Subsidiary question: repeat for **non-statutory services**

Safety and containment
For women with severe antenatal or postnatal mental disorders who present with serious risk, what service structures best provide for the **safety** of women and their children and **containment** of the disorder to allow delivery of effective care and treatment?

Specialist advice and consultation
In what ways and within what structures can **advice and consultation** be most effectively disseminated from specialist to non-specialist teams delivering care and treatment to women at risk of/or suffering from mental disorders in the antenatal or postnatal period and their children?

APPENDIX 6:

SEARCH STRATEGIES FOR THE

IDENTIFICATION OF STUDIES

The subject filter employs a combination of controlled vocabulary and free-text terms based on the following search strategy for searching DIALOG MEDLINE, but revised appropriately for other databases. The subject search uses a combination of free-text terms (including alternative spellings) and Medical Subject Heading (MeSH) terms; MeSH headings have been exploded. For databases other than MEDLINE, the search strategy has been adapted accordingly.

APMH FULL SEARCH FILTERS

MEDLINE, EMBASE, CINAHL, PsycINFO – DIALOG Datastar interface

Pregnancy and childbirth

1	PREGNANCY#.W..DE.
2	PREGNANCY-COMPLICATIONS#.W..DE.
3	PREGNANCY-TRIMESTERS#.W..DE.
4	PREGNANCY-MULTIPLE#.W..DE.
5	INFANT-NEWBORN#.W..DE.
6	PRENATAL-DIAGNOSIS#.W..DE.
7	UTERINE-MONITORING#.W..DE.
8	PELVIMETRY#.W..DE.
9	MATERNAL-HEALTH-SERVICES#.W..DE.
10	MATERNAL-CHILD-NURSING#.W..DE.
11	MATERNAL-AGE#.W..DE.
12	PERINATAL-CARE#.W..DE.
13	PARITY#.W..DE.
14	PUERPERIUM#.W..DE.
15	BREASTFEEDING#.W..DE.
16	MILK-HUMAN#.W..DE.
17	PREGNAN$4.TI,AB.
18	NEWBORN$2.TI,AB.
19	(NEW ADJ BORN$2).TI,AB.
20	(BIRTH OR CHILDBIRTH OR POSTBIRTH).TI,AB.
21	(LABOR OR LABORING).TI,AB.
22	LABOUR.TI,AB.
23	(ANTEPART$3 OR ANTE ADJ PART$3).TI,AB.

24	(PRENATAL$2 OR PRE ADJ NATAL$2).TI,AB.
25	(ANTENATAL$2 OR ANTE ADJ NATAL$2).TI,AB.
26	(PERINATAL$2 OR PERI ADJ NATAL$2).TI,AB.
27	(POSTNATAL$2 OR POST ADJ NATAL$2).TI,AB.
28	(POSTPART$2 OR POST ADJ PART$2).TI,AB.
29	PUERPERAL.TI,AB.
30	LACTAT$3.TI,AB.
31	BREASTFE$5.TI,AB.
32	(BREAST ADJ (FEED$ OR FED)).TI,AB.
33	1 OR 2 OR 3 OR 4 OR 5 OR 6 OR 7 OR 8 OR 9 OR 10 OR 11 OR 12 OR 13 OR 14 OR 15 OR 16 OR 17 OR 18 OR 19 OR 20 OR 21 OR 22 OR 23 OR 24 OR 25 OR 26 OR 27 OR 28 OR 29 OR 30 OR 31 OR 32

P&C complications – not explicit in scope

34	ABORTION-INDUCED#.W..DE.
35	MISCARR$5.TI,AB.
36	ABORTION$1.TI,AB. OR TERMINAT$3.TI,AB.
37	((FETAL OR FOETAL OR FETUS OR FOETUS OR NEONAT$2 OR INTRAUTERINE) ADJ (DEATH$1 OR DEAD)).TI,AB.
38	(STILLBORN$ OR STILL ADJ BORN$).TI,AB.
39	(STILLBIRTH$ OR STILL ADJ BIRTH$).TI,AB.
40	34 OR 35 OR 36 OR 37 OR 38 OR 39

Mental disorders

41	ADJUSTMENT-DISORDERS#.W..DE.
42	ANXIETY-DISORDERS#.W..DE.
43	DISSOCIATIVE-DISORDERS#.W..DE.
44	EATING-DISORDERS#.W..DE.
45	MOOD-DISORDERS#.W..DE.
46	NEUROTIC-DISORDERS#.W..DE.
47	PERSONALITY-DISORDERS#.W..DE.
48	SCHIZOPHRENIA-AND-DISORDERS-WITH-PSYCHOTIC-FEATURES#.W..DE.
49	SOMATOFORM-DISORDERS#.W..DE.
50	SUBSTANCE-RELATED-DISORDERS#.W..DE.
51	DEPRESSION#.W..DE. OR (SEASONAL ADJ AFFECTIVE ADJ DISORDER$2 OR DEPRESS$4 OR DYSTHYM$4).TI,AB.
52	MELANCHOL$3.TI,AB.
53	(BIPOLAR OR BI ADJ POLAR).TI,AB. AND (DISORDER$2 OR DEPRESS$4).TI,AB.

54	(CYCLOTHYMI$3 OR RAPID ADJ CYCL$3 OR ULTRADIAN NEAR CYCL$3).TI,AB.
55	(MANIA OR MANIC OR HYPOMANIA).TI,AB.
56	ANOREXIA#.W..DE.
57	(EATING NEAR DISORDER$2).TI,AB.
58	(ANOREXIA NEAR NERVOSA).TI,AB.
59	(BULIMIA#W..DE. OR BULIMI$2 OR KLEINE ADJ LEVIN OR HYPERPHAGIA).TI,AB.
60	(BING$4 OR OVEREAT$3 OR COMPULSIVE NEAR (EAT$3 OR VOMIT$3) OR FOOD$2 NEAR BING$4 OR (SELF ADJ INDUC$2 OR SELFINDUC$2) NEAR VOMIT$3 OR RESTRICT$4 NEAR EAT$3).TI,AB.
61	ANXIETY#.W..DE. OR ANXIETY-SEPARATION#.W..DE. OR PANIC#.W..DE. OR (ANXIOUS OR ANXIETY OR PANIC OR PHOBIA OR PHOBIC).TI,AB.
62	STRESS-PSYCHOLOGICAL#.W..DE.
63	(POST ADJ TRAUMATIC$2 OR POSTTRAUMATIC$2 OR STRESS ADJ DISORDER$2 OR ACUTE ADJ STRESS OR PTSD OR ASD OR DESNOS).TI,AB.
64	(COMBAT OR CONCENTRATION ADJ CAMP ADJ SYNDROME OR EXTREME ADJ STRESS OR FLASH ADJ BACK$2 OR FLASH-BACK$2).TI,AB.
65	(HYPERVIGILAN$2 OR HYPERVIGILEN$2 OR PSYCHOLOG$4 ADJ STRESS OR PSYCHO ADJ (TRAUMA OR TRAUMATIC) OR PSYCHOTRAUMA OR PSYCHOTRAUMATIC).TI,AB.
66	(RAILWAY ADJ SPINE OR RAPE NEAR TRAUMA$5 OR RE ADJ EXPERIENC$3 OR RE ADJ EXPERIENC$3 OR TORTURE ADJ SYNDROME OR TRAUMATIC ADJ NEUROS$2 OR TRAUMATIC ADJ STRESS).TI,AB.
67	TRAUMA$5.TI,AB. AND (AVOIDANCE OR GRIEF OR HORROR OR DEATH$1 OR NIGHT ADJ MARE$1 OR NIGHTMARE$1 OR EMOTION$2).TI,AB.
68	(RECURR$5 ADJ THOUGHT$2).TI,AB.
69	OBSESSIVE-BEHAVIOR#.W..DE. OR (OBSESSION OR OBSES-SIONS OR OBSESSIONAL).TI,AB.
70	(CLEAN$6 ADJ RESPONSE$2).TI,AB.
71	OCD.TI,AB.
72	OSTEOCHONDR$3.TI,AB.
73	71 NOT 72
74	COMPULSIVE-BEHAVIOR#.W..DE. OR COMPULS$5.TI,AB.
75	((SYMMETR$4 OR COUNT$3 OR ARRANG$3 OR ORDER$3 OR WASH$3 OR REPEAT$3 OR HOARD$3 OR CLEAN$3 OR CHECK$3) ADJ COMPULSI$4).TI,AB.
76	(PERSONALIT$3 NEAR (DISORDER$1 OR DIFFICULT$3)).TI,AB.
77	(ANTISOCIAL OR ANTI ADJ SOCIAL OR PSYCHOPATH$3 OR BORDERLINE OR HYSTERI$3).TI,AB.

78   (DISSOCIAT$3 NEAR (DISORDER$ OR DIFFICULT$3 OR PERSON-ALIT$3 OR DISTURB$5 OR TRAUMA$4)).TI,AB.

79   SCHIZO$9.TI,AB.

80   (PSYCHOS$2 OR PSYCHOTIC$2 OR PARANO$3).TI,AB.

81   (SOMATOFORM OR SOMATIZATION OR SOMATIC OR HYPOCHON-DRIASIS$3 OR NEURASTHENIA$3).TI,AB.

82   (CONVERSION ADJ DISORDER$1 OR HYPOCHONDRIASIS OR NEURASTHENIA).TI,AB.

83   (BODY ADJ DYSMORPHIC OR DYSMORPHOPHOBI$2 OR BRIQUET ADJ SYNDROME$1 OR SYNDROME ADJ BRIQUET).TI,AB.

84   ((ATTACH$ OR BOND OR BONDING) NEAR (AMBIVALENT OR ANXIOUS$4 OR AVOID$4 OR DIFFICULT$3 OR DISINHIBIT$3 OR DISORDER$2 OR DISORGANIS$4 OR DISRUPTIV$4 OR DISSO-CIAT$4 OR DYSREGULA$4 OR DISORIENTAT$4 OR DISTUR-BANCE$2 OR IMPAIR$5 OR INADEQUATE OR INHIBIT$3 OR INJUR$4 OR INSECUR$5 OR POOR OR STYLE$2)).TI,AB.

85   (ADJUST OR ADJUSTIVE OR ADJUSTMENT OR REACTIVE).TI,AB.

86   (DISORDER$1 OR DISTURB$5 OR DIFFICULT$3).TI,AB.

87   85 NEAR 86

88   (TRANSIENT ADJ SITUATIONAL ADJ DISTURB$5 OR TRANSIENT ADJ SITUATIONAL ADJ DISORDER$1).TI,AB.

89   KLEPTOMANI$3.TI,AB.

90   (DRUG$2 OR SUBSTANCE$2).TI,AB.

91   (ABUSE OR USE OR MISUSE OR DEPEND$6 OR ADDICT$4).TI,AB.

92   90 NEAR 91

93   (NEUROTIC$2 OR NEUROSIS).TI,AB.

94   SUICIDE#.W..DE. OR OVERDOSE#.W..DE. OR SELF-INJURIOUS-BEHAVIOR#.W..DE. OR SELF-MUTILATION#.DE.

95   (SUICID$3 OR SELF ADJ HARM$2 OR SELFHARM$2 OR SELF ADJ INJUR$4 OR SELFINJUR$4 OR SELF ADJ MUTILAT$3 OR SELFMU-TILAT$3 OR SUICID$3 OR SELF ADJ DESTRUCT$3 OR SELFDE-STRUCT$3 OR SELF ADJ POISON$3 OR SELFPOISON$3 OR SELF NEAR CUT$4 OR CUTT$4 OR OVERDOSE$2 OR SELF ADJ IMMOLAT$4 OR SELFIMMOLAT$4 OR SELF ADJ INFLICT$4 OR SELFINFLICT$4 OR AUTO ADJ MUTILAT$3 OR AUTOMUTI-LAT$3).TI,AB.

96   AFFECTIVE-SYMPTOMS#.W..DE.

97   (AFFECTIVE NEAR DISORDER$1).TI,AB.

98   MENTAL-DISORDERS.MJ.

99   (MENTAL NEAR (ILLNESS$2 OR DISEASE$1 OR DISORDER$1)).TI,AB.

100   41 OR 42 OR 43 OR 44 OR 45 OR 46 OR 47 OR 48 OR 49 OR 50 OR 51 OR 52 OR 53 OR 54 OR 55 OR 56 OR 57 OR 58 OR 59 OR 60 OR 61 OR 62 OR 63 OR 64 OR 65 OR 66 OR 67 OR 68 OR 69 OR 70 OR 73 OR 74 OR 75 OR 76 OR 77 OR 78 OR 79 OR 80 OR 81 OR 82 OR 83 OR 84 OR 87 OR 88 OR 89 OR 92 OR 93 OR 94 OR 95 OR 96 OR 97 OR 98 OR 99

Mental disorders/scales associated with P&C

101   DEPRESSION-POSTPARTUM#.W..DE.

102   ((BABY OR POSTPARTUM OR POST ADJ PARTUM OR POSTNATAL OR POST ADJ NATAL OR MATERNITY OR MATERNAL) ADJ BLUES).TI,AB.

103   101 OR 102

104   (33 OR 40) AND 100 OR 103

The result set of the above search is combined with all of the following, each on an individual basis.

Part 1

   Systematic review/meta analysis

105   META-ANALYSIS#.W..DE.

106   REVIEW-LITERATURE#.W..DE.

107   PT = META-ANALYSIS

108   ((SYSTEMATIC OR QUANTITATIVE OR METHODOLOGIC$) NEAR (OVERVIEW$4 OR REVIEW$4)).TI,AB,DE.

109   (METAANALY$3 OR META ADJ ANALY$3).TI,AB,DE.

110   (RESEARCH ADJ (REVIEW$3 OR INTEGRATION)).TI,AB,DE.

111   (REFERENCE ADJ LIST$2).AB.

112   BIBLIOGRAPHY$3.AB.

113   (PUBLISHED ADJ STUDIES).AB.

114   (RELEVANT ADJ JOURNALS).AB.

115   (SELECTION ADJ CRITERIA).AB.

116   (DATA ADJ (EXTRACTION OR SYNTHESIS)).AB.

117   (HANDSEARCH$3 OR (HAND OR MANUAL) ADJ SEARCH$3).TI,AB.

118   (MANTEL ADJ HAENSZEL OR PETO OR DERSIMONIAN OR DER ADJ SIMONIAN).TI,AB.

119   (FIXED ADJ EFFECT$2 OR RANDOM ADJ EFFECT$2).TI,AB.

120   (BIDS OR CINAHL OR COCHRANE OR INDEX ADJ MEDICUS OR ISI ADJ CITATION OR EMBASE OR MEDLINE OR PSYCINFO OR PSYC ADJ INFO OR PSYCLIT OR PSYCHLIT OR SCISEARCH OR SCIENCE ADJ CITATION OR WEB ADJ OF ADJ SCIENCE). TI,AB.

121   105 OR 106 OR 107 OR 108 OR 109 OR 110 OR 111 OR 112 OR 113 OR 114 OR 115 OR 116 OR 117 OR 118 OR 119 OR 120

122   104 AND 121

Part 2

   RCT filter

123   CLINICAL-TRIALS#.W..DE.

124   CONTROLLED-CLINICAL-TRIALS#.W..DE.

125   CROSS-OVER-STUDIES#.W..DE.

126   DOUBLE-BLIND-METHOD#.W..DE.

127   PLACEBOS#.W..DE.

128	RANDOM-ALLOCATION#.W..DE.
129	RANDOMIZED-CONTROLLED-TRIALS#.W..DE.
130	SINGLE-BLIND-METHOD#.W..DE.
131	PT = CLINICAL-TRIAL$
132	PT = CONTROLLED-CLINICAL-TRIAL
133	PT = RANDOMIZED-CONTROLLED-TRIAL
134	105 OR 106 OR 107 OR 108 OR 109 OR 110 OR 111 OR 112 OR 113 OR 114 OR 115
135	CLINICAL NEAR (TRIAL$2 OR STUDY OR STUDIES)
136	SINGL$2 OR DOUBL$2 OR TREBL$2 OR TRIPL$2
137	BLIND$3 OR MASK$3 OR DUMMY
138	118 NEAR 119
139	PLACEBO$3
140	RANDOM$8
141	116 OR 117 OR 120 OR 121 OR 122
142	ANIMAL = YES
143	HUMAN = YES
144	124 NOT (124 AND 125)
145	123 NOT 126
146	104 AND 127

Part 3-Screening

  (a) Epidemiology

147	EPIDEMIOLOGY#.DE.
148	MORBIDITY#.W..DE.
149	(MORBIDIT$3 OR PREVALENCE$1 OR INCIDENCE).ti,ab.
150	MORBIDITY.DE.
151	RECURRENCE.DE.
152	(RECURRENCE$1 OR RECURRENT DISEASE OR DISEASE COURSE).ti,ab.
153	105 OR 106 OR 107 OR 108 OR 109 OR 110
154	104 AND 111

  (b) Screening filter – UNDER REVIEW

155	MENTAL-DISORDERS-PC.DE.
156	MASS-SCREENING#.DE.
157	MULTIPHASIC-SCREENING#.DE.
158	POPULATION-SURVEILLANCE#.DE.
159	NEONATAL-SCREENING#.DE.
160	PRENATAL-DIAGNOSIS.DE.
161	PREVENTIVE-HEALTH-SERVICES#.DE.
162	DIAGNOSTIC-SERVICES#.DE.
163	DIAGNOSTIC-TESTS-ROUTINE#.DE.
164	SENSITIVITY-AND-SPECIFICITY#.DE.
165	SENSITIVITY.TI,AB,KW.

166   (FALSE ADJ NEGATIVE).TI,AB,DE.
167   (FALSE ADJ POSITIVE).TI,AB,DE.
168   PREDICTIVE-VALUE-OF-TESTS#.DE.
169   ROC-CURVE#.DE.
170   ((ANTENATAL OR ANTE ADJ NATAL OR PRENATAL OR PRE ADJ NATAL OR PERINATAL OR PERI ADJ NATAL OR POSTNATAL OR POST ADJ NATAL OR POSTPARTUM OR POST ADJ PARTUM) NEAR TEST$3).TI,AB.
171   (SCREEN$ OR ASSESS$ OR SURVEILLANCE).TI,AB.
172   PREVENT$5.TI,AB.
173   (EARLY NEAR DETECT$).TI,AB.
174   105 OR 106 OR 107 OR 108 OR 109 OR 110 OR 111 OR 112 OR 113 OR 114 OR 115 OR 116 OR 117 OR 118 OR 119 OR 120 OR 121 OR 122 OR 123
175   104 AND 124

Part 5
  Service guidance
176   FAMILY-PRACTICE#.W..DE.
177   (FAMILY PRACT$).TI,AB.
178   (GENERAL PRACT$).ti,ab.
179   PHYSICIANS-FAMILY#.W..DE.
180   PRIMARY-HEALTH-CARE#.W..DE.
181   COMMUNITY-HEALTH-SERVICES#.W..DE.
182   (COMMUNITY CARE).TI,AB,DE.
183   (SHARED CARE).TI,AB,DE.
184   (PATIENT CARE TEAM).TI,AB,DE.
185   (FAMILY AND (PHYS$ OR PRACTICE$)).TI,AB,DE.
186   ((PRIMARY NEAR CARE) OR (GENERAL NEAR PRACT$)).TI,AB,DE.
187   or/105-115
188   HOME-CARE-SERVICES#.W..DE.
189   COMMUNITY-HEALTH-SERVICES#.W..DE.
190   HOME-NURSING#.W..DE.
191   SOCIAL-SUPPORT#.W..DE.
192   (PARENT$ NEAR SUPPORT$).TI,AB.
193   (NURS$ NEAR HOME).TI,AB.
194   (HOME NEAR VISIT$).TI,AB.
195   (HEALTH NEAR VISIT$).TI,AB.
196   (DOMICIL$ NEAR NURS$).TI,AB.
197   (PUBLIC HEALTH NEAR NURS$).TI,AB.
198   (FAMIL$ NEAR SUPPORT$).TI,AB.
199   (FAMIL$ NEAR INTERVENTION$).TI,AB.
200   (SOCIAL NEXT SUPPORT$).TI,AB.
201   (HOME NEAR SUPPORT$).TI,AB.
202   (COMMUNITY-BASED OR (COMMUNITY NEXT BASED)).TI,AB.
203   or/117-131

204	DELIVERY-OF-HEALTH-CARE#.W..DE.
205	MENTAL-HEALTH-SERVICES#.W..DE.
206	MANAGED-CARE-PROGRAMS#.W..DE.
207	MENTAL-HEALTH-ASSOCIATIONS#.W..DE.
208	COMPREHENSIVE-HEALTH-CARE#.W..DE.
209	HEALTH-SERVICES-ACCESSIBILITY#.W..DE.
210	((MANAGED OR ENHANCED OR COORDINA$ OR CO ORDINA$) ADJ CARE).TI,AB.
211	(SHARED OR JOINT OR COLLABORAT$ OR INTEGRAT$ OR INTERFACE).TI,AB.
212	INTERINSTITUTIONAL-RELATIONS#.W..DE.
213	INTERPROFESSIONAL-RELATIONS#.W..DE.
214	INTERDISCIPLINARY-COMMUNICATION#.W..DE.
215	COOPERATIVE-BEHAVIOR#.W..DE.
216	PATIENT-CARE-TEAM#.W..DE.
217	"REFERRAL-AND-CONSULTATION"#.W..DE.
218	OR/133-146
219	CASE-MANAGEMENT#.W..DE.
220	CARE-MANAGEMENT#.W..DE.
221	((CASE OR CARE) AND (MANAGEMENT)) OR CPA OR (CARE PROGRAMME APPROACH) OR (ASSERTIVE COMMUNITY TREAT-MENT) OR (PACT) OR (TCL) OR (TRAINING NEAR COMMUNITY LIVING) OR (MADISION NEAR MODEL).TI,AB.
222	(CARE NEAR (COORDINAT$ OR COORDINATION)).TI,AB.
223	(ANTICIPATED RECOVERY PATHWAYS).TI,AB.
224	OR/148-152
225	MATERNAL HEALTH SERVICES
226	MATERNAL-HEALTH-SERVICES#.W..DE.
227	MATERNAL-CHILD-HEALTH-CENTERS#.W..DE.
228	(MATERN$ NEAR (CENTER$ OR SERVICE$)).TI,AB.
229	CONTINUITY-OF-CARE#.W..DE.
230	(CONTINUITY NEAR CARE).TI,AB.
231	OR/154-159
232	(PARENT$ PROGRAM$ OR PARENT$ TRAINING OR PARENT$ EDUCATION OR PARENT$ PROMOTION).TI,AB,DE.
233	MIDWIFERY#.W..DE.
234	MIDWIFERY-SERVICE#.W..DE.
235	NURSING-CARE-DELIVERY-SYSTEMS#.W..DE.
236	(MIDWIF$ NEAR TEAM$).TI,AB.
237	(MIDWIF$ MODEL$).TI,AB.
238	(MULTIDISCIPLINARY ADJ TEAM$).TI,AB.
239	(MIDWIF$ LED).TI,AB.
240	(MIDWIF$ MANAG$).TI,AB.
241	MEDICAL$ LED).TI,AB.
242	(MEDICAL MANAG$).TI,AB.

243   or/161-171
244   MBU$1.TI,AB.
245   (MOTHER NEAR (BABY OR INFANT) NEAR UNIT$).TI,AB.
246   PSYCHIATRIC-DEPARTMENT-HOSPITAL#.W..DE.
247   or/173-175
248   SPECIALITIES-MEDICAL#.W..DE.
249   (SPECIALIS$ NEAR SERVICE$).TI,AB.
250   OR/177-178
251   EDUCATION#.W..DE.
252   HEALTH-BEHAVIOR#.W..DE.
253   HEALTH-EDUCATION#.W..DE.
254   SELF-CARE#.W..DE.
255   PATIENT-EDUCATION#.W..DE.
256   PATIENT-SATISFACTION#.W..DE.
257   PATIENT-DROPOUTS#.W..DE.
258   DELIVERY-OF-HEALTH-CARE#.W..DE.
259   EDUCATIONAL-STATUS#.W..DE.
260   PATIENT-COMPLIANCE#.W..DE.
261   HEALTH-PROMOTION#.W..DE.
262   (COMPLIAN$ OR ADHEREN$).TI,AB.
263   (PATIENT NEAR (SATISFACTION OR EDUCATION)).TI,AB.
264   PATIENT$ DROPOUT$.TI,AB.
265   (TREATMENT$ NEAR REFUSAL$).TI,AB.
266   (HEALTH NEAR EDUCATION).TI,AB.
267   (HEALTH NEAR BEHAVIO$).TI,AB.
268   (SELF CARE OR SELF MANAGEMENT).TI,AB.
269   ACTION PLAN$.TI,AB.
270   EDUCAT$.TI,AB.
271   ADHER$.TI,AB.
272   COMPLY.TI,AB.
273   CONCORD$.TI,AB.
274   OR/180-202
275   OR/116,132,147,153,160,172,176,179,203.
276   104 AND 204

PREDICTION AND DETECTION SEARCH (DIAGNOSIS/ SCREENING FILTER)

MEDLINE, EMBASE, CINAHL, PsycINFO – OVID interface

Pregnancy/antenatal period

1   exp fetus monitoring/
2   exp maternal age/

3	exp maternal care/
4	exp maternal child nursing/
5	exp maternal child care/
6	exp maternal child health/
7	exp maternal health services/
8	exp multiple pregnancy/
9	exp parity/
10	exp pelvimetry/
11	exp perinatal care/
12	exp perinatal period/
13	exp pregnancy/
14	exp pregnancy complications/
15	exp pregnancy multiple/
16	exp pregnancy trimesters/
17	exp prenatal care/
18	exp prenatal diagnosis/
19	exp uterine monitoring/
20	pregnan$4.tw.
21	((anti?natal$2 or ante) adj natal$2).tw.
22	((ante?part$3 or ante) adj part$3).tw.
23	((pre?natal$2 or pre) adj natal$2).tw.
24	or/1-23

Postnatal depression

25   exp postpartum period/ or exp puerperium/ or exp postnatal care/ or exp postnatal period/ or (post natal$2 or post?natal$2 or post part$2 or post?part$2 or puerperium or (new adj mother$1)).mp.

26   exp depression/ or exp depressive disorder/ or exp major depression/ or exp seasonal affective disorder/ or exp bipolar depression/ or ((seasonal adj affective adj disorder$1) or depress$ or dysthym$4 or mood disorder$1).mp.

27   exp depression postpartum/ or exp puerperal depression/ or exp postpartum depression/

28   ((baby or post partum or post?partum or post natal$ or post?natal$ anti?natal$ or anti natal$ or anti?natal$ or matern$) adj5 blues).tw.

29   (25 and 26) or 27 or 28

Screening/diagnosis

30   exp mass screening/ or exp epidemiology/ or exp screening test/ or exp "mental health screening (saba hhcc)"/ or exp "health screening (iowa nic)"/ or exp health screening/

31   (screening or screened or screen positive or screen negative).tw.

32	exp "sensitivity and specificity"/
33	(sensitivity or specificity).tw.
34	exp diagnosis/
35	(diagnosis or diagnostic).tw.
36	(diagnosis or diagnostic).af.
37	exp pathology/
38	((pre test or pretest or post test or posttest) adj probability).tw.
39	predict$3.tw.
40	exp likelihood functions/ or maximum likelihood/ or exp maximum likelihood method/
41	likelihood ratio$.tw.
42	exp diagnostic errors/ or diagnosis, differential/ or exp "measurement issues and assessments"/
43	(false adj (negative$ or positive$)).tw.
24	or/30-43

Combined

45	and/24,29,44
46	limit 45 to yr = 2001-2005
47	remove duplicates from 46

RISK FACTORS SEARCH

MEDLINE, EMBASE, CINAHL, PsycINFO [search terms adapted for each] – DIALOG Datastar interface

Postnatal depression

1	((POSTNATAL$2 OR POST ADJ NATAL$2 OR POSTPART$2 OR POST ADJ PART$2 OR PUERPERIUM OR NEW ADJ MOTHER$1).TI,AB. OR POSTPARTUM-PERIOD#.DE.) AND (DEPRESSION#.W..DE. OR DEPRESSIVE-DISORDER#.DE. OR SEASONAL-AFFECTIVE-DISORDER#.DE. OR (SEASONAL ADJ AFFECTIVE ADJ DISORDER$2 OR DEPRESS$4 OR DYSTHYM$4).TI,AB.)
2	DEPRESSION-POSTPARTUM#.W..DE.
3	((BABY OR POSTPARTUM OR POST ADJ PARTUM OR POSTNATAL OR POST ADJ NATAL OR MATERNITY OR MATERNAL) NEAR BLUES).TI,AB.
4	PUERPERAL-DISORDERS#.DE. AND PSYCHOTIC-DISORDERS#.DE.
5	PUERPERAL.TI,AB,DE. AND PSYCHOS$2.TI,AB,DE.
6	1 OR 2 OR 3 OR 4 OR 5

Risk factors

7   RISK#.W..DE. OR RISK.DE.

8   (PREDICTOR OR PREDICTORS OR RISK ADJ FACTOR$1 OR PROG-NOS$3).TI,AB,DE.

9   (RESPON$ NEAR (TREATMENT$1 OR THERAP$3)).TI,AB.

10   PROGNOS$3.TI,AB,DE.

11   INTERPERSONAL-RELATIONS#.DE. OR LIFE-CHANGE-EVENTS#.DE. OR MARRIAGE#.W..DE. OR MATERNAL-AGE#.DE. OR PARITY#.W..DE. OR STRESS-PSYCHOLOGICAL#.DE. OR PSYCHOPATHOLOGY#.W..DE. OR SOCIAL-ENVIRONMENT#.DE. OR SOCIAL-ISOLATION#.DE. OR SOCIAL-PROBLEMS#.DE. OR SOCIAL-WELFARE#.DE. OR SOCIOECONOMIC-FACTORS#.DE.

12   (INCOME$1 OR EARNING$1 OR FINANC$5 OR OCCUPATION$2 OR SOCIAL NEAR (SUPPORT OR WELFARE OR STATUS) OR LOW ADJ STATUS OR (ADVERSE OR LIFE) ADJ (EVENT$1 OR EXPERI-ENCE$1) OR MARITAL OR MARRIAGE$1 OR HARDSHIP OR UNEMPLOY$4 OR POVERTY OR DEPRIVATION OR MISFORTUNE OR HOUSING OR RESIDENCY OR SOCIAL ADJ EXCLUSION OR PSYCHOPATHOLOGY OR STRESS$3 OR SOCIOECONOMIC OR SOCIO ADJ ECONOMIC OR ADVERSIT$3 OR PARITY).TI,AB.

13   ((RELATIONS$4 OR SUPPORT OR DYNAMICS) NEAR (SPOUSE OR FATHER OR PARTNER OR FAMILY OR PARENT$1) OR LENGTH NEAR RELATIONSHIP OR (PAST OR FAMILY OR PERSONAL) ADJ HISTORY OR FACTOR$1 OR DYSPHORIC ADJ MOOD$1 OR NEUROTIC$3 OR FIRST ADJ CHILD OR NUMBER ADJ CHIL-DREN).TI,AB.

14   7 OR 8 OR 9 OR 10 OR 11 OR 12 OR 13

Diagnostic interview

15   INTERVIEW-PSYCHOLOGICAL#.DE. OR PSYCHIATRIC-STATUS-RATING-SCALES#.DE.

16   INTERVIEW$3.TI,AB.

17   ((PSYCHOLOGICAL OR PSYCHOSOCIAL OR PSYCHO ADJ SOCIAL OR PSYCHIATRIC) ADJ (DIAGNOS$3 OR ASSESSMENT$1) OR DIAGNOS$3 ADJ (ASSESSMENT$1 OR CRITERIA) OR PSYCHODIAGNOS$3 OR PSYCHO ADJ DIAGNOS$3).TI,AB. OR DEPRESSION-DI#.DE. OR DEPRESSIVE-DISORDER-DI#.DE.

18   (MENTAL ADJ STATUS ADJ (EXAM$1 OR EXAMINATION$1) OR (ASSESSED OR ASSESSMENT$ OR PREDICTORS) WITH (DEPRESS$3 OR DIAGNOSTIC ADJ STATUS)).TI,AB.

19 (SCID OR CIS ADJ 'R' OR SADS ADJ L OR SCAN OR SCHEDULE NEAR CLINICAL ADJ ASSESSMENT NEAR NEUROPSYCHIATRY OR RDC OR RASKIN OR HDRS OR HRSD OR HAMILTON$1 OR SPI OR GOLDBERG$1 OR PITT$1 OR CIP OR COMPREHENSIVE ADJ IDENTIFICATION ADJ PROCESS OR CID).TI,AB.

20 (ICD OR INTERNATIONAL ADJ CLASSIFICATION NEAR DISEASES).TI,AB. 21 (DSM OR DIAGNOSTIC ADJ STATISTICAL ADJ MANUAL).TI,AB. OR DIAGNOSTIC-AND-STATISTICAL-MANUAL-OF-MENTAL-DISORDERS#.DE.

22 15 OR 16 OR 17 OR 18 OR 19 OR 20 OR 21

Longitudinal/prospective studies

23 LONGITUDINAL-STUDIES#.DE.
24 (LONGITUDINAL OR PROSPECTIVE$3 OR FOLLOWUP OR FOLLOW$2 ADJ UP).TI,AB.
25 23 OR 24

Combined

26 6 AND 14 AND 22 AND 25

PSYCHOTROPIC DRUGS AND HARM SEARCH (HARM FILTER)

MEDLINE, EMBASE, CINAHL, PsycINFO – OVID interface

Population groups

1 exp infant/ or exp infant, newborn/ or exp newborn/ or (infant$1 or neonat$ or new?born$ or new born$).tw.
2 exp developmental disabilities/ or exp developmental disorder/ or exp prematurity/ or ((late adj3 develop$5) or (develop$5 adj3 (disab$ or disorder$1))).tw.
3 (1 and 2) or exp infant development disorders/
4 exp fetus/ or exp "fetus (anatomy)"/ or "embryonic and fetal development"/ or (foetus or fetus or foetal or fetal).sh.
5 breast feeding/ or breast milk/ or milk human/ or exp pregnancy/ or ((breast adj (feed$ or fed or milk)) or breastfe$ or breastmilk or lactate$ or pregnan$).tw.

Psychotropic drugs

6 exp psychotropic agent/ or exp nootropic agent/ or exp psychedelic agent/ or exp psychostimulant agent/ or exp tranquilizer/ or (psychotrophic$ or nootropic$ or psychedelic$ or psychostimulant$ or tranquili?er$).tw.

7 exp antipsychotic agent/ or exp antipsychotic agents/ or exp neuroleptic agent/ or exp neuroleptic drugs/ or (anti?psycho$ or anti psycho$).tw.

8 exp antidepressant drugs/ or exp antidepressant agent/ or exp antidepressive agents/ or (antidepress$ or anti?depress$).tw.

9 antimanic agents/ or carbamazepine/ or lithium carbonate/ or lithium chloride/ or valproic acid/ or (((anti?manic or anti manic) adj5 (agent$ or drug$ or medicat$)) or mood?stabili?er$ or mood stabili?er$).tw.

10 exp anticonvulsants/ or exp anticonvulsive agent/ or exp anticonvulsive drugs/ or (anti?convuls$ or anti convuls$).tw.

11 or/6-10

Infant exposure

12 maternal exposure/ or maternal-fetal exchange/ or prenatal drug exposure/ or prenatal exposure/ or prenatal exposure delayed effects/ or breast feeding/ or breast milk/ or milk human/ or exp pregnancy/ or ((breast adj (feed$ or fed or milk)) or breastfe$ or breastmilk or lactate$ or pregnan$ or (maternal adj2 (exchange or expos$))).tw.

Infant exposure + harm + psychotropic drugs (1)

13 and/3,11-12

14 (((infant$ or neonat$ or pre natal$ or pre?natal$ or ante natal$ or ante?natal$ or in utero) adj outcome$1).tw. and 11 and 12) or ((effect$1 adj3 exposure adj3 (in utero or prenatal or pre?natal$ or ante natal$ or ante?natal$)).tw. and 11) or ((developmental adj outcome$1).tw. and 1 and 11 and 12)

15 infant development.it,tm. and 11 and 12

16 or/14-15

Harm filter

17 exp cohort studies/ or exp cohort analysis/

18 exp case-control study/ or exp case control study/

19 exp risk/ or exp risk perception/ or exp risk assessment/ or exp at risk populations/ or exp risk factors/

20 ((odds and ratio$) or (relative and risk) or (case and control)).tw.

21   exp anticonvulsants/ae, mo, ct, po, to or exp anticonvulsive agent/ae, mo, ct, po, to or antimanic agents/ae, mo, ct, po, to or carbamazepine/ae, mo, ct, po, to or lithium carbonate/ae, mo, ct, po, to or lithium chloride/ae, mo, ct, po, to or valproic acid/ae, mo, ct, po, to or exp antipsychotic agent/ae, mo, ct, po, to or exp antipsychotic agents/ae, mo, ct, po, to or exp neuroleptic agent/ae, mo, ct, po, to or exp neuroleptic drugs/ae, mo, ct, po, to or exp antidepressant drugs/ae, mo, ct, po, to or exp antidepressant agent/ae, mo, ct, po, to or exp antidepressive agents/ae, mo, ct, po, to or exp psychotropic agent/ae, mo, ct, po, to or exp nootropic agent/ae, mo, ct, po, to or exp psychedelic agent/ae, mo, ct, po, to or exp psychostimulant agent/ae, mo, ct, po, to or exp tranquilizer/ae, mo, ct, po, to

22   exp anticonvulsants/ae, ct, po, to or exp anticonvulsive agent/ae, ct, po, to or antimanic agents/ae, ct, po, to or carbamazepine/ae, ct, po, to or lithium carbonate/ae, ct, po, to or lithium chloride/ae, ct, po, to or valproic acid/ae, ct, po, to or exp antipsychotic agent/ae, ct, po, to or exp antipsychotic agents/ae, ct, po, to or exp neuroleptic agent/ae, ct, po, to or exp neuroleptic drugs/ae, ct, po, to or exp antidepressant drugs/ae, ct, po, to or exp antidepressant agent/ae, ct, po, to or exp antidepressive agents/ae, ct, po, to or exp psychotropic agent/ae, ct, po, to or exp nootropic agent/ae, ct, po, to or exp psychedelic agent/ae, ct, po, to or exp psychostimulant agent/ae, ct, po, to or exp tranquilizer/ae, ct, po, to

23   or/17-22

Infant exposure + harm + psychotropic drugs (2)

24   13 or (16 and 23)
25   24

Infant exposure/fetus/pregnant mothers + harm + psychotropic drugs

26   25 or ((or/17-20) and (or/4-5) and 11)
27   (letter or editorial$).pt.
28   (animals/ not (animals/ and human$.mp.)) or (animal$/ not (animal$/ and human$/)) or (animal not (animal and human)).po. or exp rodentia/ or exp rodent
29   26 not (or/27-28)

Health economics and quality of life search (health economics filter)

MEDLINE, EMBASE, CINAHL, PsycINFO [search terms adapted for each] – DIALOG Datastar interface
1   PREGNANCY#.W..DE.
2   PREGNANCY-COMPLICATIONS#.W..DE.

3	PREGNANCY-TRIMESTERS#.W..DE.
4	PREGNANCY-MULTIPLE#.W..DE.
5	INFANT-NEWBORN#.W..DE.
6	PRENATAL-DIAGNOSIS#.W..DE.
7	UTERINE-MONITORING#.W..DE.
8	PELVIMETRY#.W..DE.
9	MATERNAL-HEALTH-SERVICES#.W..DE.
10	MATERNAL-CHILD-NURSING#.W..DE.
11	MATERNAL-AGE#.W..DE.
12	PERINATAL-CARE#.W..DE.
13	PARITY#.W..DE.
14	PUERPERIUM#.W..DE.
15	BREASTFEEDING#.W..DE.
16	MILK-HUMAN#.W..DE.
17	PREGNAN$4.TI,AB.
18	NEWBORN$2.TI,AB.
19	(NEW ADJ BORN$2).TI,AB.
20	(BIRTH OR CHILDBIRTH OR POSTBIRTH).TI,AB.
21	(LABOR OR LABORING).TI,AB.
22	LABOUR.TI,AB.
23	(ANTEPART$3 OR ANTE ADJ PART$3).TI,AB.
24	(PRENATAL$2 OR PRE ADJ NATAL$2).TI,AB.
25	(ANTENATAL$2 OR ANTE ADJ NATAL$2).TI,AB.
26	(PERINATAL$2 OR PERI ADJ NATAL$2).TI,AB.
27	(POSTNATAL$2 OR POST ADJ NATAL$2).TI,AB.
28	(POSTPART$2 OR POST ADJ PART$2).TI,AB.
29	PUERPERAL.TI,AB.
30	LACTAT$3.TI,AB.
31	BREASTFE$5.TI,AB.
32	(BREAST ADJ (FEED OR FED OR FEEDING)).TI,AB.
33	1 OR 2 OR 3 OR 4 OR 5 OR 6 OR 7 OR 8 OR 9 OR 10 OR 11 OR 12 OR 13 OR 14 OR 15 OR 16 OR 17 OR 18 OR 19 OR 20 OR 21 OR 22 OR 23 OR 24 OR 25 OR 26 OR 27 OR 28 OR 29 OR 30 OR 31 OR 32
34	ABORTION-INDUCED#.W..DE.
35	MISCARR$5.TI,AB.
36	ABORTION$1.TI,AB.
37	((FETAL OR FOETAL OR FETUS OR FOETUS OR NEONAT$2 OR INTRAUTERINE) ADJ (DEATH$1 OR DEAD)).TI,AB.
38	(STILLBORN$ OR STILL ADJ BORN).TI,AB.
39	(STILLBIRTH$ OR STILL ADJ BIRTH).TI,AB.
40	34 OR 35 OR 36 OR 37 OR 38 OR 39
41	ADJUSTMENT-DISORDERS#.W..DE.
42	ANXIETY-DISORDERS#.W..DE.
43	DISSOCIATIVE-DISORDERS#.W..DE.
44	EATING-DISORDERS#.W..DE.

45   MOOD-DISORDERS#.W..DE.

46   NEUROTIC-DISORDERS#.W..DE.

47   PERSONALITY-DISORDERS#.W..DE.

48   SCHIZOPHRENIA-AND-DISORDERS-WITH-PSYCHOTIC-
        FEATURES#.W..DE.

49   SOMATOFORM-DISORDERS#.W..DE.

50   SUBSTANCE-RELATED-DISORDERS#.W..DE.

51   DEPRESSION#.W..DE. OR DEPRESSIVE-DISORDER#.DE. OR
        (SEASONAL ADJ AFFECTIVE ADJ DISORDER$2 OR DEPRESS$4
        OR DYSTHYM$4).TI,AB.

52   MELANCHOL$3.TI,AB.

53   (BIPOLAR OR BI ADJ POLAR).TI,AB. AND (DISORDER$2 OR
        DEPRESS$4).TI,AB.

54   (CYCLOTHYMI$3 OR RAPID ADJ CYCL$3 OR ULTRADIAN NEAR
        CYCL$3).TI,AB.

55   (MANIA OR MANIC OR HYPOMANIA).TI,AB.

56   ANOREXIA#.W..DE.

57   (EATING NEAR DISORDER$2).TI,AB.

58   (ANOREXIA NEAR NERVOSA).TI,AB.

59   (BULIMIA#W..DE. OR BULIMI$2 OR KLEINE ADJ LEVIN OR
        HYPERPHAGIA).TI,AB.

60   (BING$4 OR OVEREAT$3 OR COMPULSIVE NEAR (EAT$3 OR
        VOMIT$3) OR FOOD$2 NEAR BING$4 OR (SELF ADJ INDUC$2 OR
        SELFINDUC$2) NEAR VOMIT$3 OR RESTRICT$4 NEAR EAT$3).TI,AB.

61   ANXIETY#.W..DE.   OR   ANXIETY-SEPARATION#.W..DE.   OR
        PANIC#.W..DE. OR (ANXIOUS OR ANXIETY OR PANIC OR PHOBIA
        OR PHOBIC).TI,AB.

62   STRESS-PSYCHOLOGICAL#.W..DE.

63   (POST ADJ TRAUMATIC$2 OR POSTTRAUMATIC$2 OR STRESS
        ADJ DISORDER$2 OR ACUTE ADJ STRESS OR PTSD OR ASD OR
        DESNOS).TI,AB.

64   (COMBAT OR CONCENTRATION ADJ CAMP ADJ SYNDROME OR
        EXTREME ADJ STRESS OR FLASH ADJ BACK$2 OR FLASH-
        BACK$2).TI,AB.

65   (HYPERVIGILAN$2 OR HYPERVIGILEN$2 OR PSYCHOLOG$4 ADJ
        STRESS OR PSYCHO ADJ (TRAUMA OR TRAUMATIC) OR
        PSYCHOTRAUMA OR PSYCHOTRAUMATIC).TI,AB.

66   (RAILWAY ADJ SPINE OR RAPE NEAR TRAUMA$5 OR RE ADJ
        EXPERIENC$3 OR RE ADJ EXPERIENC$3 OR TORTURE ADJ
        SYNDROME OR TRAUMATIC ADJ NEUROS$2 OR TRAUMATIC
        ADJ STRESS).TI,AB.

67   TRAUMA$5.TI,AB. AND (AVOIDANCE OR GRIEF OR HORROR OR
        DEATH$1 OR NIGHT ADJ MARE$1 OR NIGHTMARE$1 OR
        EMOTION$2).TI,AB.

68   (RECURR$5 ADJ THOUGHT$2).TI,AB.

69   OBSESSIVE-BEHAVIOR#.W..DE. OR (OBSESSION OR OBSES-SIONS OR OBSESSIONAL).TI,AB.

70   (CLEAN$6 ADJ RESPONSE$2).TI,AB.

71   OCD.TI,AB.

72   OSTEOCHONDR$3.TI,AB.

73   71 NOT 72

74   COMPULSIVE-BEHAVIOR#.W..DE. OR COMPULS$5.TI,AB.

75   ((SYMMETR$4 OR COUNT$3 OR ARRANG$3 OR ORDER$3 OR WASH$3 OR REPEAT$3 OR HOARD$3 OR CLEAN$3 OR CHECK$3) ADJ COMPULSI$4).TI,AB.

76   (PERSONALIT$3 NEAR (DISORDER$1 OR DIFFICULT$3)).TI,AB.

77   (ANTISOCIAL OR ANTI ADJ SOCIAL OR PSYCHOPATH$3 OR BORDERLINE OR HYSTERI$3).TI,AB.

78   (DISSOCIAT$3 NEAR (DISORDER$ OR DIFFICULT$3 OR PERSONALIT$3 OR DISTURB$5 OR TRAUMA$4)).TI,AB.

79   SCHIZO$9.TI,AB.

80   (PSYCHOS$2 OR PSYCHOTIC$2 OR PARANO$3).TI,AB.

81   (SOMATOFORM OR SOMATIZATION OR SOMATIC OR HYPOCHONDRIASIS$3 OR NEURASTHENIA$3).TI,AB.

82   (CONVERSION ADJ DISORDER$1 OR HYPOCHONDRIASIS OR NEURASTHENIA).TI,AB.

83   (BODY ADJ DYSMORPHIC OR DYSMORPHOPHOBI$2 OR BRIQUET ADJ SYNDROME$1 OR SYNDROME ADJ BRIQUET).TI,AB.

84   ((ATTACH$ OR BOND OR BONDING) NEAR (AMBIVALENT OR ANXIOUS$4 OR AVOID$4 OR DIFFICULT$3 OR DISINHIBIT$3 OR DISORDER$2 OR DISORGANIS$4 OR DISRUPTIV$4 OR DISSOCIAT$4 OR DYREGULA$4 OR DISORIENTAT$4 OR DISTURBANCE$2 OR IMPAIR$5 OR INADEQUATE OR INHIBIT$3 OR INJUR$4 OR INSECUR$5 OR POOR OR STYLE$2)).TI,AB.

85   (ADJUST OR ADJUSTIVE OR ADJUSTMENT OR REACTIVE).TI,AB.

86   (DISORDER$1 OR DISTURB$5 OR DIFFICULT$3).TI,AB.

87   85 NEAR 86

88   (TRANSIENT ADJ SITUATIONAL ADJ DISTURB$5 OR TRANSIENT ADJ SITUATIONAL ADJ DISORDER$1).TI,AB.

89   KLEPTOMANI$3.TI,AB.

90   (DRUG$2 OR SUBSTANCE$2).TI,AB.

91   (ABUSE OR USE OR MISUSE OR DEPEND$6 OR ADDICT$4).TI,AB.

92   90 NEAR 91

93   (NEUROTIC$2 OR NEUROSIS).TI,AB.

94   SUICIDE#.W..DE. OR OVERDOSE#.W..DE. OR SELF-INJURIOUS-BEHAVIOR#.W..DE. OR SELF-MUTILATION#.DE.

95   (SUICID$3 OR SELF ADJ HARM$2 OR SELFHARM$2 OR SELF ADJ INJUR$4 OR SELFINJUR$4 OR SELF ADJ MUTILAT$3 OR SELFMUTILAT$3 OR SUICID$3 OR SELF ADJ DESTRUCT$3 OR SELFDESTRUCT$3 OR SELF ADJ POISON$3 OR SELFPOISON$3

	OR SELF NEAR CUT\$4 OR CUTT\$4 OR OVERDOSE\$2 OR SELF ADJ IMMOLAT\$4 OR SELFIMMOLAT\$4 OR SELF ADJ INFLICT\$4 OR SELFINFLICT\$4 OR AUTO ADJ MUTILAT\$3 OR AUTOMUTI-LAT\$3).TI,AB.
96	AFFECTIVE-SYMPTOMS#.W..DE.
97	(AFFECTIVE NEAR DISORDER\$1).TI,AB.
98	MENTAL-DISORDERS.MJ.
99	(MENTAL NEAR (ILLNESS\$2 OR DISEASE\$1 OR DISORDER\$1)).TI,AB.
100	41 OR 42 OR 43 OR 44 OR 45 OR 46 OR 47 OR 48 OR 49 OR 50 OR 51 OR 52 OR 53 OR 54 OR 55 OR 56 OR 57 OR 58 OR 59 OR 60 OR 61 OR 62 OR 63 OR 64 OR 65 OR 66 OR 67 OR 68 OR 69 OR 70 OR 73 OR 74 OR 75 OR 76 OR 77 OR 78 OR 79 OR 80 OR 81 OR 82 OR 83 OR 84 OR 87 OR 88 OR 89 OR 92 OR 93 OR 94 OR 95 OR 96 OR 97 OR 98 OR 99
101	(33 OR 40) AND 100
102	DEPRESSION-POSTPARTUM#.W..DE.
103	((BABY OR POSTPARTUM OR POST ADJ PARTUM OR POSTNATAL OR POST ADJ NATAL OR MATERNITY OR MATERNAL) ADJ BLUES).TI,AB.
104	101 OR 102 OR 103
105	COSTS-AND-COST-ANALYSIS#.W..DE.
106	ECONOMICS#.W..DE.
107	VALUE-OF-LIFE#.W..DE.
108	BURDEN NEAR DISEASE
109	BURDEN NEAR ILLNESS
110	COST OR COSTS OR COSTLY OR COSTING OR PRICE OR PRICES OR PRICING OR PHARMACOECONOMIC\$ OR EXPENDITURE\$ OR ECONOMIC\$4
111	FISCAL OR FUNDING OR FINANCIAL OR FINANCE OR BUDGET
112	RESOURCE\$ NEAR ALLOCATION\$
113	RESOURCE\$ NEAR UTILI\$
114	VALUE NEAR MONEY
115	105 OR 106 OR 107 OR 108 OR 109 OR 110 OR 111 OR 112 OR 113 OR 114
116	QUALITY-OF-LIFE#.DE.
117	116 OR QUALIT\$3 NEAR (LIFE OR SURVIVAL)
118	117 OR WELL ADJ BEING OR WELLBEING OR HEALTH ADJ STATUS OR QOL
119	104 AND (115 OR 118)
120	YEAR = 2004 OR YEAR = 2003 OR YEAR = 2002 OR YEAR = 1993 OR YEAR = 1992 OR YEAR = 1991 OR YEAR = 1990 OR YEAR = 1989 OR YEAR = 1988 OR YEAR = 1987 OR YEAR = 1986 OR YEAR = 1985 OR YEAR = 1984 OR YEAR = 2001 OR YEAR = 1983 OR YEAR = 1982 OR YEAR = 1981 OR YEAR = 1980

	OR YEAR = 2000 OR YEAR = 1999 OR YEAR = 1998 OR YEAR = 1997 OR YEAR = 1996 OR YEAR = 1995 OR YEAR = 1994
121	119 AND 120
122	ANIMAL = YES
123	HUMAN = YES
124	122 NOT (122 AND 123)
125	121 NOT 124

Details of additional searches undertaken to support the development of this guideline are available on request.

APPENDIX 7:

CLINICAL STUDY ELIGIBILITY CHECKLIST

ELIGIBILITY CHECKLIST FOR INCLUDED STUDIES

A. Inclusion criteria

All interventions
- RCT.
- Data for at least 50% of intention-to-treat population provided at end of treatment for continuous measures.
- Appropriate mental health outcomes.
- Sufficient data available for quantitative analysis (endpoint means and variance measures).
- Participants identified as at risk of, or currently experiencing, a mental health disorder in pregnancy or within one year postnatally.

Preventative interventions
- As for 'all interventions' above, no need to establish diagnosis of the trial population at randomisation.

Treatment for established diagnoses
Treatment trials are defined as trials where participants have been identified as having symptoms of a disorder either by (a) a diagnosis following a full diagnostic clinical interview or (b) by a self-report instrument ((a) and (b) to be meta-analysed separately).
- At least 70% of the population have diagnosis/are highly symptomatic of a particular disorder on entry to the trial.
- Measure of symptom severity of the disorder pre- and post-treatments that exceeds an agreed clinical threshold.

Notes
For meta-analysis, do not treat waitlist/standard care across different countries as equivalent.

APPENDIX 8:

RCT METHODOLOGICAL QUALITY CHECKLIST

Antenatal and postnatal mental health guideline Quality checklist for an RCT		
Report reference ID:		
Checklist completed by:	**Date completed:**	
SECTION 1: INTERNAL VALIDITY		
Evaluation criteria	**How well is this criterion addressed?**	
1.1	**Was the assignment of subjects to treatment groups randomised?**	
If there is no indication of randomisation, the study should be rejected. If the description of randomisation is poor, or the process used is not truly random (e.g., allocation by date, alternating between one group and another) or can otherwise be seen as flawed, the study should be given a lower quality rating.		
1.2	**Was an adequate concealment method used?**	
Centralised allocation, computerised allocation systems, or the use of coded identical containers would all be regarded as adequate methods of concealment, and may be taken as indicators of a well-conducted study. If the method of concealment used is regarded as poor, or relatively easy to subvert, the study must be given a lower quality rating, and can be rejected if the concealment method is seen as inadequate.		

SECTION 2: OVERALL ASSESSMENT	**Comments**	**Code**
2.1	**Low risk of bias**	**A**
	Moderate risk of bias **Both criteria met**	
	High risk of bias	**B**
	One or more criteria partly met	
		C
	One or more criteria not met	

APPENDIX 9:

CLINICAL STUDY DATA EXTRACTION FORMS

Study characteristics extraction form:

Ref ID	
Topic area	Epidemiology/aetiology/condition characteristics etc
	Prediction and prevention
	Psychological/psychosocial treatments
	Pharmacological/physical treatments
	Service guidance/delivery
Article type	Review	
	Meta-analysis	
	RCT	
	Other (give detail)	
	Editorial/ research digest	
Treatment(s) compared	....
Treatment aim (if specified)	preventive	general treatment	other......................
Note special population (e.g. adolescent/ substance abuse)	
Time period (e.g. ante/ post-natal)	antenatal	intrapartum	postnatal	

Appendix 9

Participant status at entry	DIAGNOSIS at entry: .... "at-risk" status at entry:			
Source/search	electronic	manual	existing review	ref list
Reference Manager	updated ✓			
Studies Database	updated ✓			
Rev Man	updated ✓		double-checked ✓	
Excluded ✓				
Notes	....			

APPENDIX 10:

RCT DATA EXTRACTION FORM

RCT data extraction form:
ID:_____   **Reference**

Treatment Group:															
	n	N		n	N		n	N		n	N				
	n	N		n	N		n	N		n	N				
	n	Mean	SD	n	Mean	SD	n	Mean	SD	n	Mean	SD			
	n	Mean	SD	n	Mean	SD	n	Mean	SD	n	Mean	SD			
Treatment Group:															
	n	N		n	N		n	N		n	N				
	n	N		n	N		n	N		n	N				

	n	Mean	SD	n	Mean	SD	n	Mean	SD	n	Mean	SD
	n	Mean	SD	n	Mean	SD	n	Mean	SD	n	Mean	SD

n = number with the event
N = number randomised

APPENDIX 11:

FORMULAE FOR CALCULATING STANDARD DEVIATIONS

The following formulae were used to calculate standard deviations (SD) where these were not available in study reports:

(n = sample size of group)

$$SD = \text{standard error} \times \sqrt{n}$$

$$SD = \frac{(\text{upper 95\% confidence interval} - \text{mean})}{1.96} \times \sqrt{n}$$

$$SD = \frac{(\text{mean}_1 - \text{mean}_2)}{\sqrt{F(\sqrt{1/n_1} + \sqrt{1/n_2})}}$$

(If F ratio is not given, then $F = t_2$)

APPENDIX 12:

QUALITY CHECKLIST FOR FULL ECONOMICS EVALUATIONS

Author: **Date of publication:**

Title:

Study design

1.	The research question is stated	Yes	No
2.	The economic importance of the research question is stated	Yes	No
3.	The viewpoint(s) of the analysis is clearly stated and justified	Yes	No
4.	The rationale for choosing the alternative programmes or interventions compared is stated	Yes	No
5.	The alternatives being compared are clearly described	Yes	No
6.	The form of economic evaluation used is stated	Yes	No
7.	The choice of form of economic evaluation used is justified in relation to the questions addressed	Yes	No

Data collection

8.	The source of effectiveness estimates used is stated	Yes	No	
9.	Details of the design and results of effectiveness study are given (if based on a single study)	Yes	No	NA
10.	Details of the method of synthesis or meta-analysis of estimates are given (if based on an overview of a number of effectiveness studies)	Yes	No	NA
11.	The primary outcome measure(s) for the economic evaluation are clearly stated	Yes	No	
12.	Methods to value health states and other benefits are stated	Yes	No	NA
13.	Details of the subjects from whom valuations were obtained are given	Yes	No	NA
14.	Indirect costs (if included) are reported separately	Yes	No	NA

308

15. The relevance of indirect costs to the study question is discussed	Yes	No	NA
16. Quantities of resources are reported separately from their unit costs	Yes	No	
17. Methods for the estimation of quantities and unit costs are described	Yes	No	
18. Currency and price data are recorded	Yes	No	
19. Details of currency, price adjustments for inflation or currency conversion are given	Yes	No	
20. Details of any model used are given	Yes	No	NA
21. The choice of model used and the key parameters on which it is based are justified	Yes	No	NA

Analysis and interpretation of results

1. Time horizon of costs and benefits is stated	Yes	No	
2. The discount rate(s) is stated	Yes	No	NA
3. The choice of rate(s) is justified	Yes	No	NA
4. An explanation is given if costs or benefits are not discounted	Yes	No	NA
5. Details of statistical tests and confidence intervals are given for stochastic data	Yes	No	NA
6. The approach to sensitivity analysis is given	Yes	No	NA
7. The choice of variables for sensitivity analysis is given	Yes	No	NA
8. The ranges over which the variables are varied are stated	Yes	No	NA
9. Relevant alternatives are compared	Yes	No	
10. Incremental analysis is reported	Yes	No	NA
11. Major outcomes are presented in a disaggregated as well as aggregated form	Yes	No	
12. The answer to the study question is given	Yes	No	
13. Conclusions follow from the data reported	Yes	No	
14. Conclusions are accompanied by the appropriate caveats	Yes	No	

Validity score: Yes/No/NA:

APPENDIX 13:
DATA EXTRACTION FORM FOR ECONOMICS STUDIES

Reviewer:	**Date of review:**
Authors:	**Publication date:**
Title:	
Country:	**Language:**

Interventions compared:

Patient population:

Setting:

Economic study design:

Perspective of the analysis:

Time frame of the analysis:

Modelling:

Source of data for effect size measures:

Primary outcome measures:

Costs included:

Source of resource use and unit costs:

Currency: **Price year:**

Discounting (costs/benefits):

Sensitivity analysis:

Effectiveness results:

Cost results:

Cost-effectiveness results:

Authors' conclusions:

Comments – limitations:

APPENDIX 14:

HEALTH ECONOMICS EVIDENCE ON MOTHER
AND BABY UNITS

BOATH2003

Boath, E., Major, K. & Cox, J. (2003) When the cradle falls II: the cost-effectiveness of treating postnatal depression in a psychiatric day hospital compared with routine primary care. *Journal of Affective Disorders, 74*, 159–166.

Study, year and country	Intervention details	Study population Study design – data source	Study type	Costs: description and values Outcomes: description and values	Results: cost effectiveness	Comments Internal validity (Yes/No/NA) Industry support
Boath et al., 2003 UK	Intervention: Specialised psychiatric parent and baby day hospital unit (PBDU) Comparator: Routine primary care (RPC) provided by GPs and health visitors with occasional referrals into secondary care	Women with a baby aged between 6 weeks and 1 year, EPDS score ≥12 and a diagnosis of major or minor depressive disorder according to RDC; exclusion criteria: puerperal psychosis, schizophrenia, history of drug or alcohol abuse, women not speaking English Data source for effect-size measures and resource use: prospective cohort study N = 30 in each arm	Cost-effectiveness analysis	Costs: Healthcare costs: Staff: GPs, health visitors, CPNs, mental health resource centre, PBDU Inpatient and day care Capital costs and equipment of PBDU Antidepressant medication Patient costs: transport, childcare Patient time losses: employment, housework, leisure Total costs (referring to 30 women per arm): PBDU group: £46,211 RPC group: £18,973 ΔC: £27,238, p < 0.001	ICER of PBDU versus RPC: £1,945 per successfully treated woman Cost-effectiveness ratio of RPC: £2,710 per successfully treated woman. Authors' conclusion: PBDU more cost effective than RPC	Perspective: societal • Currency: UK £ • Cost year: 1992/93 • Discounting: 6% for capital costs • Time horizon: 6 months • Outcome measures collected by interviews; direct and indirect cost estimates based on resource-use data derived from structured interviews, self-report scales, and retrospective analysis of

Study, year and country	Intervention details	Study population Study design – data source	Study type	Costs: description and values Outcomes: description and values	Results: cost effectiveness	Comments Internal validity (Yes/No/NA) Industry support
				Primary outcome: Number of women successfully treated; recovery defined as no longer fulfilling RDC for major or minor depressive disorder PBDU group: 21 women successfully treated RPC group: 7 women successfully treated $\Delta E = 14$, p < 0.001	Results sensitive to exclusion of costs associated with non-significantly different resource use, that is, medication and GP/health visitor costs	case-notes • Validity score: 20/5/10

APPENDIX 15:

SURVEY OF ANTENATAL AND POSTNATAL MENTAL HEALTH PRIMARY CARE SERVICES IN ENGLAND AND WALES – QUESTIONNAIRE

National Institute for Health and Clinical Excellence

National Collaborating
Centre for Mental Health

NICE GUIDELINE ON ANTENATAL AND POSTNATAL MENTAL HEALTH SERVICES

Services for Women with Antenatal and Postnatal Mental Health Problems
A Survey of NHS Primary Care Trusts by
The National Institute for Health and Clinical Excellence

Dear Chief Executive

This survey is being carried out as an essential part of the development of the NICE Guideline on Antenatal and Postnatal Mental Health by the National Collaborating Centre for Mental Health. This is one of three surveys which will help describe services for women with antenatal and postnatal mental health problems at all levels, including primary, maternity and secondary mental health services. The involvement of all PCTs is very important to achieve a complete national picture of current provision, and to support the development of NICE service guidance on antenatal and postnatal mental health. Your assistance with this is greatly appreciated.

Details of person completing the questionnaire

If necessary, please pass on to an individual in the Trust best placed to give the information requested.

Name

Position

PCT name

Address

Postcode

Telephone number

Email address

Please answer the following questions as accurately as possible. There are spaces provided for more information and comments if it is not possible to answer the questions using the options provided. If extra space is required, please attach an additional sheet.

a.   **Is there an identified lead clinician/manager within the Trust responsible for the development and/or coordination of mental health services for women with antenatal or postnatal mental health problems?**

Yes/No

Is this you?

Yes/No

If No please provide details of the individual below:

Name

Position

PCT name

Address

Postcode

Telephone number

Email address

2. What services are available for women who have identified mental health problems during pregnancy and the postnatal period?

Policies and training

2.1   Is there an agreed policy for the PCT which:

a) requires all pregnant women, and those in the postnatal period, in contact with primary care services to be routinely asked about their past or current mental health problems?

Yes / No

b) specifies that all pregnant women, and those in the postnatal period, should be asked about their mental health problems at the following times:
- on initial contact with the service   **Yes/No**
- at subsequent appointments during pregnancy   **Yes/No**
- postnatally   **Yes/No**

c) is agreed and implemented throughout the whole PCT area as follows:

- agreed   **Yes/No**
- fully implemented   **Yes/No**
- partially implemented   **Yes/No**
- not implemented   **Yes/No**

2.2 Is there a pathway/protocol within the PCT for the care of women with current mental health problems during the perinatal period?

a) Developed   **Yes/No**
b) Implemented throughout the PCT area
- fully implemented   **Yes/No**
- partially implemented   **Yes/No**
- not implemented   **Yes/No**

2.3 Is there an identified mental health training programme for health visitors in the PCT?

a) Training programme developed   **Yes/No**
b) What proportion of health visitors have received training:
- All   **Yes/No**
- Most   **Yes/No**
- Few or none   **Yes/No**

2.4 Please describe any other dedicated antenatal and postnatal mental health services in the PCT

_____
_____
_____
_____
_____
_____
_____
_____
_____

_____
_____
_____
_____
_____
_____

Services for women with severe mental health problems

Severe mental illness (SMI) refers to psychotic disorders (schizophrenia and bipolar disorder), depressive disorders and other mental disorders of sufficient severity that they significantly impair the daily personal and social functioning of an individual.

2.5 All women with SMI have access to a specialist antenatal and postnatal mental health service

Yes / No

2.6 Women with SMI who require inpatient care have access to a specialist mother and baby unit

Yes / No

If known, please indicate the number of admissions to specialist mother and baby units for the financial year 2004/2005

N = _____

3. Does the Trust have an APMH/Perinatal Mental Health Strategy?

- **Yes – Multi-agency** (If available please attach)
- **Yes – PCT only** (If available please attach)
- **No – but in preparation – multi-agency**
- **No – but in preparation – PCT only**
- **No**

Comments

Please provide any further comments or information that you feel may be relevant in the space below:

_____
_____
_____
_____
_____
_____

_____

_____

_____

_____

_____

_____

_____

_____

Signed: ____
Date: ____

Please return the completed questionnaire to (SAE enclosed):

Antenatal and Postnatal Mental Health Services Survey
NICE APMH Guideline
National Collaborating Centre for Mental Health Centre for Outcomes Research and Effectiveness
British Psychological Society
Sub-Department of Clinical Health Psychology
University College London
1-19 Torrington Place
London
WC1E 7HB

If you have any queries please contact Jenny Turner
Tel: 020 7679 5956
Fax: 020 7916 8511
Email: jenny.turner@ucl.ac.uk

APPENDIX 16:

RESULTS OF SURVEY OF ANTENATAL AND POSTNATAL MENTAL HEALTH PRIMARY CARE SERVICES IN ENGLAND AND WALES

Background

In order to inform the guideline development process, the guideline development group (GDG) commissioned a survey of the perinatal mental health services within primary care. The purpose of the survey was to investigate the current structure of mental health services for pregnant and postnatal women throughout England and Wales. The survey targeted all Primary Care Trusts (PCTs) in England and all Local Health Boards (LHBs) and NHS Trusts in Wales.

Methods

Sample
All 302 PCTs (within England), 22 LHBs and 13 NHS Trusts (within Wales) were surveyed. With regard to Welsh primary care, originally only the LHBs were to be surveyed. However, the first few responses to the survey that were received from the LHBs suggested that the NHS trusts within Wales should also be surveyed to obtain a fuller picture of the state of primary care services in Wales.

Development of survey materials

The survey was conducted via postal questionnaire. A pilot version of the questionnaire, and accompanying cover letter, were developed through an iterative process involving input from the GDG. This pilot was sent to four PCTs. Unfortunately, there were no replies from the PCTs contacted in the pilot study, despite subsequent email and telephone reminders and requests to return the survey.

Given the lack of pilot questionnaire feedback, and the time pressure surrounding the development of the guideline, the final questionnaire (see Appendix 15) was developed by the GDG simply by fine-tuning the pilot questionnaire. Questions were reworded/expanded to make the questionnaire as specific as required, and to ensure ease of understanding for those completing the questions. Therefore, the final questionnaire represented the GDG's best attempt at focusing responses on the areas of interest.

A cover letter was also devised by the group, which introduced the antenatal and postnatal mental health guideline and briefly explained the purpose and aims of the survey. The cover letter requested that the questionnaires be returned within 5 weeks of them being posted.

A mailing list for the trusts was developed via the NHS website (www.nhs.uk). This included the name of the Chief Executive, the postal address, phone number and email address of each trust.

Procedure
The questionnaire and accompanying cover letter were addressed personally to the Chief Executive of each trust and were sent with a self-addressed envelope for the return of the questionnaire.

Two weeks after posting the questionnaire, non-responding trusts were followed up with email reminders. Email reminders were sent to the email address displayed on the NHS website for each trust. Quite often, this resulted in a request for the document to be provided electronically, which was then followed through by the research assistant conducting the email reminders.

Questionnaire responses were coded and entered into a statistical package (SPSS, Version 13) for analysis. The majority of the questionnaire's questions involved mutually exclusive response options and were easy to code for analysis. Free-text comments and additional notes made on the questionnaire were coded *ad hoc* after all written responses were examined for major themes. If no comment was made, or a comment was illegible or not relevant to the question of service delivery (for example, several responses included giving a personal job description), then it was not coded. Similarly, free-text comments were not coded if they repeated information already provided in the questions specifically asked in the questionnaire.

For questionnaires that were returned with reference to more than one PCT, the information was coded once for every PCT represented in the questionnaire.

Results
This section provides a detailed analysis to responses for every question of the questionnaire. Results were analysed separately for England and Wales, and response rates for each region within each country were also analysed for completeness. These analyses are presented first, followed by the responses to specific questions asked in the questionnaire. This is followed by presentation of the coded free-text responses, with some examples of the written comments that were coded.

Region analysis
England (PCTs): 128 questionnaires were returned, which provided information regarding 144 PCTs. This corresponds to a total response rate for English primary care of 48% (144/302). Response rates for regional areas are shown in Table 58.

Wales (LHBs and NHS Trusts): Fifteen questionnaires from Wales were returned (11 from LHBs; 4 from NHS Trusts). This corresponds to a response rate of 43% (15/35) for Welsh primary care services. Response rates for regional areas in Wales are shown in Table 59.

Responses to questionnaire
Frequencies of responses for both English and Welsh primary care services, alongside each question, are displayed in Table 60 and mean numbers of admissions to mother

Table 58: Regional response rates for PCTs in England

Region (England, total N = 302)	No. PCTs represented in returned questionnaires	Response rate
London (N = 31)	9	29%
South England (N = 80)	36	45%
Midlands & East England (N = 99)	48	48%
North (N = 92)	51	55%

N = number of PCTs

and baby units (MBUs) reported by the primary care services (question 2.6) are displayed in Table 61.

Coded text responses

'*2.4. Please describe any other dedicated antenatal and postnatal mental health services in the PCT/LHB/Trust*':

Sixty-six percent (95/144) of PCTs in England and 55% (7/14) of Welsh NSH trusts and LHBs who returned the questionnaire responded to this question with additional comments (which were coded).

Most frequently, comments were made regarding types of psychological and psychosocial interventions available throughout the PCTs. Forty-five percent of English PCTs who made comments reported providing various psychological/psychosocial treatments, while no Welsh NHS trusts or LHBs reported the implementation of any interventions at all (see Tables 62 and 63 for details).

The use of the Edinburgh Postnatal Depression Scale (EPDS) as a screening tool was also reported regularly, with a few other screening tools mentioned only very occasionally. Of those PCTs who made comments here, 40% (38/95) mentioned using the EPDS as an assessment tool. Looking closer, this means that 93% (38/41) of PCTs who mentioned using any assessment tool specifically mentioned using the EPDS. The remaining 7% (3/41) reported screening for depression in the antenatal and/or postnatal period, with no mention of the specific assessment tool used, or using the Beck Depression Inventory (BDI) (2%, 1/41).

Table 59: Regional response rates for PCTs in Wales

Region (Wales, total N = 35)	No. LHBs/NHS Trusts returned questionnaires	Response rate
South East Wales (N = 14)	6	43%
Mid & West Wales (N = 12)	5	42%
North Wales (N = 9)	4	44%

Table 60: Response frequencies for each question of the survey questionnaire for both English and Welsh primary care services

Survey question	Response options	Response frequency			
		PCTs (England) (N = 144)		LHBs & NHTs (Wales) (N = 15)	
		n	%	n	%
1. Is there an identified lead clinician/manager within the Trust responsible for the development and/or coordination of mental health services for women with antenatal or postnatal mental health problems?	Yes	79	55	8	53
	No	63	44	5	33
	Missing (no response)	2	1	2	13
2.1a. Is there an agreed policy for the PCT which requires all pregnant women, and those in the postnatal period, in contact with primary care services to be routinely asked about their past or current mental health problems?	Yes	99[18,19]	69	5	33
	No	41[20]	28	8	53
	Missing (no response)	4	3	2	13
2.1b. Is there an agreed policy for the PCT which specifies that all pregnant women, and those in the postnatal period, should be asked about their mental health problems at the following times:	a) On initial contact with the service?				
	Yes	91	63	5	33
	No	33	23	5	33
	Missing (no response)	20	14	5	33

		PCTs (England) (N = 144)		LHBs & NHTs (Wales) (N = 15)	
		n	%	n	%
b) At subsequent appointments during pregnancy?	Yes	61	42	3	20
	No	55	38	7	47
	Missing (no response)	28	19	5	33
c) Postnatally?	Yes	102	71	5	33
	No	26	18	6	40
	Missing (no response)	16	11	4	27
For those PCTs and those LHBs/NHS Trusts that do not have a policy (that is, those that answered 'Yes' to Q2.1a)		(N = 99)		(N = 5)	
2.1c. Is there an agreed policy for the Trust which is agreed and implemented throughout the whole PCT as follows:	Agreed	5	5	0	0
	Fully implemented	48	48	1	20
	Partially implemented	30	30	4	80
	Not implemented	6	6	0	0
	Missing (no response)	10	10	0	0

Continued

Table 60: (*Continued*)

Survey question	Response options		Response frequency			
			PCTs (England) (N = 144)		LHBs & NHTs (Wales) (N = 15)	
			n	%	n	%
2.2a. Is there a developed pathway/protocol within the Trust for the care of women with current mental health problems during the perinatal period?	Yes		80[21]	56	2	13
	No		52[22]	36	9	60
	Missing (no response)		12[23]	8	4	27
For those PCTs and those LHBs/NHS Trusts who do have a pathway/protocol (that is, those that answered "Yes" to Q2.2a)			(N = 80)		(N = 2)	
2.2b. Is the pathway/protocol within the Trust implemented throughout the PCT area (as follows):	Fully implemented		32	40	0	0
	Partially implemented		40	50	2	100
	Not implemented		2	2.5	0	0

	Missing (no response)	6	7.5	0	0
[Answered by all]					
2.3a. Is there an identified mental health training programme for health visitors in the PCT?		(N = 144)		(N = 15)	
Yes		78[24]	54	4	27
No		56[25]	39	8	53
Missing (no response)		10[26]	7	3	20
For those PCTs and those LHBs/NHS Trusts who do have a training programme (that is, those that answered 'Yes' to Q2.3a).		(N = 78)		(N = 4)	
2.3b. What proportion of health visitors have received training?					
All		21	27	0	0
Most		50	64	3	75
Few or none		4	5	1	25
Missing (no response)		3	4	0	0

Continued

Table 60: *(Continued)*

Survey question	Response options	Response frequency			
		PCTs (England) (N = 144)		LHBs & NHTs (Wales) (N = 15)	
		n	%	n	%
Services for women with severe mental health problems					
2.5. All women with SMI have access to a specialist antenatal and postnatal mental health service	Yes	76	53	7	47
	No	62	43	5	33
	Missing (no response)	6	4	3	20
2.6. Women with SMI who require inpatient care have access to a specialist MBU, either services within the Trust, or from other providers? (See Table 61 for reported admission rates)	Yes[27]	114	79	9	60
	No	22	15	3	20
	Missing (no response)	8	6	3	20
3. Does the Trust have an antenatal and postnatal mental health strategy?	Yes – multi-agency	17	12	0	0
	Yes – PCT only	3	2	0	0
	No – but in preparation – multi-agency	43	30	1	7

No – but in preparation – PCT/LHB/ NHS Trust only	9	6	2	13
No	56	39	10	68
Missing (no response)	16	11	2	13

[18]Thirteen percent (13/99) of respondents answering 'yes' added a note to redefine the term 'policy' (for example, adjusted the word 'policy' to 'guideline' on the questionnaire, then answered 'yes'

[19]Sixteen percent (16/99) of respondents answering 'yes' added a note to say this policy was 'in development'

[20]Five percent (2/41) of respondents answering 'no' added a note to say this policy was 'in development'

[21]Nine percent (7/80) of respondents answering 'yes' added a note to say this pathway/protocol was 'in development'

[22]Seventeen percent (9/52) of respondents answering 'no' added a note to say this pathway/protocol was 'in development'

[23]Seventy-five percent (9/12) of respondents who did not answer this question added a note to say this pathway/protocol was 'in development'

[24]Six percent (5/78) of respondents answering 'yes' added a note to say this training programme was 'in development'

[25]Fourteen percent (8/56) of respondents answering 'no' added a note to say this training programme was 'in development'

[26]Ten percent (1/10) of respondents who did not answer this question added a note to say this training programme was 'in development'

[27]Percentages of those answered 'yes' (by region): London 89%, South 69%, Midlands and East 85%, North 78%

Table 61: Admissions to specialist MBUs, as reported by primary care services (question 2.6, questionnaire)

English PCTs		n (N = 144)	%	X̄	SD
No. of admissions for financial year 2004/2005	Gave a response	52	36	1.41	2.05
	Responded 'I don't know or '?''	28	19		
	Missing (no response)	64	44		
Bed days[28] for financial year 2004/2005	Gave a response	11	8	89.82	155.68
Welsh LHBs/NHS Trusts		**n (N = 15)**	%	X̄	SD
No. of admissions for financial year 2004/2005	Gave a response	5	33	0.20	0.45
	Responded 'I don't know' or '?'	1	7		
	Missing (no response)	9	60		

[28]This was not requested on the questionnaire, but since 8% of PCTs reported this either instead of, or in addition to, the number of admissions, it is reported here for completeness

X̄ = mean number of admissions per year for the trusts that answered the question

Table 62: Frequencies of reported psychological/psychosocial treatments, provided by PCTs

Treatment reported to be reported provided by PCT	Proportion of Trusts who employing this treatment	
	n (N = 43)	%
Postnatal support groups	27	63
Listening visits	17	40
CBT	6	14
Counselling	5	12
More than one of above treatments	11	26

Table 63: Frequencies of reporting cooperation with Sure Start and infant massage by the PCTs and LHBs/NHS Trusts (percentages given as proportion of primary care services that wrote a comment for Question 2.4)

Additional services reported to be provided by PCT	Proportion of Trusts who reported additional services			
	England: Total N = 95 PCTs		Wales: Total N = 14 LHBs/NHS Trusts	
	n	%	n	%
Cooperation with Sure Start	27[a]	28	1	7
Infant massage	8	8	0	0

[a]This includes some overlap with the support groups detailed in Table 62: often the postnatal support groups provided through the PCT were run in cooperation with a Sure Start programme

With regards to Welsh primary care, 29% (2/7) of those who made a comment reported using the EPDS as an assessment tool, and one LHB (14%, of 7) mentioned the 'Nottingham Tool'.

A small percentage (8%, 8/95) of PCTs also mentioned having to consider cultural aspects to their screening tools or interventions.

The frequency of referral to mental health services of women in the antenatal *and* in the postnatal period versus referring only women in the postnatal period was also examined (see Table 64).

Table 64: Frequencies of referral during the postnatal period alone versus referral during both the antenatal and postnatal periods mentioned (percentages given as proportion of primary care services that wrote a comment for Question 2.4)

Comments made in reference to:	Proportion of Trusts (of total who made a comment at all)			
	England: PCTs		Wales: LHBs/ NHS Trusts	
	n (N = 95)	%	n (N = 7)	%
Antenatal period (only, or also with reference to postnatal period)	21	22	2	29
Postnatal period only	20	21	1	14
No reference made to specific time period	54	57	4	57

Many PCTs and LHBs/NHS trusts throughout England and Wales, reported that their mental health services for women in the antenatal and postnatal periods were linked with other services, such as nearby PCTs and midwifery services, or secondary mental health trusts (see Table 8 for details).

'*Comments: Please provide any further comments or information that you feel may be relevant*':
Twenty-four percent (35/144) of English, and only 1 (7%, of 14) Welsh, primary care service providers made a comment here, which was coded.

Table 65: Frequencies of reporting various levels of an existing multidisciplinary approach to antenatal and postnatal mental health (percentages given as proportion of primary care services that reported an existing multidisciplinary approach)

Reported links with the following:	Proportion of Trusts (of total who made a comment regarding multidisciplinary approach at all)			
	England: PCTs		Wales: LHBs/NHS Trusts	
	n (N = 33)	%	n (N = 2)	%
Local primary care services only	4	12	0	0
Various other levels of care (often mentioning other primary care services also)	29	88	2	100

Table 66: Major themes of written comments from English and Welsh primary care services and frequency of reporting these problems (percentages are given as a proportion of those that wrote an additional comment here)

Comment category	Common examples of comments	England: PCTs		Wales: LHBs/NHS Trusts	
		n (N = 35)	%	n (N = 1)	%
Antenatal and postnatal mental health needs more attention	– More national work needs to be done – NICE guidance would be welcome – [Antenatal and postnatal mental health issues] should be key objective for the future	14	40	1	100
Trust short of funding/ resources	– No access to MBU in Kent – Few beds available locally – Staffing pressures	10	29	0	0

Two main themes of the comments made referred to the fact that services for antenatal and postnatal mental health need more attention in the future, and that this area was often overlooked due to funding or staffing issues (see Table 66 for some examples of written comments and frequencies of reporting these themes).

As well as the comments (for Question 2.4) regarding *existing* links with various services external to each individual PCT, 46% (16/35) of PCTs (no LHBs/NHS trusts from Wales commented here) who made an additional comment here reported future *plans to develop* links with various external services (see Table 67 for details and frequencies).

Table 67: Frequencies of reporting aims to develop various levels of a multidisciplinary approach to antenatal and postnatal mental health (percentages given as proportion of primary care services that reported aiming to develop an existing multidisciplinary approach)

Reported plans to develop links with the following:	Proportion of Trusts (of total who made a comment regarding developing a multi-disciplinary approach at all)	
	England: PCTs	
	n (N = 16)	%
Local primary care services only	1	6
Various other levels of care (often mentioning other primary care services also)	15	94

APPENDIX 17:

DECLARATIONS OF INTERESTS

BY GDG MEMBERS

With a range of practical experience relevant to antenatal and postnatal mental health in the GDG, members were appointed because of their understanding and expertise in healthcare for people with perinatal mental disorders and support for their families and carers, including: scientific issues; health research; the delivery and receipt of healthcare, along with the work of the healthcare industry; and the role of professional organisations and organisations for people with perinatal mental disorders.

To minimise and manage any potential conflicts of interest, and to avoid any public concern that commercial or other financial interests have affected the work of the GDG and influenced guidance, members of the GDG must declare as a matter of public record any interests held by themselves or their families that fall under specified categories (see below). These categories include any relationships they have with the healthcare industries, professional organisations and organisations for people with perinatal mental disorders.

Individuals invited to join the GDG were asked to declare their interests before being appointed. To allow the management of any potential conflicts of interest that might arise during the development of the guideline, GDG members were also asked to declare their interests at each GDG meeting throughout the guideline development process. The interests of all the members of the GDG are listed below, including interests declared prior to appointment and during the guideline development process.

Categories of interest

- **Paid employment**
- **Personal interests related to antenatal and postnatal mental health**: payment and/or funding from the healthcare industry, including consultancies, grants, fee-paid work and shareholdings or other beneficial interests.
- **Personal interests not specifically related to antenatal and postnatal mental health**: any other payment and/or funding from the healthcare industry, including consultancies, grants and shareholdings or other beneficial interests.
- **Non-personal interests**: funding from the healthcare industry received by the GDG member's organisation or department, but where the GDG member has not personally received payment, including fellowships and other support provided by the healthcare industry.
- **Other interests relating to antenatal and postnatal mental health**: funding from governmental or non-governmental organisations, charities, and so on, and/or ownership in a company that provides therapy or treatments likely to be covered in the guideline.

Declarations of interest	
Dr Dave Tomson	
Employment	GP and Consultant in patient-centred primary care, North Shields
Personal interests related to antenatal and postnatal mental health	None
Personal interests not specifically related to antenatal and postnatal mental health	Work for Primary Care Partners, which runs Trailblazers, an accredited training course that is part of a national network and is funded by a variety of pharmaceutical companies (approximately £20,000 between 2001 and 2005); involvement in running TIPS, a training course for specialist registrars in psychiatry, funded by Wyeth (£6,000 for running the course in 2006); receipt of a single payment for work on post-traumatic stress disorder GDG, funded by NICE (£500 in 2004)
Non-personal interests	None
Other interests related to antenatal and postnatal mental health	None
Mr Stephen Pilling	
Employment	Joint Director, NCCMH; Director, Centre for Outcomes, Research and Effectiveness, University College London; Consultant Clinical Psychologist and Deputy Head of Psychology Services, Camden and Islington Mental Health and Social Care Trust
Personal interests related to antenatal and postnatal mental health	None
Personal interests not specifically related to antenatal and postnatal mental health	Fees for lectures, including UK Psychiatric Pharmacy Group (October 2006) and at Andrew Simms Centre, Leeds (December 2006)

Declarations of interest (*Continued*)	
Non-personal interests	Grants for production of clinical guidelines and evidence-related practice: British Psychological Society Clinical Effectiveness Programme with Professor P. Fonagy and Professor S. Michie supporting production of NICE guidelines and related policy implementation work (£5.4 million, 2001–2010) Health service research grants: NHS Service Development and Organisation Research and Development Programme developing evidence-based and acceptable stepped care systems in mental healthcare, an operational research project with Professor D. Richards, Professor S. Gallivan, Dr S. Gilbody, Professor K. Lovell, Dr J. Cape, Dr P. Bower and Ms J. Leibowitz (£299,642, 2006–2009); NHS Service Development and Organisation Research and Development Programme – The 100 Ward Study: a National Survey of Psychiatric Inpatient Unit Morale with Dr S. Johnson, Professor P. Bebbington, Professor M. King, Professor S. Woods, Professor N. Wellman, Dr D. Osborn and Dr R. Arraya (£296,999, 2006–2009)
Other interests related to antenatal and postnatal mental health	None
Dr Fiona Blake	
Employment	Consultant Psychiatrist, Cambridge University Hospitals NHS Foundation Trust
Personal interests related to antenatal and postnatal mental health	None

Continued

Declarations of interest (*Continued*)	
Personal interests not specifically related to antenatal and postnatal mental health	Member of advisory panel for AstraZeneca providing advice on marketing quetiapine (£840, February 2005); Wyeth-funded APA annual meeting attendance (June 2005, expenses only)
Non-personal interests	None
Other interests related to antenatal an postnatal mental health	None
Ms Rachel Burbeck	
Employment	Systematic Reviewer, NCCMH
Personal interests related to antenatal and postnatal mental health	None
Personal interests not specifically related to antenatal and postnatal mental health	None
Non-personal interests	None
Other interests related to antenatal and postnatal mental health	None
Dr Sandra Elliott	
Employment	Consultant Clinical Psychologist, South London and Maudsley NHS Trust
Personal interests related to antenatal and postnatal mental health	Director, Postnatal Depression Trainer Training, Keele Perinatal Mental Health Education Unit (£3,000, April and November 2005)
Personal interests not specifically related to antenatal and postnatal mental health	None
Non-personal interests	None
Other interests related to antenatal and postnatal mental health	None

Declarations of interest (*Continued*)	
Dr Pauline Evans	
Employment	Senior Lecturer in Health and Social Care, University of Gloucestershire
Personal interests related to antenatal and postnatal mental health	None
Personal interests not specifically related to dementia	None
Non-personal interests	None
Other interests related to antenatal and postnatal mental health	None
Ms Josephine Foggo	
Employment	Project Manager (until August 2005), NCCMH
Personal interests related to antenatal and postnatal mental health	None
Personal interests not specifically related to antenatal and postnatal mental health	None
Non-personal interests	None
Other interests related to antenatal and postnatal mental health	None
Dr Alain Gregoire	
Employment	Consultant Perinatal Psychiatrist, Hampshire Partnership NHS Trust and University of Southampton
Personal interests related to antenatal and postnatal mental health	Some care of private inpatients and outpatients with perinatal disorders
Personal interests not specifically related to antenatal and postnatal mental health	Fees for lectures/educational events from various sponsoring pharmaceutical companies
Non-personal interests	Grant for rural research programme from National Mental Health Partnership (£63,000, 2003–2004);

Continued

Declarations of interest *(Continued)*	
	grant for research into case management for depression in primary care from Wyeth (2003, £16,000); grant from SDO NHS R&D with G. Thornicroft (Institute of Psychiatry) and S. Johnson (UCL) (£299,991, 2004 to date) (this includes a component investigating outcomes of care from MBUs and MBU mapping for the UK); occasional educational events, lectures and departmental courses sponsored by various pharmaceutical companies through Hampshire Partnership NHS Trust
Other interests related to antenatal and postnatal mental health	None
Dr Jane Hamilton	
Employment	Consultant Psychiatrist in Maternal Health, Sheffield Care Trust
Personal interests related to antenatal and postnatal mental health	None
Personal interests not specifically related to antenatal and postnatal mental health	None
Non-personal interests	None
Other interests related to antenatal and postnatal mental health	None
Mrs Claire Hesketh	
Employment	Primary Care Mental Health Services Manager, Northumberland, Tyne and Wear NHS Trust
Personal interests related to antenatal and postnatal mental health	None
Personal interests not specifically related to antenatal and postnatal mental health	None

Declarations of interest (*Continued*)	
Non-personal interests	None
Other interests related to antenatal and postnatal mental health	None
Ms Rebecca King	
Employment	Project Manager (August 2005 to August 2006), NCCMH
Personal interests related to antenatal and postnatal mental health	None
Personal interests not specifically related to antenatal and postnatal mental health	None
Non-personal interests	None
Other interests related to antenatal and postnatal mental health	None
Dr Elizabeth McDonald	
Employment	Consultant Perinatal Psychiatrist, East London and the City Mental Health NHS Trust
Personal interests relating to antenatal and postnatal mental health	Occasional lectures for healthcare professionals, for example GPs, CPNs and psychiatrists, for which honoraria from Janssen, AstraZeneca and Otsuka were received (<£500 a maximum of 2 or 3 times per year)
Personal interests not specifically related to antenatal and postnatal mental health	Support from Janssen to attend American Psychiatric Association meetings in 2002 (Philadelphia) and 2003 (San Francisco) and from AstraZeneca to attend an American Psychiatric Association meeting in 2004 (New York) (expenses only)
Non-personal interests	None
Other interests related to antenatal and postnatal mental health	None

Continued

Declarations of interest (*Continued*)	
Ms Rosa Matthews	
Employment	Systematic Reviewer (until July 2005), NCCMH
Personal interests relating to antenatal and postnatal mental health	None
Personal interests not specifically related to antenatal and postnatal mental health	None
Non-personal interests	None
Other interests related to antenatal and postnatal mental health	None
Dr Ifigeneia Mavranezouli	
Employment	Health Economist, NCCMH
Personal interests related to antenatal and postnatal mental health	None
Personal interests not specifically related to antenatal and postnatal mental health	None
Non-personal interests	None
Other interests related to antenatal and postnatal mental health	None
Mr Patrick O'Brien	
Employment	Obstetrician, University College London Hospitals NHS Foundation Trust
Personal interests related to antenatal and postnatal mental health	Medical advisor for BBC TV (approximately £3,000 per year, 2002–2005)
Personal interests not specifically related to antenatal and postnatal mental health	None
Non-personal interests	None
Other interests related to antenatal and postnatal mental health	None

Declarations of interest (*Continued*)	
Dr Donald Peebles	
Employment	Obstetrician, University College London Hospitals NHS Foundation Trust
Personal interests related to antenatal nd postnatal mental health	None
Personal interests not specifically related to antenatal and postnatal mental health	Occasional medical legal work (annual income approximately £7,000)
Non-personal interests	Research Training Fellowship funded by the Portland Hospital via University College London
Other interests related to antenatal and postnatal mental health	None
Dr Catherine Pettinari	
Employment	Project Manager (August 2006 to present), NCCMH
Personal interests relating to antenatal and postnatal mental health	None
Personal interests not specifically related to antenatal and postnatal mental health	None
Non-personal interests	None
Other interests related to antenatal and postnatal mental health	None
Mrs Sue Power	
Employment	Team Manager for Community Mental Health Team, Vale of Glamorgan County Council
Personal interests related to antenatal and postnatal mental health	None
Personal interests not specifically related to antenatal and postnatal mental health	None

Continued

Declarations of interest (*Continued*)	
Non-personal interests	None
Other interests related to antenatal and postnatal mental health	None
Mrs Yana Richens	
Employment	Consultant Midwife, University College London Hospitals NHS Foundation Trust
Personal interests related to antenatal and postnatal mental health	Editorial Board member, British Journal of Midwifery
Personal interests not specifically related to antenatal and postnatal mental health	None
Non-personal interests	None
Other interests related to antenatal and postnatal mental health	None
Mrs Ruth Rothman	
Employment	Specialist Health Visitor for Postnatal Depression and Clinical Lead for Mental Health, Southend Primary Care Trust
Personal interests related to antenatal and postnatal mental health	None
Personal interests not specifically related to antenatal and postnatal mental health	None
Non-personal interests	None
Other interests related to antenatal and postnatal mental health	None
Mrs Fiona Shaw	
Employment	Author
Personal interests related to antenatal and postnatal mental health	None
Personal interests not specifically related to antenatal and postnatal mental health	None

Declarations of interest (*Continued*)	
Non-personal interests	None
Other interests related to antenatal and postnatal mental health	None
Ms Sarah Stockton	
Employment	Information Scientist, NCCMH
Personal interests related to antenatal and postnatal mental health	None
Personal interests not specifically related to antenatal and postnatal mental health	None
Non-personal interests	None
Other interests related to antenatal and postnatal mental health	None
Dr Clare Taylor	
Employment	Editor, NCCMH
Personal interests related to antenatal and postnatal mental health	None
Personal interests not specifically related to antenatal and postnatal mental health	None
Non-personal interests	None
Other interests related to antenatal and postnatal mental health	None
Ms Lois Thomas	
Employment	Research Assistant (until September 2005), NCCMH
Personal interests related to antenatal and postnatal mental health	None
Personal interests not specifically related to antenatal and postnatal mental health	None
Non-personal interests	None
Other interests related to antenatal and postnatal mental health	None

Continued

Declarations of interest (*Continued*)	
Dr Clare Thormod	
Employment	GP, London
Personal interests related to antenatal and postnatal mental health	Provision of GP training courses in solution-focused consultation (less than £1,000 per year)
Personal interests not specifically related to antenatal and postnatal mental health	None
Non-personal interests	None
Other interests related to antenatal and postnatal mental health	None
Ms Jenny Turner	
Employment	Research Assistant (from November 2005), NCCMH
Personal interests related to antenatal and postnatal mental health	None
Personal interests not specifically related to antenatal and postnatal mental health	None
Non-personal interests	None
Other interests related to antenatal and postnatal mental health	None

10. REFERENCES

Please note that references to studies excluded from clinical review appear only in Appendix 19.

Abramowitz, J. S., Schwartz, S. A., Moore, K. M., et al. (2003) Obsessive-compulsive symptoms in pregnancy and the puerperium: a review of the literature. *Journal of Anxiety Disorders*, 17, 461–478.

Adab, N., Tudur, S. C., Vinten, J., *et al.* (2004a) Common antiepileptic drugs in pregnancy in women with epilepsy. *Cochrane Database of Systematic Reviews*, 3, CD004848.

Adab, N., Kini, U. & Vinten, J. (2004b) The longer term outcome of children born to mothers with epilepsy. *Journal of Neurology, Neurosurgery and Psychiatry*, 75, 1575–1583.

AGREE Collaboration (2003) Development and validation of an international appraisal instrument for assessing the quality of clinical practice guidelines: the AGREE project. *Quality and Safety in Health Care*, 12, 18–23.

Altshuler, L. L., Burt, V. K., McMullen, M., *et al.* (1995) Breastfeeding and sertraline: a 24-hour analysis. *The Journal of Clinical Psychiatry*, 56, 243–245.

Altshuler, L. L., Cohen, L., Szuba, M. P., *et al.* (1996) Pharmacologic management of psychiatric illness during pregnancy: dilemmas and guidelines. *The American Journal of Psychiatry*, 153, 592–606.

American Psychiatric Association (APA) (2000) *Diagnostic and Statistical Manual of Mental Disorders: DSM IV*. 4th edition. Washington, D.C.: American Psychiatric Association.

Ammaniti, M., Speranza, A. M., Tambelli, R., *et al.* (2006) A prevention and promotion intervention program in the field of mother-infant relationship. *Infant Mental Health Journal*, 27, 70–90.

Andrews, G., Slade, T. & Peters, L. (1999) Classification in psychiatry: ICD-10 versus DSM-IV. *The British Journal of Psychiatry*, 174, 3–5.

Appleby, L. (1992) Suicide in psychiatric patients: risk and prevention. *The British Journal of Psychiatry*, 161, 749–758.

Appleby, L., Warner, R., Whitton, A., *et al.* (1997) A controlled study of fluoxetine and cognitive-behavioural counselling in the treatment of postnatal depression. *British Medical Journal*, 314, 932–936.

Appleby, L., Mortensen, P. B. & Faragher, E. B. (1998) Suicide and other causes of mortality after post-partum psychiatric admission. *The British Journal of Psychiatry*, 173, 209–211.

Armstrong, K. & Edwards, H. (2003) The effects of exercise and social support on mothers reporting depressive symptoms: a pilot randomized controlled trial. *International Journal of Mental Health Nursing*, 12, 130–138.

Armstrong, K. & Edwards, H. (2004) The effectiveness of a pram-walking exercise programme in reducing depressive symptomatology for postnatal women. *International Journal of Nursing Practice*, 10, 177–194.

References

Armstrong, K. L., Fraser, J. A., Dadds, M. R., *et al.* (1999) A randomized, controlled trial of nurse home visiting to vulnerable families with newborns. *Journal of Paediatrics and Child Health*, 35, 237–244.

Arntz, A. (1994) Treatment of borderline personality disorder: a challenge for cognitive-behavioural therapy. *Behaviour Research and Therapy*, 32, 419–430.

Arroll, B., Goodyear-Smith, F., Kerse, N., *et al.* (2005) Effect of the addition of a 'help' question to two screening questions on specificity for diagnosis of depression in general practice: diagnostic validity study. *British Medical Journal*, *331*, 884.

Asker, C., Norstedt Wikner, B. & Kallen, B. (2005) Use of antiemetic drugs during pregnancy in Sweden. *European Journal of Clinical Pharmacology*, 61, 899–906.

Austin, M. P. & Lumley, J. (2003) Antenatal screening for postnatal depression: a systematic review. *Acta Psychiatrica Scandinavica*, *107*, 10–17.

Barkham, M., Rees, A., Shapiro, D. A., *et al.* (1996) Outcomes of time-limited psychotherapy in applied settings: replicating the Second Sheffield Psychotherapy Project. *Journal of Consulting and Clinical Psychology*, *64*, 1079–1085.

Bar-Oz, B., Nulman, I., Koren, G., *et al.* (2000) Anticonvulsants and breast feeding: a critical review. *Paediatric Drugs*, 2, 113–126.

Bazire, S. (2005) *Psychotropic Drug Directory 2005: The Professionals' Pocket Handbook and Aide Memoire*. Salisbury: Fivepin Publishing Ltd.

Beardslee, W. R., Bemporad, J., Keller, M. B., *et al.* (1983) Children of parents with major affective disorder: a review. *The American Journal of Psychiatry*, *140*, 825–832.

Beck, A. T., Ward, C. H., Mendelson, M., *et al.* (1961) An inventory for measuring depression. *Archives of General Psychiatry*, 4, 561–571.

Beck, A. T., Steer, R. A. & Brown, G. K. (1996) *Manual for Beck Depression Inventory-II*. San Antonio, TX: Psychological Corporation.

Beck, C. T. (2001) Predictors of postpartum depression: an update. *Nursing Research*, 50, 275–285.

Beck, C. T. & Gable, R. K. (2000) Postpartum Depression Screening Scale: development and psychometric testing. *Nursing Research*, 49, 272–282.

Beck, C. T. & Gable, R. K. (2001a) Ensuring content validity: an illustration of the process. *Journal of Nursing Measurement*, 9, 201–215.

Beck, C. T. & Gable, R. K. (2001b) Comparative analysis of the performance of the Postpartum Depression Screening Scale with two other depression instruments. *Nursing Research*, 50, 242–250.

Bennedsen, B. E., Mortensen, P. B., Olesen, A. V., *et al.* (2001) Congenital malformations, stillbirths, and infant deaths among children of women with schizophrenia. *Archives of General Psychiatry*, 58, 674–679.

Berlin, J. A. (1997) Does blinding of readers affect the results of meta-analyses? *Lancet*, *350*, 185–186.

Beutler, L. E., Clarkin, J. F. & Bongar, B. (2000) *Guidelines for the Systematic Treatment of the Depressed Patient*. New York: Oxford University Press.

Birnbaum, C. S., Cohen, L. S., Bailey, J. W., *et al.* (1999) Serum concentrations of antidepressants and benzodiazepines in nursing infants: a case series. *Pediatrics*, *104*, e11.

Bjelland, I., Dahl, A. A., Haug, T. T., *et al.* (2002) The validity of the Hospital Anxiety and Depression Scale. An updated literature review. *Journal of Psychosomatic Research. 52*, 69–77.

Blatt, S. J., Sanislow, C. A., III, Zuroff, D. C., *et al.* (1996a) Characteristics of effective therapists: further analyses of data from the National Institute of Mental Health Treatment of Depression Collaborative Research Program. *Journal of Consulting and Clinical Psychology, 64*, 1276–1284.

Blatt, S. J., Quinlan, D. M., Zuroff, D. C., *et al.* (1996b) Interpersonal factors in brief treatment of depression: further analyses of the National Institute of Mental Health Treatment of Depression Collaborative Research Program. *Journal of Consulting and Clinical Psychology, 64*, 162–171.

Boath, E., Major, K., & Cox, J. (2003) When the cradle falls II: The cost-effectiveness of treating postnatal depression in a psychiatric day hospital compared with routine primary care. *Journal of Affective Disorders, 74*, 159–166.

Boath, E. H., Pryce, A. J. & Cox, J. L. (1998) Postnatal depression: the impact on the family. *Journal of Reproductive and Infant Psychology, 16*, 199–203.

Bonari, L., Pinto, N., Ahn, E., *et al.* (2004) Perinatal risks of untreated depression during pregnancy. *Canadian Journal of Psychiatry, 49*, 726–735.

Boyce, P., Hickey, A., Gilchrist, J., *et al.* (2001) The development of a brief personality scale to measure vulnerability to postnatal depression. *Archives of Women's Mental Health, 3*, 147–153.

Boyce, P. & Hickey, A. (2005) Psychosocial risk factors to major depression after childbirth. *Social Psychiatry and Psychiatric Epidemiology, 40*, 605–612.

Boyce, P., Stubbs, J. & Todd, A. (1993) The Edinburgh Postnatal Depression Scale: validation for an Australian sample. *The Australian and New Zealand Journal of Psychiatry, 27*, 472–476.

Boyd, R. C., Le, H. N. & Somberg, R. (2005) Review of screening instruments for postpartum depression. *Archives of Women's Mental Health, 8*, 141–153.

Brent, R. L. & Beckman, D. A. (1990) Environmental teratogens. *Bulletin of the New York Academy of Medicine: Journal of Urban Health, 66*, 123–163.

Briggs, G. G., Freeman, R. K. & Yaffe, S. J. (2002) *Drugs in Pregnancy and Lactation: a Reference Guide to Fetal and Neonatal Risk.* 6th edition. Philadelphia, PA: Lippincott Williams & Wilkins.

Brinch, M., Isager, T. & Tolstrup, K. (1988) Anorexia nervosa and motherhood: reproduction pattern and mothering behavior of 50 women. *Acta Psychiatrica Scandinavica, 77*, 611–617.

British Medical Association and the Royal Pharmaceutical Society of Great Britain (2006) *British National Formulary (BNF) 51.* London: British Medical Association and the Royal Pharmaceutical Society of Great Britain.

Brockington, I. F. (1996) *Motherhood and Mental Health.* Oxford: Oxford University Press.

Brouwers, E. P., Van Baar, A. L. & Pop, V. J. (2001) Does the Edinburgh Postnatal Depression Scale measure anxiety? *Journal of Psychosomic Research, 51*, 659–663.

Brown, G. W. & Harris, T. (1978) *Social Origins of Depression: a Study of Psychiatric Disorder in Women.* London: Tavistock Publications.

References

Brown, T. A., Campbell, L. A., Lehman, C. L., *et al.* (2001) Current and lifetime comorbidity of the DSM-IV anxiety and mood disorders in a large clinical sample. *Journal of Abnormal Psychology, 110*, 585–599.

Brugha, T. S., Wheatley, S., Taub, N. A., *et al.* (2000) Pragmatic randomized trial of antenatal intervention to prevent post-natal depression by reducing psychosocial risk factors. *Psychological Medicine, 30*, 1273–1281.

Buckley, N. A. & McManus, P. R. (2002) Fatal toxicity of serotonergic and other antidepressant drugs: analysis of United Kingdom mortality data. *British Medical Journal, 326*, 1332–1333.

Bulik, C. M., Sullivan, P. F., Fear, J. L., *et al.* (1999) Fertility and reproduction in women with anorexia nervosa: a controlled study. *Journal of Clinical Psychiatry, 60*, 130–135.

Burch, K. J. & Wells, B. G. (1992) Fluoxetine/norfluoxetine concentrations in human milk. *Pediatrics, 89*, 676–677.

Calman, K. C. & Royston, G. H. (1997) Risk language and dialects. *British Medical Journal, 315*, 939–942.

Carter, F. A., Frampton, C. M. & Mulder, R. T. (2006) Cesarean section and postpartum depression: a review of the evidence examining the link. *Psychosomatic Medicine, 68*, 321–330.

Chambers, C. D., Hernandez-Diaz, S., Van Marter, L. J., *et al.* (2006) Selective serotonin-reuptake inhibitors and risk of persistent pulmonary hypertension of the newborn. *The New England Journal of Medicine, 354*, 579–587.

Chang, L., Smith, L. M., LoPresti, C., *et al.* (2004) Smaller subcortical volumes and cognitive deficits in children with prenatal methamphetamine exposure. *Psychiatry Research, 132*, 95–106.

Chee, C. Y., Lee, D. T., Chong, Y. S., *et al.* (2005) Confinement and other psychosocial factors in perinatal depression: a transcultural study in Singapore. *Journal of Affective Disorders, 89*, 157–166.

Chen, C. H., Tseng, Y. F., Chou, F. H., *et al.* (2000) Effects of support group intervention in postnatally distressed women. A controlled study in Taiwan. *Journal of Psychosomatic Research, 49*, 395–399.

Church, N. F., Brechman-Toussaint, M. L. & Hine, D. W. (2005) Do dysfunctional cognitions mediate the relationship between risk factors and postnatal depression symptomatology? *Journal of Affective Disorders, 87*, 65–72.

Clark, R., Tluczek, A. & Wenzel, A. (2003) Psychotherapy for postpartum depression: a preliminary report. *The American Journal of Orthopsychiatry, 73*, 441–454.

Clinical Standards Advisory Group (1999) *Services for People with Depression.* London: DH.

Cochrane Collaboration (2005) Review Manager (RevMan) [Computer program]. Version 4.2.7 for Windows. Oxford: The Cochrane Collaboration.

Cohen, L. S., Friedman, J. M., Jefferson, J. W., *et al.* (1994) A reevaluation of risk of in utero exposure to lithium. *The Journal of the American Medical Association, 271*, 146–150.

Cohen, L. S., Sichel, D. A., Robertson, L. M., *et al.* (1995) Postpartum prophylaxis for women with bipolar disorder. *The American Journal of Psychiatry, 152*, 1641–1645.

Cohen, L. S., Viguera, A. C., Bouffard, S. M., *et al.* (2001) Venlafaxine in the treatment of postpartum depression. *The Journal of Clinical Psychiatry, 62,* 592–596.

Cooper, P. J., Murray, L., Wilson, A., *et al.* (2003) Controlled trial of the short- and long-term effect of psychological treatment of post-partum depression. I. Impact on maternal mood. *The British Journal of Psychiatry, 182,* 412–419.

Cox, J. L., Holden, J. M. & Sagovsky, R. (1987) Detection of postnatal depression. Development of the 10-item Edinburgh Postnatal Depression Scale. *The British Journal of Psychiatry, 150,* 782–786.

Cox, J. L., Murray, D. & Chapman, G. (1993) A controlled study of the onset, duration and prevalence of postnatal depression. *The British Journal of Psychiatry, 163,* 27–31.

Creamer, M., Burgess, P. & McFarlane, A. C. (2001) Post-traumatic stress disorder: findings from the Australian National Survey of Mental Health and Well-Being. *Psychological Medicine, 31,* 1237–1247.

Crisp, A. H., Jones, M. G. & Slater, P. (1978) The Middlesex Hospital Questionnaire: a validity study. *The British Journal of Medical Psychology, 51,* 269–280.

Cubison, J. & Munro, J. (2005) Acceptability of using the EPDS as a screening tool for depression in the postnatal period. In *Screening for Perinatal Depression* (eds C. Henshaw & S. Elliot). London: Jessica Kingsley Publishers.

Curtis, L. & Netten, A. (2005) Unit Costs of Health and Social Care 2005. Canterbury: University of Kent at Canterbury, Personal Social Services Research Unit.

Czarnocka, J. & Slade, P. (2000) Prevalence and predictors of post-traumatic stress symptoms following childbirth. *The British Journal of Clinical Psychology, 39,* 35–51.

Czeizel, A. E. & Vargha, P. (2005) A case-control study of congenital abnormality and dimenhydrinate usage during pregnancy. *Archives of Gynecology and Obstetrics, 271,* 113–118.

Darwish, M., Martin, P. T., Cevallos, W. H., *et al.* (1999) Rapid disappearance of zaleplon from breast milk after oral administration to lactating women. *Journal of Clinical Pharmacology, 39,* 670–674.

Dean, C., Williams, R. J. & Brockington, I. F. (1989) Is puerperal psychosis the same as bipolar manic-depressive disorder? A family study. *Psychological Medicine, 19,* 637–647.

Deeks, J. J. (2002) Issues in the selection of a summary statistic for meta-analysis of clinical trials with binary outcomes. *Statistics in Medicine, 21,* 1575–1600.

Dennis, C. L. (2003) The effect of peer support on postpartum depression: a pilot randomized controlled trial. *Canadian Journal of Psychiatry, 48,* 115–124.

Department for Constitutional Affairs (DCA) (2005) Mental Capacity Act 2005. London: The Stationery Office Limited.

Department of Health (DH) (1999) *Effective Care Co-ordination in Mental Health Services: Modernising the Care Programme Approach – A Policy Booklet.* London: DH.

Department of Health (DH) (2001) *Treatment Choice in Psychological Therapies and Counselling: Evidence-Based Clinical Practice Guideline.* London: DH.

References

Department of Health (DH) (2002) *Women's Mental Health: into the Mainstream – Strategic Development of Mental Health Care for Women.* London: DH.

Department of Health (DH) (2004) *Organising and Delivering Psychological Therapies.* London: DH.

DerSimonian, R. & Laird, N. (1986) Meta-analysis in clinical trials. *Controlled Clinical Trials,* 7, 177–188.

Diav-Citrin, O., Okotore, B., Lucarelli, K., *et al.* (1999) Pregnancy outcome following first-trimester exposure to zopiclone: a prospective controlled cohort study. *American Journal of Perinatology,* 16, 157–160.

Diav-Citrin, O., Shechtman, S., Aharonovich, A. *et al.* (2003) Pregnancy outcome after gestational exposure to loratadine or antihistamines: a prospective controlled cohort study. *The Journal of Allergy and Clinical Immunology,* 111, 1239–1243.

Dolovich, L. R., Addis, A., Vaillancourt, J. M., *et al.* (1998) Benzodiazepine use in pregnancy and major malformations or oral cleft: meta-analysis of cohort and case-control studies. *British Medical Journal,* 317, 839–843.

Drummond, M. F. & Jefferson, T. O. (1996) Guidelines for authors and peer reviewers of economic submissions to the BMJ. The BMJ Economic Evaluation Working Party. *British Medical Journal,* 313, 275–283.

Duncan, S., Mercho, S., Lopes-Cendes, I., *et al.* (2001) Repeated neural tube defects and valproate monotherapy suggest a pharmacogenetic abnormality. *Epilepsia,* 42, 750–753.

Eberhard-Gran, M., Eskild, A. & Opjordsmoen, S. (2006) Use of psychotropic medications in treating mood disorders during lactation: practical recommendations. *CNS Drugs,* 20, 187–198.

Eccles, M., Freemantle, N. & Mason, J. (1998) North of England evidence based guidelines development project: methods of developing guidelines for efficient drug use in primary care. *British Medical Journal,* 316, 1232–1235.

Edwards, A., Elwyn, G., Covey, J., *et al.* (2001) Presenting risk information – a review of the effects of 'framing' and other manipulations on patient outcomes. *Journal of Health Communication,* 6, 61–82.

Egan, G. (1990) *The Skilled Helper: a Systematic Approach to Effective Helping.* Pacific Grove, CA: Brooks/Cole.

Elliot, R. (1998) Editor's introduction: a guide to the empirically supported treatments controversy. *Psychotherapy Research,* 8, 115–125.

Elliott, S. A., Leverton, T. J., Sanjack, M., *et al.* (2000) Promoting mental health after childbirth: a controlled trial of primary prevention of postnatal depression. *The British Journal of Clinical Psychology,* 39, 223–241.

Epperson, C. N., Terman, M., Terman, J. S., *et al.* (2004) Randomized clinical trial of bright light therapy for antepartum depression: preliminary findings. *The Journal of Clinical Psychiatry,* 65, 421–425.

Epstein, R. M., Alper, B. S., & Quill, T. E. (2004) Communicating evidence for participatory decision making. *The Journal of the American Medical Association,* 291, 2359–2366.

Ericson, A., Kallen, B. & Wiholm, B. (1999) Delivery outcome after the use of antidepressants in early pregnancy. *European Journal of Clinical Pharmacology*, *55*, 503–508.

Eros, E., Czeizel, A. E., Rockenbauer, M., *et al.* (2002) A population-based case-control teratologic study of nitrazepam, medazepam, tofisopam, alprazolum and clonazepam treatment during pregnancy. *European Journal of Obstetrics, Gynecology and Reproductive Biology*, *101*, 147–154.

Evans, J., Heron, J., Francomb, H., *et al.* (2001) Cohort study of depressed mood during pregnancy and after childbirth. *British Medical Journal*, *323*, 257–260.

Fahy, T. A. & Morrison, J. J. (1993) The clinical significance of eating disorders in obstetrics. *British Journal of Obstetrics and Gynaecology*, *100*, 708–710.

Field, T., Pickens, J., Prodromidis, M., *et al.* (2000) Targeting adolescent mothers with depressive symptoms for early intervention. *Adolescence*, *35*, 381–414.

Gagnon, A. J. (2000) Individual or group antenatal education for childbirth/parenthood. *Cochrane Database of Systematic Reviews*, *4*, CD002869.

Gallivan, S., Utley, M., Treasure, T., *et al.* (2002) Booked inpatient admissions and hospital capacity: mathematical modelling study. *British Medical Journal*, *324*, 280–282.

Gamble, J., Creedy, D., Moyle, W., *et al.* (2005) Effectiveness of a counseling intervention after a traumatic childbirth: a randomized controlled trial. *Birth: Issues in Perinatal Care*, *32*, 11–19.

Garner, D. M. & Garfinkel, P. E. (1979) The Eating Attitudes Test: an index of the symptoms of anorexia nervosa. *Psychological Medicine*, *9*, 273–279.

Gavin, N. I., Gaynes, B. N., Lohr, K. N., *et al.* (2005) Perinatal depression: a systematic review of prevalence and incidence. *Obstetrics and Gynecology*, *106*, 1071–1083.

Gaynes, B. N., Gavin, N., Meltzer-Brody, S., *et al.* (2005) Perinatal depression: prevalence, screening accuracy, and screening outcomes. *Evidence Report/Technology Assessment (Summary)*, 1–8.

Gelder, M. G., Lopez-Ibor, J. J. & Andreasen, N. C. (2000) *New Oxford Textbook of Psychiatry*. Oxford: Oxford University Press.

Gentile, S. (2004) Clinical utilization of atypical antipsychotics in pregnancy and lactation. *The Annals of Pharmacotherapy*, *38*, 1265–1271.

Gigerenzer, G. & Edwards, A. (2003) Simple tools for understanding risks: from innumeracy to insight. *British Medical Journal*, *327*, 741–744.

Gillick v West Norfolk and Wisbech Area Health Authority [1985] 3 All ER 402 (HL).

Gissler, M., Berg, C., Bouvier-Colle, M. H., *et al.* (2005) Injury deaths, suicides and homicides associated with pregnancy, Finland 1987–2000. *European Journal of Public Health*, *15*, 459–463.

Goldberg, D., Privett, M., Ustun, B., *et al.* (1998) The effects of detection and treatment on the outcome of major depression in primary care: a naturalistic study in 15 cities. *The British Journal of General Practice*, *48*, 1840–1844.

Goldberg, D. P. (1972) *The Detection of Psychiatric Illness by Questionnaire*, London: Oxford University Press.

Goldberg, D. P. & Bridges, K. (1988) Somatic presentations of psychiatric illness in primary care setting. *Journal of Psychosomatic Research*, *32*, 137–144.

Goldberg, D. P. & Huxley, P. (1992) *Common Mental Disorders: A Bio-Social Model.* London: Tavistock/Routledge.

Goldberg, D. P., Cooper, B., Eastwood, M. R., *et al.* (1970) A standardised psychiatric interview for use in community surveys. *British Journal of Preventive and Social Medicine, 24,* 18–23.

Goldberg, D. P., Jenkins, L., Millar, T., *et al.* (1993) The ability of trainee general practitioners to identify psychological distress among their patients. *Psychological Medicine, 23,* 185–193.

Goodwin, N., 6, P., Peck, E., *et al.* (2004) *Managing Across Diverse Networks of Care: Lessons from Other Sectors.* Policy Report to the NHS SDO R & D Programme, Health Services Management Centre, University of Birmingham.

Gorman, L. L. & O'Hara, M. W. (2006) Prevention of postpartum depression in high risk women, unpublished.

GRADE Working Group (2004) Grading quality of evidence and strength of recommendations. *British Medical Journal, 328,* 1490–1494.

Green, J. M. (2005) What is the EPDS measuring and how should we use it in research? In *Screening for Perinatal Depression* (eds C. Henshaw & S. Elliot). London: Jessica Kingsley Publishers.

Gregoire, A. J., Kumar, R., Everitt, B., *et al.* (1996) Transdermal oestrogen for treatment of severe postnatal depression. *Lancet, 347,* 918–919.

Grimes, D. A. & Snively, G. R. (1999) Patients' understanding of medical risks: implications for genetic counseling. *Obstetrics and Gynecology, 93,* 910–914.

Haddad, P. M., Pal, B. R., Clarke, P., *et al.* (2005) Neonatal symptoms following maternal paroxetine treatment: serotonin toxicity or paroxetine discontinuation syndrome? *Journal of Psychopharmacology, 19,* 554–557.

Hagan, R., Evans, S. F. & Pope, S. (2004) Preventing postnatal depression in mothers of very preterm infants: a randomised controlled trial. *BJOG: an International Journal of Obstetrics and Gynaecology, 111,* 641–647.

Hardy, G. E., Cahill, J., Shapiro, D. A., *et al.* (2001) Client interpersonal and cognitive styles as predictors of response to time-limited cognitive therapy for depression. *Journal of Consulting and Clinical Psychology, 69,* 841–845.

Harlow, B. L., Vitonis, A. F., Sparen, P., *et al.* (2007) Incidence of hospitalization for postpartum psychotic and bipolar episodes in women with and without prior prepregnancy or prenatal psychiatric hospitalizations. *Archives of General Psychiatry, 64,* 42–48.

Harris, B., Fung, H., Johns, S., *et al.* (1989) Transient post-partum thyroid dysfunction and postnatal depression. *Journal of Affective Disorders, 17,* 243–249.

Harris, B., Oretti, R., Lazarus, J., *et al.* (2002) Randomised trial of thyroxine to prevent postnatal depression in thyroid-antibody-positive women. *The British Journal of Psychiatry, 180,* 327–330.

Harrison-Hohner, J., Coste, V., Dorato, L., *et al.* (2001) Prenatal calcium supplementation and postpartum depression: an ancillary study to a randomized trial of calcium for prevention of preeclampsia. *Archives of Women's Mental Health, 3,* 141–146.

Hay, D. F., Pawlby, S., Sharp, D., *et al.* (2001) Intellectual problems shown by 11-year-old children whose mothers had postnatal depression. *Journal of Child Psychology and Psychiatry, 42,* 871–889.

Hayes, B. A. (2001) Perinatal depression: a randomized controlled trial of an antenatal education intervention for primiparas. *Birth: Issues in Perinatal Care, 28*, 28–35.

Hedegaard, M., Henriksen, T. B., Sabroe, S., *et al.* (1993) Psychological distress in pregnancy and preterm delivery. *British Medical Journal, 307*, 234–239.

Heinicke, C. M., Fineman, N. R., Ruth, G., *et al.* (1999) Relationship-based intervention with at-risk mothers: outcome in the first year of life. *Infant Mental Health Journal, 20*, 349–374.

Hemels, M. E., Einarson, A., Koren, G., *et al.* (2005) Antidepressant use during pregnancy and the rates of spontaneous abortions: a meta-analysis. *The Annals of Pharmacotherapy, 39*, 803–809.

Hendrick, V., Altshuler, L. L. & Suri, R. (1998) Hormonal changes in the postpartum and implications for postpartum depression. *Psychosomatics, 39*, 93–101.

Hendrick, V., Smith, L. M., Suri, R., *et al.* (2003) Birth outcomes after prenatal exposure to antidepressant medication. *American Journal of Obstetrics and Gynecology, 188*, 812–815.

Heron, J., O'Connor, T. G., Evans, J., *et al.* (2004) The course of anxiety and depression through pregnancy and the postpartum in a community sample. *Journal of Affective Disorders, 80*, 65–73.

Hertzberg, T. & Wahlbeck, K. (1999) The impact of pregnancy and puerperium on panic disorder: a review. Journal of Psychosomatic Obstetrics and Gynaecology, *20*, 59–64.

Hickey, A. R., Boyce, P. M., Ellwood, D., *et al.* (1997) Early discharge and risk for postnatal depression. *The Medical Journal of Australia, 167*, 244–247.

Higgins, J. P. & Thompson, S. G. (2002) Quantifying heterogeneity in a meta-analysis. *Statistics in Medicine, 21*, 1539–1558.

Hipwell, A. E. & Kumar, R. (1996) Maternal psychopathology and prediction of outcome based on mother-infant interaction ratings (BMIS). *The British Journal of Psychiatry, 169*, 655–661.

Hiscock, H. & Wake, M. (2002) Randomised controlled trial of behavioural infant sleep intervention to improve infant sleep and maternal mood. *British Medical Journal, 324*, 1062–1065.

Hodnett, E. D., Lowe, N. K., Hannah, M. E. *et al.*, (2002) Effectiveness of nurses as providers of birth labor support in North American hospitals: a randomized controlled trial. *The Journal of the American Medical Association, 288*, 1373–1381.

Hoffrage, U. & Gigerenzer, G. (1998) Using natural frequencies to improve diagnostic inferences. *Academic Medicine, 73*, 538–540.

Holden, J. M., Sagovsky, R. & Cox, J. L. (1989) Counselling in a general practice setting: controlled study of health visitor intervention in treatment of postnatal depression. *British Medical Journal, 298*, 223–226.

Hollon, S. D., Shelton, R. C., Wisniewski, S., *et al.* (2006) Presenting characteristics of depressed outpatients as a function of recurrence: preliminary findings from the STAR*D clinical trial. *Journal of Psychiatric Research, 40*, 59–69.

Holmes, L. B., Harvey, E. A., Coull, B. A., *et al.* (2001) The teratogenicity of anticonvulsant drugs. *The New England Journal of Medicine, 344*, 1132–1138.

Holmes, L. B., Wyszynski, D. F., Baldwin, E. J., *et al.* (2006) Increased risks for non-syndromic cleft palate among infants exposed to lamotrigine during pregnancy. *Birth Defects Research Part A: Clinical and Molecular Teratology*, 76, 318.

Honey, K. L., Bennett, P. & Morgan, M. (2002) A brief psycho-educational group intervention for postnatal depression. *The British Journal of Clinical Psychology*, 41, 405–409.

Horowitz, J. A., Bell, M., Trybulski, J., *et al.* (2001) Promoting responsiveness between mothers with depressive symptoms and their infants. *Journal of Nursing Scholarship*, 33, 323–329.

Howard, L. M. (2005) Fertility and pregnancy in women with psychotic disorders. *European Journal of Obstetrics, Gynecology and Reproductive Biology*, 119, 3–10.

Howell, E. A., Mora, P. & Leventhal, H. (2006) Correlates of early postpartum depressive symptoms. *Maternal and Child Health Journal*, 10, 149–157.

Hughes, P., Turton, P., Hopper, E., *et al.* (2002) Assessment of guidelines for good practice in psychosocial care of mothers after stillbirth: a cohort study. *Lancet*, 360, 114–118.

Huizink, A. C., Robles de Medina, P. G., Mulder, E. J., *et al.* (2003) Stress during pregnancy is associated with developmental outcome in infancy. *Journal of Child Psychology and Psychiatry*, 44, 810–818.

Isenberg, K. E. (1990) Excretion of fluoxetine in human breast milk. *The Journal of Clinical Psychiatry*, 51, 169.

Jablensky, A. V., Morgan, V., Zubrick, S. R., *et al.* (2005) Pregnancy, delivery, and neonatal complications in a population cohort of women with schizophrenia and major affective disorders. *The American Journal of Psychiatry*, 162, 79–91.

Jadad, A. R., Moore, R. A. & Carroll, D. (1996) Assessing the quality of reports of randomised clinical trials: is blinding necessary? *Controlled Clinical Trials*, 17, 1–12.

Jesse, D. E., Walcott-McQuigg, J., Mariella, A., *et al.* (2005) Risks and protective factors associated with symptoms of depression in low-income African American and Caucasian women during pregnancy. *Journal of Midwifery and Women's Health*, 50, 405–410.

Jomeen, J. & Martin, C. R. (2005) Confirmation of an occluded anxiety component within the Edinburgh Postnatal Depression Scale (EPDS) during early pregnancy. *Journal of Reproductive and Infant Psychology*, 23, 143–154.

Jones, I. & Craddock, N. (2001) Familiarity of the puerperal trigger in bipolar disorder: results of a family study. *The American Journal of Psychiatry*, 158, 913–917.

Kallen, B. (2004) Neonate characteristics after maternal use of antidepressants in late pregnancy. *Archives of Pediatrics and Adolescent Medicine*, 158, 312–316.

Kallen, B. & Mottet, I. (2003) Delivery outcome after the use of meclozine in early pregnancy. *The European Journal of Epidemiology*, 18, 665–669.

Kallen, B. & Tandberg, A. (1983) Lithium and pregnancy. A cohort study on manic-depressive women. *Acta Psychiatrica Scandinavica*, 68, 134–139.

Karasu, T. B. (1986) The specificity versus nonspecificity dilemma: toward identifying therapeutic change agents. *The American Journal of Psychiatry*, 143, 687–695.

Keles, N. (2004) Treatment of allergic rhinitis during pregnancy. *American Journal of Rhinology*, *18*, 23–28.

Kendell, R. E., Chalmers, J. C. & Platz, C. (1987) Epidemiology of puerperal psychoses. *The British Journal of Psychiatry*, *150*, 662–673.

Killaspy, H., Bebbington, P., Blizard, R., *et al.* (2006) The REACT study: randomised evaluation of assertive community treatment in north London. *British Medical Journal*, *332*, 815–820.

Kisely, S., Gater, R. & Goldberg, D. P. (1995) Results from the Manchester Centre. In *Mental Illness in General Health Care: an International Study* (eds T. B. Üstün & N. Sartorius). Chichester: Wiley.

Klerman, G. L., Weissman, M. M., Rounsaville, B. J., *et al.* (1984) *Interpersonal Psychotherapy of Depression*. New York: Basic Books.

Koro, C. E., Fedder, D. O., L'Italien, G. J., *et al.* (2002) Assessment of independent effect of olanzapine and risperidone on risk of diabetes among patients with schizophrenia: population based nested case-control study. *British Medical Journal*, *325*, 243.

Kouba, S., Hallstrom, T., Lindholm, C., *et al.* (2005) Pregnancy and neonatal outcomes in women with eating disorders. *Obstetrics and Gynecology*, *105*, 255–260.

Kroenke, K., Spitzer, R. L. & Williams, J. B. (2003) The Patient Health Questionnaire-2: validity of a two-item depression screener. *Medical Care*, *41*, 1284–1292.

Kumar, R. (1989) Postpartum psychosis. *Bailliere's Clinical Obstetrics and Gynaecology*, *3*, 823–838.

Kutcher, J. S., Engle, A., Firth, J., *et al.* (2003) Bendectin and birth defects. II: Ecological analyses. Birth Defects Research. *Part A, Clinical and Molecular Teratology*, *67*, 88–97.

Laine, K., Heikkinen, T., Ekblad, U., *et al.* (2003) Effects of exposure to selective serotonin reuptake inhibitors during pregnancy on serotonergic symptoms in newborns and cord blood monoamine and prolactin concentrations. *Archives of General Psychiatry*, *60*, 720–726.

Lavender, T. & Walkinshaw, S. A. (1998) Can midwives reduce postpartum psychological morbidity? A randomized trial. *Birth*, *25*, 215–219.

Lawrie, T. A., Hofmeyr, G. J., De Jager, M., *et al.* (1998) The effect of norethisterone enanthate on postnatal depression: a randomised placebo-controlled trial. *Women's Health Issues*, *8*, 199–200.

Lester, B. M., Cucca, J., Andreozzi, L., *et al.* (1993) Possible association between fluoxetine hydrochloride and colic in an infant. *Journal of the American Academy of Child and Adolescent Psychiatry*, *32*, 1253–1255.

Leverton, T. J. & Elliott, S. A. (2000) Is the EPDS a magic wand?: 1. A comparison of the Edinburgh Postnatal Depression Scale and health visitor report as predictors of diagnosis on the Present State Examination. *Journal of Reproductive and Infant Psychology*, *18*, 279–296.

Lewis, G. & Drife, J. (2004) Why Mothers Die 2000–2002: *The Sixth Report of Confidential Enquiries into Maternal Deaths in the United Kingdom*. London: CEMACH/Royal College of Obstetricians and Gynaecologists.

Lindhout, D. & Schmidt, D. (1986) In-utero exposure to valproate and neural tube defects. *Lancet, 1,* 1392–1393.

Llewellyn, A., Stowe, Z. N. & Strader, J. R., Jr. (1998) The use of lithium and management of women with bipolar disorder during pregnancy and lactation. *The Journal of Clinical Psychiatry, 59,* Suppl 6, 57–64.

Llorente, A. M., Jensen, C. L., Voigt, R. G., *et al.* (2003) Effect of maternal docosahexaenoic acid supplementation on postpartum depression and information processing. *American Journal of Obstetrics and Gynecology, 188,* 1348–1353.

Lobel, M., Dunkel-Schetter, C., & Scrimshaw, S. C. (1992) Prenatal maternal stress and prematurity: a prospective study of socioeconomically disadvantaged women. *Health Psychology, 11,* 32–40.

Lou, H. C., Hansen, D., Nordentoft, M., *et al.* (1994) Prenatal stressors of human life affect fetal brain development. *Developmental Medicine and Child Neurology, 36,* 826–832.

Lovestone, S. & Kumar, R. (1993) Postnatal psychiatric illness: the impact on partners. *The British Journal of Psychiatry, 163,* 210–216.

Ludlow, J. P., Evans, S. F. & Hulse, G. (2004) Obstetric and perinatal outcomes in pregnancies associated with illicit substance abuse. *The Australian and New Zealand Journal of Obstetrics and Gynaecology, 44,* 302–306.

Lumley, J., Watson, L., Watson, M., *et al.* (2001) Periconceptional supplementation with folate and/or multivitamins for preventing neural tube defects. *Cochrane Database of Systematic Reviews, 2,* CD001056.

McElhatton, P. R. (1994) The effects of benzodiazepine use during pregnancy and lactation. *Reproductive Toxicology, 8,* 461–475.

McKenna, K., Koren, G., Tetelbaum, M., *et al.* (2005) Pregnancy outcome of women using atypical antipsychotic drugs: a prospective comparative study. *The Journal of Clinical Psychiatry, 66,* 444–449.

Malek-Ahmadi, P. (2001) Olanzapine in pregnancy. *The Annals of Pharmacotherapy, 35,* 1294–1295.

Manber, R., Schnyer, R. N., Allen, J. J., *et al.* (2004) Acupuncture: a promising treatment for depression during pregnancy. *Journal of Affective Disorders, 83,* 89–95.

Mann, T. (1996) *Clinical Guidelines: Using Clinical Guidelines to Improve Patient Care Within the NHS.* Leeds: NHS Executive.

Mann, T. (1999) *A National Service Framework for Mental Health. Modern Standards and Service Models.* London: DH.

Marcenko, M. O. & Spence, M. (1994) Home visitation services for at-risk pregnant and postpartum women: a randomized trial. *The American Journal of Orthopsychiatry, 64,* 468–478.

Marteau, T. M. (1989) Psychological costs of screening. *British Medical Journal, 299,* 527.

Matalon, S., Schechtman, S., Goldzweig, G., *et al.* (2002) The teratogenic effect of carbamazepine: a meta-analysis of 1255 exposures. *Reproductive Toxicology, 16,* 9–17.

Matthey, S., Barnett, B., Kavanagh, D. J., *et al.* (2001) Validation of the Edinburgh Postnatal Depression Scale for men, and comparison of item endorsement with their partners. *Journal of Affective Disorders, 64,* 175–184.

Mazzeo, S. E., Slof-Op't Landt, M. C., Jones, I., *et al.* (2006) Associations among postpartum depression, eating disorders, and perfectionism in a population-based sample of adult women. *The International Journal of Eating Disorders, 39,* 202–211.

Mazzotta, P. & Magee, L. A. (2000) A risk-benefit assessment of pharmacological and nonpharmacological treatments for nausea and vomiting of pregnancy. *Drugs, 59,* 781–800.

Meltzer, H., Gill, B., Petticrew, M., *et al.* (1995a) *Economic Activity and Social Functioning of Adults with Psychiatric Disorders.* London: HMSO.

Meltzer, H., Gill, B., Petticrew, M., *et al.* (1995b) *The Prevalence of Psychiatric Morbidity Among Adults Living in Private Households.* London: HMSO.

Meyer, E. C., Coll, C. T., Lester, B. M., *et al.* (1994) Family-based intervention improves maternal psychological well-being and feeding interaction of preterm infants. *Pediatrics, 93,* 241–246.

MHRA (2005) Zopiclone 7.5 mg Tablets (Zopiclone) PL 08215/0049. Available at: http://www.mhra.gov.uk/home/groups/l-unit1/documents/websiteresources/con 223057.pdf

Middlemiss, C., Dawson, A. J., Gough, N., *et al.* (1989) A randomised study of a domiciliary antenatal care scheme: maternal psychological effects. *Midwifery, 5,* 69–74.

Milgrom, J., Negri, L. M., Gemmill, A. W., *et al.* (2005) A randomized controlled trial of psychological interventions for postnatal depression. *The British Journal of Clinical Psychology, 44,* 529–542.

Miller, L. J. (1995) Use of electroconvulsive therapy during pregnancy. *Obstetrical and Gynecological Survey, 50,* 10–11.

Misri, S. & Milis, L. (2004) Obsessive-compulsive disorder in the postpartum: open-label trial of quetiapine augmentation. *Journal of Clinical Psychopharmacology, 24,* 624–627.

Misri, S., Kostaras, X., Fox, D., *et al.* (2000) The impact of partner support in the treatment of postpartum depression. *Canadian Journal of Psychiatry, 45,* 554–558.

Misri, S., Reebye, P., Corral, M., *et al.* (2004) The use of paroxetine and cognitive-behavioral therapy in postpartum depression and anxiety: a randomized controlled trial. *The Journal of Clinical Psychiatry, 65,* 1236–1241.

Mitchell, E. A., Thompson, J. M., Stewart, A. W., *et al.* (1992) Postnatal depression and SIDS: a prospective study. *Journal of Paediatrics and Child Health, 28,* Suppl 1, S13–S16.

Mitchell, J. T. (1983) When disaster strikes...The critical incident stress debriefing process. *Journal of Emergency Medical Services, 8,* 36–39.

Morgan, J. F., Lacey, J. H. & Sedgwick, P. M. (1999) Impact of pregnancy on bulimia nervosa. *The British Journal of Psychiatry, 174,* 135–140.

Morrow, J., Russell, A., Guthrie, E., *et al.* (2006) Malformation risks of antiepileptic drugs in pregnancy: a prospective study from the UK Epilepsy and Pregnancy Register. *Journal of Neurology, Neurosurgery and Psychiatry, 77,* 193–198.

Munk-Olsen, T., Laursen, T.M., Pedersen, C., B., *et al.* (2006) New parents and mental disorders: a population-based register study. *Journal of the American Medical Association, 296,* 2582–2589.

Murray, D. & Cox, J. L. (1990) Screening for depression during pregnancy with the Edinburgh Depression Scale (EPDS). *Journal of Reproductive and Infant Psychology, 8,* 99–107.

Murray, L. & Carothers, A. D. (1990) The validation of the Edinburgh Post-natal Depression Scale on a community sample. *The British Journal of Psychiatry, 157,* 288–290.

Murray, L., Stanley, C., Hooper, R., *et al.* (1996) The role of infant factors in postnatal depression and mother-infant interactions. *Developmental Medicine and Child Neurology, 38,* 109–119.

Nager, A., Johansson, L. M. & Sundquist, K. (2005) Are sociodemographic factors and year of delivery associated with hospital admission for postpartum psychosis? A study of 500,000 first-time mothers. *Acta Psychiatrica Scandinavica, 112,* 47–53.

Nakano, K. K. (1973) Anencephaly: a review. *Developmental Medicine and Child Neurology. 15,* 383–400.

Narrow, W. E., Rae, D. S., Robins, L. N., *et al.* (2002) Revised prevalence estimates of mental disorders in the United States: using a clinical significance criterion to reconcile 2 surveys' estimates. *Archives of General Psychiatry, 59,* 115–123.

Nasrallah, H. A. (2006) Metabolic findings from the CATIE trial and their relation to tolerability. *CNS Spectrums, 11,* 32–39.

National Collaborating Centre for Mental Health (NCCMH) (2004) *Depression: Management of Depression in Primary and Secondary Care.* London & Leicester: The British Psychological Society and Royal College of Psychiatrists.

National Collaborating Centre for Mental Health (NCCMH) (2005) *Post-Traumatic Stress Disorder: The Management of PTSD in Adults and Children in Primary and Secondary Care.* London & Leicester: Royal College of Psychiatrists and The British Psychological Society.

National Collaborating Centre for Mental Health (NCCMH) (2006) *Bipolar Disorder: The Management of Bipolar Disorder in Adults, Children and Adolescents, in Primary and Secondary Care,* in press. London & Leicester: The British Psychological Society and Royal College of Psychiatrists.

National Screening Committee (2004) National Screening Committee Policy. http://www.nsc.nhs.uk/

National Teratology Information Service (NTIS) (2005) *Use of Paroxetine in Pregnancy.* Newcastle upon Tyne: NTIS, Regional Drug and Therapeutics Centre.

Nelson, K. & Holmes, L. B. (1989) Malformations due to presumed spontaneous mutations in newborn infants. *The New England Journal of Medicine, 320,* 19–23.

Newport, D. J., Viguera, A. C., Beach, A.J. *et al.* (2005) Lithium placental passage and obstetrical outcome: implications for clinical management during late pregnancy. *The American Journal of Psychiatry, 162,* 2162–2170.

NICE (2002) *Schizophrenia: Core interventions in the Treatment and Management of Schizophrenia in Primary and Secondary Care.* NICE Clinical Guideline 1. London: National Institute for Clinical Excellence.

NICE (2003) *Guidance on the Use of Electroconvulsive Therapy.*NICE Technology Appraisal 59. London: National Institute for Clinical Excellence.

NICE (2004a) *Depression: Management of Depression in Primary and Secondary Care.* NICE Clinical Guideline 23. London: National Institute for Clinical Excellence.

NICE (2004b) *Eating Disorders: Core Interventions in the Treatment and Management of Anorexia Nervosa, Bulimia Nervosa and Related Eating Disorders.* NICE Clinical Guideline 9. London: National Institute for Clinical Excellence.

NICE (2004c) *Anxiety: Management of Anxiety (Panic Disorder, with or without Agoraphobia, and Generalised Anxiety Disorder) in Adults in Primary, Secondary and Community Care.* NICE Clinical Guideline 22. London: National Institute for Clinical Excellence.

NICE (2004d) *Guide to the Methods of Technology Appraisal.* London: National Institute for Health and Clinical Excellence.

NICE (2004e) *The Guideline Development Process – An Overview for Stakeholders, the Public and the NHS. London:* National Institute for Health and Clinical Excellence.

NICE (2005a) *Post-Traumatic Stress Disorder: The Management of PTSD in Adults and Children in Primary and Secondary Care.* NICE Clinical Guideline 26. London: National Institute for Health and Clinical Excellence.

NICE (2005b) *Guideline Development Methods: Information for National Collaborating Centres and Guideline Developers.* London: National Institute for Health and Clinical Excellence.

NICE (2005c) *Obsessive-Compulsive Disorder: Core Interventions in the Treatment of Obsessive-Compulsive Disorder and Body Dysmorphic Disorder.* NICE Clinical Guideline 31. London: National Institute for Health and Clinical Excellence.

NICE (2005d) *Violence: the Short-Term Management of Disturbed/Violent Behaviour in In-Patient Psychiatric Settings and Emergency Departments.* NICE Clinical Guideline No. 25. London: National Institute for Health and Clinical Excellence.

NICE (2006) *Bipolar Disorder: The Management of Bipolar Disorder in Adults, Children and Adolescents, in Primary and Secondary Care.* NICE Clinical Guideline 38. London: National Institute for Health and Clinical Excellence.

Nonacs, R. & Cohen, L. S. (1998) Postpartum mood disorders: diagnosis and treatment guidelines. *The Journal of Clinical Psychiatry*, 59, 34–40.

Nonacs, R. M., Soares, C. N., Viguera, A. C., *et al.* (2005) Bupropion SR for the treatment of postpartum depression: a pilot study. *The International Journal of Neuropsychopharmacology*, 8, 445–449.

Norcross, J. C. (ed.) (2002) *Psychotherapy Relationships That Work: Therapist Contributions and Responsiveness to Patients.* New York: Oxford University Press.

References

Nordentoft, M., Lou, H. C., Hansen, D., *et al.* (1996) Intrauterine growth retardation and premature delivery: the influence of maternal smoking and psychosocial factors. *American Journal of Public Health, 86*, 347–354.

Nulman, I., Rovet, J., Stewart, D. E., *et al.* (2002) Child development following exposure to tricyclic antidepressants or fluoxetine throughout fetal life: a prospective, controlled study. *The American Journal of Psychiatry, 159*, 1889–1895.

Oates, M. (2000) *Perinatal Maternal Mental Health Services. Council Report CR88.* London: Royal College of Psychiatrists.

Oberlander, T. F., Warburton, W., Misri, S., *et al.* (2006) Neonatal outcomes after prenatal exposure to selective serotonin reuptake inhibitor antidepressants and maternal depression using population-based linked health data. *Archives of General Psychiatry, 63*, 898–906.

O'Brien, M. D. & Gilmour-White, S. K. (2005) Management of epilepsy in women. *Postgraduate Medical Journal, 81*, 278–285.

O'Connor, A. M., Stacey, D., Entwistle, V., *et al.* (2003a) Decision aids for people facing health treatment or screening decisions. *Cochrane Database of Systematic Reviews, 2*, CD001431.

O'Connor, T. G., Heron, J., Golding, J., *et al.* (2003b) Maternal antenatal anxiety and behavioural/emotional problems in children: a test of a programming hypothesis. *Journal of Child Psychology and Psychiatry, and Allied Disciplines, 44*, 1025–1036.

Office for National Statistics (2006) http://www.statistics.gov.uk [accessed June 2006]

O'Hara, M. W. & Swain, A. M. (1996) Rates and risk of postpartum depression – a meta-analysis. *International Review of Psychiatry, 8*, 37–54.

O'Hara, M. W., Zekoski, E. M., Philipps, L. H., *et al.* (1990) Controlled prospective study of postpartum mood disorders: comparison of childbearing and nonchildbearing women. *Journal of Abnormal Psychology, 99*, 3–15.

O'Hara, M. W., Stuart, S., Gorman, L. L., *et al.* (2000) Efficacy of interpersonal psychotherapy for postpartum depression. *Archives of General Psychiatry, 57*, 1039–1045.

Olde, E., Van Der Hart, O., Kleber, R., *et al.* (2006) Posttraumatic stress following childbirth: a review. *Clinical Psychology Review, 26*, 1–16.

Omtzigt, J. G., Los, F. J., Grobbee, D. E., *et al.* (1992) The risk of spina bifida aperta after first-trimester exposure to valproate in a prenatal cohort. *Neurology, 42*, 119–125.

Onozawa, K., Glover, V., Adams, D., *et al.* (2001) Infant massage improves mother-infant interaction for mothers with postnatal depression. *Journal of Affective Disorders, 63*, 201–207.

Patel, R. R., Murphy, D. J. & Peters, T. J. (2005) Operative delivery and postnatal depression: a cohort study. *British Medical Journal, 330*, 879.

Patton, S. W., Misri, S., Corral, M. R., *et al.* (2002) Antipsychotic medication during pregnancy and lactation in women with schizophrenia: evaluating the risk. *Canadian Journal of Psychiatry, 47*, 959–965.

Peckham, C. S. & Dezateux, C. (1998) Issues underlying the evaluation of screening programmes. *British Medical Bulletin, 54,* 767–778.

Pedersen, L., Skriver, M. V., Norgaard, M., *et al.* (2006) Maternal use of Loratadine during pregnancy and risk of hypospadias in offspring. *International Journal of Medical Sciences, 3,* 21–25.

Petrou, S., Cooper, P., Murray, L., *et al.* (2002) Economic costs of post-natal d epression in a high-risk British cohort. *The British Journal of Psychiatry, 181,* 505–512.

Prendergast, J. & Austin, M. P. (2001) Early childhood nurse-delivered cognitive behavioural counselling for post-natal depression. *Australasian Psychiatry, 9,* 255–259.

Priest, S. R., Henderson, J., Evans, S. F., *et al.* (2003) Stress debriefing after childbirth: a randomised controlled trial. *The Medical Journal of Australia, 178,* 542–545.

Radloff, L. S. (1977) The CES-D Scale: a self-report depression scale for research in the general population. *Applied Psychological Measurement, 1,* 385–401.

Rambeck, B., Specht, U. & Wolf, P. (1996) Pharmacokinetic interactions of the new antiepileptic drugs. *Clinical Pharmacokinetics, 31,* 309–324.

Rector, N. A., Bagby, R. M., Segal, Z. V., *et al.* (2000) Self-criticism and dependency in depressed patients treated with cognitive therapy or pharmacotherapy. *Cognitive Therapy and Research, 24,* 571–584.

Reid, M., Glazener, C., Murray, G. D., *et al.* (2002) A two-centred pragmatic randomised controlled trial of two interventions of postnatal support. BJOG: An International Journal of Obstetrics and Gynaecology, *109,* 1164–1170.

Revicki, D. A. & Wood, M. (1998) Patient-assigned health state utilities for depression-related outcomes: differences by depression severity and antidepressant medications. *Journal of Affective Disorders, 48,* 25–36.

Roberts, J., Sword, W., Watt, S., *et al.* (2001) Costs of postpartum care: examining associations from the Ontario mother and infant survey. *The Canadian Journal of Nursing Research, 33,* 19–34.

Robertson, E., Grace, S., Wallington, T., *et al.* (2004) Antenatal risk factors for postpartum depression: a synthesis of recent literature. *General Hospital Psychiatry, 26,* 289–295.

Robertson, E., Jones, I., Haque, S., *et al.* (2005) Risk of puerperal and non-puerperal recurrence of illness following bipolar affective puerperal (post-partum) psychosis. *The British Journal of Psychiatry, 186,* 258–259.

Rogers, C. R. (1957) The necessary and sufficient conditions of therapeutic personality change. *Journal of Consulting Psychology, 21,* 95–103.

Roth, A. & Fonagy, P. (2004) What Works for Whom?: A Critical Review of Psychotherapy Research, New York: Guilford Press.

Rubin, E. T., Lee, A. & Ito, S. (2004) When breastfeeding mothers need CNS-acting drugs. *The Canadian Journal of Clinical Pharmacology, 11,* e257–e266.

Rubovits, P. (1996) Project CHILD: An intervention program for psychotic mothers and their young children. In *Parental Psychiatric Disorder: Distressed Parents and their Families* (eds M. Gopfert, J. Webster & M. V. Seeman). Cambridge: Cambridge University Press.

Rush, A. J., Giles, D. E., Schlesser, M. A., *et al.* (1986) The Inventory for Depressive Symptomatology (IDS): preliminary findings. *Psychiatry Research, 18*, 65–87.

Ryding, E. L., Wirén, E., Johansson, G., *et al.* (2004) Group counseling for mothers after emergency cesarean section: a randomized controlled trial of intervention. *Birth, 31*, 247–253.

Sanderson, C. A., Cowden, B., Hall, D. M., *et al.* (2002) Is postnatal depression a risk factor for sudden infant death? *The British Journal of General Practice, 52*, 636–640.

Say, R., Murtagh, M. & Thomson, R. (2006) Patients' preference for involvement in medical decision making: a narrative review. *Patient Education and Counseling, 60*, 102–114.

Schatz, M., Zeiger, R. S., Harden, K., *et al.* (1997) The safety of asthma and allergy medications during pregnancy. *The Journal of Allergy and Clinical Immunology, 100*, 301–306.

Schneider, M. L., Roughton, E. C., Koehler, A. J., *et al.* (1999) Growth and development following prenatal stress exposure in primates: an examination of ontogenetic vulnerability. *Child Development, 70*, 263–274.

Scialli, A. R. (2005) Counseling. *Reprotox in a Nutshell January 2005*. Downloaded from http://reprotox.org/docs/nutshell01_05.pdf July 2005.

Segal, Z. V., Kennedy, S. H. & Cohen, N. L. (2001a) Clinical guidelines for the treatment of depressive disorders. V. Combining psychotherapy and pharmacotherapy. *Canadian Journal of Psychiatry, 46*, Suppl 1, 59S–62S.

Segal, Z. V., Whitney, D. K. & Lam, R. W. (2001b) Clinical guidelines for the treatment of depressive disorders. III. Psychotherapy. *Canadian Journal of Psychiatry, 46*, Suppl 1, 29S–37S.

Sernyak, M. J., Leslie, D. L., Alarcon, R. D., *et al.* (2002) Association of diabetes mellitus with use of atypical neuroleptics in the treatment of schizophrenia. *The American Journal of Psychiatry, 159*, 561–566.

Shakespeare, J. (2001) *Evaluation of Screening for Postnatal Depression Against the National Screening Committee Handbook Criteria*. National Screening Committee, UK.

Shakespeare, J., Blake, F. & Garcia, J. (2003) A qualitative study of the acceptability of routine screening of postnatal women using the Edinburgh Postnatal Depression Scale. *The British Journal of General Practice, 53*, 614–619.

Sharma, V., Smith, A. & Khan, M. (2004) The relationship between duration of labour, time of delivery, and puerperal psychosis. *Journal of Affective Disorders, 83*, 215–220.

Sharp, D., Hay, D. F., Pawlby, S., *et al.* (1995) The impact of postnatal depression on boys' intellectual development. *Journal of Child Psychology and Psychiatry, 36*, 1315–1336.

Sholomskas, D. E., Wickamaratne, P. J., Dogolo, L., *et al.* (1993) Postpartum onset of panic disorder: a coincidental event? *The Journal of Clinical Psychiatry, 54*, 476–480.

Simon, G. E., Goldberg, D. P., Von Korff, M., *et al.* (2002) Understanding cross-national differences in depression prevalence. *Psychological Medicine, 32*, 585–594.

Slone, D., Siskind, V., Heinonen, O. P., *et al.* (1977) Antenatal exposure to the phenothiazines in relation to congenital malformations, perinatal mortality rate, birthweight, and intelligence quotient score. *American Journal of Obstetrics and Gynecology, 128,* 486–488.

Small, R., Lumley, J., Donohue, L., *et al.* (2000) Randomised controlled trial of midwife led debriefing to reduce maternal depression after operative childbirth. *British Medical Journal, 321,* 1043–1047.

Smith, L., Yonekura, M.L., Wallace, T., *et al.* (2003) Effects of prenatal methamphetamine exposure on fetal growth and drug withdrawal symptoms in infants born at term. *Journal of Developmental and Behavioural Pediatrics, 24,* 17–23.

Sotsky, S. M., Glass, D. R., Shea, M. T., *et al.* (1991) Patient predictors of response to psychotherapy and pharmacotherapy: findings in the NIMH Treatment of Depression Collaborative Research Program. *The American Journal of Psychiatry, 148,* 997–1008.

Spencer, J. P., Gonzalez, L. S., III & Barnhart, D. J. (2001) Medications in the breast-feeding mother. *American Family Physician, 64,* 119–126.

Spigset, O., Carleborg, L., Norstrom, A., *et al.* (1996) Paroxetine level in breast milk. *The Journal of Clinical Psychiatry, 57,* 39.

Spigset, O., Carieborg, L., Ohman, R., *et al.* (1997) Excretion of citalopram in breast milk. *British Journal of Clinical Pharmacology, 44,* 295–298.

Spinelli, M. G. (1997) Interpersonal psychotherapy for depressed antepartum women: a pilot study. *The American Journal of Psychiatry, 154,* 1028–1030.

Spinelli, M. G. & Endicott, J. (2003) Controlled clinical trial of interpersonal psychotherapy versus parenting education program for depressed pregnant women. *The American Journal of Psychiatry, 160,* 555–562.

Spitzer, R. L., Kroenke, K., & Williams, J. B. (1999) Validation and utility of a self-report version of PRIME-MD: the PHQ primary care study. Primary Care Evaluation of Mental Disorders. Patient Health Questionnaire. *The Journal of the American Medical Association, 282,* 1737–1744.

Stamp, G. E., Williams, A. S. & Crowther, C. A. (1995) Evaluation of antenatal and postnatal support to overcome postnatal depression: a randomized, controlled trial. *Birth, 22,* 138–143.

Stein, A., Woolley, H., Senior, R., *et al.* (2006) Treating disturbances in the relationship between mothers with bulimic eating disorders and their infants: a randomized, controlled trial of video feedback. *The American Journal of Psychiatry, 163,* 899–906.

Stein, G. & Van Den Akker, O. (1992) The retrospective diagnosis of postnatal depression by questionnaire. *Journal of Psychosomatic Research, 36,* 67–75.

Stein, M. B., Walker, J. R., Hazen, A. L., *et al.* (1997) Full and partial posttraumatic stress disorder: findings from a community survey. *The American Journal of Psychiatry, 154,* 1114–1119.

Stowe, Z. N., Casarella, J., Landry, J., *et al.* (1995) Sertraline in the treatment of women with postpartum major depression. *Depression, 3,* 49–55.

Surkan, P. J., Peterson, K. E., Hughes, M. D., *et al.* (2006) The role of social networks and support in postpartum women's depression: a multiethnic urban sample. *Maternal and Child Health Journal*, *10*, 375–383.

Taddio, A., Ito, S. & Koren, G. (1996) Excretion of fluoxetine and its metabolite, norfluoxetine, in human breast milk. *Journal of Clinical Pharmacology*, *36*, 42–47.

Terp, I. M. & Mortensen, P. B. (1998) Post-partum psychoses. Clinical diagnoses and relative risk of admission after parturition. *The British Journal of Psychiatry*, *172*, 521–526.

Terp, I. M., Engholm, G., Moller, H. *et al.* (1999) A follow-up study of postpartum psychoses: prognosis and risk factors for readmission. *Acta Psychiatrica Scandinavica*, *100*, 40–46.

Thompson, C., Ostler, K., Peveler, R. C., *et al.* (2001) Dimensional perspective on the recognition of depressive symptoms in primary care: The Hampshire Depression Project 3. *The British Journal of Psychiatry*, *179*, 317–323.

Thomson, R., Edwards, A. & Grey, J. (2005) Risk communication in the clinical consultation. *Clinical Medicine*, *5*, 465–69.

Truax, C. B. & Carkhuff, R. R. (1967) *Toward Effective Counseling and Psychotherapy*. Chicago: Aldine.

Turton, P., Hughes, P., Bolton, H., *et al.* (1999) Incidence and demographic correlates of eating disorder symptoms in a pregnant population. *The International Journal of Eating Disorders*, *26*, 448–452.

Turton, P., Hughes, P., Evans, C. D., *et al.* (2001) Incidence, correlates and predictors of post-traumatic stress disorder in the pregnancy after stillbirth. *The British Journal of Psychiatry*. *178*, 556–560.

Turton, P., Badenhorst, W., Hughes, P., *et al.* (2006) Psychological impact of stillbirth on fathers in the subsequent pregnancy and puerperium. *The British Journal of Psychiatry*, *188*, 165–172.

Üstün, T. B. & Sartorius, N. (eds) (1995) *Mental Illness in General Health Care: An International Study*. Chichester: Wiley.

Van Den Bergh, B. R., Mennes, M., Oosterlaan, J., *et al.* (2005) High antenatal maternal anxiety is related to impulsivity during performance on cognitive tasks in 14- and 15-year-olds. *Neuroscience and Biobehavioural Reviews*, *29*, 259–269.

Veiel, H. O. (1990) The Mannheim Interview on Social Support. Reliability and validity data from three samples. *Social Psychiatry and Psychiatric Epidemiology*, *25*, 250–259.

Viguera, A. C., Nonacs, R., Cohen, L. S., *et al.* (2000) Risk of recurrence of bipolar disorder in pregnant and nonpregnant women after discontinuing lithium maintenance. *The American Journal of Psychiatry*, *157*, 179–184.

Wadhwa, P. D., Sandman, C. A., Porto, M. *et al.* (1993) The association between prenatal stress and infant birthweight and gestational age at birth: a prospective investigation. *American Journal of Obstetrics and Gynecology*, *169*, 858–865.

Walsh, B. T., Seidman, S. N., Sysko, R., *et al.* (2002) Placebo response in studies of major depression: variable, substantial, and growing. *The Journal of the American Medical Association*, *287*, 1840–1847.

Webb, R., Abel, K., Pickles, A., *et al.* (2005) Mortality in offspring of parents with psychotic disorders: a critical review and meta-analysis. *The American Journal of Psychiatry, 162,* 1045–1056.

Webster, J., Pritchard, M. A., Linnane, J. W., *et al.* (2001) Postnatal depression: use of health services and satisfaction with health-care providers. *Journal of Quality in Clinical Practice, 21,* 144–148.

Webster, J., Linnane, J., Roberts, J., *et al.* (2003) IDentify, Educate and Alert (IDEA) trial: an intervention to reduce postnatal depression. *BJOG: an International Journal of Obstetrics and Gynaecology, 110,* 842–846.

Weissman, M. M., Markowitz, J. C. & Klerman, G. L. (2000) *Comprehensive Guide to Interpersonal Psychotherapy.* New York: Basic Books.

Weissman, A. M., Levy, B. T., Hartz, A. J., *et al.* (2004) Pooled analysis of antidepressant levels in lactating mothers, breast milk, and nursing infants. *The American Journal of Psychiatry, 161,* 1066–1078.

Wenzel, A., Haugen, E. N., Jackson, L. C., *et al.* (2003) Prevalence of generalized anxiety at eight weeks postpartum. *Archives of Women's Mental Health, 6,* 43–49.

Whooley, M. A., Avins, A. L., Miranda, J., *et al.* (1997) Case-finding instruments for depression. Two questions are as good as many. *Journal of General Internal Medicine, 12,* 439–445.

Wickberg, B. & Hwang, C. P. (1996) Counselling of postnatal depression: a controlled study on a population based Swedish sample. *Journal of Affective Disorders, 39,* 209–216.

Wide, K., Winbladh, B., Tomson, T., *et al.* (2000) Psychomotor development and minor anomalies in children exposed to antiepileptic drugs in utero: a prospective population-based study. *Developmental Medicine and Child Neurology, 42,* 87–92.

Wieck, A. (2004) Teratogenic syndromes. In *Adverse Syndromes and Psychiatric Drugs: a Clinical Guide* (eds P. M. Haddad, S. Durson & W. Deakin). Oxford: Oxford University Press.

Wieck, A., Kumar, R., Hirst, A. D., *et al.* (1991) Increased sensitivity of dopamine receptors and recurrence of affective psychosis after childbirth. *British Medical Journal, 303,* 613–616.

Wiggins, M., Oakley, A., Roberts, I., *et al.* (2005) Postnatal support for mothers living in disadvantaged inner city areas: a randomised controlled trial. *Journal of Epidemiology and Community Health, 59,* 288–295.

Williams, J. W., Jr, Kerber, C. A., Mulrow, C. D., *et al.* (1995) Depressive disorders in primary care: prevalence, functional disability, and identification. *Journal of General Internal Medicine, 10,* 7–12.

Wisner, K. L. & Wheeler, S. B. (1994) Prevention of recurrent postpartum major depression. *Hospital and Community Psychiatry, 45,* 1191–1196.

Wisner, K. L., Perel, J. M. & Findling, R. L. (1996) Antidepressant treatment during breast-feeding. *The American Journal of Psychiatry, 153,* 1132–1137.

Wisner, K. L., Perel, J. M., Peindl, K. S., *et al.* (2001) Prevention of recurrent postpartum depression: a randomized clinical trial. *The Journal of Clinical Psychiatry, 62,* 82–86.

Wisner, K. L., Hanusa, B. H., Peindl, K. S., *et al.* (2004a) Prevention of postpartum episodes in women with bipolar disorder. *Biological Psychiatry, 56,* 592–596.

Wisner, K. L., Perel, J. M., Peindl, K. S., *et al.* (2004b) Prevention of postpartum depression: a pilot randomized clinical trial. *The American Journal of Psychiatry, 161,* 1290–1292.

World Health Organization (WHO) (1992) *The ICD-10 Classification of Mental and Behavioural Disorders: Clinical Descriptions and Diagnostic Guidelines.* Geneva: WHO.

Wright, S., Dawling, S. & Ashford, J. J. (1991) Excretion of fluvoxamine in breast milk. *British Journal of Clinical Pharmacology, 31,* 209.

Zelkowitz, P. & Milet, T. H. (1995) Screening for post-partum depression in a community sample. *Canadian Journal of Psychiatry, 40,* 80–86.

Zigmond, A. S. & Snaith, R. P. (1983) The hospital anxiety and depression scale. *Acta Psychiatrica Scandinavica, 67,* 361–370.

Zlotnick, C., Johnson, S. L., Miller, I. W., *et al.* (2001) Postpartum depression in women receiving public assistance: pilot study of an interpersonal-therapy-oriented group intervention. *The American Journal of Psychiatry, 158,* 638–640.

Zung, W. W. (1965) A self-rating depression scale. *Archives of General Psychiatry, 12,* 63–70.

11. ABBREVIATIONS

ALSPAC	Avon Longitudinal Study of Parents and Children
AN	antenatal
BDI	Beck Depression Inventory
BNF	British National Formulary
BPDS	Bromley Postnatal Depression Scale
CAMHS	Child and Adolescent Mental Health Services
CBT	cognitive behavioural therapy
CCEI	Crown-Crisp Experiential Index
CES-D	Center for Epidemiologic Studies Depression Scale
CGI	Clinical Global Improvement
CI	confidence interval
CINAHL	Cumulative Index to Nursing and Allied Health Literature
CISD	critical-incident stress debriefing
CIS-R	Clinical Interview Schedule – Revised
CPN	community psychiatric nurse
DH	Department of Health
DMC	Dyadic Mutuality Code
DSM	Diagnostic and Statistical Manual of Mental Disorders (versions III-R and IV-TR)
ECT	electroconvulsive therapy
EMBASE	Excerpta Medica database
EPDS	Edinburgh Postnatal Depression Scale
GAD	generalised anxiety disorder
GDG	Guideline Development Group
GHQ	General Health Questionnaire (D: depression)
GP	general practitioner
GRP	Guideline Review Panel
HOME	Home Observation for Measurement of the Environment (Inventory)
HRQoL	health-related quality of life
HRSD	Hamilton Rating Scale for Depression
HTA	health technology assessment
ICD	International Classification of Diseases (10th edition)
ICER	incremental cost-effectiveness ratio

IDS	Inventory of Depressive Symptomatology
IPT	interpersonal psychotherapy
K	number of trials contributing to the summary statistic
LHB	Local Health Board
MDD	major depressive disorder
MBU	mother and baby unit
MEDLINE	Compiled by the US National Library of Medicine and published on the web by Community of Science, MEDLINE is a source of life sciences and biomedical bibliographic information
MHRA	Medicines and Healthcare products Regulatory Agency
MMR	major malformation rate
MPN	months postnatally
n	number of participants
NCCMH	National Collaborating Centre for Mental Health
NHS	National Health Service
NHS EED	National Health Service Economic Evaluation Database
NICE	National Institute for Health and Clinical Excellence
NNT	number needed to treat (B: benefit; H: harm)
NSC	National Screening Committee
NSF	National Service Framework
OCD	obsessive-compulsive disorder
OHE HEED	Office of Health Economics, Health Economics Evaluation Database
OR	odds ratio
p	probability
PBDU	parent and baby day hospital unit
PCT	Primary Care Trust
PDSS	Postnatal Depression Screening Scale
PHQ	Patient Health Questionnaire
PICO	patient, intervention, comparison and outcome
PN	postnatal
PsycINFO	An abstract (not full text) database of psychological literature from the 1800s to the present
PTSD	post-traumatic stress disorder
QALY	quality adjusted life years

RCT	randomised controlled trial
RDC	research diagnostic criteria
RPC	routine primary care
RR	relative risk
SADS	Schedule for Affective Disorders and Schizophrenia
SAS	Spielberger State/Trait Anxiety Scale
SCID	Structured Clinical Interview for DSM (II, III or IV)
SD	standard deviation
SE	standard error
SF-36	36-Item Short Form Questionnaire
SIGH-SAD	Structured Interview Guide for the Hamilton Depression Rating Scale – Seasonal Affective Disorder version
SMD	standardised mean difference
SR	systematic review
SSRI	selective serotonin reuptake inhibitor
STAI	State-Trait Anxiety Inventory
TCA	tricyclic antidepressant
WHO	World Health Organization
WMD	weighted mean difference